A Muslim Archipelago:
Islam and Politics in Southeast Asia

Max L. Gross

NDIC PRESS

National Defense Intelligence College
Washington, DC
March 2007

The National Defense Intelligence College supports and encourages research on intelligence issues that distills lessons and improves Intelligence Community capabilities for policy-level and operational consumers.

This book has been many years in the making, as the author explains in his Preface, though he wrote most of the actual text during his year as senior Research Fellow with the Center for Strategic Intelligence Research. The author was for many years Dean of the School of Intelligence Studies at the Joint Military Intelligence College. Even though it may appear that the book could have been written by any good historian or Southeast Asia regional specialist, this work is illuminated by the author's more than three decades of service within the national Intelligence Community. His regional expertise often has been applied to special assessments for the Community. With a knowledge of Islam unparalleled among his peers and an unquenchable thirst for determining how the goals of this religion might play out in areas far from the focus of most policymakers' current attention, the author has made the most of this opportunity to acquaint the Intelligence Community and a broader readership with a strategic appreciation of a region in the throes of reconciling secular and religious forces.

This publication has been approved for unrestricted distribution by the Office of Security Review, Department of Defense.

William.Spracher@dia.mil, Editor
Center for Strategic Intelligence Research

CONTENTS

FOREWORD

Southeast Asia continues to beckon policymakers and scholars alike to revisit its history in spite of the tomes of appraisals already written, deconstructive or otherwise. Because of a significant presence of Muslims in the region, and particularly in the wake of 9/11, it invariably attracts the attention of foreign powers drawn by the specter of terrorism and focused on rooting out radical Islamist groups said to be working with al-Qa'eda.

Dr. Max Gross has written an impressive account of the role of Islam in the politics of Southeast Asia, anchored by a strong historical perspective and a comprehensive treatment of current affairs. The result is very much a post-9/11 book. The origins of Jemaah Islamiyah and its connections with al-Qa'eda are carefully detailed. Yet, unlike much of the post-9/11 analysis of the Muslim world, Dr. Gross's research has been successful in placing the phenomenon of terrorism within a larger perspective. While recognizing that al-Qa'eda's influence on regional terror networks remains unclear, it behooves us to be reminded that, regardless of the nature and extent of the linkages, to dismiss terrorism as a serious threat to security would be naïve to the point of recklessness.

The Muslim Archipelago is a profoundly Islamic region, and Jemaah Islamiyah is only a small portion of this reality. The attention Dr. Gross pays to ABIM in Malaysia, of which I was a part, and the civil Islam movement in Indonesia, of which the late Nurcholish Madjid was a principal spokesman, is greatly appreciated. Those unfamiliar with the background and role of the traditional Islamic PAS party in Malaysia, as well as the Darul Islam movement in Indonesia, will find the author's account highly beneficial. The MNLF, the MILF, and Abu Sayyaf in the Philippines, as well as the various Islamic movements in southern Thailand, are also carefully explained.

As a retired career employee of the U.S. Department of Defense, Dr. Gross has paid much attention to security issues, highlighting the conflicts that continue to beset us and efforts by the governments of the region to resolve them even as final settlements remain elusive. In the discourse of the impact of Islam in the region, there is a tendency to view Islam in bipolar terms, the upshot of which is to lump organizations founded on Islamic precepts as being radical with a tendency of associating with terrorist bodies. This orientation prevents one from discerning between mainstream political Islam and its more extremist peripheries. It is therefore refreshing that Dr. Gross does not fall prey to this stereotyping and remains strictly objective in his assessment.

For my part, however, perhaps from having been actively involved in the political process pertaining to security matters in Southeast Asia, it would be disingenuous to profess non-partisanship in my overall assessment of the situation. I dare say that many in the region still view the U.S. policy on terror as being marked by that Wilsonian *machismo* that has led it to miss the woods for the trees. This is not to suggest that the terrorism-related discourse is an exercise in futility or that it should be abandoned altogether. While it is true that terrorism from afar has stoked the domestic radical fire and led to acts of violence, governments in the region have hijacked the war on terror for their own political ends. On the pretext of fighting terrorism, many regional leaders have blatantly consolidated their political powers, further entrenching the insidious forms of soft-authoritarianism that they have consistently opposed and sought to reform.

Just as sound policies for engaging Muslims cannot be formulated without a thorough understanding of history, this understanding will not come about from clichéd notions of Islam. Dr. Gross' book, therefore, is not merely an academic exercise but is highly instructive in helping to devise an approach for those who have an interest in seeing long-term stability in the region.

As I have come to know Dr. Gross over the past several months, I have found him a scholar with a deep knowledge of Islam. With this book he has made a formidable contribution to the field, and I have no hesitation in recommending this work to those interested in learning about the role of Islam in the politics of Southeast Asia.

Anwar Ibrahim
Washington, DC

Anwar Ibrahim is former Finance Minister and Deputy Prime Minister of Malaysia. During academic year 2005-2006, he was Distinguished Visiting Professor at the Prince Alwaleed Bin Talal Center for Muslim-Christian Understanding at Georgetown University.

A Commentary on
A MUSLIM ARCHIPELAGO: ISLAM AND POLITICS IN SOUTHEAST ASIA
Allen L. Keiswetter

Dr. Max Gross, a trained historian, has written a baseline history of Islam in Southeast Asia. Starting with basic questions such as how did Islam come to this region, he connects the interaction of local authorities, colonial powers, and governments with the challenge Islam has presented to governance for more than a thousand years. Especially strong are the introductory and concluding chapters. The former provides a short scan of the history of the expansion of Islam into Southeast Asia and of the relationship of colonial legacies of the British, Dutch, Portuguese, Spanish, and Americans to Islam today in the region. The last chapter traces the development of the idea of an Islamic state from the time of Mohammad in Medina to its present-day role in the politics of Southeast Asia.

Still, this is a book with a contemporary focus. Dr. Gross's purpose is to use history to explain today's Islamic insurgencies in Indonesia, Malaysia, Thailand, and the Philippines and to offer perspectives for the future. These four countries fall along a spectrum. Indonesia, the world's largest Muslim country, is about 90 percent Muslim, and the conflicts which Dr. Gross examines are largely between a secularization of Islam, especially Sukarno's *Pancasila* mixing Islam and nationalism, and the much more traditional Islamic orthopraxy among the Acehnese and others. Malaysia has a different context; its population is 53 percent Muslim, and the central question concerns accommodation between the majority Muslims and the minority Christians and ethnic Chinese. In Thailand and the Philippines, where the Muslims are minorities themselves (approximately four and five percent respectively), the question is political accommodation in the opposite direction. Underlying most of these conflicts are separatist histories based not only on religious differences but also on geographic, ethnic, racial, and social disparities.

This book's unique contribution is that it brings together in one reference a mass of information on the insurgencies in Southeast Asia. The country accounts are detailed and thorough as to events, organizations, dates, and participants. The chronological context provides Dr. Gross the opportunity to give his insights about historical causality. His accounting highlights the interaction of the insurgencies within Southeast Asia and their international connections outside the region. Especially good are the detailed presentations in the chapters on Indonesia and the Philippines.

Against this baseline the stage is set for further research and analysis. Two things in particular come to mind. The first is the need to answer further analytical questions from the information Dr. Gross has presented. How are the histories similar and different and why? What strategies have been most successful in dealing with the insurgencies? To what extent is the motivation of the insurgents religious and to what extent is it based on other factors? The second involves further inquiry in line with the book's subtitle "Islam and Politics in Southeast Asia." While politics is comprehensively covered, of interest would be additional research about the non-political factors regarding the insurgents, such as their similarities and differences in Islamic belief and practice, their economic situations, and their prospects and hopes for the future.

Even a brief glance at the new Army Field Manual on counterinsurgency makes clear that the questions answered and inspired by this book are not marginal to the concerns of intelligence analysts. In its final draft, its chapter on intelligence concludes with the following:

> What makes intelligence analysis for COIN [counterinsurgency operations] so distinct and so challenging is the amount of cultural information that must be gathered and understood. However, to truly grasp the environment of operations, commanders and their staffs must expend at least as much effort understanding the people they are supporting as [they do in understanding] the enemy. All this information is essential to get at the root causes of the insurgency and to determine the best ways to combat it.

Dr. Gross has made an excellent contribution to what is needed, and further analysis and research will, one hopes, provide even further insight.

Allen L. Keiswetter is a faculty member at the National Defense Intelligence College, on contract from Pearson Analytical Solutions, and Adjunct Scholar at the Middle East Institute. He teaches courses on Islam and on the Middle East.

A Commentary on
A MUSLIM ARCHIPELAGO: ISLAM AND POLITICS IN SOUTHEAST ASIA
Roger E. Biesel

Islam has come to the forefront of the world's consciousness following al-Qa'ida's attacks on the United States on September 11, 2001, and subsequently those in London, Madrid, and Indonesia. In the West, Revolutionary Islamism has become as reviled an ideology as revolutionary Communism was prior to 1991. With Islam as such a potent force in international relations, it is apropos that this richly documented and insightful work by one of Washington's leading Islamic scholars should arrive now. In his discussion of Islam, Dr. Gross' focus is not on the Arab world, as some might expect, but on that area where the largest number of Muslims in the world dwell—Southeast Asia. Because Asia continues to advance as the fastest growing region in the world, the author's focus on the Islamic phenomenon there takes on important meaning.

Dr. Gross is well qualified to address this topic. With a career spanning over 40 years as a scholar and lecturer on Islam, he presently provides lectures at U.S. government offices in Washington. Having traveled widely in the Muslim world, he currently serves at the Center for Christian-Muslim Understanding with the faculty of his alma mater, Georgetown University. Dr. Gross' previous work at Washington's American University and George Washington University on Islam, international relations of the Middle East, and the Arab-Israeli conflict is widely recognized. He has published extensively on these same subjects while also supporting works of other scholars with his informed contributions.

This timely, well-written work is delightfully understandable and an easy read despite its size and the complexity of the subject matter. Those who may have thought of Islam as a totally Middle East and Arab entity will come away with another point of view. The author's "General Considerations" set the scene, clarifying how the ethnic Malay character of the region has created a substantially different approach to Islam from that of the Arabs. While Islam in the Arab world and South Asia came about largely by the sword and military conquest, Southeast Asia's experience was totally different—largely one of gradual, peaceful assimilation through trade and intermarriage. Thus, Islam in Southeast Asia was overlaid onto already existing rich and colorful sets of beliefs and tribal superstitions that varied widely from region to region. A brief historic overview is followed with discussion of Europe's impact on the region and its influence in the formation of the two major Islamic countries in the region—Malaysia and Indonesia. For those seeking deeper historical treatment, the author addresses the four key Islamic populations in the region—Malaysia, Thailand, Indonesia, and the Philippines—up to the present time.

Islam's colorfulness and variety make any broad generalities or characterizations about it inaccurate. Similar to Christians, Jews, Buddhists, Hindus, or other faiths, most followers of Islam are not fanatics, extremists, or revolutionaries. While all Muslims share a common religious belief, their behavior varies widely. One unique characteristic of Islam is that it is totally centered on God—state and religion melt together. Muslims believe that the Koran, Islam's holy book, and Muslim law alone are adequate to govern the relations of man. Only four truisms apply to Islam: that all Muslims believe in the same Abrahamic God that Jews and Christians worship; that they believe Muhammad was God's complete and final prophet; that they believe in the power of prayer—five times a day is mandatory; and that they believe in the Last Judgment. Beyond that, *Dar al Islam*, the House of Islam, is more diverse than it is homogeneous. The diversity of Islam becomes more understandable when considering that some 1.2 billion people of every race are Muslim—from China to Senegal, from the former Soviet Union to Nigeria, plus some seven million in Europe and several million Americans—with only about 20% Arab.

Since its founding some 1,400 years ago, Islam has been a source of conflict, violence, and fanaticism. The bombings and shootings of the new millennium in Southeast Asia that have been killing Muslims by the score and the bloody Shiite-Sunni standoff in present-day Iraq are but recent examples. Nevertheless, Islam also has been a source of generosity, unbelievable beauty, ingenious technological innovation, and inspiration to both kings and the disenfranchised alike.

Dr. Gross' emphasis on Southeast Asia takes on added meaning when considering that two of the world's three largest Muslim populations reside there—196 million in Indonesia, 138 million in Pakistan, and 114 million in Bangladesh. This compares with the 350-plus million residing in Arab countries of the Middle East and North Africa. In addition, non-Arab countries hosting populations exceeding 50% Muslim include Afghanistan, Iran, Mali, Malaysia, and Turkey. Also, many Arabs in Egypt, Lebanon, Palestine, and Syria are Christian—not Muslim. Similarly, the vast majority of Muslims in Southeast Asia are not "Arabic" despite recent efforts by oil-rich Saudis to export their more fundamental Islamic beliefs to the region.

In this age of globalization and global interdependence, tolerance of diversity becomes increasingly crucial. A calm, law-abiding Muslim population in the West and content, secure, non-Muslim religious minorities in the Islamic world can be barriers to the belief that every region belongs to just one faith or culture. Although the principle of human rights is reason enough for tolerance, religious diversity will safeguard all against the "clash of civilizations," the clash between Islam and the West that extremists want. The fissure between two great civilizations which occurred during the Crusades in the 1100-1500 time frame has outlived any useful meaning and should not be replayed.

As we proceed into the 21st century, leveling the playing field between the West and the Islamic world and leaving our grandchildren a legacy of understanding and tolerance are absolutely essential, even more so in the Muslim world. Muslims have come to experience life in the West in terms of being free to interpret their own religion. To resist suspicion of being a "fifth column," they need to interact more openly with other faiths and in a more generous spirit. For one, they need to stop treating non-Muslim minorities residing in Islamic lands as second-class citizens. Following such traditional Muslim theocracy in this regard has no place in a modern Islamic state. The assertion that Islam is incompatible with democracy and modernity makes Dr. Gross' latest work all the more important. He helps us place global events and our fears into a balanced context—something never more important than it is today.

Roger E. Biesel is a Southeast Asia analyst at the Defense Intelligence Agency who has in recent years been focused on the role of Islam in the region.

AUTHOR'S PREFACE

On 10-11 September 2003, the Center for the Study of Intelligence hosted a conference in Charlottesville, Virginia, to discuss the subject "Intelligence for a New Era in American Foreign Policy." One of the recommendations from that conference, in the context of "Proposals for Change" within the Intelligence Community, was as follows:

> The U.S. government was a big actor in creating the broad and institutional knowledge base necessary for conducting the Cold War. Could we replicate that in some way today? We need to create, among other things, an atlas of Islam…a knowledge base. We ought to do it as a national project.[1]

This research study responds to this recommendation, albeit at a somewhat more modest level than "a national project." Additionally, in order to narrow the focus, the current study focuses only on the countries of Southeast Asia—Indonesia, Malaysia, the Philippines, and Thailand. The current volume is a projected Volume One of a multi-volume study. The final result is intended to be a global compendium, attempting to assess the role and place of Islam in the contemporary world. As this work ends, the author begins research on a second volume tentatively titled "Islam in South Asia."

For more than 20 years the author taught a course at the National Defense Intelligence College on "Islam in the Contemporary World." Through the years, students in this course have conducted research and written papers on the place of Islam in a country of choice. Other students chose a particular Islamist group to examine with an eye to assessing its particular significance. Altogether, more than 250 papers have been amassed.

The current study is inspired by the efforts of all these students, but is significantly supplemented by the author's own research and experience over even more years of study and teaching about Islam. In writing their papers, students responded to a standard set of five questions:

1. How did Islam come to the country? Or how did the country come to be predominately Islamic?
2. How central has Islam (as opposed to other political ideologies) been in the political history of the country as it has come into modern times?
3. What is the official policy of the current government of the country toward Islam? Why does the government have such a policy? And what are the benefits and costs to the government for maintaining such a policy?

---

[1] Central Intelligence Agency, *Intelligence for a New Area in American Foreign Policy*, Center for the Study of Intelligence Conference Report, 10-11 September 2003, Charlottesville, Virginia (Washington, DC: Center for the Study of Intelligence, January 2004), 20.

4. What principal Islamist movements exist within the country (or in exile) that are working to change the current political status quo (or maintain it)? If there is more than one, why the multiplicity of movements? What animates the adherents of these movements, and what is/are their goal(s)?

5. What is your prognosis concerning the future of contemporary Islamic movements in the country of your study?

The current study follows this same thematic approach, although much integration across the region being examined (Southeast Asia) was necessary. A copy of these five questions sat before the author constantly during the more than one year required to complete this study.

The chief concern about Islam for intelligence personnel and national policy-makers is not its spiritual or religious dimensions but rather its political aspects. Since the 1979 Iranian revolution, and more particularly since the shocking attacks on the New York World Trade Center and the Pentagon in Washington, DC, on September 11, 2001, this political aspect of Islam has assumed a new importance that was not so readily apparent in the earlier decades of the 20th century. Islam as a political factor in world politics, particularly in the Muslim world itself, during the post-September 11, 2001, era is the principal focus of this study. Factors other than Islam—nationalism, modernization, globalization, secular political ideologies, and the impact of external powers—are of course also part of the political milieu of every Muslim country. The aim of this study has been to achieve a balanced assessment in which the impact of the Islamic political factor is measured as one of several other factors operating in the politics of the Muslim world.

Student authors who contributed to my thinking on Southeast Asia include: Paul E. Belt, Shawn P. Boudreau, William R. Bray, Jimmy L. Briggs, Robert J. Briggs, Ray M. Ceralde, Shannon L. Cornwell, Robert A. Dahlke, Steven E. Daskal, Howard C. Davis, Susan L. Davis, Andrew J. Furne, Mary P. Gibson, Cecil D. Giddens, Robert E. Hagen, Richard W. Hayden, Victor R. Jolin, Jason A. Kotara, Jennifer Laun, Kevin M. Lucey, Bill A. Miller, Elaine M. Parks, Kelly Parks, Steven F. Rue, Houston S. Roby, Rachel Schindel-Gombis, Margaret Silberstern, Sherril L. Stramara, and Danny R. Thornton. I have reread each of these student papers in the preparation for this study. They will see little of their work in the final product, however, as I found it necessary to go far beyond their own modest term papers in my research. Nevertheless, each one was a source of inspiration, a source of ideas, and a pointer to useful sources.

As one who has spent a career as a specialist in the Middle East, the author is conscious of his limitations in writing about Southeast Asia. However, contact with a number of such regional specialists, such as Anwar Ibrahim and Eugene Martin, who have read and commented on various parts of the study, has been helpful. Friends David Dennis and Jennifer Noyon also have read and commented on different parts of the text. I thank my wife, Nasrine, for her patience and support. The author assumes full responsibility for any limitations of the study, of which he is sure there are many.

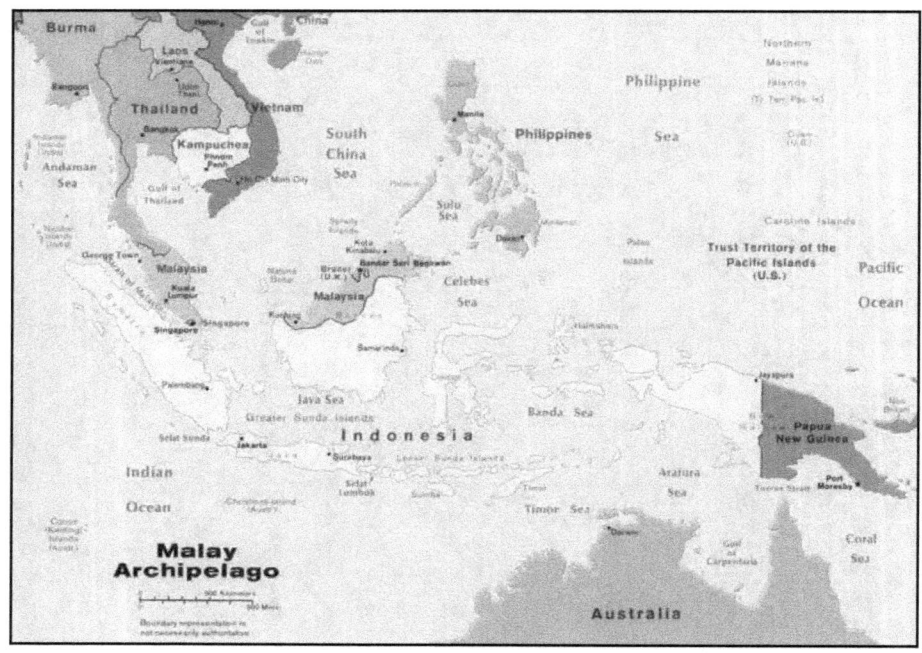

The Malay Archipelago, a region more commonly known as Southeast Asia.
Source: CIA.

CHAPTER 1

ISLAM IN SOUTHEAST ASIA: HISTORICAL BACKGROUND

GENERAL CONSIDERATIONS

The Malay peninsula and Indonesian archipelago of southeast Asia, extending from southern Thailand in the west and the southwestern portions of the Philippines in the east, constitute a highly populated geographic region where Islam is well established. The Muslim Hui people of central China (as opposed to the Uygurs of western China) and the Cham people of Cambodia and Vietnam may also be thought of as belonging to this same regional grouping.

Table 1 Muslim Population in Southeast Asia			
Country	**Total Population (millions)**	**Percent Muslims**	**Muslim Population (millions)**
Brunei	0.4	67.2	0.3
Cambodia	13.4	> 0.1	0.1
China	1298	1.4	18.2
Indonesia	238.5	88	210
Malaysia	23.5	52.9	12.4
Singapore	4.4	14	0.6
Philippines	86.2	5	4.3
Thailand	64.9	3.8	2.5
Vietnam	82.7	> 0.01	0.1

Source: Central Intelligence Agency, *The World Fact Book, 2004*. Washington, DC: Central Intelligence Agency, 2004. Intelink URL: *http://www.cia.gov/references/csfo/cfactbook/index.html*. Percentages cross-referenced with Richard V. Weekes. *The Muslim Peoples: An Ethnographic Survey* (Westport, CT: Greenwood Press, 1984)

The modern state of Indonesia is the largest country in the world in terms of its Muslim population, although at least 12 percent of its population is non-Muslim. Malaysia, a much less populous state, is politically dominated by its Muslim Malay population, despite the fact that Malay Muslims constitute barely a majority in the country. In Thailand and the Philippines, the Muslim populations constitute small minorities of about four to five percent. Nevertheless, these minorities are large and concentrated enough to be politically significant in each country. The Hui people of China, who number approximately 9.2 million, are numerically significant but constitute less than one percent of the vast Chinese population of nearly 1.4 billion. The small Sultanate of Brunei, famous for the fabulous wealth its ruler derives from rich petroleum deposits found under its soil, constitutes only a tiny fraction of the large Muslim community in southeast Asia. The Cham Muslims of Cambodia, who numbered approximately 300,000 in the mid-1970s, saw their numbers drop to slightly more than 100,000 due to the intense persecution they suffered at the hands of the Khmer Rouge between 1975 and 1979.[1]

Islam and "Malayness"

In general, the term "Muslim" in southeast Asia also means Malay. Although Indonesia and the Philippines together constitute a complex island archipelago (Indonesia itself consists of 13,667 islands spread over three time zones, although only five of these can be considered major population centers), populated by a large number of ethnic groups (more than 50 in the case of Indonesia, more than ten in the Philippines, and at least ten in Malaysia), the process of Islamization in the region has also been perceived as a process of Malayization in that, particularly in the early period of Islamization, the Malay language served as the *lingua franca* of the loose confederation of trading sultanates that firmly established Islam in the region. This process was unintentionally reinforced by the Dutch administration of the Netherlands East Indies that promoted the use of Malay throughout the islands.[2] Today, *Bahasa Indonesia*, the formally adopted national language of Indonesia, is but a variant of the Malay language spoken in Malaysia (*Bahasa Malaysia*), whose purpose is to knit the multiethnic and multilingual, diverse population of Indonesia together. Similarly, both the Muslim minorities in Thailand's five southernmost provinces of Pattani, Songkhla, Satun, Yala, and Narathiwat and the Philippine's two substantially Muslim-populated southwestern regions identify themselves as Malays rather than as Thais or Filipinos. Even the Cham Muslims of Cambodia and Vietnam carry identities as being of Malay origin. Only the thoroughly Sinicized Hui Muslims of central China lack such a Malay identity, although no doubt some of their original numbers were of Malay origin. To be a Muslim in southeast Asia, therefore, carries an ethnic as well as a religious identity and makes adherence to Islam all the more relevant politically.

The Potential of Malay Unity

The contemporary militant Islamist group in the region, *Jemaah Islamiyah*, has as its stated goal the unification of these Muslim Malay people into a single Islamic state,

---

[1] Zachary Abuza, *Militant Islam in Southeast Asia: Crucible of Terror* (Boulder, CO: Lynn Reinner Publishers, 2003), 81.

[2] Robert Day McAmis, *Malay Muslims* (Grand Rapids, MI: William B. Eerdmans Publishing Co., 2002), 47.

comprising not only Indonesia and Malaysia, but also the southern Thai and Philippine provinces. There is no indication that the Cham of Cambodia and Vietnam are included in this ambition, but Cham Muslims from Cambodia are active in the movement. The Hui of China are probably excluded from the Islamist vision of *Jemaah Islamiyah*, but their presence could weigh in with regard to Chinese policy toward the Muslim peoples of southeast Asia. The *Jemaah Islamiyah* and its affiliate groups (e.g., Abu Sayyaf in the Philippines) stand accused of numerous acts of terrorism in southeast Asia and have been linked to bin Ladin's *al-Qa'ida* organization. Accordingly, the *Jemaah Islamiyah* has been targeted in the U.S.-sponsored Global War on Terrorism (GWOT) and is strongly opposed by the four major state regimes in the region affected by the *Jemaah Islamiyah* ambition. In the face of such fierce opposition, it seems unlikely that the self-defeating terrorist tactics adopted by the *Jemaah Islamiyah* can have any short-term prospect of success.

The *Jemaah Islamiyah* vision of a unified Muslim Malay Southeast Asia is not all that different, however, from that of revolutionary Indonesian leader Sukarno. His original stated objective also envisioned a political union of the same scattered territories, albeit under a nationalist, rather than a religious/ideological, banner. Although the original BPUPKI[3] constitutional document did not include the Muslim portions of Thailand nor the Philippines, it did include all of what is now contemporary Malaysia as well as Portuguese Timor (East Timor), and subsequent interregional politics suggests that the Muslim (Malay) areas of the Philippines and Thailand were not wholly outside of Sukarno's scope. His famous *Pancasila* doctrine, which remains institutionalized in Indonesian constitutional practice, was his way of preempting efforts of some to make Indonesia an Islamic state governed by Islamic law (*Shari'a*) and to base it on nationalist principles instead. The result has been the ironic situation in which Malaysia with a population that is 53 percent Muslim is "officially" an Islamic state, whereas the much larger Indonesia with a population that is 88 percent Muslim is not.

The vision of a politically unified East Indies, including the Malay peninsula, however, may have been less a Japanese-empowered indigenous political movement than a legacy of Dutch imperial attitudes which from the beginning sought a monopoly on the spice trade in the East Indies and jealously guarded Holland's dominant position in southeast Asia as best it could. The Netherlands did not prove to be the strongest of the competing European imperial powers. It never seriously challenged Spanish control of the Philippines, never replaced Portuguese control of East Timor, proved unable to

---

[3] *Badan Penyelidik Usaha Persiapan Kemerdekaan Indonesia* (BPUPKI) was a committee established under the auspices of the Japanese colonial administration in March 1945, shortly before the surrender of the Japanese to the United States on August 15, 1945, to draw up a constitution for an independent, post-war Indonesia. The committee members included Sukarno, Muhammad Hatta, and other leading members of the Indonesian independence movement that successfully resisted the reimposition of Dutch rule after World War II. Japan gained a certain degree of Malay support during the war on both the Malay peninsula and the Indonesian archipelago by promising independence and a unified Malay state within the envisioned Greater East Asia Coprosperity Sphere following victory against the allies. The vision of *Raya Indonesia* (Greater Indonesia) remained part of Sukarno's policy throughout his period of rule, which ended in 1965.

challenge Thai hegemony over the northern Malay states, and finally proved unable to resist British inroads in the territories that were to become Malaysia. The result has been a divided region with different governance and administrative traditions that constitute more the legacy of the imperial past than of indigenous political evolution.

Factors Promoting Disunity

Yet another factor promoting political disunity has been the variety of autonomy or even independence movements that have characterized especially modern Indonesian political history. The almost continuous rebellion of Aceh in northwestern Sumatra and the independence movement of the Molucca Islands (*Republik Maluku Selatan*) in the mid-1950s are two of the most obvious examples of this tendency. The *Darul Islam* movement of the early 1950s in which an effort to establish an independent Islamic state governed by the *Shari'a* in western Java was yet another example of a different type. Comprised of thousands of islands, the Indonesian archipelago exhibits powerful centripetal political tendencies. When the European powers began arriving in the region in the 16th century, what they found was a large number of states—some Islamic sultanates, others Hindu/Buddhist rajas. As European power began to wane in the early 20th century, and especially after World War II, it was perhaps natural that regions of the East Indies that had once been states sought to revive their identity as independent states. In departing, the Dutch took note of this tendency and sought to empower it. Whereas Dutch administrators in the late 19th and early 20th centuries busied themselves with consolidating their rule, eliminating legacies of the old independent states that had characterized the East Indies and building the infrastructure of a modern, consolidated unitary state, as it became clear after World War II that the Dutch could no longer maintain their position in the region, they began restoring and recognizing a series of 15 states (e.g., East Indonesia, West Kalimantan, East Sumatra, Negara Madura, Daerah Banjar in Kalimantan (Borneo), Pasundan (west Java), and others). This was in advance of signing a treaty with the new revolutionary government of Indonesia that the Dutch would do only if the new state was organized as a federal system that continued to recognize the Dutch Crown, remained tied to Holland economically, and whose states could deal with the Dutch independently.

The ink was barely dry on the December 27, 1949, treaty that transferred sovereignty from the Netherlands to the new United States of Indonesia (*Republik Indonesia Serikat*) than the new states the Dutch had created began to dissolve themselves, either voluntarily or in response to threats by the revolutionary army of Indonesia. On August 17, 1950, the federal system, which the Dutch had demanded, was formally abolished and a new constitution, closely modeled on the original constitution of 1945 defining the Republic of Indonesia as a unitary state with a strong central government based in Jakarta, was proclaimed. The original consolidating tendency of the Dutch colonial authority was restored with subsequent pain and hardship to many citizens of the new country who opposed this tendency.

The struggle between the forces of centralization and those of decentralization has been a characteristic feature of the history of southeast Asia. Over time, the forces of centralization have generally prevailed. Whether such a tendency will always be the case cannot be known with any certainty. Islam is a factor that works both ways. As the history of southeast Asia demonstrates, Muslims desirous of residing in a state where *Shari'a* prevails can be satisfied with a small state, but they also can labor on behalf of a large, strong, centralized state. What tendency Muslims are likely to favor in southeast Asia is an important theme of this work.

HISTORICAL OVERVIEW

Role of Trade

Most sources trace the introduction of Islam into southeast Asia back no further than the 10th or 11th centuries, but a case can be made that the Arab, Persian, and later Indian traders that were the primary propagators of the faith into the region were active as early as the 7th century and certainly by the 9th century, when T'ang Chinese fashions were all the rage in Abbasid Baghdad.[4] Gradually these merchants settled in regions where they established their businesses, married within the indigenous population, and raised families according to Islamic law. The new faith spread slowly among the established Hindu and Buddhist populations of the region, gradually leading to the conversion of some local rulers and the establishment of a number of Muslim kingdoms (sultanates) throughout the region during the 14th and 15th centuries. The first major state of this type to be established was the Sultanate of Malacca in the mid-15th century,[5] although several other ruling families had converted earlier. With the establishment of a strong Muslim state in Malacca as a linchpin for trade throughout the archipelago, Islam gradually permeated the ports and capital cities of various other kingdoms in the Malay peninsula and eastern archipelago long before effectively penetrating the agricultural populations of the interior or the more easterly islands.

Prior to Malacca on the Malay peninsula, a sultanate had been established at Aceh on the northwest coast of Sumatra as early as 1250, but following Malacca more coastal Islamic states quickly came into being in the late 15th and early 16th centuries: Patani in what is now southern Thailand; Johore and Perak on the Malay peninsula; Bantam, Mataram, and Demak on Java; Brunei in Borneo; and Makassar in Sulawesi. In the 17th century too, inland Muslim sultanates, such as that of Minangkabau in

---

[4] Marshall G.S. Hodgson, *The Venture of Islam,* Volume 1 (Chicago, IL: University of Chicago Press, 1974), 233.

[5] B.R. Pearn., *An Introduction to the History of South-East Asia* (Berhad, Malaysia: Longman Malaysia SDN, 1970), 26–34. The strategically located Malacca was a center for Arab, Persian, Indian and Chinese traders moving their goods between various trade centers. Due to the prevailing winds, Malacca hosted ships and their crews for weeks at a time while they waited for winds to shift. Beginning about 1402 Paramesawar, a new Hindu Prince of Malacca, began asserting his strength against regional enemies, leading him to assert his status as an independent ruler and ultimately declaring himself a Muslim prior to his death in 1424, taking the name Megat Iskander Shah. That the conversion was contested was evidenced by the power struggle between his two sons following his death. The issue was not settled until 1446 when Kasim prevailed for Islam and took the name Muzaffar Shah and the title of Sultan.

Central Sumatra, began to be established.[6] The movement included what is now the Philippines, where Islam was well established on Sulu and Basilan islands and on Mindanao in the south and was spreading into the north at the time of the arrival of the Spaniards in the 16th century.[7] A Muslim sultan by the name of Suleiman had just established himself in Manila at the time of the arrival of the Spanish fleet in 1571,[8] and it is likely the whole Philippine archipelago would have been more strongly influenced by Islam had the Spanish intervention not occurred.[9]

Yet another direction of this movement was mainland China, where Arab and Persian merchants and mariners also gradually settled in various coastal port cities, especially Canton, bringing their religion with them. Marrying local Han Chinese women, but raising families within the Islamic tradition, these merchant/traders lived in specially designated "barbarian settlements" which may have corresponded to the various sultanates being established elsewhere in Southeast Asia. Their numbers only increased as families grew and as more foreign Muslims continued to settle in China until the 14th century. The establishment of the Ming Dynasty, which overthrew the former Mongol dynasty in 1368, led to a period of severe backlash against foreign presence in China, in which Muslim immigrants were forced either to depart or assimilate (abandon foreign languages). Barbara Pillsbury notes, "It was during this period (the Ming Dynasty, 1368–1644) that the Muslims in China became Sinicized, acculturating to Han Chinese ways through the adoption of Han surnames, clothing and food habits and through speaking Chinese as their everyday language."[10] They did not abandon their religion, however, but continued to increase in numbers, even as they became "increasingly similar, physically as well as culturally, to the Han."[11] Gradually, the Muslims ceased to be thought of as foreigners, but a unique Chinese people, the *huihui*, or *Hui*, as opposed to the vast *Han* majority in China.

The partial Islamization of the Champa kingdom in central Vietnam followed this same pattern. Originally established as a Hindu kingdom by Malay immigrants originating in today's Indonesia, probably from Aceh, the Champa kingdom, whose capital was at Indrapura (Tra Kiêu) near modern Da Nang, flourished from the 5th

---

[6] Anthony H. Johns, "Indonesia: Islam and Cultural Pluralism," in *Islam in Asia: Religion, Politics and Society*, ed. by John L. Esposito (New York: Oxford University Press, 1987), 205.

[7] Lela Garner Noble, "The Philippines: Autonomy for the Muslims," in *Islam in Asia: Religion, Politics and Society*, ed. by John L. Esposito (New York: Oxford University Press, 1987), 97.

[8] Charles Kimball, "The Long Road from Mecca to Manila," in *History of Thailand and Southeast Asia*. URL: *http://www.guidetothailand.com/thailand-history/mecca_manila.htm*. The name Manila is allegedly derived from the Arabic term *Ma'man Allah* (safe/secure place of Allah). Ismail al-Farouki. "Islamic Renaissance in Contemporary Society," in Muhammad Mumtaz Ali, ed., *Modern Islamic Movements: Models, Problems and Prospects* (Kuala Lumpur: A.S. Noordeen, 2000), 5.

[9] Ira M. Lapidus, *A History of Islamic Societies* (Cambridge, UK: Cambridge University Press, 1988), 469–470, provides an excellent account of the Islamization process in Southeast Asia.

[10] Barbara Pillsbury, "Hui" in *The Muslim Peoples: An Ethnographic Survey*, ed. by Richard V. Weekes (Westport, CT: Greenwood Press, 1984), 333.

[11] Pillsbury, "Hui," 333.

century C.E. until 1471, when it was destroyed by the Vietnamese in the course of that kingdom's southward expansion. At that time most of the Cham who had become Muslim fled to Angkor (modern Cambodia), where they were given refuge by the Khmer king. There they continue to live today in scattered, isolated Muslim settlements in the larger Buddhist, Khmer culture. Before the fall of the Champa kingdom, its prosperity had rested in involvement in the east-west trade between China and India, plus a kinship and perhaps religious alliance with the Malays of Malacca and the Indonesian archipelago to which they were closely linked both politically and economically.[12] A small number of Muslim Cham continues to reside in central and southern coastal Vietnam.

Role of Islamic Schools/Missionary Activity

A primary means by which Islam spread throughout southeast Asia was the *pondok* (*pesantren* in Indonesia), a Malay term for an Islamic religious school corresponding to the *madrasa* in the central Islamic lands. Hajj Ahmad Kamar suggests that "people were attracted by provisions in the *Qur'an* and the *Hadith* that mankind should be ranked on a basis of interpersonal equality,"[13] that is, by the egalitarian ethos of the faith as opposed to the rigid caste structure associated with Hinduism. Islam was spread by *'ulama* who opened such religious training centers, where they trained students in Islamic doctrine. The students then returned to their district villages and communities, where they in turn spread the word of the *Qur'an*. The connection of Islam with the seagoing international trade of the era was also clearly relevant.[14]

Role of Sufism

Most sources agree that the Islam the native Malay population of this region found agreeable and attractive was also closely associated with Sufi (Islamic mysticism) teachings or, perhaps more apt, with that understanding of Islam that enables the believer to maintain diverse approaches to the experience of religious truth while affirming the oneness of God and the truth of the Islamic message. The association of Islam and mysticism enabled converts to maintain elements of traditional Hindu-Buddhist-animist practice and also accept the basic values and tenets of Islam as well. The result has been an Islam that has been historically syncretic and characterized by tolerance of diverse points of views, combined with legacies of pre-Islamic practice. The noted British anthropologist Clifford Geertz provided an example of this syncretism from a field visit he made to Java in 1960. A typical prayer offered by a Javanese villager to

---

[12] Ronald Provencher, "Cham" in Richard V. Weekes, ed., *Muslim Peoples: A World Ethnographic Survey*, 2d ed. (Westport, CT: Greenwood Press, 1984), 199.

[13] Hj. Ahmad Kamar, "Islam in Peninsular Malaysia," in *Muslims in China and South-East Asia*. URL: *http://www.erols.com/zenithco/index.html*. Accessed 10 April 1998.

[14] For an excellent discussion of the Islamization process in Southeast Asia, see Lapidus, *History of Islamic Societies*, 469.

begin a feast included invocations to the guardian spirits of the village, the household angel of the kitchen, the ancestors of all the guests, and the spirits of the fields, waters, and a nearby volcano. But the prayer ended dramatically with the phrase, "There is no god but Allah and Muhammad is the Prophet of Allah."[15]

ENTER THE EUROPEANS

It is difficult to estimate the spread of Islam in Southeast Asia by the time of the arrival of the West European powers in the region in the 16th century. What first the Portuguese, then later the Spanish, the Dutch, and the English merchantmen who explored these lands, found was a series of mainly coastal Muslim sultanates which dominated the east-west sea trade routes that linked China with India and the Middle East beyond, but remained in competition with other Hindu and Buddhist kingdoms that still existed in the region. What is clear, however, is that entry of the Western powers into southeast Asia helped to spur the advance of Islam over the next few centuries, even as the Europeans consolidated political and economic control over the region. As the Europeans made use of missionaries to attempt to win the hearts and minds of natives to support European colonial rule, so also Islamic missionary activity proved even more successful in promoting a unifying mechanism for resisting the permanence of European rule. As a result, although the Europeans succeeded until the 20th century in dominating southeast Asia politically, militarily, and economically, they proved unable to dominate the region culturally.

On the other hand, the modern states of southeast Asia owe their existence more to the interaction of West European powers in the region during the 16th to 20th centuries than to indigenous political evolution. The Philippines as a state are that collection of East Indian islands over which Spain was able to establish authority beginning in the 16th century. Indonesia is a product of Dutch control, whereas Malaysia (including its provinces of Sabah and Sarawak on the Indonesian island of Borneo) is a legacy of British colonial rule. Thailand (Kingdom of Siam) remained relatively free from European imperial outreach and indeed was often a very strong kingdom capable of exerting imperial ambitions of its own over parts of the Malay peninsula. As a result, when each of these states emerged from European colonial control as modern, independent nation states in the mid-20th century, the multi-tribal and multiethnic, yet nearly overwhelmingly Malay and Muslim, population of the region was almost irrevocably divided by modern boundaries and different governing and administrative traditions.

Portugal

The first European colonizers on the scene were the Portuguese. Their success at capturing Malacca in 1511 had the effect of disrupting the unity of the Muslim-

---

[15] Clifford Geertz, *The Religion of Java* (Chicago: University of Chicago Press, 1960), 40–41.

dominated network of trading states centered upon this strategic city that had come into being during the 15th century. Nevertheless, the Portuguese were unable to assert control or even ascendancy over the whole region. Instead, they pursued a policy of shifting alliances with native Muslim and Hindu rulers to shore up and maintain their position against others who sought to dislodge them, especially the Sultanate of Aceh, which remained a constant threat to Portuguese control of Malacca during the period of Portuguese rule.[16]

Spain

Another key competitor to Portugal at this time was Spain, whose fleet, sent from Mexico in 1565, began to take control of the Philippines (named after King Philip II of Spain). It eventually displaced in 1571 the Sultan of Manila, whose former seat of authority was made the seat of Spanish rule in the colony. Unlike the Portuguese, who used missionaries relatively unsuccessfully in an effort to convert native Malays and draw them into loyalty to Portuguese rule, the Spanish used the Church as a mechanism of administration in the Philippines. Although economic and trading interests were of concern, ultimate conversion of Filipinos to Christianity was a major goal of Spanish policy. Overall, Spain's occupation of most of the Philippine Islands occurred with very little bloodshed, because the native inhabitants offered little armed resistance. Two areas that did offer resistance, however, were the Igorot, the highland tribal peoples on the main northern island of Luzon, and the Muslim inhabitants of the southern areas of Mindanao, Basilan, and the Sulu archipelago. Both of these peoples remained detached and alienated from Spanish rule in the Philippines until its end in 1898, with the Moors, or Moros, as the Spanish labeled them, preferring independence from Spanish rule and providing unceasing resistance to Spanish control.

Spain also moved in quickly on various Portuguese interests, taking over the island of Ternate in the eastern Spice Islands in 1574 following a popular revolt against the Portuguese governor and in 1578 successfully placing its own candidate of choice as the new Sultan of Brunei on the north coast of Borneo. The sudden death in 1578 of the King of Portugal in Morocco led King Philip II of Spain to assert a personal claim to the throne of Portugal, which he succeeded in having recognized in 1580. Under Philip, Portuguese colonial interests in Southeast Asia were not vigorously pursued, but rather than slowly falling before Spanish ambitions it was now the Netherlands and England, both enemies of Spain in this era, that quickly moved in on Portugal's interests in the region.

---

[16] On the Portuguese effort in Southeast Asia, see Lapidus, *History of Islamic Societies*, 470–471, and *Malaysia: A Country Study*, 17–20.

Holland

Following the Dutch declaration of independence from the Spanish empire in 1581 and the English defeat of the Spanish Armada in 1588, both Holland and England emerged as significant maritime powers, building faster and better ships than the Spanish or Portuguese. In Southeast Asia the Dutch in particular moved quickly to seize Portuguese possessions. The Dutch United East India Company, established in 1602 and chartered by the Dutch parliament, was the agency for advancing these interests. In 1619, the Company, which had forged alliances with the Sultans of Johore (Malaysia) and Aceh (Sumatra) against the Portuguese, established a permanent base at Batavia (modern Jakarta) on the north coast of Java, from which they sought to control the sea lanes through the archipelago. In January 1641, in coordination with the Sultan of Johore, the Dutch finally were able to overcome the Portuguese fortress at Malacca. Henceforth, the Dutch were the preeminent European power controlling trade in Southeast Asia and dominating local rulers until the coming of the English in the latter decades of the 18th century.[17]

England

Concentrating its attentions on the Indian subcontinent, the English East India Company was content not to compete seriously with the Dutch in southeast Asia until increased trade between southern China and English India in the mid-18th century led the Company in 1773–75 to seek basing facilities on the northern coast of Borneo, where the Dutch had shown little interest, and on the Sulu archipelago whose sultan, though technically a subject of the Spanish governor in Manila, remained eager to assert his independence. A decade later, in 1785, the Company moved to establish a permanent naval base in the eastern Indian Ocean, negotiating a treaty with the Sultan of Kedah on the northern Malay Peninsula in which it was granted the Island of Penang. In this case the Sultan of Kedah was seeking an alliance that would strengthen his hand against the king of Siam (Thailand), to whom he was tributary. The 1795 occupation of Holland by the forces of revolutionary France strengthened the English hand further, when the Dutch government in exile in London agreed to permit English officials to take over all Dutch territories overseas temporarily in order to deny them to the French.

A key figure at this time was Thomas Stamford Raffles, an English East India Company official, stationed at Penang, who became lieutenant governor of Java during the period of temporary English rule over the Dutch East Indies. Unhappy with his government's decision to return the East Indies to Holland after the demise of Napoleon, he played a shrewd political game with the Sultan of Johore (Malaysia) who, in 1819, leased to the English East India Company the right to establish a settlement on the swampy and largely uninhabited island of Singapore. In a very short

---

[17] On Dutch operations in Southeast Asia, see Lapidus, *History of Islamic Societies*, 471–473.

time, this settlement flourished, in part because of its highly strategic location on the Strait of Malacca, but also due to Raffles' own excellent administrative abilities, and became the dominant trading entrepôt of the region. Unable to resist these English inroads into its previously unchallenged domain, Holland agreed in 1824 to an Anglo-Dutch treaty which defined the Malay peninsula and Singapore as being in the English sphere of influence, and England accepted the remainder of the Dutch East Indies that eventually became Indonesia as being solely a sphere of Dutch influence. On this basis, the groundwork was laid for the eventual establishment of the two major Malay states: Malaysia and Indonesia.

THE FORMATION OF MALAYSIA

Consolidation of English Authority

In 1826, following the treaty with Holland, the English joined their five coastal holdings on the peninsula (Penang, Wellesley [Perei], Dindings, Malacca, and Singapore) into a single administrative unit called the "Straits Settlements." At first headquartered in Penang, the administrative center was soon moved to Singapore in 1832. A subordinate unit of the English East India Company headquartered in Calcutta until 1857, the Straits Settlements was then taken over by the British Indian government until being made a Crown Colony under the Colonial Office in 1867.

The remainder of the peninsula consisted of the ten sultanates (including Patani, today a part of Thailand) into which it had been divided for years. From the perspective of the King of Siam (Thailand), however, these Islamic states had been established in traditional Thai lands, and with the retreat of Dutch power in the peninsula the Siamese king sought to assert Thai primacy over as many of them as possible. The Malay sultans responded by seeking English support for their independent status. Fearful of offending the King of Siam whose alliance the English wished to maintain against Burma, or later against the French in Indochina, yet not wishing to create hostile neighboring Islamic states, the various governors of the Straits Settlements walked a tightrope of diplomacy throughout the 19th century with regard to the Malay states. The long-term result was deeper and deeper involvement in the affairs of the Malay sultans until 1874, when the English governor at Singapore succeeded in beginning the process of establishing, in exchange for English support, English residents whose counsel "must be asked and acted upon on all questions other than those touching Malay custom and religion."[18] The first residents were established with the west coast Sultans of Perak, Negeri Sembilan, and Selangor. Later, in 1888, the Sultan of Pahang, a large east coast state, also requested and received a resident. The remaining six Malay sultanate—Kedah, Terengganu, Kelantan, Perlis, and Patani—all in the north and paying tribute to the King of Siam, as well as Johore in the south, next to Singapore, held aloof and refused to accept an English resident. The northern states were the poorest and least developed on the peninsula and have remained so until

---

[18] *Malaysia: A Country Study*, 30.

today, whereas Johore was and remains relatively prosperous. The sultans of each, however, resisted compromising their independence to the English, even after 1909, when King Chulalongkorn of Siam ceded to England suzerainty over all the northern sultanates except Patani.

Mechanisms of English Supervision

The resident system did have the impact of reducing the independence of the sultans that accepted them. The English residents "scrupulously maintained the etiquette and ceremony of Malay courts and gave government employment" to the relatives of the sultans and their retainers.[19] Meanwhile, payment of subsidies to make up for lost revenues that accrued from such English-desired reforms as the abolition of slavery or the suppression of piracy had the long-term impact of transforming the sultans and their governments into appendages of the English administration.

The grouping of four so-called "protected" sultanates into a State Council headed by the governor of the Straits Settlements, but from which the five "unprotected" sultanates held aloof, formed the basis of the future government of Malaysia. Through the State Council the British residents were gradually able to introduce modern Western concepts of governance and administration. Finally, in 1896 the British administration was able to persuade the sultans under their protection to sign a formal Treaty of Federation, which established a federal, but nevertheless unitary, central government headed by a so-called Resident General, a single British official in charge of the residents of each of the Federated Sultanates and appointed by the Governor of the Straits Settlements. In this manner a British-controlled central government was brought into being, but the appearances of traditional Muslim governance were also maintained. In 1909, Kuala Lumpur was selected as a seat of government for a new Federal Council, headed by the Resident General, who was entrusted with modern governance responsibilities for what was now called the Federation of Malay States.

Economic Transformation

This political transformation was closely associated with economic developments that were taking place during this same period. The rapid expansion of the tin mining industry after 1848, then of rubber plantations beginning in the early 20th century, and finally of iron mining and palm oil plantations, radically transformed the traditional pastoral Malay economy centered around small village life. The wealth generated by this economic development eased the political change that gradually transformed the sultans under British protection into something more like government functionaries than independent rulers.

---

[19] *Malaysia: A Country Study*, 30.

At the same time, economic change had far less social impact on the rural Malay way of life than might have been expected. Because Malays were generally perceived not to be sufficiently adaptable to work in the new industrial sectors of the Malay economy, the British, other Western, Chinese, and Japanese investors who provided capital to fund these new economic ventures relied heavily on the import of Chinese labor, which greatly augmented the small, already established Chinese community that lived in many coastal towns of the Malay peninsula, especially the Straits Settlements. The British also relied heavily on immigrants from India and Sri Lanka who served in the British police and armed forces of the Malay Federation. Indian immigrants also played many private sector roles as well, such as truck, bus, and taxi drivers, night watchmen and rubber plantation workers. This immigration was so substantial that by the 1930s the demographic portrait of the Malay peninsula had changed radically. Whereas the population at the beginning of the 19th century had been almost wholly Malay, by the mid-20th century Malays constituted only about 50 percent in their own country, Chinese about 35 percent, and Indians (both Hindu and Muslim) 10 percent. This major demographic change would also have serious political ramifications in the future.

The economic and demographic changes noted above were confined almost entirely to the west coast of the Malay peninsula, within the area defined as the Federation of Malay States. The unfederated Malay states along the east coast were far less affected, the population consisting almost entirely of Malay rural villagers living in settlements of less than 1,000 people. The same condition was generally true of the two territories on North Borneo — Sabah and Sarawak — that were also to become part of modern Malaysia. These were originally parts of the Sultanate of Brunei whose ruler, in 1841, in return for services rendered in helping suppress a local revolt against him, awarded the western territory — today called Sarawak — to James Brooke, a former British East India Company officer and man of independent wealth, in return for an annual subsidy. This concession remained in the hands of the Brooke family until 1946, when Britain transformed Sarawak into a Crown Colony.

The territory to the northeast of Brunei (later to be called Sabah) the sultan leased in 1865 to a United States venture, the American Trading Company of Borneo. This company failed, however, and sold its lease to a Hong Kong-based British firm that eventually took the name British North Borneo Company. The European investors soon found themselves in a dispute with the Sultan of Sulu (Philippines), who also laid claim to the leased territory that he argued the Sultan of Brunei had no right to lease. The situation was complicated by the determination of the Spanish rulers of the Philippines to force the submission of the Muslim Sultan of Sulu once and for all and to annex all territories claimed by him, including the land controlled by the North Borneo Company. To protect this British interest, the British government granted the company a royal charter in 1881. An 1885 treaty among Britain, Spain, and Germany finally settled the dispute by recognizing Spanish control of Sulu in exchange for Spain's dropping any claims to territory in Borneo. The British then moved quickly to establish, in 1888, a protectorate arrangement, similar to that already in effect for the federated Malay states, with Sarawak, the Sultan of Brunei, and the British North

Borneo Company jurisdiction, and in 1891 an Anglo-Dutch arrangement delineated a border agreement between Dutch and British territories on Borneo. The way was made, therefore, for these territories (except for Brunei) to become part of modern Malaysia in 1963.

Continuing Role of Malay "Custom and Religion"

A feature of British governance in Malaya was careful avoidance of questions "touching on Malay custom and religion" that remained in the hands of the traditional sultans. An important result of this policy was the strong persistence of traditional society and Malay customs and mores, particularly in the poorer but more independent states of the "unfederated sultans" (Perlis, Kedah, Terengganu, and Kelantan in the north, and Johore in the south). In contrast, the peoples of the Federation of Malay States as well as the Straits Settlements were undergoing rapid social and economic change associated with the development of big businesses, improved transportation networks, electrification, better public health facilities, and greater educational opportunities. The primary agents as well as the chief beneficiaries of these changes, however, were the growing European, Chinese, and Indian immigrant communities, far more than the Malays themselves. Increasingly, the lands of the Malay peninsula were becoming a complex, pluralistic, and bifurcated society over which the Malay sultans, in cooperation with the British, continued to be dominant politically, but in which the immigrant communities were dominant economically and commercially.

Growth of Diversity in English Malaya

Not surprisingly, as the Malay peninsula moved closer to political independence during the 1940s and 1950s, this imbalance became a prominent issue. Emerging political parties tended to be ethnically based, with Chinese and Indian parties generally seeking greater political influence and Malay parties seeking an improved economic status for the indigenous Malay population, but not at the cost of reduced Malay political status. The Japanese occupation during World War II (1942 – 1945) greatly aggravated ethnic relations, particularly between the Malays and the Chinese. Closely allied with the British and mainland Chinese, the Chinese community bitterly opposed the Japanese occupation, and resistance groups against it were predominately Chinese in composition and leadership. To curry local support, the Japanese demonstrated strong favoritism toward Malays and sought to empower a growing Malay nationalist movement that went so far as to envision an eventual political union with the Indonesian archipelago. The animosities raised during the war did not end with the defeat of the Japanese in 1945, but continued to animate Malayan politics for a number of years to come.

World War II

The relative ease by which the Japanese overran the British in the Malay peninsula and the Dutch in the East Indies in 1942 gravely weakened the prestige of both colonial powers in the eyes of the local populations. The weak post-war financial positions of both European powers, as well as the war weariness of their citizens, moreover, made it difficult to restore their former authority in both areas. Yet both tried. As the British returned to the Malay peninsula, the government was determined to weaken the status of the Malays who were perceived to have collaborated with the Japanese during the war. In April 1946 it announced the creation of a new entity called the Malayan Union that united the former federated and unfederated states—along with Penang and Malacca of the former Straits Settlements—into a single Crown Colony under a British governor, and in which the former quasi-independent sultanates were totally suppressed. Singapore was withheld from the Union as a separate British Crown colony. The Union arrangement, moreover, defined all inhabitants of the new political entity as equal citizens, regardless of ethnicity, and English along with Malay was adopted as official languages of the country.

Assertion of Malay Hegemony

This step by the British authorities provoked a powerful and unified reaction among Malays, who feared that such a system would entrench ethnic Chinese domination of the economy and lead to Chinese political domination. In March 1946, even before the proclamation of the Malayan Union, a general meeting of Malay organizations was convened in Kuala Lumpur for the purpose of opposing the Union. The chief result of the meeting was the establishment of the United Malay National Organization (UMNO), a political party that succeeded in combating the Malayan Union, led the country into independence, and continues to be Malaysia's leading political party through today.

The formation of the UMNO was challenged by a counter-organization of non-Malay figures and secular political parties called the All-Malayan Council of Joint Action (AMCJA), which supported the Malayan Union, at least in principle. The association of the Malay Communist Party (CPM) with the Chinese-dominated organization, the insistence by the AMCJA that Singapore with its large Chinese majority be included in the Malayan Union, as well as the unified forcefulness of the Malay-dominated UMNO soon led the British to reverse their policy. In February 1948, the colonial authority announced the formation, in place of the Malayan Union, of a Federation of Malaya. In this new formula, the nine Malay sultans retained their former status and powers, especially with regard to Malay customs (*adat*) and religion. Joined with them were two new states, Penang and Malacca, formerly part of the Straits Settlements, which would have elected governors rather than hereditary sultans. Singapore with its 1.5 million Chinese inhabitants remained apart from the federation as a British Crown Colony, which ensured a Malay majority in the new Malay state.

The "Emergency"

The change in British policy emboldened the opponents of this policy, especially the Malaysian Communist Party and other left-wing groups, which so recently had been engaged in insurgent operations against the Japanese, to resort to "armed struggle" in an effort to overturn the established—as they viewed it—Anglo/Malay-dominated society and replace it with a more egalitarian political order as envisioned in the Malayan Union. "Terrorist" operations against remote rubber plantations and mines, culminating in the assassination of the British High Commissioner in October 1951, began almost immediately after implementation of the federation plan, leading the British in June 1948 to proclaim a state of emergency. The "Emergency," which was declared at an end only in 1960, although it was basically contained by the early 1950s, had the impact of delaying self-rule for the Federation that Britain had promised in 1948, but it did not stop it.

Movement toward Independence

In 1954, negotiations aimed at granting Malayan self-rule resumed, but the issue of communal equality remained a principal obstacle. In light of the Emergency and the sweep of Chinese Communist-inspired insurgencies in East Asia, the Malays were more insistent than ever that non-Malays not be granted full citizenship, and that pro-Malay economic incentives be institutionalized. The British continued to take the view that ethnic Chinese and Indians that had been in Malaya for generations were in fact there to stay and should be considered full citizens with equal rights in the country. Compromise was finally achieved by UMNO leader Tunku Abdul Rahman,[20] who formed an alliance relationship with counterpart conservative parties—the Malayan Chinese Association (MCA) and the Malayan Indian Congress (MIC)—in the other major Malayan ethnic communities. Together these parties proved able to dominate federal elections, both at the local and national levels, and to reach a compromise on ethnic issues that was minimally acceptable to all parties. These principles were enshrined in a Constitution drawn up between June and October 1956 and implemented on August 15, 1957, when the independence of Malaya was announced.

Independent Malaya

In the Constitution, the issue of citizenship was addressed by defining all persons born on the peninsula as citizens and requiring naturalization for all others. Malay desires were satisfied by the formal adoption of Malay (Bahasa Malaysia) as the

---

[20] Tunku Abdul Rahman, a member of the family of the Sultan of Kedah and a graduate of Cambridge University, became leader of UMNO in 1951, succeeding Dato Onn bin Ja'afar who resigned from the party after his failure to transform it from an all-Malay organization into a multiethnic party. *Malaysia: A Country Study*, 52.

official national language[21] and of Islam as the official religion of the state, although the freedom of the other religious communities was also guaranteed. The traditional role of the sultans was finessed by establishing the state as a constitutional monarchy. By the terms of the Constitution, the nine sultans chose one of their own as the paramount ruler, or king (*yang di-pertuan agong*), every five years. Although the King and the sultans retained their traditional privileges "touching on Malay custom and religion," they were otherwise made subordinate to a prime minister who was to be chosen by a popularly elected House of Representatives (*Dewan Rakyat*). The constitution also provided for an appointed Senate (*Dewan Negara*) with limited powers similar to those of the British House of Lords. Besides these provision, the Constitution also retained "special privileges for Malays in the civil service, scholarships, business enterprises, licenses, and the reservation of some land for their exclusive use."[22]

Table 2 Malaysian Kings (*Yang Di-Pertuan Agong*)		
Name of Individual	**Dates as King**	**Hereditary Title**
Abdul-Rahman	1957 – 1960	Sultan of Negeri Sembilan
Hisamuddin Alam Shah	1 Apr – 1 Sep 1960	Sultan of Senangor
Syed Putra	1960 – 1965	Raja of Perlis
Ismail Nasiruddin	1965 – 1970	Sultan of Terengganu
Abdul Halim	1970 – 1975	Sultan of Kedah
Yahya Petra	1975 – 1979	Sultan of Kelantan
Ahmad Shah al-Mustain Billah	1979 – 1984	Sultan of Pehang
Iskandar	1984 – 1989	Sultan of Johore
Aylan Mahibbudin Shah	1989 – 1994	Sultan of Perak
Jaafar	1994 – 1999	Sultan of Negeri Sembilan
Salahuddin Abdul-Aziz Shah	1999 – 2001	Sultan of Selangor
Syed Sirajuddin	2001 – Present	Raja of Perlis
Source: Table constructed from web pages associated with URL: *http://en.wikipedia.org/wiki/Yang-di-Pertuan_Agong*. Accessed 1 December 2004.		

---

[21] English was also considered a national language for a 10-year period.

[22] *Malaysia: A Country Study*, 53.

Singapore remained apart from the now independent Federation of Malaya, but it too was granted self-rule as part of the British Commonwealth in 1959. Now free to pursue an independent policy, its new Chinese leader, Lee Kwan-Yew, head of the island's left-wing People's Action Party (PAP), advocated incorporation into the Federation upon which resource—poor Singapore was dependent for almost everything, including its water, food, and electricity. Fearful that the large Chinese population of the island would tip the demographic balance against Malay dominance, the Malayan government remained reluctant. A British-sponsored suggestion that the inclusion of Crown Colonies Sarawak, Brunei, and North Borneo (Sabah), as well as Singapore, into an enlarged Federation, a step that helped to maintain the ethnic balance, tended to neutralize Malay opposition. Accordingly, following a lengthy political process which included amendments to the Malay Constitution to protect the rights of the Iban, Kadazan, and other ethnic minorities in the Borneo territories, and a referendum in each of the joining states, the merger was finally achieved with the formal establishment of the enlarged state of Malaysia on September 16, 1963.

Malaysia

The merger joined the original nine Malay sultanates, each characterized by a hereditary ruler, with the three former Straits Settlements—Penang, Malacca, and Singapore—and two states in North Borneo-Sarawak and Sabah-each of which was headed by an elected governor. Only the Sultanate of Brunei chose not to join the Federation. Increasingly wealthy from the revenues generated by the substantial oil reserves in his small territory, the sultan preferred not to be one of ten equal hereditary members of the Federation nor to share his oil wealth at the decision of the federal government. The adherence of Singapore to the Federation also proved to be short-lived. Despite efforts of its governor, Lee Kwan-Yew, to demonstrate the "Malay" character of the Chinese presence in Singapore and Malaysia, his real agenda was to achieve ethnic equality of all the Malaysian peoples, an attitude many Malays perceived as threatening to the special privileges they held in the Malaysian Constitution. Accordingly, in August 1965, just two years after the merger of Singapore into Malaysia, the two decided on divorce by mutual consent, and the island resumed its status as an independent, sovereign state.

Opposition to Independent Malaysia

The new Malaysian state did not come into being without significant opposition, however. The enthusiasm of the inhabitants of Sarawak and Sabah was far weaker than the proponents of the merger had expected, and the Sultan of Brunei succeeded holding aloof from it. The incorporation of Singapore proved unworkable as well. Still another opponent was the government of the Philippines, which resurrected the claim that Sabah was Filipino territory on the grounds that it originally had been part of the Sultanate of Sulu. Although Philippine President Diosdado Macapagal (1961 – 1965) formally accepted the results of the Sabah referendum that favored joining the North

Borneo territory to Malaysia, the issue remained a bone of contention between Kuala Lumpur and Manila for a number of years.

The major opposition to the enlarged Malaysian state was the government of Indonesia, then headed by President Sukarno. Strongly imbued with an anti-colonialist orientation that perceived the division of the Malay world to be the result of European imperialism, Sukarno was a champion of a "greater Indonesia" (*Raya* Indonesia) concept that hoped to unify the entire Malay world, from Patani in southern Thailand to Mindanao in the southwest Philippines, into a single Muslim Malay state under his own leadership. A revolutionary leader who had displaced the Dutch from Indonesia, Sukarno perceived Malaysia to be largely a British creation aimed at frustrating Malay union and its expansion into the "Indonesian territories" as an exercise in "neocolonialism." Unable to prevent the expansion of Malaysia by diplomatic means, he infiltrated Indonesian soldiers into Sabah, Sarawak, Singapore, and the Malay peninsula, where, within hours of the proclamation of the Federation of Malaysia in September 1963, they began to carry out acts of sabotage and terrorism. The aim was to spark a popular uprising against the government of Malaysia and in favor of union with Indonesia. The effort failed, but left Indonesia and Malaysia in a state of conflict until the overthrow of Sukarno on September 30, 1965. As it gradually became clear that the new military government of Indonesia under General Suharto had ended Sukarno's policy and accepted the new political status quo in the region, a treaty of peace and mutual recognition that brought a formal end to the hostilities was signed on August 11, 1966.

THE FORMATION OF INDONESIA

When after the defeat of Napoleon the Dutch returned to the East Indies in 1816, it was the Dutch government that reasserted colonial rule rather than the Dutch United East India Company that had been dissolved in 1799, and ownership of all Company properties had been assumed by the government of the Netherlands. Whereas the Company, operating out of Batavia (Jakarta), rather like one of the many other states on Java and the other islands of the archipelago, had working relations—sometimes friendly, sometimes hostile—with the sultans and rajas of these states and mainly sought to obtain profits as well as a dominant position politically and militarily, the new governor-general of all Dutch possessions in the East Indies came as a ruler with a bureaucratic staff determined to take charge and compel obedience.

Resistance to Dutch Rule

To maximize its profits, the Company had sought to monopolize trade in those items in which it specialized—spices in the first instance, but also textiles, coffee, and tea, as the years progressed. Although the rural peasantry may have suffered exploitation, their masters, the various Muslim and Hindu/Buddhist aristocracies that ruled them, profited from their relationship with the Company. The new Dutch government administration, however, introduced new concepts—cash crops and taxation—that, although they maximized profits for Holland, tended to circumvent the aristocracy and oppress the peasantry. Moreover, it created a firm determination to organize economic production around a centrally-controlled system of plantations, headed by Dutch administrators. A general preference for relying on imported Chinese labor also had the impact of further impoverishing the rural peasantry. Accumulating discontent with the new Dutch rule gave rise to a general uprising against it in 1825. The Java War of 1825–1830, as it came to be known, was led by a coalition of the Javanese aristocracy (traditional sultans and rajas), but had strong peasant support, and cost an estimated 200,000 Javanese lives before the Dutch succeeded in containing it by 1830.

The Dutch victory in this war consolidated Dutch rule in Java and paved the way for extension of this rule over the remaining islands of the archipelago that were not otherwise colonized by another European power.[23] Dutch success came as the result of building a series of small fortresses across Java, manned by small mobile units, that gradually enabled the Dutch to exert direct authority over the entire island. Although in the immediate aftermath of the Java War the Dutch authorities retreated somewhat from the system of direct rule they were in the process of establishing, over the longer run the system of indirect rule they established fairly rapidly evolved into a system of direct rule. Under the Dutch governor-general, Java was organized into a number of residencies (the final number was 16), each of which was administered by a Dutch "resident." Beneath each of the residents, the jurisdiction under his control was further divided into a number of *bupati* (regencies). At this level, the government was confided to a Javanese official, assisted by a Dutch "advisor," conceptualized at first as a "younger brother" of the *bupati*, but over time the actual representative of the resident for whom both were employed.

Like the British on the Malay peninsula, the Dutch at first recognized and sought to take advantage of the native authority invested in the traditional sultans and rajas of Java. Whether the *bupati* were reigning sultans or not, those whom the Dutch appointed to positions of responsibility and authority were drawn from what came to be known as the *priyayi* (aristocratic) class, the families of the sultans and rajas, a class of families whose status in Indonesian society was rooted both in royal descent and government service. The dominant aristocracy, however, was the Dutch governing establishment whose purpose was to organize Java economically in order to derive maximum profits for the home government.

The Cultivation System

The "Cultivation System," adopted by governor-general Johannes van den Bosch in 1830, a highly centralized economic system that sought to set aside one-fifth of the

---

[23] During this period (1820–1837), the Dutch were also involved in the Padri War in the Aceh district of western Sumatra. This was less an uprising against the Dutch than Dutch involvement in a dispute between local religious leaders. The Dutch role in this conflict drew that nation more deeply into the internal affairs of Sumatra than heretofore had been the case.

Sultan's palace in Jogjakarta, Java, Indonesia, September 2000.
Source: NGA Research Center—Ground Photography Collection.

land as plantations producing designated cash crops for export solely for the benefit of the Dutch treasury, was the mechanism for achieving this end.[24] Although designed to leave 80 percent of the land in the hands of the native Malay rulers, the placing of responsibility for returning one-fifth of their predetermined annual revenues, regardless of harvest yield, to the Dutch authorities, in the hands of the *bupati* administrators, had the long-term impact of subordinating the *priyayi* class, while impoverishing the peasantry. Under pressure of the Cultivation System, the former ruling class of Java was gradually turned into a salaried bureaucratic aristocracy. The only exception was the Sultanate of Jogjakarta (central Java) that continues to this day.

The Liberal Policy

Despite the benefit to the home government, a liberal Dutch administration in 1870 began to dismantle the Cultivation System in favor of what was called the "Liberal Policy." Up to this point, all crops had been shipped to Holland by the Netherlands Trading Company (NHM), which held a monopoly on the Cultivation System. The new policy enabled and empowered other European investors to acquire land under long-term leasehold. The policy had the impact of returning capital to the Dutch East Indies, rather than solely extracting it. Another impact was the gradual conversion of products exported from rice, coffee, sugar, tea, and tobacco to new industrial raw materials, such as rubber, copra, tin, and petroleum. Yet another feature of the new economic system was increased interest in the other islands of the archipelago, so that rapid economic development was accompanied by increased territorial expansion. A new legal instrument—the Short

---

[24] Between 1840 and 1880, revenues from the Dutch East Indies (about 18 million guldens per annum) constituted approximately one-third of the annual Dutch budget.

Declaration—imposed on local rulers the requirement of accepting the authority of Batavia. In this way, by 1910 Dutch authority had been extended over all of those territories that were eventually to become Indonesia. New communications systems—roads and railways in Java and Sumatra, and regular seaborne shipping services-linked Java to the more remote islands of the archipelago.

The Ethical Policy

The success of the Liberal Policy in organizing a more modern economic sector, as it did in the Malayan peninsula, primarily benefited the immigrant community, mainly European and Chinese, but did little to alter the traditional, largely subsistence economy of wet-rice cultivation that characterized the local Indonesian economy. The vast gap between these two sectors of the Dutch East Indies led some to advocate a more "ethical" policy toward the native inhabitants of the Dutch colony. A new liberal Dutch government beginning in 1901 embarked on just such a path, which it called the "Ethical Policy." The aim of the policy was to divert some of the wealth generated by the profitable colony back into improved health services, education, and agricultural extension work designed to strengthen and modernize the village economy. Another aspect of the policy was to provide incentives for inhabitants of relatively overpopulated Java to migrate and take up residence on other, relatively underpopulated islands of the archipelago. This policy, which continued to be carried on by independent Indonesia after 1945, was in effect a Javanese colonization of the archipelago, designed to facilitate both economic and political expansion of the government in Batavia.

Despite its good intentions, the Ethical Policy achieved little success in terms of its stated aims. The agricultural extension programs aimed mainly at improving the existing subsistence wet-rice cultivation rather than replacing it and did little to diminish the growing gap that was apparent between the traditional and modern sectors of Indonesian society. Significant expansion of schools and medical training facilities, meanwhile, served mainly the ambitions of the *priyayi* class who tended to be frustrated when, upon graduation, they found their subsequent careers limited by "Dutch-only" racial barriers that led some to feel increasingly embittered about continuing Dutch rule.

Emergence of Civil Society

Meanwhile, another aspect of the Ethical Policy led to the creation in 1903 of representative councils, composed of European, Indonesians and Chinese, in each residency, whose function was solely advisory and not legislative; in 1918 of a central People's Council to advise the governor-general in Batavia; and in 1925 of similar advisory councils at the *bupati* level. Designed to buttress the colonial authority rather than undermine it, the advisory councils gave a voice to some who sought to influence Dutch rule on behalf of the native Indonesian populations.

Growing opposition to Dutch rule in the early 20th century arose mainly among lower members of the *priyayi* class – low-ranking government employees, impoverished aristocrats, schoolteachers, native doctors – most of whom were beneficiaries of the new Ethical Policy but whose ambitions were frustrated by the stronghold maintained by the Dutch/upper-*priyayi* class over the levers of political and economic power. Probably facilitated by the Ethical Policy, which encouraged formation of such civil society groups, a number of organizations sprang into existence representing a variety of perspectives. All sources agree that the first of these was *Budi Utomo* (Noble Endeavor), established in 1908 among students of the School for Training Native Doctors in Batavia. Of interest was the decision of this Javanese organization to adopt Malay, the lingua franca of the archipelago, rather than Javanese as its language of discussion, implying a commitment to a larger political concept than just Java. A minority organization comprised of lower *priyari*, its appeal was limited, and *Budi Utomo* did not endure long.

Sarekat Islam. Other organizations emerged quickly, however. Among these was the Islamic Traders' Association, established in 1909, in an effort to compete more effectively with competition from the close-knit Chinese community. In 1912, this organization restructured under the name *Sarekat Islam* (Islamic Union) with the goal of becoming a mass organization. Under the leadership of a former *priyayi* official of the Dutch government, Haji Umar Said Cokroaminoto, who cast himself as a charismatic, if not divine, figure, *Sarekat Islam* quickly grew into an organization claiming 360,000 members with some 80 branches throughout the archipelago by 1914. Committed to Islamic teaching as well as general Muslim prosperity, the organization also gained membership because of a decidedly anti-Chinese appeal.[25]

The Indies Party. Yet another political movement established in 1910 was the Indies Party that advocated an "Indies nationalism" and self-government for the people of the Indies in place of the foreign Dutch rule. Led by a mixed-blood Eurasian named Dowes Dekker (he took the name Danudirja Setyabuddhi in 1946 after Indonesian independence), his more radical activities led to his exile in Holland in 1913 along with a few of his associates, and the end of his party. In Holland, however, he associated himself during the early 1920s with an organization, the Indonesian Alliance of Students, which advocated the same principles.

Muhammadiyah. Still another Muslim group organized in 1912 was the Muhammadiyah. Although established in Jogjakarta, it had its early strength in Sumatra, where one of its leaders, Muhammad Hatta (later a close associate of revolutionary leader Sukarno), had his roots. The Muhammadiyah represented the modernist or reformist trend in Islam that sought to implement the very influential ideas of the Egyptian scholar Muhammad Abduh (d. 1905) and his disciple Rashid

---

[25] Pearn, *Introduction to the History of South-East Asia*, 202–205. Future revolutionary leader Ahmad Sukarno, a Muslim native of Bali, grew up in the home of Haji Umar Said Cokroaminoto and was strongly influenced by his example and by the model of *Sarekat Islam*.

Rida (d. 1935), the principal publicist of the former's concepts through his Arabic journal *al-Manar* (Lighthouse). As elsewhere in the Islamic world, where this powerful strain of thought was influential, the reformist movement was based on four major ideas (as adapted for the Dutch East Indies):

1. The development of a modern and sophisticated understanding of Islam that was in harmony with the principles of Western science and material progress,

2. The purification of Islamic practice, such as the elimination of animist and Hindu/Buddhist elements of Javanese culture that were at variance with Islamic teachings,

3. The encouragement of piety and a serious attitude to the carrying out of religious obligations, and

4. The provision of social services to the Muslim community that the Dutch were unwilling to provide.

Other aspects of the Egyptian reform movement were reopening "the gates of *ijtihad* (rational, independent thinking about the *Qur'an* and *hadith*) and abandonment of *taqlid* (uncritical acceptance of established, traditional interpretation about the *Qu'ran* and *hadith* as delineated by the four orthodox *madhhab*, or schools of Islamic jurisprudence, in Islam, and the Shafi'i school in particular, which predominates in southeast Asia). Among other things, the modernist movement advocated the training of a new, modern `ulama` educated in the principles of scientific modernism and a progressive understanding of Islam.

Like the Muslim Brotherhood in Egypt (established in 1928 on the same principles), the Muhammadiyah organized itself as primarily a philanthropic organization supporting a network of modern schools and other institutions such as orphanages and hospitals. The sectors of the population from which its membership was primarily drawn was the lower middle classes of small and medium-sized towns and cities, merchants and, increasingly later, white-collar professionals, clerks, and civil servants.[26] Adherents of the Muhammadiyah way were generally called *santri* Muslims, as opposed to the more syncretic *abhangen* Muslims.

Communist Party. The year 1914 also saw the formation of the Indies Social-Democratic Association (ISDV), which in 1920 became the Communist Association of the Indies and in 1924 the Indonesian Communist Party (PKI). Active among trade unionists and rural villagers and strongly backed by the Communist International in Moscow, the party contributed to its own undoing in 1926–27 by instigating rural uprisings in Java and Sumatra. The government crackdown against the party caused it to nearly disappear and not to reappear until the years after independence.

---

[26] Greg Barton, "Islam and Politics in the New Indonesia," in Jason F. Isaacson and Colin Rubenstein, eds., *Islam in Asia: Changing Political Realities* (New Brunswick, NJ: Transaction Publishers, 2002), 6.

Nahdlatul Ulama. In 1926, yet another mass Islamic organization came into being. This was the *Nahdlatul Ulama* (renaissance of the *Ulama*), established by leading traditional `ulama in east Java. The appearance in 1912 of the Muhammadiyah, which was highly critical of the practice and teaching of the traditional `ulama, had not immediately appeared threatening to them, but over time it did, and the *Nahdlatul Ulama* was their reaction. A goal of the new organization was to defend the traditional practices of Indonesian Muslims (generally called *abhangen*–Muslims continuing to practice pre-Islamic rituals, as opposed to *santri*–Muslims opposed to such practices), such as praying at the tombs of men considered to be saints and invoking the blessing of one's ancestors, which the Muhammadiyah scorned as being un-Islamic. The *abhangen* `ulama felt scorned by the arrogant attitude displayed by many of the *santri* toward them. Moreover, the new and more modern schools being operated by the Muhammadiyah held the potential for making obsolete the traditional *pesantren* (traditional Islam boarding schools) that were run by the *abhangen* `ulama. In an effort to facilitate networking and cooperation among the traditional `ulama and their *pesantren*, this new organization sought to defend the traditional values of Indonesian Islam. Although the rural-based NU always remained a looser and less homogeneous organization than the more urban-based Muhammadiyah, it too quickly enjoyed rapid growth and participation and became much the larger organization.

Nationalist Party. The most significant of these new organizations over the longer term, however, was the Indonesian Union, established in 1927 and soon converted into the Indonesian Nationalist Party (PNI) the following year. Founded by a group of graduates of the technical college at Bandung, this movement strongly reflected the imprint of its first leader, Ahmad Sukarno, a Balinesian-born Muslim who became independent Indonesia's first president in 1945. The party's appeal, like that of Sukarno himself, was its ability to attract elements of all sectors of Indonesian society. Modernist, traditionalist, religious, secularist, Islamic and Marxist all at the same time, Sukarno's party was first and foremost a nationalist party in a land where no strong sense of nationhood existed, but for which the cause of independence and self-rule, it was argued, transcended the great diversity of Indonesian society. The rapid success of the party in recruiting membership, its non-cooperation with the Dutch East Indies government, and its declared determination to send the Dutch authorities home as soon as possible made it a threat to the Dutch authorities, and in 1929 and again in 1933 Sukarno and a number of his colleagues were arrested, tried, convicted, and sentenced to periods of exile. Without their leadership, the party foundered but did not die. Its strength was in eclipse, however, at the time of the March 1942 Japanese occupation of the Dutch East Indies during World War II.

World War II

As was the case in the Malay peninsula, the Japanese occupiers deposed and interned the previous European colonial government and hired many native Indonesians to assist them in running their own administration. Also similar to their policy on the

Malay peninsula, the Japanese cultivated the opponents of Dutch rule. These included PNI leader Sukarno and Muhammadiyah leader Muhammad Hatta, both of whom held significant positions in the occupation authority and proved to be true collaborators with the Japanese.[27] Both played this role, however, in the longer-term interest of achieving Indonesian independence. Accordingly, in August 1945, on the eve of Japanese surrender to the United States, the two men were summoned by the Japanese authorities in Saigon, Vietnam, and informed of Japan's intent to transfer power to them. Returning to Jakarta (Batavia), Sukarno, waiting a few days until officially informed of the Japanese surrender, proclaimed Indonesian independence on August 17, 1945.

War for Independence

Recognition of Indonesian independence was not obtained solely by declaring it, however. Holland was determined to reclaim its colony but, devastated itself by its own Nazi occupation during World War II, required help to do so. As they had during the Napoleonic wars 130 years before, British troops were dispatched to disarm and repatriate remaining Japanese troops on the islands, liberate Europeans held in internment camps, and maintain general law and order. The first two tasks were accomplished without great difficulty, but the third proved more difficult. Fearful that the ultimate British goal was to restore Dutch rule, Sukarno and Hatta moved quickly to consolidate their leadership and to organize forces capable of meeting the challenge to Indonesian independence. Two institutions started during the war under Japanese auspices were transformed into a makeshift government. The first, a 135-man committee (BPUPKI) established in March 1945 to begin drawing up a constitution, was transformed into the Central Indonesian National Committee (KNIP) that began the process of administering the country. The second, a paramilitary organization raised by the Japanese, called the Sukarela Tentara Pembela Tanah Air (PETA)—today considered the forerunner organization of the Indonesian Armed Forces (ABRI, later TNI)—was rallied to defend Indonesian independence.

In the tense situation that emerged, law and order tended to break down and legitimate revolutionary activities became difficult to discern from other acts of criminal violence. Youthful gangs (*pemuda*) emerged that threatened Dutch settlers and members of the old *priyayi* elite that had collaborated with either the Dutch or the Japanese. Dutch armed groups, meanwhile, mobilized to defend their lives and their properties and to attack supporters of the new Indonesian government. Clashes between *santri* and *abhangen* groups occurred, and groups with separatist or leftist agendas, contrary to the objectives of Sukarno's government, proliferated. Although it required nearly a decade for Sukarno to bring order out of this growing chaos, the event that guaranteed it would be him rather than the Dutch or British who would play this role occurred soon after his declaration of independence.

---

[27] Pearn, *Introduction to the History of South-East Asia*, 213-215, 218-219.

Typical interior room at the Sultan's palace, in Yogyakarta, Java, Indonesia, September 2000.
Source: NGA Research Center—Ground Photography Collection.

This was the Battle of Surabaya (October 24–November 24, 1945) in Java. British troops clashing with *pemuda* animated by the cause of *jihad* suffered a significant military disaster in which their commander and hundreds of troops were killed. British Indian Army troops attempting to retake Surabaya on November 20–24 found themselves attacked by both PETA forces and thousands of *jihad*-inspired *pemuda*. Sukarno and Hatta flew in to try to halt a massacre of the outnumbered British troops, but the battle was not ended until a division of British troops landed, supported by naval and aerial bombardments. Unwilling or unable to carry the battle further and preoccupied with the problem of reestablishing its own position on the Malay peninsula, Britain reached the conclusion that Holland had no choice but to negotiate an agreement with the new Indonesian government.

In 1947 and early 1948, a major insertion of new Dutch forces throughout the archipelago, coupled with a blockade uneasily supported by the Western powers, left the nationalists on the verge of defeat, their territory reduced to roughly a third of Java by the time the UN was able to arrange a cease-fire. By mid-1948, Sukarno and other senior leaders had been arrested and sent into internal exile on Sumatra.[28]

Despite military successes, the Dutch were losing their grip on the East Indies. Suppressing the insurgency was costing the Dutch over $1 million a day which they could ill afford. The patience of their allies, especially the United States, was also growing thin. When the Dutch arrested the nationalist leadership in 1948, the UN

---

[28] Robert B. Asprey, *War in the Shadows: The Guerrilla in History*, Vol II (Garden City, NY: Doubleday & Co., 1975), 760–765.

Security Council demanded an immediate cease-fire and the release of the republican leaders, and was backed up by a Truman Administration threat to halt Marshall Plan aid to the Netherlands if they failed to comply. Meanwhile, Indonesia's ability to field an army and organize its population was maturing. Facing economic collapse and

abandonment by their allies, the Dutch agreed to new negotiations in April 1949 that culminated in a grant of independence in December.[29]

A Fragile Independence

The December 1949 grant of sovereignty by the Netherlands established a federal United States of Indonesia, of which the Sukarno regime on Java was but one of sixteen political units. Once Dutch forces withdrew, this federal system was quickly reorganized as the unitary Republic of Indonesia in 1950. The new government, fatigued by four years of war, was soon beset by an unsuccessful revolt by the *Darul Islam* movement in western Java, southern Sulawesi, and Aceh. This revolt sought to create an Islamic state with greater representation from the outer islands (especially Sulawesi, the Moluccas, and Sumatra), rather than the secular state dominated by Sukarno and the Javanese elite surrounding him. The rebels hoped to lure the more conservative Hatta (who was from Sumatra) away from Sukarno, but failed in this gamble as well as in their military confrontation with Sukarno's tough, loyal army. The *Darul Islam* was only the first of a series of Islamically-inspired revolts in the outer islands that continued throughout the Sukarno years. As Sukarno's personalist rule moved the country further toward the Left and increased the dominance of secularists and his Javanese followers, the endemic unrest continued.[30]

---

[29] Asprey, *War in the Shadows*, 765–767.

[30] Pearn, *Introduction to the History of South-East Asia*, 225–227; and Hinton, 54.

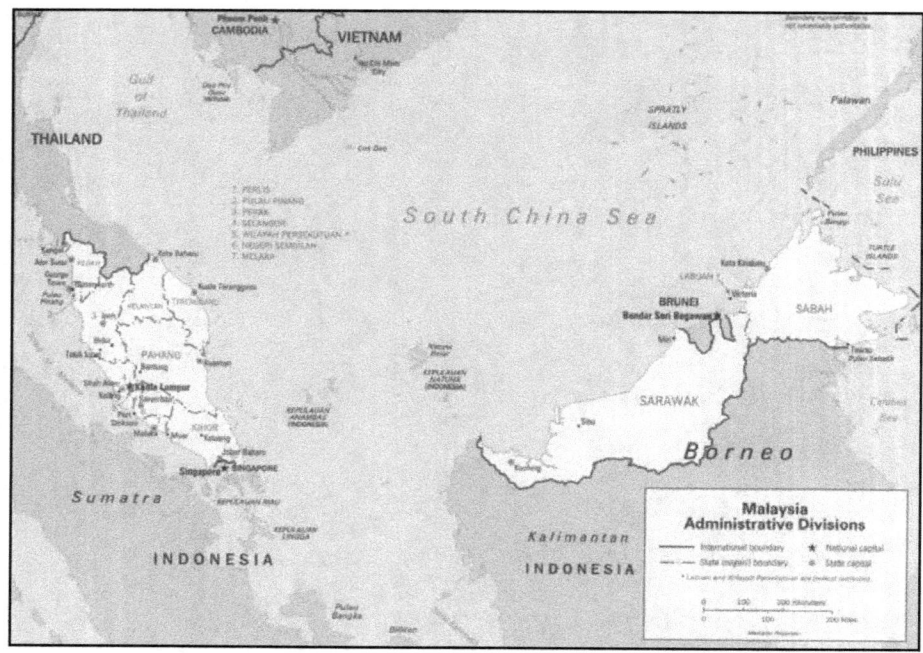

Map of Malaysia
Source: CIA.

CHAPTER 2

ISLAM IN MALAYSIA

The basic question for Malaysia remains to be answered: Can there be an increased development of a sense of Islamic identity while still maintaining the delicate communal balance that has made Malaysia the thriving nation it is today?

— Fred Van der Mehden

The major fault line in Malaysian politics, as in Malaysian society, is the country's demographic division between its slight majority of native Malays and other Malaysian citizens mainly of Chinese or Indian origin. Viewed another way, the fault line is between its majority native Muslim population (Malays and others of Indian/Pakistani/Bangladeshi origin) and its large non-Muslim minority population, primarily Chinese in origin. Still another way to view the fault line is to draw it between more economically disadvantaged and class-driven traditional society of Muslim Malays, especially in the northern and eastern states of the country, and the far more modern, egalitarian, and economically developed, largely non-Malay sector of society, especially in the western and southern parts of the country. Although one must beware of drawing these categorizations too monolithically (there are rich Malays as well as impoverished Chinese), they do form the basis of the fundamental political debate that characterizes Malaysian society.

ESTABLISHMENT OF MALAY HEGEMONY

In a very real sense, the late 1940s conflict over the Malayan Union and the ultimately victorious Federation of Malaya concepts of how the future Malay peninsula should be organized represented a civil war over this fault line in which the traditional Muslim Malay sector emerged as dominant. In part this was due to British military intervention against the insurgents organized and led by the Chinese-based Malay Communist Party (CPM) that proved to be the most diehard champion of the National Union.

Credit also should be given to the United Malay National Organization (UMNO) that Malay leaders brought into being in 1946 to protect and advance Malay interests and to defend the Federation as opposed to the Union concept. Emerging as Malaysia's dominant political party from that time till the present, its leadership historically kept the focus on Malay national rather than Islamic political interests and in general on the economic development of the country. Fundamentally a conservative party that kept its focus on the secular interests of all, it proved able to reach across Malaysia's ethnic and sectarian divisions and to form alliances with counterpart parties among the Chinese and Indian communities. Together, the UMNO, the MCA (Malaysian Chinese Association), and the MIC (Malaysian Indian Congress) have been able to dominate Malaysia politically throughout its history. As a result, despite many undercurrents of division and potential conflicts, Malaysia has remained a relatively stable, democratic, constitutionally based, parliamentary state that has experienced rapid economic development and significant national prosperity.

Undercurrents of Dissatisfaction

The fissures in Malaysian society erupted in large-scale rioting in Kuala Lumpur, however, over a two-week period in May 1969. The unanticipated violence followed national elections in which the UMNO/MCA/MIC alliance failed to secure a parliamentary majority (the alliance received 49.1 percent of the vote). Jubilant supporters of the opposition parties, mainly Chinese, took to the streets in celebration. Accused of taunting onlooking Malays with racial epithets, the celebrants were set upon. Although confined mainly to the nation's capital, the communal violence could not be ended for two weeks and resulted in hundreds of casualties, mainly Chinese and Indians.

The Kuala Lumpur riots of May 1969 proved to be a wake-up call to Malaysia's ruling establishment and a watershed in the country's modern history. As a result, the government set in motion a number of reforms, and various societal reactions also occurred. Among the steps taken by the ruling UMNO were a declaration of a state of emergency (which has never been officially lifted), a suspension of parliament for nearly two years, temporary administration of the country by a specially established National Operations Council (NOC), and amendment of the Sedition Act of 1948 (created by the British to deal with the communist insurgency) to prohibit public questioning of the special status of Malays or of Islam, the powers of the Malay sultans, the status of Malay as the national language, and the laws of citizenship, particularly with reference to non-Malays. With the reconvening of parliament in 1972, the latter provisions of the Sedition Act were formally written into the Constitution. Politically, the UMNO, aware of its diminished strength as demonstrated in the 1969 elections, embarked on a campaign to form alliances with a greater number of political parties than just the MCA and MIC. The result in 1974 was the establishment of the *Barisan Nasional* (National Front), a coalition of ten parties, headed by the UMNO that has successfully dominated national elections since that time.

The Malay Response: The New Economic Policy

Although the riots could have been interpreted as highlighting a need to promote greater political equality in Malaysian society, the UMNO-dominated government that sought to promote stability by strengthening its own hand politically concluded otherwise. The causes of the May 1969 violence were attributed mainly to the grievances and frustrations of the Malay element of society that were primarily economic in nature. The solution was found in the adoption of the New Economic Policy (NEP), promulgated in 1971, that sought to address these grievances by pursuing policies favorable to Malay economic interests. Statistics indicated that in 1969 the Malay share of national corporate wealth was 2.3 percent, whereas the Chinese share was 34.3 percent as opposed to the 63.3 percent that belonged to foreign (primarily British) owners.[31] The NEP was a long-term, 20-year plan that spanned four five-year plans, ending in 1990. The stated goal was two-fold-to end poverty in the country, which affected mainly Malays who constituted the largest number of poor—and to strengthen the Malay share of the national wealth of the country through powerful affirmative action programs discriminating in their favor. The goal by 1990 was for Malays to own 30 percent of the national wealth (24 percent had been reached by 2003), Chinese 40 percent, and foreign owners 30 percent.[32] The heart of the program was a series of massive public expenditure programs directed mainly at rural Malays aimed generally at urbanizing them.[33] Among these programs was an ambitious one to gradually buy out foreign interests whose shares were sold on favorable terms to Malay entrepreneurial investors.[34]

Although the NEP fell short of its originally stated goals, its overall impact on Malaysian society for the next three decades was profound. For the next twenty-five years, until the general Asian economic crisis in 1997, the already partially modernized economy grew at an unprecedented rate of an average 7 percent per year—8 percent per annum between 1985 and 1995—making Malaysia one of the most prosperous nations in southeast Asia. Previously based primarily on plantation and mining activities, with rubber and tin being the principal exports, under the NEP the Malaysian economy underwent a great diversification that reduced its dependence on overseas commodities markets. Palm oil, tropical hardwoods, petroleum, natural gas, and manufactured items, particularly electronics and semiconductors, but also its own Proton Saga automobile, were all added to the list of Malaysian exports.

Social Impacts of the NEP

More telling, however, was the social transformation produced by the NEP. In order to prepare Malays for the enhanced role they were being empowered to play in Malaysia's economy, under the NEP a number of new scientific, technical, and vocational schools were established as well as middle schools and four universities, in all of which Malays were given preferential admission quotas. Whereas in 1965 only 21 percent of enrollment in the country's single University of Malaya were Malays, by 1977 three-quarters of all students admitted to the country's now five universities were

---

[31] Zachary Abuza, *Militant Islam in Southeast Asia: Crucible of Terror* (Boulder, CO: Lynn Reinner Publishers, 2003), 50. Frederica M. Bunge. ed. *Malaysia: A Country Study*, 4th edition. HQ, Department of the Army, DA PAM 550-45 (Washington, DC: U.S. Government Printing Office, 1985), 147.

[32] By 1990, the relative share had changed to 20.3 percent for Malays, 46 percent for Chinese and Indian, and 35 percent for foreign ownership. *The Far East and Australasia*, 2003 (London and New York: Europa Publications, 2003), 787.

[33] *Malaysia: A Country Study*, 63–64. A.B. Shamsul, "Bureaucratic Management of Identity in a Modern State: 'Malayness' in Postwar Malaysia," in Dru C. Gladney, ed., *Making Majorities: Constituting the Nation in Japan, Korea, China, Malaysia, Fiji, Turkey, and the United States* (Stanford, CA: Stanford University Press, 1998), 145.

[34] *Malaysia: A Country Study*, 144–148.

Malay.[35] Many other Malay as well as Chinese students were sent abroad to secure advanced education, Australia being a favored venue for many.

GROWTH OF THE ISLAMIC MOVEMENT

Closely associated with this vast educational expansion was a youth movement, especially among Malays, that was perhaps the counterpart of those counter-cultural youth movements that flourished in many countries during the 1970s—in the late and post-Vietnam war eras. In the case of Malaysia, the movement took the form of increased interest in religion, or perhaps better to say, the Islamic component of the Malay identity. Although empowered by the ruling establishment, the movement had a clear anti-establishment cast, identified with opposition to the American role in Vietnam and to imperialism in general, and tended to find meaning and enthusiasm in the rediscovery of Islam. Many movements emerged, but three in particular have garnered the most attention.

Jamaat Tabligh

The first was *Jamaat Tabligh*, an Indian-based missionary movement (*dakwah* in Malay, *dawa'* in Arabic) that had been established in India in the 1920s, came to Malaysia during the 1950s to conduct its work primarily in the Indian Muslim community, but in the 1970s found its appeal increasingly popular in Malay village communities and youth in general.[36] Self-consciously apolitical, *Jamaat Tabligh* missionaries placed emphasis on personal morality, piety, and strict observance of the ritual requirements of Islam. This implied eating and dressing in an "Arabic" fashion in imitation of what was believed to be the Prophet Muhammad's style, characteristics that separated the youthful adherents from their Malay elders. Mosque-based in its operations, *Jamaat Tabligh* groups either built or took over existing mosques that became centers of worship and further missionary activity. Simple and inoffensive in its approach, the movement was not perceived to be threatening and was at least tolerated if not actually encouraged by Malaysian authorities.

Darul Arqam

Yet a second was the *Darul Arqam* movement, founded in 1968 by a former Malay government schoolteacher and political activist, Ashaari Muhammad. Far more cultic than *Jamaat Tabligh*, *Darul Arqam* established an Islamic commune on eight acres of

---

[35] *Malaysia: A Country Study*, 123.

[36] Jomo Kwame Sundaram and Ahmed Shabery Cheek, "The Politics of Malaysia's Islamic Resurgence," in *Third World Quarterly*, 10, No. 2 (April 1988), 846. Also Greg Barton, "Islam, Society, Politics and Change in Malaysia," in *Islam in Asia: Changing Political Realities*, ed. by Jason F. Isaacson and Colin Rubinstein (New Brunswick, NJ: Transaction Books, 2002), 104.

land near the village of Sungei Penchala outside Kuala Lumpur. The commune was the forerunner of no less then 40 other communities, 200 schools, charitable associations, and dispensaries specializing in the "Islamic" rehabilitation of young drug addicts established by the organization in Malaysia, Thailand, and Indonesia before its suppression for heresy by the Malaysian government in 1994.[37] Similar to *Jamaat Tabligh* in the type of lifestyle it demanded of its adepts-Arabic style dress, turbans, eating with hands, avoidance of tables, chairs, and televisions—it nevertheless differed by requiring them to live in a closed community, separate from the rest of the society. Organizational self-sufficiency was a principal goal of *Darul Arqam*, and the production of *halal* meat and other Islamic goods emerged as a key attribute of the group that enabled it to become a successful business enterprise with branches throughout southeast Asia.[38] At the time of its 1994 suppression it was estimated to have around 10,000 members and assets estimated at $120 million.[39] Avowedly apolitical, like *Jamaat Tabligh*, it nevertheless was innately critical of the larger society in which it sought to take root. Sharply critical of other Islamic movements in Malaysia, which Ashaari Muhammad claimed only theorized, shouted slogans, and conducted seminars, *Darul Arqam* sought to reestablish a "true" Islamic community in the here and now through a formal renunciation of the larger society in which it lived.[40]

ABIM

More important in the longer run than either *Jamaat Tabligh* or *Darul Arqam*, however, was the Malaysian Islamic Youth Movement—*Angkatan Belia Islam Malaysia* (ABIM) that, as it grew and matured, played an increasingly important political role in Malaysian society. Formally established in 1971 at the country's then single University of Malaya for the purpose of "building a society that is based on the principles of Islam,"[41] ABIM experienced rapid growth and claimed membership of 40,000 in addition to many other supporters by the early 1980s.[42] Receiving its strongest support from Malay youth in Malaysia's burgeoning institutions of higher learning in the 1970s, especially in the country's more highly developed and urbanized western states (Negeri Sembilan, Selangor, and Perak), ABIM may have achieved success because of its relatively intellectual appeal. Highly critical of groups like

---

[37] Gilles Kepel, *Jihad: The Trail of Political Islam*, 92.

[38] Barton, "Islam, Society, Politics and Change in Malaysia," 105.

[39] Kepel, *Jihad: The Trail of Political Islam*, 94.

[40] Sundaram and Cheek, "The Politics of Malaysia's Islamic Resurgence," 847. Arqam was one of the Prophet Muhammad's companions in Mecca who had assisted him during his night flight to Medina in 622 AD. Like the *Takfir wa Higra* movement in Egypt that also made renunciation of the old sinful society (*takfir*) and emigration (*Hijra*) to a new place the symbol of their movement, in a similar way Ashaari Muhammad invoked the house of Arqam (*Darul Arqam*) as a symbol of renouncing society and finding refuge in a safe place. Barton, "Islam, Society, Politics and Change in Malaysia," 105.

[41] Barton, "Islam, Society, Politics and Change in Malaysia," 111.

[42] Daniel Pipes, *In the Path of God: Islam and Political Power* (New York: Basic Books, Inc., Publishers, 1983), 251. *Malaysia: A Country Study*, 213.

Jamaat Tabligh and *Darul Arqam* for focusing on "mindless ritual practices" and "unthinking obedience to *Shari'a* law," ABIM placed the emphasis on economic and social concerns, how to achieve justice in these areas, and how to make Islam a vibrant way of life.[43] Study groups, seminars, conferences, and other educational venues, precisely those activities so sharply criticized by *Darul Arqam*, were the heart of ABIM activity that served to raise the consciousness of members, facilitate dialogue among them, and promote a deeper understanding of Islam and issues affecting Malaysia.[44] Strongly influenced by the examples of *Jamiyat-i Islami* in Pakistan and the *Ikhwan al-Muslimin* (Muslim Brotherhood) of Egypt, both organizations that opposed modern secularism and its political manifestation, nationalism, ABIM took a strong stand against the UMNO-sponsored National Economic Policy, which it saw as an expression of Malay nationalism. Instead, it advocated the gradual transformation of all of Malaysia into an Islamic state, governed by the *Shari'a* which, it argued, was inherently and historically multicultural in spirit and aimed at achieving social justice for all members of society. Economically, ABIM argued, government policy should be aimed at helping the poor in all sectors of society, not just among the Malays.[45]

Despite an original intention to remain a civil society organization, fundamentally aloof from politics, like *Jamaat Tabligh* and *Darul Arqam*, ABIM was quickly drawn into a political role. In part this was due to the charismatic leadership of Anwar Ibrahim, one of ABIM's founders (he was 25 years of age in 1971) who became its president from 1974 to 1982. Whether it was his intention to play a political role or not, his leadership of ABIM cast him into the political spotlight, led to his political co-optation by Prime Minister Mahathir Mohammed in 1982, and his designation as Mahathir's eventual successor prior to being rudely dropped from favor and transformed into a criminal behind bars in 1998. Probably a more profound reason behind ABIM's ascent into political relevance was the successful UMNO co-optation in 1972 of Malaysia's main Islamic opposition party, the *Parti Islam seMalaysia* (PAS), into the expanded 10-party *Basilan Nasional* (National Front) coalition that continued to dominate Malaysia politically in the years after the May 1969 riots in Kuala Lumpur. Although PAS justified its decision to join the *Basilan Nasional* on the basis of strengthening Malay solidarity in order to implement the NEP, its joining the coalition had the impact of removing it from its traditional role of opposition to the UMNO at a time of rapid Islamic resurgence in the country. The absence of PAS from its traditional opposition role created a vacuum that ABIM was in a position to fill.

PAS — The Islamic Party

Although UMNO had dominated Malaysian politics throughout the country's history, it had never gained the support of all Malays. In large part this was because it was correctly perceived as representing the Malay aristocratic classes associated

---

[43] Pipes, *In the Path of God*, 251.

[44] Barton, "Islam, Society, Politics and Change in Malaysia,"113.

[45] Pipes, *In the Path of God*, 251.

with the traditional sultans from which its principal leaders were drawn,[46] the ruling administrative elite of the government whose loyalty it commanded because of its patronage, and its willingness to accommodate multiculturalism.[47] Established in 1951 as an opposition Malay party by former members of UMNO's religious bureau, PAS leaders objected to the secular nationalist leanings of UMNO and from the beginning articulated their goal of making an Islamic state out of Malaysia.[48] Never a particularly strong political party at the national level, its strength was rooted in the economically disadvantaged, largely Malay-inhabited northern and eastern states, particularly Kelantan and Terengganu, over both of which the party gained political control in the first country-wide elections in 1959. Dominated by Islamic teachers (`ulama) in the traditional *pondoks* of northern and eastern Malaysia, the administration of which became a principal PAS activity, PAS was in many ways analogous to *Nahlatul Ulama* in Indonesia.[49] That is, it represented the traditional, more folk, Islam of historic southeast Asia rather than the more puritan or modernistic Islam of *Jamaat Tabligh*, *Darul Arqam*, or ABIM that was to come later. At the same time, PAS was more chauvinistically Malay than was UMNO, but because it opposed the more secular, nationalist approach of UMNO it had no choice but place its stress on the Islamic aspect of Malay nationalism.

Islam and the UMNO

Despite its dominance, UMNO exerted great pressure on PAS in the 1960s in an effort to eliminate it politically. It succeeded in recapturing control of the state government of Terengganu in 1961 and launched an unsuccessful, large-scale campaign to gain control of Kelantan from PAS in the fateful elections of 1969 that produced the Kuala Lumpur race riots of May of that year. Meanwhile, in 1962 the UMNO-controlled government had gravely weakened the Islamic party by arresting its leader, Dr. Burhanuddin al-Helmy, and a number of other PAS leaders for alleged solidarity with Indonesian President Sukarno in his efforts to undermine the creation of Malaysia.[50] Following the 1969 race riots and the adoption of the overtly pro-Malay New Economic Policy, the UMNO appeared to have realized its objective of eliminating PAS as a political competitor by drawing it into the *Barisan Nasional* coalition in 1972, but this was only a temporary reprieve from an Islamically-based opposition.

---

[46] Malaysia's first three prime ministers—Tunku Abdul Rahman (1963–1970), Tun Abdul Razak (1970–1976), and Dato Hussein Onn (1976–1981)—were all scions of the royal house of Kedah, or in the case of Onn married into it. Not until the election of Dr. Mahathir Mohammed, a "commoner" (also from Kedah), as head of UMNO and Prime Minister in 1981 was this pattern broken. The choice of the non-aristocratic Mahathir did not eliminate the perception of whom the party represented, however.

[47] Yong Mun Cheong, "The Political Structures of the Independent States," in Nicholas Tarling, ed., *The Cambridge History of Southeast Asia, Vol. 2, Part 2, From World War II to the Present* (New York: Cambridge University Press, 1999), 83.

[48] Barton, "Islam, Society, Politics and Change in Malaysia," 116.

[49] Abuza, *Militant Islam in Southeast Asia*, 52. Barton, "Islam, Society, Politics and Change in Malaysia," 117.

[50] Sundaram and Cheek, "The Politics of Malaysia's Islamic Resurgence," 849.

Given the success of the UMNO in co-opting PAS politically, the flourishing of Islamist movements in Malaysia in the 1970s can only be explained as a social phenomenon among young Malays who were increasingly alienated by the social and economic changes affecting the country, in part as a result of the energies released by the NEP. Although ABIM, *Darul-Arqam, Jamaat Tabligh*, and other groups like them were all civil society movements, the government clearly saw them, especially ABIM, as potentially threatening politically. Later, Prime Minister Mahathir Mohammed established his reputation in 1974-1976, when, as education minister, he cracked down on Islamic activism on the university campuses by placing restraints on free speech and assembly and by ordering the arrest of ABIM leader Anwar Ibrahim for organizing a demonstration against the government's lack of attention to rural poverty.[51]

The arrest of Ibrahim only strengthened the appeal of ABIM among modern Malays, however, and transformed Ibrahim into a figure of national stature. Even so, UMNO appeared to remain in the ascendant by virtue of its defeat of PAS in Kelantan state elections in 1977, depriving PAS of political control anywhere in the country. The political humiliation of the rural-based PAS, however, marked the beginning of a new openness to personalities of the urban-based ABIM, the entry of many of these individuals into positions of leadership in PAS, and the gradual transformation of PAS into a more modern, less `ulama-centered organization that espoused an even sharper critique of the UMNO-dominated government.[52]

The essence of the ABIM critique was that Islam should be understood not just to be the religion of the Malays, but a universal religion whose full implementation as the governing principle of the state would be good for all the peoples of Malaysia, Muslim or not. Multiracialism and multiculturalism, according to the ABIM argument, were characteristic of Islam, and Islam rather than Malay political dominance was the key to establishing a stable and prospering Malaysia. An aspect of this argument was a sharp critique of the UMNO's NEP initiatives on the grounds they were based on Malay ethnic chauvinism rather than the good of all the people of Malaysia. ABIM, which adopted the slogan "Islam as the Solution to the Problems of a Multi-Racial Society," claimed to stand for a broader, more all-encompassing, and modern vision of Malaysia's future than UMNO, which it was gradually linking to the program of UMNO's principal competitor, the PAS.[53] Anwar Ibrahim, the charismatic leader of ABIM, was the most effective articulator of this view that gained both him and ABIM significant favorable attention in the country's Chinese and Indian communities and appeared to position him as a potential future challenger to UMNO's historic political dominance.

---

[51] Abuza, *Militant Islam in Southeast Asia*, 53.

[52] Barton, "Islam, Society, Politics and Change in Malaysia," 114.

[53] Mohammad Abu Bakar, "Islam, Civil Society, and Ethnic Relations in Malaysia," in Nakamura Mitsuo, Sharon Siddique, and Omar Farouk Bajunid, eds., *Islam and Civil Society in Southeast Asia* (Singapore: Institute of Southeast Asian Studies, 2001), 65–66.

MAHATHIR GOES ISLAMIC

A change in UMNO's leadership in 1981 in which former Prime Minister and Party leader Dato Hussein Onn was replaced by Dr. Mahathir Mohammad brought a significant change in the way that the ruling party dealt with its PAS/ABIM challenge. In March 1982 Mahathir shocked the country by announcing that 34-year-old ABIM leader Anwar Ibrahim was leaving his organization to join UMNO. Ibrahim's decision was undoubtedly affected by intra-ABIM politics in that, coincidentally with his decision to joint forces with Mahathir, his ABIM colleague and rival, Terengganu-based Hajji Abdul Hadi Awang, was named head of PAS.[54] Ibrahim explained his decision by saying that he was satisfied with UMNO's commitment to Islamic values,[55] and indeed he was right. A part of their agreement was that if Mahathir was not prepared to transform Malaysia into an "Islamic state," he was at least prepared to advance a number of initiatives to make Malaysia more Islamic in character.[56]

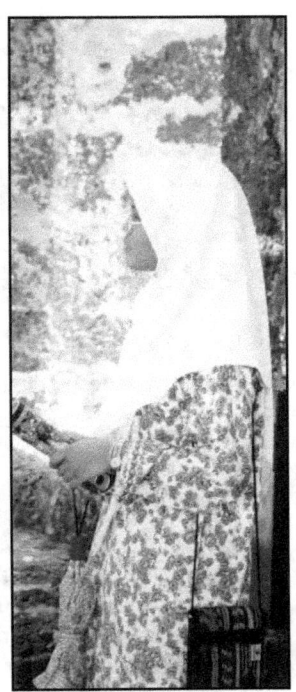

Muslim woman dressed in traditional garb, Malacca, Malaysia, May 2001.
Source: NGA Research Center — Ground Photography Collection.

Islamic Policies

Very quickly after the co-optation of Anwar Ibrahim into the UMNO, a number of measures aimed at strengthening Islamic values in Malaysian society began to be implemented. Among these were the establishment of an Islamic bank, the International Islamic University of Malaysia (IIUM),[57] an Islamic insurance company, a network of Islamic pawn shops, a ban on gambling, a ban on the import of beef not slaughtered in accordance with Islamic rules, greatly increased Islamic content on radio and television, introduction of Arabic script (*jawi*) into the primary school curriculum, the suspension of the government-run meal program in public primary schools during the month of fasting (*Ramadan*), mandatory teaching of Islam both in elementary schools and in institutions of higher learning, a ban on smoking in all government offices, and training courses on

---

[54] Barton, "Islam, Society, Politics and Change in Malaysia," 118. Yet another factor at work at this time was the 1979 Iranian revolution, led by Iran's `ulama, which was quite favorably viewed by the `ulama-based PAS and those ABIM leaders who were joining PAS. This was in contrast with the UMNO and other ABIM leaders such as Anwar Ibrahim whose contacts were close with the oil-producing states of Saudi Arabia and Kuwait and who intellectually were more in tune with Sunni Islamic movements, such as the *Jamiyat-i Islami* of Pakistan and the *Ikhwan al-Muslimeen* of Egypt. Barton, "Islam, Society, Politics and Change in Malaysia," 115.

[55] *Malaysia: A Country Study*, 213.

[56] Barton, "Islam, Society, Politics and Change in Malaysia," 118.

[57] For details on the IIUM, one can visit the university's website at *http://www.iiu.edu.my/*.

An Islamic mosque in Kota Baru, Kelantan, northern Malaysia, March 2004.
Source: NGA Research Center—Ground Photography Collection.

Islamic ethics for all government civil servants.[58] All of
these changes had the impact of promoting a more Islamic veneer to the commercially
vibrant Malaysian society, but more importantly they had the impact of requiring the
employment of many religious studies graduates whose services were needed to ensure
that the new Islamic institutions were operating in accordance with the *Shari'a*.[59]
Another impact was the gradual disappearance of ABIM as an organized body gaining
popular attention by its critiques of government policy and also the virtual eclipse of
PAS, at least for the moment, as a political opposition movement to the UMNO and
the *Barisan Nasional*.[60]

Another aspect of the change toward being a more Islamic country was a noticeable
increase in Malaysia's interest in its role as a member of the Organization of the
Islamic Conference (OIC), as opposed to the active roles it had previously played as
a member of the British Commonwealth and the Non-Aligned Movement (NAM). In
addition, it also began to lend support to many Muslim movements elsewhere in the
Islamic world—e.g. the Palestine cause, the Arakanese in Myanmar, the Chechens
in Russia, and the Bosnians.[61]

The Comeback of PAS

Although PAS as a potential political alternative to the ruling establishment headed
by UMNO and Prime Minister Mahathir Mohammed remained in virtual eclipse
during the 1980s, it began to make a comeback in the 1990s. In part, this was due

---

[58] Abu Bakar, "Islam, Civil Society, and Ethnic Relations in Malaysia," 69. Pipes, *In the Path of God*,
251. Milne, 53.

[59] Kepel, *Jihad: The Trail of Political Islam*, 93–94.

[60] Barton, "Islam, Society, Politics and Change in Malaysia," 116. In the April 1982 general elections in
which Anwar Ibrahim had joined the UMNO and campaigned for them, PAS strength dropped to only 14.5
percent of the popular vote. *Malaysia: A Country Study*, 226.

[61] Abuza, *Militant Islam in Southeast Asia*, 54.

to the increasingly repressive character of the ruling establishment during this same period. Always a party that sought near hegemonic political dominance, but especially within the Malay community, the UMNO under Mahathir's leadership exerted even greater energy to press its advantage. Among the mechanisms used was selective use of the Internal Security Act provision of the state of emergency condition (that had not been lifted since its declaration following the 1969 riots) to arrest dissident opponents of the ruling regime. In addition, almost monopolistic control of Malaysia's media outlets and the judiciary, financial patronage to manipulate the electoral process, and gerrymandering of electoral districts to ensure UMNO and *Barisan Nasional* control of the political process gave Mahathir almost authoritarian control over the political system.[62] Unable to challenge UMNO on Islamic grounds, PAS leaders, many now former ABIM activists, increasingly were able to portray PAS as the liberal (rather than the conservative) party in Malay politics that opposed the authoritarianism and increasing corruption associated with UMNO and BN rule.

A split within UMNO in 1987 was necessary for the door to open to a revival of PAS political fortunes, however. Unable to successfully challenge Mahathir's leadership of UMNO, political rival Tenku Razaleigh Hamza broke away with a number of other UMNO deputies in 1988 to form his own party, *Semangat 46* (Spirit of [19]46) and entered into a coalition with PAS and the Chinese-based Democratic Action Party (DAP), the alternative socialist-oriented counterpart of PAS in the Chinese community otherwise dominated by UMNO ally, the MCA. Although the new coalition was unable to defeat UMNO and the BN in the 1990 general elections, it did make serious inroads into its voting strength.[63] Moreover, the BN lost control of two state governments, Sabah and Kelantan, the latter of which was taken over by PAS after an interval of 13 years.

Under the leadership of PAS leader, Nik Aziz Nik Mat, the new PAS government of Kelantan moved quickly to adopt the *Shari'a* as the prevailing law of the state and banned gambling, closed nightclubs, restricted the sale of alcohol, and imposed the death sentence for apostasy.[64] Although PAS had advocated implementation of the *Shari'a* since its establishment in 1951, it had failed to do so when previously in power. Now it did so but immediately came into conflict with the UMNO-dominated federal government that enforced its position that no state decision in criminal law would be valid without being sustained at the federal level by the courts of the UMNO-controlled judiciary system. The death penalty for apostasy, for example, came into conflict with the constitutional provision guaranteeing freedom of religion. This position, however, brought the Mahathir government into direct conflict with the federal constitution that assigned all "matters touching on Malay custom and religion" to the traditional sultans who continued to serve as hereditary governors of nine of the thirteen Malaysian

---

[62] Barton, "Islam, Society, Politics and Change in Malaysia," 120–132.

[63] The BN gained only 53 percent of the votes, as opposed to 71 percent in 1986. Barton, "Islam, Society, Politics and Change in Malaysia," 124–125.

[64] Abuza, *Militant Islam in Southeast Asia*, 54.

states. Accordingly, Mahathir embarked on a campaign to undermine these established powers and restrict the already diminished authority of the sultans.

Mahathir Strikes Back

Mahathir had actually begun his effort to limit the powers of the hereditary rulers as early as 1983, when he proposed a constitutional amendment that would remove the requirement of their assent for approval of any legislation at the state level. In part, the conflict over this issue was the basis of his rivalry with Kelantan aristocrat Tenku Razaleigh Hamza, who unsuccessfully tried to unseat him as UMNO leader in 1987, leading to the formation of the breakaway *Semangat 46* political party. Weakened, but still victorious in the 1990 elections, Mahathir revived his campaign to eliminate the remaining power of the sultans, and the conflict with Kelantan state provided the venue for doing so. Orchestrating a vicious campaign of innuendo against the personal qualities of many of the sultans in the UMNO-controlled media, the UMNO leadership subtlely prepared public opinion and undermined popular support for them as much as possible. In a series of measures, Mahathir succeeded in adopting a "code of conduct" for the sultans, which forbade them from being involved in politics, and in rescinding a historic law requiring government officials to accord special treatment to them. Finally, in May 1994, he was able to obtain approval in the House of Representatives for a constitutional amendment that decisively eliminated the power of the sultans to block legislation by withholding assent.[65]

Despite the outrage provoked in the traditional sectors of Malay society by these measures, the UMNO/BN coalition won its largest election victory in the history of the country in the 1995 elections. In large part the incumbent regime's popularity was due to the phenomenal economic growth most of the country had been experiencing for more than two decades, but especially in the early 1990s. In the large Chinese community, moreover, the move to adopt *Shari'a* was perceived as threatening, even though the number of Chinese in Kelantan state was very small. The election augmented UMNO's and Mahathir's powers even more completely, and in September 1997 he continued his attack on state powers by convening a conference to promote the centralization of the administration of the *Shari'a*, historically and constitutionally a state matter, into the hands of the federal government.[66]

IMPACT OF THE ASIAN FINANCIAL CRISIS

It was just at this moment, however, that Malaysia was hit by the Asian financial crisis of 1997. In mid-July 1997 the [Malaysian] ringgit began to depreciate, placing sudden pressure on the many firms and investors who had borrowed in foreign currency, making foreign credits suddenly much more difficult to obtain. The Malaysian crisis

---

[65] *The Far East and Australasia, 2003*, 766–767.

[66] *The Far East and Australasia, 2003*, 767.

was precipitated by simple contagion from events in Thailand, but the markets soon focused on what were seen as structural problems in the Malaysian system, notably overexpenditure on prestige infrastructure projects and opacity in the economy, partly as a result of corruption, partly a result of the formal policy of promoting the economic development of the Malay community. The ringgit's decline became catastrophic in October, when it lost 40 percent of its previous value within a month.[67]

The economic crisis provoked a political crisis within Malaysia, particularly between Mahathir and his deputy prime minister and finance minister, Anwar Ibrahim. Whereas Ibrahim viewed the crisis more in domestic terms and argued that inefficient companies subsidized by the government under the NEP should be allowed to fail, Mahathir instead perceived the crisis as resulting from an international conspiracy aimed at compromising Malaysian independence. In addition, Ibrahim favored strong anti-corruption measures in order to restore international confidence, a stance that placed him at odds with a number of UMNO tycoons. Although both agreed that austerity measures were necessary, it became apparent that the two differed on where cost cutting should occur. In the end, Mahathir implemented cost reductions mainly by reducing government salaries, while preserving as much as he could of his government's grandiose infrastructure projects in which the fortunes of friends and relatives was at stake.

The Firing of Anwar Ibrahim

Long considered Mahathir's natural and designated successor when the former retired from office, former ABIM leader Anwar Ibrahim unwisely, but probably with integrity, stood in opposition to his mentor, a stance Mahathir, probably also unwisely, clearly perceived as being a move to accelerate the political transition process. The recent abrupt collapse of the Suharto regime in neighboring Indonesia in May 1998, due to popular pressures brought on by the Asian financial collapse, may also have been a factor influencing both men. Accordingly, in early September 1998 Mahathir again shocked the nation by suddenly announcing Ibrahim's dismissal from all his government positions and from membership in UMNO. Despite the storm of controversy provoked by this precipitous action, the storm only deepened, when three weeks later Ibrahim was abruptly arrested and charged with several clearly trumped-up counts of illegal behavior, including corruption. Allegations of police brutality against Ibrahim within prison inflamed tensions even more. Throughout his trial, in which the court eventually declared him guilty in April 1999 and sentenced him to fifteen years

---

[67] *The Far East and Australasia, 2003,* 767.

in prison,[68] riot police had to hold at bay large numbers of protestors who maintained a more or less permanent vigil.

Politically, Ibrahim had been popular, particularly with Malaysian youth, and his association with UMNO had kept many of them loyal to the party. To these, Mahathir's perceived cruel treatment of Ibrahim was emblematic of the autocratic character, including total emasculation of the judiciary, of the now long-serving prime minister. Following the arrest of Ibrahim and during and after his trial, large numbers of his supporters began to defect from UMNO and flocked to PAS, quickly reviving the main Malay opposition party's challenge to historic UMNO dominance.[69] Aware of this relative loss of support, but also taking into account the partial recovery of the Malaysian economy by late 1998, Mahathir again surprised the country by advancing the date of federal elections from April 2000 to November 1999.

The Price of Victory

Although, as expected, Mahathir and the UMNO continued to dominate Malaysian politics in the 1999 elections, PAS and a coalition of allied opposition parties grouped into a *Barisan Alternatif* political front made serious inroads at the expense of the *Barisan Nasional*, leaving UMNO with only 57 percent of the seats in parliament, as opposed to the 65 percent the party had controlled since 1995. More importantly, PAS regained control of Terengganu state that it had lost, seemingly irrevocably, in 1961, and it posed serious challenges to UMNO control in several other, largely Malay states (Perlis, Perak, and Kedah-Mahathir's home state) in the north and east of the country. The significance of winning in Terengganu was that, unlike relatively impoverished and underdeveloped Kelantan (both having Malay majorities of about 95 percent), Terengganu had become a significant petroleum and gas-producing state in which the sharing of revenues derived from these resources between the federal government and the state was a matter of bitter dispute. Soon after the PAS victory, Mahathir's government required that all royalties derived from offshore platforms facing Terengganu go to the central treasury, overnight reducing Terengganu's budget by 80 percent. Although the move provoked outrage in Terengganu state and made it more difficult for PAS to govern effectively, it also made state authorities more highly

---

[68] Ibrahim was released from prison on September 2, 2004, precisely six years to the day from his dismissal from office as deputy prime minister and finance minister. The release was ordered by Malaysia's Federal Court, which by a two-to-one vote found the original court decision "flawed." Mahathir's successor as Prime Minister, Abdullah Badawi, was said not to have intervened to influence the court's decision. Mahathir himself had retired as prime minister in October 2003.

[69] Ten months after Ibrahim's arrest, PAS membership rolls were said to have jumped by 20 percent—to 120,000. By 2001, PAS claimed to have 800,000 members. In contrast, UMNO membership was said to be 2.7 million souls. PAS remained a relatively small opposition party; yet the strength of its opposition was significantly augmented as a result of the Anwar Ibrahim case. Abuza, *Militant Islam in Southeast Asia*, 56–57.

dependent on the largess of Kuala Lumpur, and PAS leaders dependent on the good will of UMNO leaders to maintain themselves.

MILITANT ISLAM IN MALAYSIA

A feature of Islamic resurgence and growing Islamization in Malaysia in the years after 1969 was also the undercurrent of militant Islamic fundamentalism. The dilemma of Malay politics has been how the dominant Malay ruling elite can maintain control of the country in association with Chinese and Indian elites without alienating the support of the Malay majority in the country and also maintain support of a majority of Malays without alienating the large and economically significant Chinese and Indian communities in the country. Through the years UMNO has effectively balanced the inherent tensions in this dilemma by focusing on economic development-centered in the Chinese community and by diverting the surplus wealth generated by this economic development to help ameliorate the relatively underdeveloped Malay community. The more Islamically-oriented PAS, on the other hand, remained a minority party because it was a more chauvinistically Malay party that found it difficult to gain the trust of a sufficient number of Chinese or Indians (non-Muslims) to be victorious electorally at the national level, although it could win in the Malay-majority states in the north and east. With the growing Islamization of the ethnic Malay community, which ought to have strengthened the appeal of PAS to the ordinary Malay, UMNO could only cope with this challenge, or so Mahathir believed, by co-opting the Islamic movement for its, and his, own purposes, i.e., to maintain UMNO's political hegemony over the Islamic party within the Malay community (PAS), while maintaining sufficient support in the Chinese and Indian communities to assure UMNO electoral supremacy. Increasingly, as Mahathir pursued an Islamization policy, however, his style of leadership was forced into what one political scientist has called a "repressive, responsive" approach[70] toward governance. Although Malaysia remained a democracy, the ruling party increasingly relied on authoritarian methods to maintain its hegemony, while seeking to be responsive to the perceived needs and desires of the communities it governed.

Early Incidents

It was in this context that some Malays developed a more militant posture toward the ruling regime. The first major instance of a government crackdown on Islamic elements apparently inciting violent action against it was in 1984, when the Mahathir government took action to imprison a number of PAS youth leaders who, influenced by the example of the Iranian revolution of 1979, were advocating a similar revolution in Malaysia. Then in November 1985, in a second incident, government forces surrounded and attacked the village of Memali in the Baling district of Kedah state. There, under the leadership of a PAS extremist, Ustaz Ibrahim, the village had

---

[70] Harold Crouch, *Government and Society in Malaysia* (Ithaca, NY: Cornell University Press, 236-247).

been organized into an Islamic commune, perhaps on the model of *Darul Arqam*, and refused to recognize any higher political authority. Well-armed to defend itself, the Memali commune evoked a government response remarkably analogous to that of the Syrian government in the city of Hamah in February 1982 or the U.S. government to the Branch Davidian cult in Waco, Texas, in February 1993. The standoff resulted in an attack by government forces, which resulted in the deaths of 14 villagers and four policemen as well as the arrest of 160 commune members, including children.[71]

Lure of the Afghan *Jihad*

Although data are sparse, it was also during this period—the mid-1980s—that recruiters based in Pakistan, probably part of the Peshawar-based *Maktab al-Khidmat*,[72] (MAK) headed by the Arab professor Abdullah Azzam, began traveling in Southeast Asia seeking young Muslim recruits to participate in jihadist activities against the Soviet occupation of Afghanistan. Indonesian and Filipino Muslim youth may have proved more responsive to these appeals than Malaysians, but Malaysia itself, as well as Singapore, soon emerged as major transit points and processing centers for individuals from Southeast Asia moving to and from Pakistan and Afghanistan.

There were several reasons for this phenomenon. First, the Malaysian government embarked on its own Islamization campaign, and like most Muslim governments, was supportive of the Afghan resistance to the Soviet occupation. Secondly, as a relatively open society, particularly in comparison to neighboring Indonesia under Suharto or the Philippines under Marcos, the trafficking in persons, money transfers, or arms shipments could occur with little monitoring or state concern. Thirdly, as a country with a flourishing economy, Malaysia had a large requirement for foreign labor. This circumstance led the Mahathir government to ease visa restrictions for entry into Malaysia, especially for people from Muslim countries, in the decade plus prior to the Asian financial crisis of 1997. Finally, most of the work associated with support for the Afghan resistance was in the hands of foreign elements in Malaysia-Arabs in the first instance, but also increasingly with the passage of time militant Islamic exiles mainly from Indonesia. As a result, the recruitment, training, supporting, and sending of Southeast Asian youth to Pakistan and Afghanistan was work the government could tolerate and even empower; it was not work for which the government had specific responsibility. Such conditions continued in Malaysia, even after the Soviet withdrawal from Afghanistan, and the *Maktab al-Khidmat* was gradually transformed into a new organization called *al-Qa'ida*.

---

[71] Barton, "Islam, Society, Politics and Change in Malaysia," 119.

[72] Literally *Maktab al-Khidmat l'il-Mujahideen al-Arab* (Office of Services of the Arab Mujahideen).

Jemaah Islamiyah

The specific Indonesians involved with and who came to be associated with the Malaysian-based (until 1998), al-Qa'ida-linked, pan-Southeast Asian Islamist organization, *Jemaah Islamiyah* (JI), formally established on January 1, 1993,[73] had mostly come to Malaysia in the mid-1980s, fleeing the Suharto regime. Although their numbers were many,[74] of special note were Abdullah Sungkar (1936–1999), founder and leader of JI, and two key associates, Abu Bakar Ba'asyir (b. 1938) and Muhammad Iqbal Rahman (aka Fikiruddin, aka Abu Jibril). Yet another individual, significant for the important leadership role he eventually came to play, was a young 20-year-old, Riduan Isamuddin (aka Hambali, b. 1966).

Although Hambali may not have been entirely typical of the many who went to Pakistan and Afghanistan and returned to Southeast Asia imbued with the *jihad*ist spirit, the pattern is typical enough to be used as a paradigm for many of the others who followed the same path. Said to have arrived in Malaysia in 1985 in flight from Indonesia, he is alleged to have had university studies as his primary goal. He was, however, recruited to join the *jihad* in Afghanistan, where he served for an apparent three-year period between 1988 and 1990. There he is said to have met and worked with Usama bin Ladin, a close associate of Abdullah Azzam, and subsequently the latter's successor following his death in November 1989.

On his return to Malaysia in late 1990–early 1991, Hambali lived an apparently simple life as a roadside kebab seller, butcher, and later as a peddler and itinerant preacher. Although he lived in virtual poverty, he made use of his traveling to preach, spot recruits, raise funds, and organize travel of recruits being sent either to Pakistan or the Philippines.[75] Among those who traveled to Pakistan at this

---

[73] Other sources give varying dates for the formal establishment of *Jemaah Islamiyah*, from 1989 to 1995. In November 2002, a document found on the computer of Imam Sumudra known as the PUPJI document (Constitution of *Jemaah Islamiyah*) established the founding date of the organization as January 1, 1993. See below, Chapter 4, 101. I had earlier selected 1992 as reflecting the historical progress of events, as noted in the paragraphs that follow, which indicate that 1992 was the likely date.

[74] Abuza gives the number as around 800. Abuza, *Militant Islam in Southeast Asia*, 125.

[75] Biographical data on Hambali are very incomplete. This perspective is based largely on a journalistic account: Baradan Kuppusamy, "Hambali: The Driven Man," from *Asia Times Online*, 19 August 2003. URL: *www.atimes.com/atimes/Southeast_Asia?EH19Ae06.html*, accessed 2 November 2004. The details in this article have been closely cross-checked with other journalistic accounts of Hambali, however.

time to meet Usama bin Ladin was Abdullah Sungkar.[76] Soon after his return, he, Ba'asyir, Fikiruddin, Hambali, and others moved from diverse places of residence to the coastal village of Sungei Manggis in southern Malaysia, a ferry ride away from Indonesia across the Strait of Malacca. The *Jemaah Islamiyah* movement, of which these men were the central leadership, dates from this gathering at Sungei Manggis in early 1992.[77]

Roots of *Jemaah Islamiyah*

The concept of *jemaah islamiyah* was not a new one dating from this moment, however. Both Sungkar and Ba'asyir considered themselves the spiritual heirs of Sekarmadji Kartosuwirjo—the founder-leader of the Indonesian *Darul Islam* movement in western Java whose struggle to create an "Islamic state" in Indonesia was brutally crushed by the Sukarno regime during the 1950s.[78] Believing that the *Darul Islam* movement had failed because Indonesian society (*jemaah*) was not yet ready, both Sungkar and Ba'asir spoke of the need of a longer-term process to foster the creation of a *jemaah islamiyah* (Islamic society) as a necessary prelude to establishing an Islamic state. In furtherance of this goal, and in time-honored Indonesian tradition, the two in 1972 established an Islamic boarding school (*pesantren*), called *al-Mukmin* in Ngruki (suburb of Solo). Starting with 30 students, the institution had grown to 1,900 students by the year 2000. The later *Jemaah Islamiyah* organization, founded by Sungkar and

---

[76] This may have been Sungkar's second trip out of Malaysia since his arrival in 1985, as well as his first meeting with bin Ladin. The exchange must have occurred between April and December 1991, the brief period that bin Ladin lived primarily in Peshawar, Pakistan, after his surreptitious departure from Saudi Arabia and later decision to settle in Sudan. This brief period, which is virtually ignored in the plethora of bin Ladin/*al-Qa'ida* literature that has appeared since September 2001, may well have been the true starting point of *al-Qa'ida* as an organization striving for global reach. Another visitor to bin Ladin at this time was the soon-to-be Filipino Abu Sayyaf leader, Abdurrajak Abubakar Janjalani. Upon the latter's departure from Pakistan in December 1991—the same time as bin Ladin's departure for Khartoum-Janjalani was accompanied by an individual, sent with him by bin Ladin, whom the United States less than two years later would know by the name of Ramzi Yousef. The Abu Sayyaf group in the Philippines dates from early 1992, following Janjalani's return home from Pakistan, although bin Ladin had established earlier contact with the Filipino Muslims in 1988 when he had sent his brother-in-law, Muhammad Jamal Khalifa, to the Philippines to obtain recruits for the war in Afghanistan. Rohan Gunaratna, *Inside al-Qaeda: Global Network of Terror* (New York: Columbia University Press, 2002), 178; Abuza, *Militant Islam in Southeast Asia*, 92. Unlike Sungkar, Janjalani had traveled to Afghanistan before. He was part of an alleged 300 Filipino recruits to have been brought to Pakistan in the mid-1980s to participate in the *jihad* against the Soviet occupation of Afghanistan. There is no evidence that Hambali traveled to Pakistan at this time with Sungkar, but in light of subsequent events it seems reasonable that he did. The only account dealing at all with this brief period of bin Ladin's stay in Pakistan is that found in Adam Robinson, *Bin Ladin: Behind the Mask of the Terrorist* (New York: Arcade Publishing, 2001), 133–134. Even this account is virtually devoid of comment on bin Ladin's activities during this period, however.

[77] Gunaratna, *Inside al-Qaeda*, 195.

[78] Abuza, *Militant Islam in Southeast Asia*, 126.

Muslim tourists at St. Paul Hill, Malacca, Malaysia, May 2001.
Source: NGA Research Center—Ground Photography Collection.

Ba'asir in 1992, was to be heavily populated by graduates of this institution.[79] Like the Muhammadiyah mass organization of Indonesia, the curriculum of *al-Mukmin* was strongly influenced by the modernist arguments of Muhammad Abduh and Rashid Rida. Unlike the Muhammadiyah, however, Sungkar and Ba'asir placed emphasis on the incompatibility of a society that adhered to God's laws (*Shari'a*) and the society that did not. A true Islamic state could come into being only by a *jemaah islamiyah* that was characterized by strength—strength of faith, strength of brotherhood, and military strength—a strength that would enable the faithful society ultimately to crush its enemies, as the *Darul Islam* movement had earlier been crushed in the 1950s. Arrested and imprisoned for four years by the Suharto regime for "subversive" activities in 1978, Sungkar and Ba'asyir fled to Malaysia in 1985 on learning they were about to be arrested again.[80]

Objectives of *Jemaah Islamiyah*

The decision to formally organize a group called *Jemaah Islamiyah* in Malaysia in 1992–93 obviously came as a result of meetings with bin Ladin in Peshawar and

---

[79] See, for instance, the roster of JI activists provided by the Brussels-based International Crisis Group, "Indonesia Backgrounder: How the *Jemaah Islamiyah* Terrorist Network Operates," from *ICG Online*, 11 December 2002. URL: *http://www.crisisweb.org/home/index.cfm?id-1397&1-1*. Accessed 12 December 2004.

[80] Abuza, *Militant Islam in Southeast Asia*, 126–127.

probably also funding from him. The primary focus of the organization, however, was not Malaysia, but the use of Malaysia as a convenient and reasonably secure transit point for the conduct of operations elsewhere, primarily in the Philippines and Indonesia. If the definition of a terrorist organization requires that the group first be assigned responsibility for an act of terrorism, then JI could not be effectively identified as such until August 2000, when it conducted its first-known terrorist operation—the assassination of the Philippine ambassador in Jakarta.[81] By this time, the leadership cadre of JI and many of its other activists had returned to Indonesia, following the collapse of the Suharto regime in May 1998. The period of the 1990s was primarily a time of organizing, recruiting, training, planning, and developing of the financial and logistical infrastructure to support violent actions that would come later and in which the Malaysia of Prime Minister Mahathir Mohammed served as a relatively free safe-haven for such intrigues.

The principal operational leaders of this effort appear to have been Hambali and another Indonesian, Muhammad Iqbal Rahman (aka Abu Jabril), who served as head of training for all JI cadres operating in Southeast Asia.[82] Under their leadership, contacts were made and JI cells (*fiah*) established throughout Southeast Asia for the purposes of training and taking responsibility for unique types of operations (arms training, explosives manufacture, media activities, etc.). These *fiah*, in turn, were grouped into four *mantiqi*: one for peninsular Malaysia, southern Thailand, and Singapore; the second for all Indonesia, except for Borneo (Kalimantan, Sabah, Sarawak, and Brunei); the third for the Philippines, all Borneo, and Sulawesi in eastern Malaysia; and the fourth for Australia and Papua (Irian Jaya). Each of the *mantiqi* was headed by a Hanbali lieutenant.[83]

Until the departure of the JI leadership to Indonesia in 1998, the Malaysian *mantiqi* was the largest part of the growing JI organization as well as its focal point. It was here that links were maintained with the *al-Qa'ida* organization, first in Sudan, but later in Afghanistan and Pakistan, and with the fighting groups in the Philippines and Indonesia. The Malaysian *mantiqi* was also the financial center of the JI and primary meeting place for JI and *al-Qa'ida* planners. Through the Malaysian *mantiqi*, which also included Singapore, passed the approximately 100 recruits who traveled to Pakistan and Afghanistan during this period. Other recruits were sent to the Philippines to receive training from *al-Qa'ida* and other trainers. The Malaysian *mantiqi* also operated its own training camp in Negeri Sembilan.

---

[81] In fact, the existence of *Jemaah Islamiyah* became known only in December 2001, when a tape detailing plans of the Singapore cell was discovered in the home of *al-Qa'ida* military commander Muhammad Atef (Abu Hafs al-Misri) in Kabul, Afghanistan. See below, Chapter 4, 100-101. *Jemaah Islamiyah* operations prior to this date were unattributed.

[82] A detailed description of JI organizing activities during this period is provided by Abuza, *Militant Islam in Southeast Asia*, 125–140, on which this account is largely based.

[83] Abuza, *Militant Islam in Southeast Asia*, 132.

Sultan's palace in Kota Baru, Malacca, Malaysia, March 2004.
Source: NGA Research Center — Ground Photography Collection.

Jemaah Islamiyah and *al-Qa'ida*

Finally, the Malaysian *mantiqi* also established a number of front companies that were used to channel funds from *al-Qa'ida* as well as to procure weapons and materials used in bomb-making. One of these, called the Konsojaya Trading Company, established in June 1994 by Hambali, *al-Qa'ida* operative Wali Khan Amin Shah, Afghan investor Mehdat Abdul Salam Shabana, Saudi investor Hemaid H.Al-Ghamdi, and four others, appears to have been set up primarily to support OPLAN Bojinka in the Philippines — the abortive plan led by New York World Trade Center bombing planner, Ramzi Yousef, to assassinate U.S. President Clinton and Pope John XXXIII, and to bomb simultaneously 11 U.S. aircraft over the Pacific sometime in early 1995.[84]

Even after the departure of the JI leadership to Indonesia in 1998, the Malaysian *mantiqi* continued to play a central role in coordinating JI and *al-Qa'ida* operations. Key planning for the October 2000 bombing of the American ship USS Cole in the port of Aden, as well as the September 11, 2001, aircraft attacks on New York's World

---

[84] Gunaratna, *Inside al-Qaeda*, 195; Abuza, *Militant Islam in Southeast Asia*, 129.

51

Trade Center and the Pentagon in Washington, DC, took place under JI cover at a meeting in Kuala Lumpur on January 5, 2000.[85]

The KMM—JI's Malaysian Counterpart

Although *Jemaah Islamiyah* emerged on Malaysian soil, it did not attract too many Malays. Two small groups of Malaysians were said to have been sent to Pakistan and Afghanistan prior to the Soviet withdrawal in 1989. Others followed, but in small numbers, during the 1990s. Among those who had the experience of *jihad* and thus could call themselves *mujahidin*, many continued to carry the legacy with them. Some of these,[86] along with others, on October 12, 1995, formed a new militant organization called the Malaysian Mujahidin Group (*Kampulan Mujahidin Malaysia*—KMM), under the leadership of Afghan veteran Zainon Ismail. The formation of the KMM followed the Malaysian elections of 1995 in which Mahathir's UMNO secured its largest electoral victory ever, leaving some associated with the new KMM to abandon hope that a "true" Islamic state could ever be established through democratic means, nor that PAS could ever win at the national level electorally. Accordingly, KMM established itself as a covert organization dedicated to overthrowing the UMNO-led government by force in the interest of establishing Malaysia once and for all as an Islamic state.

The precise relationship between KMM and *Jemaah Islamiyah* is unclear, as was the relationship between KMM and PAS. Although KMM was an independent group, some of its members also belonged to *Jemaah Islamiyah*, and most KMM members were supporters of PAS, if not members, but were disillusioned by PAS's continuing commitment to work through the democratic process. A key KMM leader, moreover, was the son of Kelantan-based PAS leader Nik Aziz Nik Mat-Nik Adli Nik Aziz-the latter said to have served six years in Afghanistan between 1990 and 1996.[87] Returning to teach Arabic in his father's PAS-operated school in Kelantan's capital, Kota Baru, Nik Adli became increasingly involved with the KMM and allegedly committed to a violent overthrow of the Malaysian government. Later charges against him included the purchase of a large number of weapons and explosive materials from Thailand in 1999, close and continuing contacts with the JI leadership, including Hambali, the dispatching

---

[85] Among the attendees at the meeting were (1) Khalid al-Mihdar and (2) Nawaf al-Hazmi, two of the hijackers who flew American Airlines Flight 77 into the Pentagon. Other attendees included (3) Ramzi bin al-Shibh of the Hamburg *al-Qa'ida* cell, a close associate of September 11 leader Muhammad Atta who allegedly failed to be a twentieth hijacker because of his inability later to obtain a visa enabling him to enter the United States; (4) Khalid Shaikh Muhammad, overall planner of both the USS Cole operation and the 9/11 operation; (5) Tawfiq bin Atash, an alleged key operative associated with the attack on the USS Cole; (6) Fahad al-Quso, the alleged key planner behind the August 1998 bombing of two U.S. embassies in East Africa; (7) Ahmad Hikmat Shakir, a key *al-Qa'ida* operative of Iraqi origin; and (8) Hambali. Abuza, *Militant Islam in Southeast Asia*, 123.

[86] Abuza says the number was 45. Abuza, *Militant Islam in Southeast Asia*, 124.

[87] Gunaratna, *Inside al-Qaeda*, 196.

of KMM members to train in MILF camps in the Philippines, and participating in battles against Christians in the Maluku Islands (Indonesia), also in 1999 and early 2000.[88]

Demise of the KMM

The KMM was uncovered during the summer of 2001. A bank robbery in May of that year in which police killed two and detained six KMM members led to confessions implicating others. Although the KMM leadership may not have authorized its members to conduct this crime, they nevertheless were revealed as a result of the failure of the bank operation. On August 4, 2001, Zainon Ismail, Nik Adli, and eight other alleged members of the KMM (seven of whom were also PAS members) were detained for attempting to violently overthrow the Malaysian government and establish an Islamic state. The police also linked KMM to a number of other crimes, as enumerated above.[89] Following the September 11 attacks on the United States and growing evidence of deeper involvement in terrorist activities, many more were arrested. Altogether, 68 members of KMM were eventually identified and imprisoned under the provisions of the all-embracing Internal Security Act of 1948.

A year before, and under similar circumstances, yet another militant group called *Al-Ma'unah*, apparently unconnected to KMM, had been uncovered, when in July 2000 members of the group had seized weapons from military stockpiles in northern Perak State. In the ensuing four-day standoff, two government officials were killed before the group surrendered. The leader of the group, Mohammed Amin Razali, was a Malay who had served too in Afghanistan in the 1980s. Also influenced by the model of the Indonesian movement of the 1950s but not apparently affiliated with *Jemaah Islamiyah Darul Islam* or its leadership, Razali had returned to Malaysia to form his own cult-like group, four of whose members, including himself, were sentenced to death on December 27, 2001, for plotting the violent overthrow of the Malaysian government.[90]

---

[88] Some critics of the Mahathir regime argued that the charges against Nik Adli were trumped up as a means of discrediting his father and PAS in general. Although PAS continually disclaimed any connection with KMM and Nik Aziz did nothing to defend his son, the allegation that UMNO might transform the troubles of Nik Adli into political advantage against PAS was credible. Abuza, *Militant Islam in Southeast Asia*, 125.

[89] Abuza, *Militant Islam in Southeast Asia*, 156.

[90] Abuza, *Militant Islam in Southeast Asia*, 125. An editorial in the UMNO-oriented Kuala Lumpur *New Straits Times* interpreted the incident as follows: "[I]t would appear that the Al-Mu'unah movement is perhaps a manifestation of an irrational extremism and militancy within PAS itself...In terms of size, it may be a small element. Nevertheless, it is a dangerous development, for, as shown by the fanatical actions of the Al-Mu'unah members, it imperils national security, bordering on lunacy and threatening to bring about the disintegration of Malaysia. Agreed, this development may not have been endorsed or encouraged by the PAS leadership. But does it matter? It was from within the larynx of the party's leadership that the hate emanated. As observed by Prime Minister *Datu*k Seri Dr. Mahathir Mohammad, Al-Mu'unah is the direct result of PAS's campaign of hatred for the Government." *New Straits Times* (Internet Version in English), July 21, 2000. Document ID SEP20000721000072, accessed on Intelink June 5, 2000.

IMPACT OF THE 9/11 ATTACKS ON MALAYSIA

Although the *al-Qa'ida*-sponsored attacks on the United States on September 11, 2001, raised the possibility that Malaysia could be identified as a country that harbored international terrorists, particularly after it became known that two of the aircraft hijackers had resided in Malaysia and attended the January 2000 meeting in Kuala Lumpur where at least a part of the planning for the operation had occurred, the event in fact proved a political boon to Prime Minister Mahathir Mohammed and the UMNO. Mahathir immediately condemned the September 11 attacks and promised to fight terrorism within Malaysia. He moved quickly to suppress the just discovered KMM organization and promised close cooperation with the United States on tracing *al-Qa'ida* fund transfers in Malaysia. He also moved quickly to close down a key *al-Qa'ida* website (*www.alneda.com*) that was hosted on a Kuala Lumpur internet server. Close cooperation with the United States brought an invitation for a state visit to Washington, DC, in May 2002, the first such visit since 1994, where Mahathir signed a formal agreement with U.S. President George W. Bush to cooperate in combating terrorism.

While mending and consolidating ties with Washington, Mahathir also preserved his credentials as a Malaysian nationalist leader. He publicly rebuffed a formal request from the United States to hand over several hundred people on a U.S. list of terrorist suspects, stating that he would only do so if "the United States provided direct evidence that they had committed a crime within the United States."[91] Terrorists charged with committing crimes in Malaysia, he asserted, would be tried in Malaysian courts in accordance with Malaysian law.[92] He also reflected the views of many Malays and Muslims around the world by strongly criticizing the U.S. military response to the September 11 attacks by invading Afghanistan, while failing to make concerted "efforts...to find the reasons why these terrorists chose to resort to violence in the first place."[93]

Mahathir's primary political response to the September 11 attacks, however, was domestic. He adroitly used the crisis to link PAS in the minds of Malay voters with Islamic extremism, terrorism, the KMM, and JI, whose presence in Malaysia and its links to *al-Qa'ida* he finally became able to admit. Declaring on September 29, 2001, that Malaysia was already an Islamic state,[94] Mahathir sought to brand PAS as Taliban-like extremists who wanted to implement an extremist form of Islam and carry Malaysia backward rather than forward in its development.[95] Although this

---

[91] Abuza, *Militant Islam in Southeast Asia*, 213.

[92] On the other hand, an Oregon-based terrorist suspect, Ahmed Ibrahim Bilal, who was found to be studying at Malaysia's International Islamic University, was immediately deported to the United States. Abuza, *Militant Islam in Southeast Asia*, 213.

[93] Patrick Senayah, "U.S.-led Bombings of Afghanistan Won't Resolve Terrorism: Dr. M." Kuala Lumpur *New Straits Times*, October 14, 2001.

[94] Talk given by Patricia Martinez (University of Malaysia) at the U.S. Department of State, April 1, 2004.

[95] Abuza, *Militant Islam in Southeast Asia*, 216.

political strategy may have been only marginally successful among Malays, it worked well with the country's non-Malay voters.[96] In the March 2004 general elections, *Barisan Nasional* candidates received 64 percent of the votes and won 90 percent of the seats in the Malaysian Parliament.[97] Although PAS retained control of Kelantan state, UMNO also regained control of Terengganu state, where it immediately began reversing *Shari'a* provisions (bans on traditional female dancing, unisex hair salons, separate male and female checkout lines in stores) that PAS had implemented—as it had previously in Kelantan in the early 1990s.[98]

Retirement of Mahathir Mohammed

By the time of the 2004 general elections, however, Mahathir Mohammed was gone, having stepped down from all his offices except his seat in Parliament in October 2003. Succeeding him was his Deputy Prime Minister, Abdullah Ahmad Badawi, former foreign minister and education minister in successive Mahathir governments. Mahathir had designated him Deputy Prime Minister after the dismissal and arrest of his predecessor, Anwar Ibrahim, in 1998. In the run-up to the 2004 elections, there was considerable doubt that Bedawi, an apparently less forceful individual than Mahathir, could play the dominant role in Malaysian politics that had characterized Mahathir's 22 years as Prime Minister.

Badawi succeeded, however, in separating himself, at least temporarily, from Mahathir's political shadow. Running on a platform that promised to address problems of alleged corruption, cronyism, government inefficiency, and continuing rural poverty, Badawi surprised potential voters by arresting two key industrial leaders on charges of corruption prior to the election, and by reversing a Mahathir decision on the award of a major contract to build a railroad line that was widely believed to have been originally awarded for political rather than economic considerations.[99] These measures that demonstrated an intent to govern in a way that responded to some of the dissatisfactions with the Mahathir regime no doubt contributed to his landslide election victory in April 2004. Badawi's release of Anwar Ibrahim from prison later in the year (September 2) may also have been aimed at strengthening his popular base. Whether Badawi could survive the long knives of inter-party politics within the UMNO remained to be seen.

In selecting Badawi as his political successor, Mahathir appeared to have done well. From the standpoint of the Islamic factor in Malaysian politics, just as his co-optation

---

[96] Talk given by Heng Pek Koon (American University) at the U.S. Department of State, April 1, 2004.

[97] Talk given by Osman Bakar (Georgetown University) at the U.S. Department of State, April 1, 2004.

[98] Ioannis Gatsiounis, "Malaysia: Tug-of-War over Terengganu," *Asia Times Online*, May 7, 2004. URL: *http://www.atimes.com/atimes/Southeast_Asia/FG07Ae01.html*.

[99] Ioannis Gatsionnu, "Malaysia: Abdullah boleh-or Can He?" *Asia Times Online*, March 2, 2004. URL: *http://www.atimes.com/atimes/Southeast_Asia/FC02Ae05.html*. Accessed December 29, 2004.

of Anwar Ibrahim in 1982 had served him well politically, so his choice of Badawi in 1998 had the appearance of being a political master stroke. Unlike Ibrahim, who had been an Islamic enthusiast, Badawi was formally educated in Islamic studies. Running on a slogan called *Islam Hadhari* (Civilized Islam) that called upon Malaysians to embrace modernity and the information age and to attend government schools rather than the traditional *pondoks*, generally run by the traditional (usually PAS-supporting) `*ulama*, he would be a hard man to debate on Islamic grounds.

OUTLOOK

With the election of 2004, the UMNO and the *Barisan Nasional* continued to maintain the strong grasp on Malaysian politics it had held since the country gained independence in 1957. Challenged by a revival of Islamic sentiment since the 1970s, the party responded by co-opting Islamic values into its mechanism of governance. However, it had sought to embrace a vision of Islam that coexists with rapid economic development and prosperity. As a result, those with a more "fundamentalist" orientation have continued to be marginalized politically. This pattern is likely to endure for the foreseeable future. The Chinese and Indian elements of the electorate almost guarantee it, as does the ever growing urban, middle class Malay sector. As the 1995 landslide election of UMNO helped to give birth to the militant KMM movement, the frustrated reaction of the same PAS-related elements may give birth to a renewed militant element following the 2004 election. The regime is more alert to the threat to political stability posed by such a development in the post-9/11 world. Malaysian politics is likely to continue to be a rocky road, but continuity is likely to prevail over discontinuity — as it has in the past — for the foreseeable future

Kampung King Mosque in Melaka, across Strait of Malacca from Sumatra, Indonesia, March 2004.
Source: NGA Research Center — Ground Photography Collection.

56

Map of Thailand.
Source: CIA.

CHAPTER 3

ISLAM IN THAILAND

For the Malay Muslims of southern Thailand the question has always been how to participate in the political process of a state based on a Buddhist cosmology... The process of national integration is synonymous with "cultural disintegration" from the perspective of many Malay Muslims.

—Surin Pitsuwan

THE SULTANATE OF PATANI

The Malay Sultanate of Patani, situated in today's southern Thailand, was established in the mid-15th century, soon after the foundation of the Sultanate of Malacca. The date usually given for the conversion to Islam of the previously existing *raja* of Langkasuka is 1457.[100] The sultanate was situated on the east coast of the Malay peninsula and coincided with the present-day Thai provinces of Pattani,[101] Yala, and Narathiwat.[102]

Like the other Muslim sultanates established in southeast Asia during this era, Patani was a trading state that facilitated east-west trade between China and other locations in the Far East with ports to the west. Its capital city, Patani, was located at the mouth of a river that drained into an extensive rice plain, and was strategically positioned to serve as the eastern terminus of an overland trading route across the peninsula.[103] Its relative remote location on the northeast coast of the Malay peninsula isolated it from the advance of the Portuguese, Spanish, Dutch, and finally British trading settlements that began to be established in the region during the 16th century.

The Decline of Patani

Although Patani flourished in the century after the Portuguese capture of Malacca in 1511, it began to decline economically in the early 17th century, about the time the Dutch established their permanent settlement at Batavia (Jakarta). Despite its economic decline, it emerged during the same century, along with Aceh in northwestern Sumatra,

---

[100] W.K. Che Man. *Muslim Separatism: The Moros of Southern Philippines and the Malays of Southern Thailand* (New York: Oxford University Press, 1990), 34.

[101] The modern Thai province and city is spelled Pattani. The conventional Malay spelling of the traditional sultanate and its capital city is Patani. This difference in usage is followed in this study.

[102] The fourth southern Thai province that is mostly Malay Muslim, Satun, was originally a part of the sultanate of Kedah (Malaysia), whose ruler formally ceded that portion of his sultanate to the Siamese king in 1843.

[103] *Encyclopedia of Asian History.* Ed. by Ainslie T. Embree (New York: Charles Scribner's Sons, 1988), 220.

as a principal center of Islamic scholarship and learning in southeast Asia, developing the reputation of being the "Cradle of Islam" on the Malay peninsula.[104]

An interesting aspect of Patani's history during this period (1584 to mid-1600s) was rule by four successive queens (*sultanah*).[105] The eventual threat to Patani's independence came, not from advancing European power in the region, but from the expanding and consolidating Buddhist Siamese (Thai) Kingdom of Ayutthaya to the north.[106] Although the sultan of Patani succeeded in defending himself from a number of attacks in the mid-18th century, he finally succumbed to Siamese power in 1785 — the same year the Sultan of Kedah leased the island of Penang to the English East India Company and was forced to pay annual tribute to the King of Ayutthaya, along with his fellow rulers to the south (the sultans of Kedah, Perlis, Kelantan, and Terengganu).

PATANI UNDER THAI RULE

The expansionist Chakkri dynasty, that continues to preside over Thailand today and was building its new capital at Bangkok during this period, likely would have sought the submission of the whole Malay peninsula had it not encountered the English

---

[104] *First Encyclopaedia of Islam, 1913–1936*, Vol VI, eds. M. Th. Houtsma, A.J. Wensinck, E. Levi-Provencal, H.A.R. Gibb, and W. Heffening (New York: E.J. Brill, 1993), 1035. Also, Peter Chalk, "Militant Islamic Separatism in Southern Thailand," in Jason F. Isaacson and Colin Rubenstein, eds., *Islam in Asia: Changing Political Realities* (New Brunswick, NJ: Transaction Publishers, 2002), 165.

[105] Known as (1) *Ratu Hijau* (the Green Queen), (2) *Ratu Biru* (the Blue Queen), (3) *Ratu Ungu* (the Violet Queen), and (4) *Ratu Kuning* (the Yellow Queen), the period of their rule constitutes the "golden age" of Patani history, when the sultanate expanded its borders to include Kelantan and Terengganu, making it the most powerful Malay state after Johor in the south. Aside from a famed literary tradition that developed in this era and continues to this day [Virginia Matheson Hooker, "Patani," in *New Encyclopedia of Islam*, ed. by C.E. Bosworth, E. van Donzel, W.P. Heinrichs, and G. LeComte, Vol. 8 (Leiden: E.J. Brill, 1995) 285–286], Patani was famous for gun casting, of which two famous cannon measuring over six meters in length today grace the entrance of the Thai Ministry of Defense in Bangkok. See "The End of Langkasuka: The Rise and Fall of the Malay Kingdom of Patani," *Sejarah Melayu: A History of the Malay Peninsula*. URL: *http://www.sabrizain.demon.co.uk/malaya/kedah3.htm*. Accessed January 3, 2005.

[106] Siam officially took the name Thailand (land of the free) only in 1939. Although the Tai (Thai) people who migrated from southern China gradually conquered the land of Siam in the 13th century, exerting their hegemony on other peoples previously inhabiting the land, it was not until the 20th century that considerations of nationalism — i.e., that Siam was the land of the Thai people-led to a formal decision to change the name of the country. Barbara Leitch LePoer, ed. *Thailand: A Country Study* (Washington, DC: HQ U.S. Army, 1987), 28. For contemporary writers looking backward, use of the term "Siam/Siamese" often seems archaic. Therefore, the term "Thai" is sometimes used in the text of this work, when (as a more modern coinage) use of the term "Siamese" actually would be more correct. Hopefully an esthetic balance has been achieved.

presence on the peninsula.[107] The British presence was in fact welcomed by the Thai king as a useful ally against arch-enemy Burma. As a result, a balance of power emerged that resulted over the long term in the emergence of independent Malaysia. The sultanate of Patani was not to be a part of this process, however. After a number of rebellions against Thai rule during the years 1791–1808, the Thai king partitioned Patani into seven smaller states,[108] each with its own new *sultan* or *raja* appointed by the king but administered by the nearby Buddhist *raja* of Ligor (Songkhla). Although this measure of divide and rule made it easier to assure Thai domination of the region, it did not prevent yet another uprising in 1832, and again in 1838, that the Thai government suppressed with particular brutality, devastating the countryside and transforming the once prosperous sultanate into the economically backward region it has since remained.

Following the revolt of 1838, the region of Pattani remained relatively quiescent under Thai rule, perhaps in part because the central government left it alone and engaged in minimum interference in local affairs. This changed during the latter years of modernizing Thai monarch, Chulalongkorn (Rama V, 1868–1910), who, among other things, placed an emphasis on modern communications, including the railroad that was completed as far as the Malay border soon after his death. He also began the development of a modern education system. Although the new system of government schools did not reach Pattani during his reign, it would eventually pose a challenge to the traditional `ulama-run *pondok* schools whereby Islamic tradition was transmitted.

Most importantly for Pattani was the king's effort, beginning in 1893, to implement a more modern system of government administration. In 1902, the seven states into which the old sultanate of Patani had been divided in 1808 were reconsolidated into a single province under the direction of a Siamese High Commissioner. Although each former state retained its Malay ruler, each ruler was advised by a Siamese officer who reported directly to the Siamese High Commissioner in Pattani. This system, which closely resembled the "residency" system established by the Dutch in Java in the 1830s and the British in some of the Malay states beginning in 1874, had as its aim the elimination of traditional indirect forms of rule and the consolidation of central authority as a basis for more uniform rule throughout the kingdom. All officials, including the local rulers, moreover, were salaried and forbidden to collect fees for

---

[107] The Thai view is that once the authority of Siam had extended over the whole of the Malay peninsula, whose local rulers held their title from the King of Siam. The conversion or changeover of many of these rulers and peoples to Islam was part of an expression of rebellion or independence from Thai suzerainty. Behind this conversion to Islam were the expansionist policies of the sultan of Malacca who was challenging Thai hegemony on the peninsula. Beset by many other challenges, the kings of Siam were never able to reassert their hegemony over parts of the peninsula until the emergence of the Chakkri dynasty in 1767. See Sir John Malcolm, "Malcolm (4 Kings)," *LoveToKnow 1911 Online Encyclopedia*. (c)2003,2004 LoveToKnow, URL: *http://65.191encyclopedia.org/M/MA/MALCOLM_4_KINGS_.htm*. Accessed January 3, 2005.

[108] Pattani, Nhongchik, Reman, Rangae, Saiburi, Yala and Yaring. "Briefing: A brief introduction to the Malay Kingdom of Patani," from *Islamic Human Rights Commission Online*. URL: *http://www.ihrc.org.uk/show.php?id-1342*. Accessed January 3, 2005.

services rendered or to exact forced labor. In this manner, as in the neighboring Malay states and in the Dutch East Indies, the traditional Muslim ruling class was transformed into a salaried sector of the Siamese central government.[109]

Consolidation of Thai Rule

The new administration was not implemented in Pattani without resistance, however, and in 1906 the province was redivided into four provinces as a means of combating the unified resistance demonstrated by the native Malays to the changes being imposed on their region. Later, the division of old Patani was reduced to the three provinces that continue to exist today.

Control of provincial administration was of growing importance to the Thai government, largely because of increasing pressure being exerted on Siam by France and Britain. The French occupation of Cochin China in 1863 had forced Siam to formally relinquish its claim to Cambodia in 1867—except for the provinces of Siem Reap and Battambang. Then in 1885, Britain completed its conquest of Burma, annexing portions of northern Burma claimed by the Thai monarchy. Meanwhile, as France consolidated its control of all of Vietnam in the 1880s, it began to assert claims on Thai-controlled Laos, which Siam was forcibly forced to cede to French control in 1893. Then in 1907, France forced Thailand to cede Battambang and Siem Reap to Cambodia.

Under pressure from Britain to define the border between Siam and the Malay states over which it had increasing influence, King Chulalongkorn did so in 1909 by abandoning his claims to Perlis, Kedah, Kelantan, and Terengganu in return for a major loan to complete his railroad to the Malayan frontier. Pattani, always a troublesome region with very few Thais or Buddhists among its residents, remained a part of Siam. The conclusion of the Anglo-Siamese Treaty of 1909 that delineated this border brought an end to European imperial expansion in southeast Asia, as both England and France began to view Siam as a convenient buffer, reducing friction between the two rivals that soon would be allies in World War I. At the same time, the final borders of the Siamese state were drawn, receiving international recognition as such, and Siam was poised to evolve as a territorially-based, modern nation state, rather than as an empire of the Thai kings whose borders historically had ebbed and flowed depending on the strength of the monarchy.

Continued Pattani Resistance

The period between 1909 and the Siamese revolution of 1932 witnessed a number of uprisings against Thai rule in the Pattani region. Close intermarital links between

---

[109] Clive Christie, *A Modern History of Southeast Asia* (New York: I.B. Tauris, 2000), 175.

the Patani and Kelantan royal families led Siamese authorities to suspect "outside" intervention and support from Kelantan, and accordingly to strengthen policies of centralization, especially in the areas of taxation, education, and in requiring use of the Thai languages, both in schools and government offices. Such policies only strengthened opposition to Thai rule and helped to provoke violent outbreaks, such as the Patani revolt of February-March 1923.[110]

UNDER THE THAI REVOLUTIONARY REGIME

The Siamese revolution that occurred by a bloodless *coup d'état* in June 1932 brought to power in Bangkok a group of younger, "nationalist" military and civilian leaders whose action was directed, not against the king who remains the symbol of the Thai nation until today, but against his coterie of conservative royal ministers, whom the revolutionaries felt were holding the country back from emerging as a modern nation state. Their goal, which they moved quickly and successfully to implement, was to transform the traditional absolute monarchy into a limited constitutional monarchy, governed increasingly by representative institutions such as the unicameral National Assembly that the "promoters" rapidly brought into being within a year.

Although the unity of the new nationalist leadership soon broke down over various issues and has never provided the country with a truly "stable" government, the leaders remained unified on the "nationalist" character of their revolution, an attitude that led to a change in the name of the state to "Thailand" in 1939, and a view that all citizens of the Thai state (no longer simply subjects of the Thai king) were Thai nationals who should participate fully in the institutions and culture of the Thai people.

Although the policies of the new nationalist leaders of Thailand were almost wholly secular in nature, Thai culture is overwhelmingly Theravada Buddhist in orientation, a circumstance that led the Malay Muslims of Pattani to feel even more marginalized in the larger society whose new leadership clearly wanted them to be a part. The replacement of civilian leadership by a more authoritarian military leadership in 1938 accelerated this nationalization process even further.[111]

World War II

During World War II, as the Japanese invaded southeast Asia in late 1941, taking over French Indochina, the Philippines, the Malay peninsula, and the Dutch East Indies

---

[110] Christie, *A Modern History of Southeast Asia: Decolonization, Nationalism and Separatism* (London: Tauris Academic Studies, 1996), 175–176.

[111] LePoer, Barbara Leitch, ed. *Thailand: A Country Study*. Department of the Army Pamphlet 550–53 (Washington, DC: Federal Research Division, Library of Congress, 1987), 26–28. Also Christie, *Modern History of Southeast Asia*, 176–177.

in early 1942, the ultranationalist Thai military regime of Phibun (later Field Marshal Luang Plaek Phibunsongkhram), probably as much because of ideological affinity as well as reasons of *Realpolitik*, allied itself with Japan and permitted Japanese forces to enter the Malay peninsula from the north in 1941 at the coast near Pattani.[112] As a reward for its cooperation, Thailand received from the Japanese during the war parts of its former territories in Laos, Cambodia, and Burma as well as the four Malay states of Kelantan, Terengganu, Kedah, and Perlis. The Thai alliance with Japan and its January 1942 declaration of war against Britain and the United States,[113] not to mention the recovery of the Malay states, made Britain and Thailand antagonists during the war. As a result, whereas most Malays during the war collaborated with the Japanese with the nationalistic aim of eventually securing their independence from the British or the Dutch, many Pattani Malays collaborated with the British against the Thai regime.

The leader of this movement was Tenku Mahmud Mahyiddeen, the second son of the last *sultan* (or *raja*) of Patani, Tenku Abdul Kadir, who had been sent into exile by the Thai government earlier in the century. A member of the Kelantan civil service from 1933, Tenku Mahmud escaped with the British army to India following the Japanese invasion. "There he played a leading role recruiting Malay volunteers for Force 136, the organization that was coordinating guerrilla activity in Malaya against the Japanese."[114] The bulk of this activity took place in the Pattani region of southern Thailand, where anti-Thai sentiment was strong, and where the British were planning for a counter-invasion of the Malay peninsula.

Last Gasp Toward Patani Secession

Tenku Mahmud hoped that British success in the war would lead to a liberation of Patani from Thai rule. Indeed in November 1945, shortly after the end of the war, seven leading members of the traditional Malay ruling elite of Patani addressed a formal petition to London requesting "that the British Government may have the kindness to release our country and ourselves from the pressure of Siam, because we do not wish to remain any longer under the Siamese Government."[115]

---

[112] Christie, *Modern History of Southeast Asia*, 178.

[113] An interesting and significant sidelight of the Thai declaration of war against the United States was that it was never formally presented in Washington by the Thai ambassador—Seni Pramoj, later Prime Minister of Thailand after the war—who instead organized and led a "Free Thai Movement" that cooperated with the United States Office of Strategic Services (OSS) during the war. Accordingly, the United States never declared war on Thailand and at the end of the war did not consider it a belligerent. *Thailand: A Country Study*, 30.

[114] Christie, *Modern History of Southeast Asia*, 178.

[115] Full text in Christie, *Modern History of Southeast Asia*, 227–230. Notably, the text asks neither for Pattani independence or affiliation with the Malay Federation. It consists mainly of a detailing of Patani grievances with Thai rule and a request for liberation from Thai rule.

The moment was probably the most opportune time the Malay Muslims of Patani have had before or since to realize their general desire for secession from Thailand. It is clear that the British government seriously considered the proposal, and some members of the government favored a positive response as a means of "punishing" Thailand for its stance in the war. In the end, however, it made no response to the proposal. The reasons for this were perhaps several.

A 1944 change of government in Thailand had brought to power new leaders who gradually were able to repudiate the former regime's agreements with Japan and covertly give free access to allied agents operating in Thailand. Thus Thailand had effectively changed sides during the war, and could claim it no longer was the hostile power it had been at the start of the war.

Moreover, British support for the Malay Union in British Malaya as a means of "punishing" the Malays for their general support of the Japanese during the war probably worked to the detriment of the Patani Malays, whose cause was not unrelated to the cause of their fellow Malays lower on the peninsula. The powerful Malay nationalist response that led Britain to reverse its position on the Malay Union in favor of a Malay Federation in February 1948 was echoed in the Patani region as well. But here it was expressed as bitterness, for it was too late. In January 1946, Britain and Thailand had signed a post-war treaty in which the latter agreeably returned Kelantan, Terengganu, Kedah, and Perlis, as well as portions of Burma it had taken over during the war, to the British in return for no further territorial concessions.[116]

Finally, a key indirect role probably had been played by the United States, which in the latter stages of World War II began to view Thailand as a key linchpin of its strategic interests in southeast Asia. The U.S. communicated to Britain that it was not "prepared to accept any post-war arrangement that would impair Thai sovereignty."[117]

New "Islam-Friendly" Policies Toward Pattani

The new Thai government that had covertly switched sides in the war with Japan was also prepared to deal differently and more constructively with its southern Malay-Muslim population than its predecessor regime had been. Perhaps influenced by the threat that Britain might lay claim to the Pattani region for the Malay Federation, it enacted in late 1945 a "Patronage of Islam Act," which sought to integrate Islam into the structure of state governance.

Among other things, the Act established a formal Islamic hierarchical structure comprised of state-appointed `ulama headed by a *chularajmontri* (chief cleric) appointed by the King himself. Also established by the Act was a National Council for

---

[116] Christie, *Modern History of Southeast Asia*, 181.
[117] Christie, *Modern History of Southeast Asia*, 181.

Islamic Affairs and Provincial Councils for Islamic Affairs "in every province where there are a substantial number of Thai Muslims." Very quickly, in 1946 and 1947, the government allowed itself to be influenced by these new institutions to restore certain prohibitions that had been imposed by the pro-Japanese regime-Friday as a religious holiday in Muslim areas and the applicability of Islamic law for Muslims in the areas of marriage, family, and inheritance. In addition, the government worked closely with the new Islamic institutions to develop regulations for the registering of mosques, election of mosque councils, and the appointment of mosque officials.[118]

Although the civilian leadership responsible for these reforms was overthrown by *coup* d'état in November 1947 by the same military clique it had replaced in 1944, an event that energized Pattani leaders to make renewed efforts to gain international recognition for separation from Thailand, the new regime did not reverse these reforms that continue to form the basis of the relationship between the Thai state and Islam until today.

The Continuing Language Issue

One area the more liberal civilian leaders had not touched, however, and the new military *junta* assiduously avoided, was the language issue-that Thai rather than Malay should be the language of instruction in Thai schools. The language issue, rather than Islam itself, increasingly became the point of contention between Pattani separatists and state authorities until the last years of the 20th century. The reforms, by integrating Islamic law, or at least portions of it, into the structure of state authority for Muslims, in fact transformed Thailand into a relatively "Islam-friendly" state into which "Thai" Muslims possessed equal opportunity and even perhaps some advantages with regard to access to higher education and social mobility, but "Malay Muslims" continued to experience prejudice and unequal treatment with respect to the larger society.

The Growth of Islam in Thailand

The "Islam-friendly" reforms of the late 1940s had the long-term effect of actually facilitating Muslim immigration into Thailand, mainly from India (including Pakistan/Bangladesh) and China. Hence, today an estimated 300,000 of the country's 2.5 million Muslims who reside primarily in northern Thailand and in the region of Bangkok practice Islam freely but otherwise are gradually assimilated into Thai culture through education and intermarriage.[119]

---

[118] Christie, *Modern History of Southeast Asia*, 182.

[119] Preeda Prapertchob, "Islam and Civil Society in Thailand: The Role of NGOs," in *Islam and Civil Society in Southeast Asia*, ed. by Nakamura Mitsuo, Sharon Siddique, and Omar Farouk Bajunid (Singapore: Institute of Southeast Asian Studies, 2001), 111–112.

A high degree of assimilation has also been achieved in the southwestern Malay province of Satun, across the Malaysian border from Kedah, where an absence of lines of communication forms an effective barrier between the province and its southern Malaysian neighbor.[120]

In the southeastern Malay provinces of Pattani, Yala, and Narathiwat, it has been a different story. Although there are many examples of individuals and families who have successfully assimilated into Thai society,[121] a critical mass remains that resists assimilation, attempts to demonstrate ignorance of the Thai language, and keeps alive the dream of separation from Thailand.

Diminished Significance of Pattani Issue During Cold War

The eruption in 1948 of the Communist insurgency in Malaya and the emergence of the Thai-Malay border area as a haven of refuge for the mainly Chinese communist insurgents placed a premium on close British-Thai relations in order to secure the Thai-Malay border. The issue of Pattani separatism was accordingly overshadowed by issues that from the larger international perspective seemed far more significant, and Pattani separatist hopes that had seemed so near to fruition only three years before now appeared to be dashed forever.

Despite continued Thai efforts to achieve assimilation of the old Patani region, it has until now "remained a 'zone of dissidence,' with intermittent outbreaks of guerrilla activity and, at best, only a sullen submission to Thai rule."[122] A key to maintaining the traditional Muslim-Malay culture of this region was the continued flourishing of the long-established *pondok* system of private Islamic boarding schools.[123] Despite the earlier establishment of government schools that provided a mandatory seven-year curriculum in the Thai language, including Buddhist as well as Islamic religious instruction, the *pondok* system continued to flourish.[124]

---

[120] Christie, *Modern History of Southeast Asia*, 187.

[121] Notable examples are Dr. Surin Pitsuwan, who served as Thai Foreign Minister in the late 1990s, and Wan Muhammad Noor Matha, former President (Speaker) of the Thai National Assembly. Prapertchob, "Islam and Civil Society in Thailand," 104–105.

[122] Christie, *Modern History of Southeast Asia*, 187.

[123] See Hasan Madmarn, *The Pondok and the Madrasah in Patani* (Bangi: Universiti Kebangsaan Malaysia Press, 1999).

[124] Parents typically sent their children for the first seven years to the government-operated elementary school, then on to the *pondok* for intermediate and higher education, if they could afford it and wished such a destiny for their (usually male) child. See Department of the Army, *Ethnographic Study Series: Minority Groups in Thailand*, Chapter 16, "The Malays" (Washington, DC: HQ, Department of the Army, February 1970), 1029–1030. This 54-page chapter is a fine ethnographic survey of the Malay Muslims of southern Thailand and is highly recommended as a detailed overview of Malay social life in Thailand. See also Madmarn, *The Pondok and the Madrasah in Patani*, 74.

Beginning in 1960 the Thai government undertook steps to bring the *pondok* schools under state supervision as well. A key aspect of the program was a requirement that all *pondoks* be registered with the Ministry of Education and add to their curricula certain secular subjects required of all Thai schools. Although Malay was not eliminated as a language of instruction, registration required Thai to be added as a second language of instruction. Registered schools were eligible to receive state funding and were subject to state inspections, but could remain "private" schools. They were also obliged to provide educational authorities with lists of teachers and pupils. Unregistered schools were considered to be operating "illegally" and subject to closure. As a result, some 150 of an estimated 355 schools then operating closed in protest, but by 1971 some 400 *pondoks* were registered as "legal" private schools. In 2004, it was alleged that 127 unregistered *pondoks* were still operating in the Malay region of southern Thailand.[125]

If the *pondok* system remained the primary means used by southern Malays to preserve and transmit Islamic teachings and Malay culture, the clear effort by Thai authorities in the early 1960s to gradually compromise the independent character of these schools led some political activists to devise new means to pursue the cause of Malay separatism. It was just at this time and in apparent reaction to this effort that a variety of new political organizations, some with a militant agenda, sprang up to pursue the struggle to preserve Malay heritage in other ways.

The *Barisan Revolusi Nasional*

One of the first was the National Revolutionary Front (*Barisan Revolusi Nasional*—BRN), established by a group of former *pondok* teachers and led by Ustaz Haji Abdul Karim, himself the owner of a *pondok* in Narathiwat province, who, rather than submit to Thai authority, took to the jungle to organize a revolutionary opposition.[126] Identified in 2004 as the "largest and best organized of the three main insurgent factions operating in southern Thailand,[127] the BRN from the beginning was fully committed to armed struggle, totally denying the legitimacy of Thai rule over Muslim Malays, and committed to the reconstruction of a Muslim-Malay state of Pattani in southern Thailand. The emergence of the BRN coincided with the end of "the Emergency" in neighboring Malaya. It may have reflected a change of strategy in the Communist Party of Malaya (CPM), with which the BRN became closely allied, to focus on Pattani national liberation as a prologue to the establishment of a unified, socialist Malay

---

[125] Madmarn, *The Pondok and the Madrasah in Patani*, 74. Also Anthony Davis, "Thailand Confronts Separatist Violence in its Muslim South," *Jane's Intelligence Review*, March 2004, 21–22.

[126] Anthony Davis, "Southern Thai Insurgency Gains Fresh Momentum," *Jane's Intelligence Review*, August 2004, 19.

[127] Davis, "Southern Thai Insurgency Gains Fresh Momentum," 19.

nation "stretching from Pattani to Singapore, governed by one head of state and united under one common flag." Such was the identical view of both parties.[128]

Its alliance with the CPM, its socialist program, and its emphasis on Malay nationalism tended to identify the BRN as a secular rather than Islamist party, although its manifestos continued to be cast in religious terminology-Islamic socialism being the promotion of a just and prosperous society sanctioned by God and Malay nationalism being an expression of God's oneness and unity. The BRN was in many respects a "national" or "people's" liberation movement typical of many such movements throughout the "Third World" in the 1960s and 1970s that benefited in varying degrees from Soviet or communist-bloc support. Like other groups with whom it competed in striving for the liberation of Pattani from Thai rule, it engaged in a variety of violent actions-ambushes, assassinations, kidnappings, extortion, sabotage, and bomb attacks-generally designed to promote an atmosphere of lawlessness in the region, a sense of insecurity for ethnic Thais living there, and an intolerable burden for Thai officials trying to govern the area. The main targets were those symbols of Thai authority that were "considered to pose the greatest threat to Malay-Muslim culture and identity," in particular schools, teachers, local government officials and administrators, and Buddhist settlers in the south.[129]

PULO

Although the BRN made its mark in the 1960s and 1970s as a viable insurgent organization, its strong left-wing agenda did not enable it to achieve mass appeal among the essentially conservative Malay-Muslim population of southern Thailand, and it was eventually overshadowed by a competing insurgent group, the Pattani United Liberation Organization (PULO). Organized "in 1968 by Kabir Abdul Rahman, an Islamic scholar who had become disillusioned with what he saw as the 'limited' and 'ineffectual' nature of the established Malay opposition in Pattani," PULO "grouped together a younger, more militant generation of Thai Muslims—many of whom had been radicalized while studying overseas—becoming an active insurgency with the politicization of Malay students in the early 1970s."[130]

The growth of PULO coincided with the efflorescence of Islamic revivalism in neighboring Malaysia during the 1970s and reflected a similar trend that soon followed

---

[128] Peter Chalk, "Militant Islamic Separatism in Southern Thailand," in Jason F. Isaacson and Colin Rubenstein, eds., *Islam in Asia: Changing Political Realities* (New Brunswick, NJ: Transaction Publishers, 2002), 169–170.

[129] Chalk, "Militant Islamic Separatism in Southern Thailand," 168–169.

[130] Chalk, "Militant Islamic Separatism in Southern Thailand," 171.

in the Malay regions of southern Thailand during this same period.[131] Eschewing the left-wing rhetoric of the BRN, PULO positioned itself as a more strictly Malay-Muslim nationalist organization that sought and received its external support from sources in the Muslim world. Libya and Syria were two countries that provided degrees of support, and some PULO fighters received training from the Palestine Liberation Organization (PLO) in Lebanon.[132]

More importantly, PULO received strong popular support from Malays in Malaysia and more specifically from the Islamic opposition party in Malaysia, the *Parti Islam seMalaysia* (PAS) that controlled neighboring Kelantan state and for which support for Muslim separatism in Thailand served as a useful rallying cry. Although the ruling United Malay National Organization (UMNO) that governed Malaysia found it in the national interest to collaborate closely with neighboring Thailand over the security of their joint border, the issue remained a delicate one that the Malaysian government could not push too vigorously without augmenting popular support for its PAS rival.

Accordingly, despite close joint Thai-Malaysian cooperation over border security, Kelantan especially remained a safe haven for PULO activists and a transit point for fund transfers and fighters moving in and out of Thailand. Ostensibly an organization that "placed priority on improving the standard of education among the southern Malay population as well as fostering and nurturing their political consciousness and national sentiments," PULO, possibly in part to keep pace with the BRN and other rival organizations, sanctioned violence as part of its secessionist struggle. PULO violence was carried out by its military arm, the Pattani United Liberation Army (PULA), which claimed responsibility for a number of bombing and arson attacks on the same types of targets—symbols of Thai rule-in southern Thailand, as well as occasionally in Bangkok.[133]

Other Resistance Groups

Although the BRN and PULO were the principal resistance movements against continuing Thai rule in southern Thailand during the 1960s–1980s, a weakness of the resistance movement in general was the plethora of other movements that also emerged, either as break-away movements or as new initiatives in other sectors of Malay-Muslim Thailand. Among these were the *Barisan Nasional Pembebasan*

---

[131] Prapertchob, "Islam and Civil Society in Thailand," 109, notes that the 1979 Islamic revolution in Iran and the global Islamic resurgence that that revolution represented was the key watershed event for the revival of Islamic sentiments in southern Thailand, symbolized by the widespread appearance of female *hijab*, a type of attire that in the past had not been widespread, but "limited only to the time of prayer or for the old people in the rural areas or for people who had performed the *hajj* and during particular Muslim festivities and ceremonies."

[132] Zachary Abuza, *Militant Islam in Southeast Asia: Crucible of Terror* (Boulder, CO: Lynn Reinner Publishers, 2003), 79.

[133] Chalk, "Militant Islamic Separatism in Southern Thailand," 172.

(BNPP), formed in 1971; the *Sabil-illah*, established in 1975–1976; and Black December 1902, a shadowy organization that simply reflected the date when the old Pattani sultanate was formally incorporated into the Thai kingdom.[134]

The Other Side of the Coin

Adding to the complexity of the situation, yet another wholly different organization dating from the early 1960s was the Thai Muslim Student Association (TMSA), "established to promote and preserve the collective interests of the *ummah* in Thailand in general and the educated Muslim youths in particular." Somewhat analogous to the Malaysian Islamic Youth Movement (ABIM), established in neighboring Malaysia a decade later, the TMSA sought to avoid conflict with the government, and instead to win the respect of Thai authorities for Malay culture as part of the diverse nature of Thai society.

Placing an emphasis on leadership training through seminars, workshops and student work camps, especially in rural areas, the TMSA sought to respond to liberal trends in Thai society that were prepared to accept Islam as a component of Thai culture and to permit the Malay Muslims the maximum degree of self-government. Many products of this organization did indeed emerge as successful politicians, university professors, executives, senior government officials, and businessmen, including the former Thai foreign minister, Dr. Surin Pitsuwan, and President of the Thai National Assembly, Wan Muhammad Noor Matha. As an organization of student activists, the TMSA was also deeply involved in the pan-Thai student revolution of the early 1970s that finally toppled the military dictatorship of Thanom Kittikachorn in 1973.[135]

Thai Countermeasures

Despite the persistence of Malay-Muslim insurgent activity in southern Thailand from the 1960s through the 1980s, Thai government authority, focused on its Fourth Army Region Southern Border Provinces Administration Center (SBPAC) headquartered in Pattani, managed to prevent the resistance from becoming the large-scale popular movement PULO in particular sought to make it. Although Thai forces were often brutal toward villages thought to be harboring insurgents, Thai policy in general remained assimilation, permitting Muslims to practice their religion freely. This included adjudicating legal cases between Muslims in Islamic courts in accordance with Islamic law, fostering Muslim upward mobility within Thai society for those who

---

[134] Chalk, "Militant Islamic Separatism in Southern Thailand," 182–183.

[135] Prapertchob, "Islam and Civil Society in Thailand," 105–106.

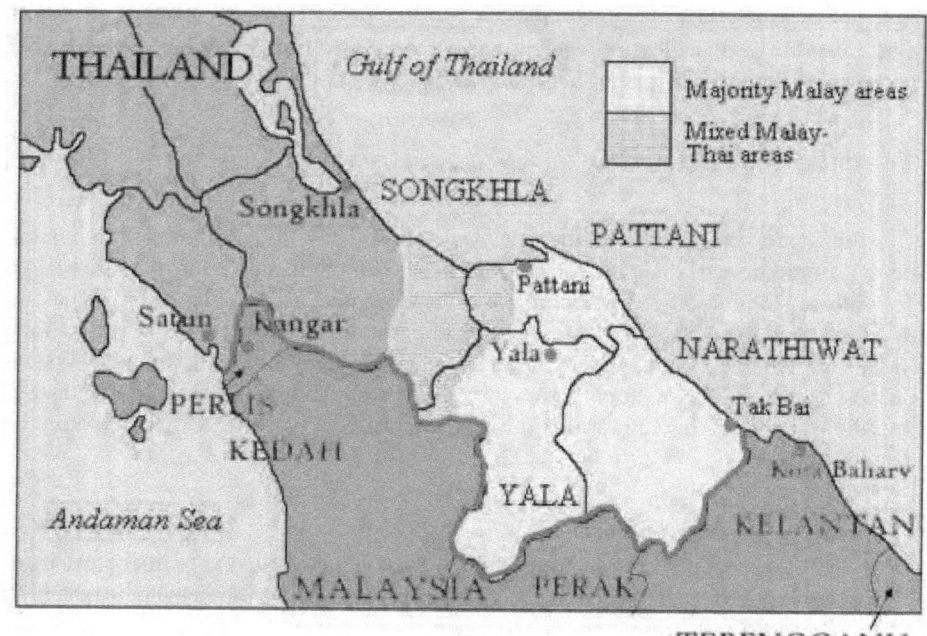

Predominantly Muslim Sectors of Southern Thailand and Northern Malaysia.
Source: Author.

adapted to Thai cultural norms, and generating projects designed to raise the economic standards of the Muslim inhabitants of southern Thailand.[136]

The combination of approaches led in the 1980s to a gradual overcoming of the insurgency so that by the end of the decade Muslim insurgents were assessed to number no more than 300–500, whereas at their peak in the mid-1970s they had numbered on the order of 3,000. The insurgency seemed over, and in 1993 the Thai government offered amnesty to those willing to lay down their arms. Nearly half accepted these terms, leaving the estimated remaining 150–200 Malay militants officially defined as outlaws, drug smugglers, gun-runners, bank robbers, terrorists—all of which they were—hiding out in the jungles of southern Thailand or northern Malaysia.[137]

---

[136] Thai policy toward the insurgency finally came to be based on Prime Minister's Orders 66/2523 and 65/2525, issued by the government of Prime Minister Prem Tinsulanonda in the late 1970s. Directed primarily against the Thai Communist Party (TCP) threat, a far more significant insurgent threat than that of the Malay-Muslim south, the same principles were applied in the south as elsewhere in the country, with considerable short-term success. Targeting sources of corruption and class differentiation in Thai society as well as the militant movements opposed to the government, the policy stressed economic development and maximum political participation at the local level. See Paragraph 6, "Thai Government Policies," in *Primer: Muslim Separatism in Southern Thailand.* Prepared by the Virtual Information Center of HQ USCINCPAC. URL: *http://www.vic-info.org/SEAsia/ThailandPage.htm.* Accessed February 3, 2005.

[137] Abuza, *Militant Islam in Southeast Asia,* 78.

Although instances of insurgent violence-bombings of schools, drive-by shootings, and arson attacks—continued during the 1990s, these were far more sporadic, less part of a pattern or concerted strategy, and more easily construed solely as criminal acts. From the standpoint of the Thai government and most analysts observing Thai affairs, Thailand had effectively contained the Malay-Muslim separatist movement, as it had the communist insurgency in other parts of the country, with successful policies aimed at dealing harshly with the insurgents and seeking to eliminate the perceived causes and rationale for the insurgent activity.

FROM NATIONALISM TO ISLAM

With regard to southern Thailand, however, this judgment proved to be premature. In fact, Malay-Muslim separatist sentiment was passing through a quiet phase as it slowly transformed from one form into another—from what had been a largely nationalistic, ethnic Malay-based resistance to a cause that was more deeply rooted in Islamic religious sentiment. According to Prapertchob, this transformation began in the early 1980s, fully a decade after its appearance in neighboring Malaysia.

Largely inspired, in Prapertchob's view, by the success of the Iranian revolution, the movement manifested itself in several ways. The most obvious manifestation was the *hijab* movement, a widespread tendency for Muslim women who previously had had no such tradition in southern Thailand to adopt a head covering and long, full-bodied dress for all aspects of their public lives. A second was the widespread proliferation of the apolitical *Jemaat Tabligh* and *Darul Arqam* movements, apparently with Thai government support, that had flourished in neighboring Malaysia in the 1970s and now spread into Thailand in the 1980s.[138] Increased mosque attendance, the building of a significant number of new mosques, and construction of the Saudi-funded Yala Islamic College were yet other manifestations of this Islamic revival.

Less noticed during this quiet period of the late 1980s and early 1990s was the gradual disappearance of young men who might otherwise have been engaged in insurgent operations in southern Thailand. Although unnoted at the time, their absence became apparent as they began to return from Afghanistan and perhaps other fighting fronts in the early to mid-1990s. Again, as in neighboring Malaysia, in 1995 a group of these Afghan veterans coalesced into a new organization, GMIP (*Gerakan Mujahideen Islam Pattani*, or Pattani Islamic Mujahideen Movement), under the leadership of Afghan veteran Nasori "Sori" Saesaeng (aka Wae Ka Raeh).[139]

---

[138] Prapertchob, "Islam and Civil Society in Thailand," 109–111.
[139] Davis, "Thailand Faces up to Southern Extremist Threat," 13.

Formation of GMIP

The appearance of GMIP in southern Thailand almost simultaneously with the formation of a parallel organization, the KMM (*Kampulan Mujahidin Malaysia*), in neighboring Kelantan state cannot be explained as pure coincidence. The common experience of studying and training in Afghanistan and/or Pakistan and association, whether formal or informal, with *Jemaah Islamiyah* and *al-Qa'ida* suggests a commonality of purpose and commitment to mutual support, if not a more formal alliance or union as parts of a single larger organization.

As with the Malaysian KMM, the period 1995–2000 was a time of training, preparation, and planning for the GMIP. The year 1995 also brought a split in the old PULO and the formation of a more militant new PULO, also called the BNB (*Barisan Nasional Baru*), as well as yet another small radical group called the *Tantra Jihad Islam* (TIJ). Although historically loath to coordinate their operational activities, in mid-1997 the groups did come together to form *Bersatu* (Solidarity), a tactical alliance between the old, more nationalist groups in an effort to "refocus national and regional attention on the 'southern question.'"[140] Following their agreement, during the period August 1997–January 1998 no fewer than 33 separate attacks were carried out against symbols of Thai rule in southern Thailand, resulting in nine deaths, several dozen injuries, and considerable economic damage in a campaign of violence the region had not seen since the early 1980s.[141] Although the Thai government responded forcefully to contain this new outbreak of insurgent activity, its success in doing so by early 1998 was in part due to new Malaysian cooperation in arresting insurgent leaders taking refuge in neighboring Kelantan state. Whereas Malaysian Prime Minister Mahathir Mohammed previously had adopted a general hands-off attitude toward Malay insurgent activity in Thailand, on this occasion he responded decisively to Thai appeals to guarantee the security of their common border.[142]

The *Bersati*-led outbreak of violence coincided with the 1997 Asian financial crisis that had the impact of undermining the political leadership of both Thailand and Malaysia, and in this situation Malaysia's Mahathir perceived cracking down on insurgent refugees from Thailand as a means of striking out against his own political rival, the *Parti Islam seMalaysia* (PAS).Centered on Kelantan state, PAS both gave safe haven to the rebels from Thailand and was gaining political strength at Mahathir's expense due to the Asian financial crisis.

The failure of the *Bersati* uprising undermined the continuing appeal of the traditional separatist parties, as many traditional activists began surrendering to Thai authorities or fled abroad into exile. As would soon become apparent, ongoing resistance to Thai authority in southern Thailand would increasingly express itself in Islamist

---

[140] Chalk, "Militant Islamic Separatism in Southern Thailand," 175, 183.

[141] Chalk, "Militant Islamic Separatism in Southern Thailand," 175.

[142] Chalk, "Militant Islamic Separatism in Southern Thailand," 176.

rather than nationalist terms. This was not apparent at the moment, however, as Thai government authorities tended to be confident that Malay separatist sentiments had been compromised and that any continuing insurgent-like activities—drug-running as a money-making activity, illegal arms trafficking, bank robberies, assassinations, bombings—were solely ongoing criminal activity characteristic of the economically backward southern region of the country.

REVIVAL OF THE INSURGENCY

Later reporting indicated that the late 1990s was a period of intensive training for new cadres of Islamist militants in southern Thailand that involved members of the KMM in Malaysia and others who "spoke Malay with an Indonesian accent." Instruction was said to take place covertly at night in buildings in both urban and rural areas and included classes relating to the history of the Malay sultanate of Patani, the concept of *jihad*, and physical as well as weapons training. Maintaining the clandestine nature of the activities of the assembled cadres was said to have been of paramount concern. Most instructors and trainees wore ski masks to conceal individual identities, and the greatest stress was placed on the importance of security.[143]

Although Thai authorities until early 2005 remained in denial concerning the possibility of linkages between Thai separatists and the transnational *Jemaah Islamiyah* (JI), it seems likely that this clandestine jihadist training activity in southern Thailand was JI-related, involving Thai Muslim, Malaysian, Indonesian, possibly Filipino, and perhaps jihadist Muslims of even other nationalities.

Although instances of bombings and other insurgent-type activities continued sporadically during this period, Thai authorities persisted in asserting that although terrorist groups continued to exist in the south they lacked the organization and financial support to mount a viable insurgent threat, as they had in the 1960s into the 1980s. Accordingly, during the summer of 2001, soon after the election of tycoon Thaksin Shinawatra as the new Prime Minister of Thailand, the government began the process of dismantling its Southern Border Provinces Administration Center (SBPAC) that had long been the focus of Thai anti-insurgency operations in the south.[144]

Thai Government Remains in Denial

Incredibly, this decision of the Thai government followed the first operation carried out by the *Jemaah Islamiyah* in Thailand on April 7, 2001, the bombing of the Hat Yai train station and hotel in Yala that resulted in the death of a young boy, injuries to

---

[143] Davis, "Southern Thai Insurgency Gains Fresh Momentum," 16–17.

[144] GlobalSecurity.org. "Thailand Islamic Insurgency," 3–4. URL: *http://www.globalsecurity.org/military/world/war/thailand2.htm*. Accessed February 1, 2005.

several passengers, and severe property damage.[145] Blamed by the Thai government on PULO, which immediately denied responsibility, Thai authorities appeared unaware of the JI insurgent training, planning, and preparations that had been underway in the south for several years.

In his recent book, *Imperial Hubris*, former lead U.S. Central Intelligence Agency analyst on *al-Qa'ida*, Michael Scheuer, observed that

> Since 11 September 2001, the tone of bin Ladin's rhetoric toward young males has changed; where it was once critical and meant to shame young men into action, it is now supportive and complimentary. The change probably is due to the steady flow of young men to the dozen or so Islamist insurgencies now being fought in the world...in late 2001, [*al-Qa'ida*] sent fighters home from Afghanistan because they were not needed in that phase of the war....[146]

In Scheuer's analysis, a key purpose of the September 11, 2001, attacks on targets in the United States was to inspire Islamist insurgent movements around the world, such as those in Thailand, Indonesia, the Philippines, Burma, Kashmir, Afghanistan, Chechnya, Xinxiang, Iraq, Saudi Arabia, Yemen, Somalia, Egypt, Algeria, etc. If Muslims could attack key nodes of power in the heart of the greatest power on earth, the action seemed to say, then surely Muslims engaged in even more just causes than the attack on the United States could achieve great things in their own areas of operation.

In the case of southern Thailand, Scheurer's analysis appears to have merit. Although nothing is known about the numbers of Malay Thais that may have returned from Afghanistan after the U.S. offensive there in late 2001, the simultaneous large-scale arrest of Islamic militants in Singapore, Malaysia, Indonesia, Brunei, and the Philippines at this time led many *Jemaah Islamiyah* suspects throughout southeast Asia to flee to southern Thailand, where they received safe haven from sympathetic elements there.[147] Among those finding such safe havens was JI leader Hambali who, in January 2002, was able to convene a meeting in Bangkok, where planning was

---

[145] Abuza, 80. Although the train bombing in Yala may have been meant to signal the beginning of the renewed insurgency in southern Thailand that actually began in December 2001, the almost concurrent arrest of a number of KMM members and general uncovering of that organization in May in neighboring Kelantan state may have forced a reappraisal and a delay until conditions were more propitious.

[146] Anonymous [Michael Scheuer], *Imperial Hubris: Why the West Is Losing the War on Terror* (Washington, DC: Brassey's, Inc., 2004), 133–134.

[147] Anthony L. Smith, "Trouble in Thailand's Muslim South: Separatism, not Global Terrorism," in *Asia-Pacific Security Studies*, 3, 10 (December 2004), 3. Available online at URL: *http://www.apcss.org/Publications/APCSS/Trouble%20in%20Thailands%20Muslim%20South.pdf*. Accessed February 1, 2005. Although the author of this article still perceives the post-9/11 renewed insurgency in traditional Malay separatist terms, he does recognize that the insurgency possessed new elements and that these types of "coordinated action[s have] never been so well executed."

76

begun for a number of terrorist operations, including the eventual October 12, 2002, bombings in Bali, Indonesia.[148] What can be said with certainty is that on December 24, 2001, five carefully coordinated and almost simultaneous attacks on police posts in all three Malay provinces of southern Thailand marked the opening strikes of a renewed insurgency in southern Thailand that continued unabated, reaching a crescendo of insurgent actions during 2004.

Nature of the New Insurgency

The different nature of the renewed insurgency was noted by one commentator:

> ...up until 2001, separatism and unrest were all but dead in the south. Hence the surprise and uncertainty voiced by many Thais, both Muslim and Buddhist, to the escalation of violence. Local people appear "confused," as one resident of Yala put it. Senator Aumar Toryib of Narathiwat says the local people still don't know who is behind the violence.[149]

Yet another close observer of the insurgency observed:

> In late 2001 GMIP leaflets scattered in districts of Yala urged holy war and support for Osama bin Ladin in the service of the separatist cause... Beginning in December 2001 and continuing through 2002, a succession of assassinations of individual policemen, teachers, local officials and suspected informers has been punctuated by larger attacks on police posts. The pattern has persisted in 2003 along with several incidents that seized national attention.

> Since they began on 24 December 2001, the attacks have repeatedly involved coordinated groups of masked men armed with AK-47 rifles and often mounted on motorbikes, staging near simultaneous attacks on widely separated police posts. This suggests a degree of planning, tactical competence and aggression that has no precedent in the military lacklustre histories of PULO or BRN.[150]

---

[148] Abuza, 158. Among those present at the meeting were Muklas (Indonesian), Noordin Azari Husin (Indonesian), Noordin Mohamad Top (Indonesian), and Wan Min (Malaysian), all of whom were to play later important roles in bombings in Indonesia in 2002, 2003, and 2004. International Crisis Group. "Southern Thailand: Insurgency, not Jihad," *Asia Report* No. 98, 18 May 2005. URL: *http://www.crisisgroup.org/library/documents/asia/south_east_asia/098_southern_thailand_indurgency_not_jihad..pdf.* Accessed June 6, 2005.

[149] Julian Gearing, "Terror in Thailand: 'Ghosts' and Jihadis" from Asia Times Online. URL: *http://www.atimes.com/atimes/Southeast_Asia/FD03Ae05.html.* Accessed November 2, 2004.

[150] Davis, "Thailand Faces up to Southern Extremist Threat," 13.

So clandestine was the nature of the renewed insurgency that analysts and journalists commenting on it were somewhat at a loss to account for the new vigor of the anti-government violence. In a sense, the commentators were only following the analysis of the Thai government itself that remained in denial, for a time at least, that it faced any more serious challenge than the common criminality to which it had relegated the Malay insurgency in the early 1990s.

Thaksin Finally Reacts

In July 2002, however, Prime Minister Thaksin suddenly reversed his position and ordered the Army, Civilian Military Police (CPM 43), and Ministry of Interior to reestablish their previously dismantled intelligence apparatus and control headquarters, and renamed Southern Border Provinces Peace Building Command (SBPPBC). In addition, a coordinating center was established within the Thai National Security Council in Bangkok. Although this increased focus on the terrorism problem in Thailand led to a number of high-level arrests of JI operatives, including JI operations leader, Hambali, on August 11, 2003, the Thai leadership, even in 2004, continued to decouple insurgency-related actions in Thailand with "international terrorist groups," including *Jemaah Islamiyah*.[151]

The restored SBPPBC did not immediately cope effectively with the renewed insurgency, however. Indeed, almost as if in retaliation for the arrests of *Jemaah Islamiyah* leaders in 2003, the insurgency grew in intensity during 2004. A particularly spectacular attack occurred on Sunday, January 4, 2004, in which about 30 Malay insurgents attacked a Thai Army post in Narathiwat, killed four soldiers, and seized 413 firearms, including two general-purpose machine guns and a number of rocket-propelled grenade launchers. At the same moment—about 1:30 in the afternoon—other insurgents torched 20 government schools and two police posts scattered across 11 of the 13 districts of Narathiwat province. Other diversions, such as the burning of tires on highways and the setting of charges and grenades on bridges, took place simultaneously in neighboring Yala province. The operation was well-planned and was completed within 20 minutes. Felled trees protected the two trucks used to carry away the arsenal of weapons as did scattered nails on all the approach roads to the Army post. No fewer than 200 insurgents were estimated to have been required to carry out the entire operation, which was obviously most carefully planned and coordinated.[152]

Although the Thaksin government, recognizing the import of the incident, responded by immediately declaring martial law throughout the south, dispatching 3,000 additional troops to the region, and launching a massive dragnet to arrest individuals suspected of being involved in recent acts of insurgent violence, the attention-getting

---

[151] GlobalSecurity.org, "Thailand Islamic Insurgency," 3–5.
[152] Davis, "Thailand Confronts Separatist Violence in its Muslim South," 20, and Davis, "Southern Thai Insurgency Gains Fresh Momentum," 18, 23.

attacks of January 4 proved only the opening shots of a seemingly unending campaign of bombings, assassinations, arson attacks, raids aimed at seizing arms, and pin-prick attacks on military installations that continued on an almost daily basis throughout 2004 and into 2005.[153]

Focusing on the traditional, unlicensed *pondoks* that government authorities believed to be the seedbed of the renewed resistance, they arrested both teachers and students on the slightest pretexts, but found such arrests had little impact on insurgent activities.[154] On only one occasion, on April 28, 2004, did Thai security forces manage to close in on elements of the resistance, when they surrounded some 108 young fighters armed with knives and a few firearms in Pattani's historic Krue Se mosque and systematically killed them all.[155] In hindsight, some speculated that for the insurgents the Kreu Se "massacre" had been in fact a "suicide operation" designed to highlight the lack of respect Thai authorities held for Pattani's most holy place. The young age of most of the dead, the lightness of their arms when in fact hundreds of captured weapons were held by the insurgents, the *jihad*ist-related literature found on their persons after their deaths, and the cries of "Allahu Akbar" that arose from them as they engaged in the fight all pointed to this conclusion.[156]

Although for a few days Thai authorities congratulated themselves on the achievement of this victory, it soon became apparent that the incident had no impact on the level of violence in southern Thailand. Another unfortunate incident on October 24, 2004, held the potential for even further strengthening the insurgency and undermining Thai legitimacy in southern Thailand. The death by suffocation of 78 Muslim men from about 1,300 arrested, after they had been crammed into army trucks for a long five-hour drive from Tak Bai in Narathiwat province to the army camp at Pattani, affected many families and produced widespread outrage against the security forces and the government. The 1,300 men had been part of a crowd of about 2,000 people that had been demonstrating against the arrest of six men on charges of stealing government firearms. Over the course of a long day, the crowd had grown and become increasingly unruly. Although the Army affirmed that it had not used live ammunition, the bringing of water cannon and tear gas to the scene provoked pandemonium, leading to charges of significant police brutality, including nine deaths, as Thai officials sought to arrest any who resisted them.[157]

---

[153] Davis, "Southern Thai Insurgency Gains Fresh Momentum", 17–18.

[154] Anthony Davis, "School System Forms the Frontline in Thailand's Southern Unrest," in *Jane's Intelligence Review* (November 2004), 10–11.

[155] Alan Sipress, "Thai Forces Were Ready for Attacks," *The Washington Post*, April 29, 2004, A19.

[156] Davis, "Southern Thai Insurgency Gains Fresh Momentum," 14–15.

[157] Alisa Tang, "At Least 78 Die after Thailand Riot," in *Northwest Herald Online*, October 28, 2004. URL: *http://www.nwherald.com/MainSection/other/290433813785258.php*. Accessed October 28, 2004. Marwaan Macan-Marker, "Suffocation Deaths Inflame Thai South," *Asia Times Online*, October 28, 2004. URL: *http://atimes01.atimes.com/Southeast_Asia/FJ28Ae01.html*. Accessed November 2, 2004. Also Alan Sipress, "Relatives Seek Bodies of Thai Muslim Demonstrators," *The Washington Post*, October 28, 2004, A20.

The incident, which produced international headlines, provoked outrage among the Malay-Muslim population of southern Thailand as well as in neighboring Malaysia, where Prime Minister Badawi felt compelled to issue a statement saying, "We hope that the situation there [Narathiwat province] does not worsen and spread to other provinces and that it will be contained quickly."[158] Only a rash of retaliatory killings and bombings followed, however, as the insurgency continued.

Reelection of Thaksin

The massive landslide reelection of Prime Minister Thaksin Shinawatra and his Thai Rak Thai (TRT) populist party in the February 5, 2005, elections, in which he gained 374 out of a possible 500 seats in the Thai parliament, promised to give Thailand a degree of political stability the country had not known since the revolution of 1932. One area that would remain recalcitrant, however, was the Malay-Muslim south. The TRT, which had held six of the 11 parliamentary seats from the three violence-racked provinces of Pattani, Narathiwat, and Yala, gained none in the 2005 election.

Indeed, soon after his massive reelection, Thaksin moved quickly to address the problem of southern Thailand by establishing a National Reconciliation Commission, headed by former prime minister Anand Panyarachun. The stated aim of the commission was to soften the policy of the Thai government regarding the southern Muslims in an effort to achieve reconciliation by dialogue rather than compliance by force. It remained to be seen whether this approach would prove fruitful.[159]

A Retrospective

In his study of separatist movements in Southeast Asia, Clive Christie notes several reasons for their failure in the post-World War II period. Foremost among them has been "the general priority given by the states" of the region "to regional stability." Since nearly all states in southeast Asia are "vulnerable to regional discontents and separatist impulses"—the Arakanese and Karen in Burma, the Muong montagnards in Vietnam, the South Moluccans, the Ambonese and Achenese of Indonesia, the Muslims of the Philippines, as well as the Pattani Malay Muslims of southern Thailand-state policy in each has generally held aloof from interfering in the "internal" affairs of its neighbors. Thus, the UMNO-headed government of Malaysia has refrained from supporting the Malay-Muslim cause in southern Thailand, although the minority Malay party, PAS, governing Kelantan state, has done so, at least in providing Thai Malay Muslim insurgents a safe haven and refuge. In this respect, Christie notes, the "history of Southeast Asia since the Second World War has been very different from that of

---

[158] Anil Netto, "Malaysia Rages over Muslim Killings," *Asia Times Online*, October 30, 2004. URL: *http://www.atimes.com/atimes/Southeast_Asia/FJ30Ae02.html*. Accessed November 2, 2004.

[159] Marwaan Macan-Markar, "Softly-Softly in Thailand," in *Asia Times Online*, 21 May 2005. URL: *http://www.atimes.com/atimes/Southeast_Asia/GE21Ae01.html*. Accessed 3 June 2005.

South Asia, where the states of the region have rarely hesitated to exploit the separatist difficulties of their neighbors."[160] In Southeast Asia, the principle of non-interference was also enshrined in the 1967 formation of the Association of Southeast Asian Nations (ASEAN), whose stated purpose is to foster political stability, regional cooperation, and economic development among the member states of the organization.

So too, Christie notes, the United States-led, general international focus on the containment of communist movements in the region, not only in Vietnam, placed regional separatist movements in a secondary, if not tertiary, position as annoying distractions to the far more important Cold War struggle being played out in Southeast Asia during the post-World War II period. Separatist movements like that of the Malay Muslims of southern Thailand were a source of instability that needed to be contained if Thailand were to emerge as a strong and prosperous, Western-oriented state capable of resisting the communist threat, both within and on its borders.[161] U.S. policy, therefore, contributed to the marginalization of the Malay Muslim issue in Thai politics.

The gradual political evolution of most states in the region into "authoritarian democracies"—states with democratic processes dominated by a single ruling party, such as the UMNO in Malaysia or Golkar in Indonesia, often closely associated with the military—placing a stress on rapid economic development, has also been injurious to minority views, such as those of the Malay Muslims of southern Thailand, whose interests contradict those of the largely Buddhist Thai ruling elite. Unable to achieve recognition of their right of self-determination in the immediate post-World War II period, their cause has largely been subsumed by "larger" issues. The partial success of successive Thai governments, moreover, in achieving at least some degree of assimilation of mainly urban members of its Malay Muslim population has also tended to undermine the separatist cause, as it was intended to do.

OUTLOOK

Yet, as developments in the post-September 11, 2001, era have demonstrated, the cause of Malay Muslim separatism in southern Thailand persists. As Christie notes, to some degree the persistence of any separatist movement is strengthened if individuals involved in it are closely linked to a historical state, which of course the Muslims of southern Thailand are. The fact that Pattani Muslims are on the periphery of the Thai state, on the border with ethnically identical Malaysia, rather than located in the central part of the state, also contributes to the endurance of Malay Muslim resistance to submission to Thai rule. Culturally, despite official Thai assimilationist policies, Malays are often referred to by the general Thai public as *khaek* (foreigners), an attitude that generates alienation rather than overcoming it.[162] Resistance to Thai rule

---

[160] Christie, *Modern History of Southeast Asia*, 195.

[161] Christie, *Modern History of Southeast Asia*, 199–202.

[162] Christie, *Modern History of Southeast Asia*, 192–193.

has now endured for more than two centuries and is likely to pose a difficult problem for Thai authority for many years to come.

When Christie was preparing his study of separatism in southeast Asia during the mid-1990s, Pattani Muslim separatism, or "dissidence," as he prefers to call it, was in a quiet phase. "The continuing failure of Patani Malay resistance to achieve its separatist goals," he writes, did not "mean that Thai rule had been accepted in the region." Indeed, he argues, "Patani Muslims have—ever since the Thais began their policies of administrative, political, religious and educational integration—attempted to live within their own world as if the Thai state did not exist." This process he calls a classic case of "internal *hijra*, or withdrawal from and non-recognition of *kafir* [infidel] authority."[163]

He could not know of the renewed insurgency that was to follow, but he did anticipate it by noting the potential for a "resurgence of populism, this time in a religious guise." "Populism" he defines as a "process of mass mobilization on the basis of ideas, or one fundamental idea, designed to appeal to the prejudices of as large a section of the population as possible." Often, he argues, populist movements "have the quality of an overall simplicity of appeal, an inherent 'anti-elite' bias, and, quite often, a lack of intellectual coherence."[164] "Always hovering in the wings," he notes, "is the possibility that the creation of an Islamic state in Malaysia or a triumph of Islamic radicalism in the wider Islamic world might again open up the joint issues of Malay and Islamic irredentism in Patani."[165]

The perceived triumph of the Islamist-based struggle against the Soviet occupation of Afghanistan in the 1980s does indeed appear to have inspired other struggles against perceived foreign "occupations" of Islamic lands in other parts of the world. In the case of Thailand, although more than a decade was to pass before the renewed struggle appeared there, the *al-Qa'ida* strike against the United States on September 11, 2001, appears to have been an igniter of a renewed insurgency in the southern provinces of that country.

A key difference between the renewed 21st century Islamist-based insurgency and the previous, more nationalist-based insurgency of the 1960s and 1970s was the "disturbingly opaque" nature of the conflict for which "no organization has claimed responsibility."[166] Anthony Davis, a close observer of the insurgency in Thailand, reached the conclusion that the primary actors in the new insurgency were the old pan-Malay BRN, which still maintained a substantial infrastructure in the Thailand-Malaysia border area; the GMIP association of veterans of the war in Afghanistan;

---

[163] Christie, *Modern History of Southeast Asia*, 189.
[164] Christie, *Modern History of Southeast Asia*, 205–206.
[165] Christie, *Modern History of Southeast Asia*, 190.
[166] Davis, "School System Forms the Frontline in Thailand's Southern Unrest," 10.

and the small but still militant New PULO.[167] Whether this was the case or not, the actors in the insurgency were a new generation of insurgents that had been engaged in planning and training for several years before the outbreak of the insurgency in 2001. What was also clear was that, whereas the previous generation had been engaged in a "struggle for national liberation," the new generation was engaged in a *jihad*, a "give me liberty or give me death" type of struggle that was posing a difficult challenge for the Thai central government.[168]

---

[167] Davis, "Southern Thai Insurgency Gains Fresh Momentum," 15.

[168] Since these words were penned, the International Crisis Group in Brussels published its study, "Southern Thailand: Insurgency, not Jihad," that reached precisely the opposite conclusion. The author leaves it to the reader to compare these two analyses and reach his/her own conclusion. The ICG report, which has the benefit of drawing from police and interrogation reports of captured Islamic militants, is rich in detail but perhaps is too cautious in challenging the official policy position of the Thai government. *Asia Report* No. 98, 18 May 2005. URL: *http://www.crisisgroup.org/library/documents/asia/south_east_asia/098_southern_thailand_indurgency_not_jihad..pdf*. Accessed June 6, 2005.

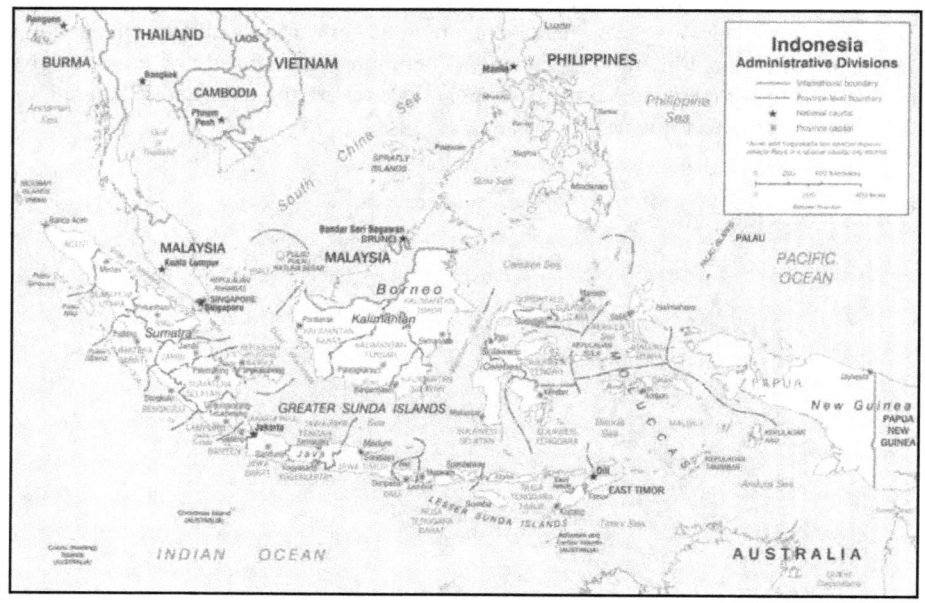

Map of Indonesia.
Source: CIA.

CHAPTER 4

ISLAM IN INDONESIA

There will be no reform in Indonesia over the long-term unless Islam is recognized as the powerful moral force it is.

—Daniel Lev

The politics of the modern, independent state of Indonesia has consisted largely of the interactions of an almost exclusively male elite of approximately 2,000 individuals.[169] Most of these men are members of the traditional *priyayi* class, descendants of the historic *sultans* and *rajas* and their families that were drawn into collaboration with the Dutch rulers during the colonial era. In this sense they constitute a continuation of the political elite that has governed the Indonesian islands for centuries, whether independently in much smaller states, or jointly at the top echelons of a unified, independent Indonesia.

Most members of this ruling elite, moreover, are *abhangen* Muslims, although a few are also Hindu, Buddhist, or even Christian. Unlike *santri* Muslims who strive to practice their religion by limiting it to the guidance provided by the *Qur'an*, the *hadith*, and the Shafi'i school of Islamic law, *abhangen* Muslims take a broader view and incorporate within Islam religious practices that predate the arrival of Islam in the Indonesian archipelago. In general, these practices are referred to as *kebatinan*, a word that relates to the Arabic *batin* (hidden), that is, the "inner" side of religion (as opposed to its external manifestations and requirements). These practices involve ceremonies that relate to the spirits that dwell in the *kris*, the dagger carried by most Indonesian men; ceremonies that take note of *Semar*, the guardian spirit of Java; attention to the prophecies of *Joyoboyo*, an Indonesian counterpart of Nostradamas in the West; and ceremonial offerings to *Lara Kidul*, the Queen of the Indonesian Ocean. Perhaps of even greater import is the *wayang*, or shadow puppet show which unites the traditional Hindu *Ramayana* and *Mahabharata* epics with figures from Islamic history to teach about the meaning and purpose of life, of the constant struggle between good and evil, and even of transmitting government policies. Constantly staged on birthdays, weddings, important religious occasions, or as ritual entertainment during family feasts, the *wayang* is an ever-present aspect of Indonesian *abhangen* life and a primary means of transmitting traditional values from one generation to the next.[170]

---

[169] Lee Khoon Choy, *A Fragile Nation: The Indonesian Crisis* (Singapore: World Scientific Publishing Company, 1999), 7.

[170] Lee Khoon Choy, 41–147. Lee's chapter is a detailed and fascinating investigation of "Javanese" mysticism (*kebatinan*) in which the author, Singapore's ambassador to Indonesia during the early 1970s, took a special interest. As Java constitutes approximately 50 percent of the total population of Indonesia, and Indonesia may be conceptualized as a Javanese "empire," inherited from the Dutch who built it, its culture and the values associated with that culture tend to be salient in any discussion of Indonesian "culture," even though other islands of the archipelago express cultural norms quite at variance with those of Java.

FORMATION OF THE STATE IDEOLOGY

As *abhangen* Muslims, Indonesia's dominant political class has tended to identify with the *Nahdlatul Ulama*, the mass movement of Indonesia's *abhangen* Muslims, established in 1926 in opposition to the more *santri*-oriented Muhammadiyah. Broadly tolerant of religious expression in all its forms, the *abhangen* elite has not only relied on *Nahdlatul Ulama* as a counterweight to the influence of Muhammadiyah in Indonesian politics, but also, in the interest of national unity, has held fast to an even broader ideological doctrine designed to promote inclusiveness among all of Indonesia's diverse peoples. This is the doctrine of *Pancasila*, first put forward by President Ahmed Sukarno in 1945, and captured in the national slogan inscribed on the Indonesian state crest, *Bhinneka Tanggut Ika* (Unity in Diversity).

Somewhat reminiscent of Sun Yat-sen's espousal of *San Min Chu Yi* (Three Peoples' Principles) as the basis for a unified, modernizing, and democratic China, Sukarno's *Pancasila* enumerated five principles as the basis of governance in Indonesia:

1. Belief in one God
2. Humanitarianism
3. National unity
4. Representative government
5. Social justice for all

Pancasila, like the six principles of Atatürkism in Turkey, remains today the official guiding ideology of Indonesia. Nevertheless, implementing its principles and ensuring its primacy did not come easily and faced many challenges following the declaration of Indonesian independence.

The first challenge was the Dutch, who in the late 1940s sought vigorously, though unsuccessfully, to reestablish their rule over the East Indies after World War II. Following this challenge came that posed by the tendency toward decentralization, which threatened to fragment the archipelago into several states. Perhaps even more challenging, however, was the *Darul Islam* movement that denied the legitimacy of *Pancasila* and sought instead the establishment of Indonesia as an Islamic state. Like the republican government of Sukarno, however, the *Darul Islam* movement opposed the potential fragmentation of Indonesia and supported the maintenance of its unity.

THE ISLAMIC ALTERNATIVE

During World War II, the Japanese occupation authority had sought to rally Muslim opinion against the Western powers by organizing in October 1943 a Consultative Council of Indonesian Muslims (*Masyumi-Majlis Syura Muslimin Indonesia*), that sought to unify the *Nahdlatul Ulama* and Muhammadiyah mass organizations. Although *Masyumi* refused to authorize Muslims to bow toward the Japanese emperor and rejected Japan's request to declare the war against the Allies a *jihad*, the new combined organization did collaborate with the occupation authorities and continued after the war as one of independent Indonesia's major political parties. Toward the end of the war, as Japan moved increasingly to the defensive, the occupation authorities began raising a number of military and paramilitary units to assist in the defense of the archipelego. In addition to PETA, the forerunner of the Indonesian Armed Forces (ABRI/TNI), *Masyumi* was also authorized in December 1944 to organize an "Islamic" military force which took the name *Barisan Hizbullah* (Party of God Front).[171]

Following the surrender of the Japanese, the *Hizbullah* fought alongside PETA against the Dutch, but in 1947 some members of *Hizbullah* broke away, taking the new name *Darul Islam* (House of Islam) and calling its armed elements the Indonesian Islamic Army. Following the Dutch agreement to recognize Indonesian sovereignty in December 1949, the *Darul Islam* based in West Java refused to recognize the authority of the new republican government led by Sukarno and proclaimed instead an independent Islamic state (*Negara Islam Indonesia*) in what is now Pasundan province. Under the leadership of Soekarmadji Kartosuwiryo, *Darul Islam* found support in Aceh, South Sulawesi, and other areas of the country outside of Java and posed a serious insurgency problem for the government until its leader's capture and execution in 1962.[172]

In addition to these problems and in part because of them, the new government remained extremely fragmented for a number of years, with the legislature's 232 seats being divided among many parties. The largest party represented, the Muslim *Masyumi*, had only 49 seats—and that party soon split in 1952, with the more traditionalist members of the old *Nahdlutal Ulama* (NU) recreating their own party.[173]

Six cabinets were formed in the 1950–57 period, reflecting the constantly shifting balance of power between the competing political parties. In addition, Sukarno faced a growing challenge from the Communist Party of the Indies (PKI) that dominated the powerful Central All-Indonesia Workers Organization (SOBSI) and a rejuvenated Indonesian Peasant Front (BNI), as well as more peaceful competition from the social democratic Indonesian Socialist Party (PSI). These parties shared his goal of a unified, secular, and socialist Indonesia, but were bitterly opposed by the Islamic parties, such as *Masyumi* and the NU, not to mention the *Darul Islam*.

Sukarno's growing impatience with the byzantine complexities of party politics and continuing regional and religious unrest led to his decision in 1956 that the democratic political process needed to be discarded. In 1957, the military and the PKI both became

---

[171] William H. Frederick and Robert L. Worden, *Indonesia: A Country Study*, Department of the Army Pamphlet 550–39 (Washington, DC: U.S. Government Printing Office, 1993), 41–42. Also Anthony H. Johns, "Indonesia: Islam and Cultural Perspectives," in *Islam in Asia: Religion, Politics, and Society*, ed. John L. Esposito (New York: Oxford University Press, 1987), 208–209.

[172] Lee Khoon Choy, 157–158.

[173] *Indonesia: A Country Study*, 49.

more dominant players in the economy and control of the nation as the restlessness of the outer islands increased. On March 14, 1957, Sukarno declared martial law, ending Indonesia's brief experiment with parliamentary democracy.[174] Sukarno referred to his new authoritarian approach to governance as "guided democracy," but he increasingly relied on the Army and the PKI (Communist Party) to balance the power of the Islamic parties, continuing Dutch influence, and regional secessionists.

After a major anti-Sukarno revolt led by civilian and military opponents of the President's growing authoritarianism in February 1958, Sukarno undertook a major purge of regional and ideological opponents. Many officers from the outer islands were forced to resign, leaving the military increasingly Javanese and loyal to Sukarno.[175] This episode and its aftermath both reflected and expanded the centralization of politico-military control in the hands of the secular Javanese at the expense of both traditional Muslims and non-Javanese. Outer island leaders complained of their commodity-based export economies being exploited for the development of import-dominated Java. Their complaints were largely ignored until they became violent, at which point the Army would suppress them. The growing power of the Army, however, especially in the outer islands, increasingly led Sukarno to look to the Java-based Communist Party as a means of balancing the increasing power of the military. In August 1960, moreover, he formally declared illegal the *Masjumi* Muslim party, as well as several others which had participated in the 1958 revolt against him and refused to submit to his concept of "guided democracy."[176]

FALL OF SUKARNO

During the "guided democracy" years (1958–1965), Sukarno relied on the Army and the Communist Party to keep the Islamic parties and regional separatists at bay. Increasingly he leaned even more closely on the Communist Party to keep the Army at bay. During this period, four other features characterized Sukarno's style of rule: a growing personality cult culminating in his self-appointment as "President for Life" in 1963; a sharply deteriorating economy characterized by hyperinflation and food shortages, as Sukarno spent massive amounts on expensive government buildings, public monuments, and military adventurism; a strong foreign policy alignment with Beijing, Phnom Penh, Hanoi, and P'yongyang "in order to combat Neocolonialism, Colonialism, and Imperialism"; and an aggressive foreign policy aimed at securing control of West New Guinea (Irian Jaya under Indonesian rule) from the Dutch in 1962 and confontation with the new state of Malaysia that had come into being on September 16, 1963.[177]

---

[174] *Indonesia: A Country Study*, 50.
[175] *Indonesia: A Country Study*, 50, and Sundhaussen, 434–438.
[176] *Indonesia: A Country Study*, 51.
[177] *Indonesia: A Country Study*, 51–54.

Communist Party aggressiveness in enforcing its policies—such as redistribution of land to the rural peasantry in areas of the country where it was strong-taking advantage of Sukarno's reliance on the party, provoked hostility in other sectors of Indonesian society. The *denouement* arrived in September 1965 in what came to be called the *Gestapu* coup. Pro-communist officers allegedly murdered five generals whom they claimed were plotting a *coup d'état* and seized the Indonesian state radio station to announce that fact. If the aim of the involved officers was to launch a *coup d'état* of their own, they failed miserably. Other anti-communist Army units under the leadership of General Suharto intervened immediately and took charge, ending the threat. News of the alleged communist *coup d'état* provoked a country-wide uprising against Indonesian communists, however, and over the next two months literally hundreds of thousands of Indonesians alleged to be communists, especially in Jawa (East) Timur and on Bali, as well as in parts of Sumatra—all also strongholds of traditional separatist sentiment—were killed. Members of the *Nahdlatul Ulama*'s youth branch, *Ansor*, were particularly active in these mob killings, which targeted Indonesia's wealthy, capitalist Chinese community as well.[178]

Although Sukarno lived on and technically continued to serve as President of Indonesia until his death in June 1970, the liquidation of the PKI and the simultaneous purge of pro-Sukarno elements in the Armed Forces had the result of undermining his authority and transferring real ruling authority to the Army. Sukarno capitulated to the inevitability of his loss on March 11, 1966, when he signed an executive order transferring his executive authorities to General Suharto. A year later, on March 12, 1967, the change of power was carried a step further, when the Provisional People's Consultative Assembly (MPR(S)) recognized Suharto as "Acting President" in place of the former President Sukarno.

ASCENDANCY OF THE "NEW ORDER"

Under Suharto, the Armed Forces (ABRI/TNI) came into ascendancy in Indonesian politics. Nevertheless, the institutions of republican government remained. Suharto and the Army took the view that economic development was the most important objective of state policy and treated the anarchic politics that had characterized Sukarno's rule as a disruptive force that needed to be tamed. To do so, Suharto first restructured the political party system, forcing the traditional parties to merge into two electoral coalitions: the United Development Party (PPP) into which all the Islamic parties were required to unite,[179] and the Indonesian Democratic Party (PDI) comprising the non-Muslim and secular parties. The old PKI (Communist Party of Indonesia) was banned.

---

[178] *Indonesia: A Country Study*, 54–57.

[179] The four components of the PPP were *Nahdlatul Ulama*, the Muslim Party of Indonesia (PMI), the Islamic Association Party of Indonesia (PSII), and the Islamic Educational Movement (Perti). PMI was a resurrected version of the banned *Masjumi*, a largely *santri*-oriented party that represented the modernizing values of the non-political Muhammadiyah organization. NU and PMI were the dominant partners in the PPP. *Indonesia: A Country Study*, 242–243.

The centerpiece of his political strategy was the creation by 1973 of a government party, *Golangan Karya*, popularly known as "Golkar," a coalition of such "functional groups" as trade unions, women, and students. Its key component was the bureaucracy, as all government workers and officials from the capital down to the smallest village were expected to be members, and its basic purpose was to serve as "a framework within which the military could mobilize civilian support" for its policies.[180]Throughout the duration of Suharto's rule (1965–1998), Golkar succeeded in dominating Indonesia's electoral process, typically controlling approximately 70 percent of seats in the National Assembly, elected every four years.

If the Islamic parties felt that Suharto would reward their support in helping to overturn the old Sukarno regime, they were wrong in their calculation. Suharto, even more forcefully than his successor, reinforced the marginalization of Islam in politics by forcing through the parliament in 1984 an act that required every political and social organization, including the Islam-based PPP, to proclaim the "civil religion" of *Pancasila* as its "sole ideological principle." Meanwhile, the government crushed opposition by sentencing vocally dissident Muslims to long prison terms for subversion. Under Suharto's rule, the NU, while paying lip service to *Pancasila*, gradually withdrew from the political arena and rededicated itself to strictly religious, social, and cultural pursuits.

At the same time, Suharto was not insensitive to the Islamic character of the society over which he ruled. As early as February 1968, his New Order government authorized the formation of a new Islamic party, *Partai Muslimin Indonesia* (PMI-Indonesian Muslim Party, also known as *Parmesi*) on condition that no former senior Masyumi leaders could occupy leadership positions in it.[181] What Suharto seemed to be seeking was an Islamic party that would support rather than challenge the legitimacy of the state that was based on the principles of *Pancasila* rather than strictly on *shari`a*. In this case, he was assisted by the emergence of an intellectual trend that began to take root during the late 1960s and early 1970s. Centered on individuals associated with the *Himpunan Mahasiswa Islam* (HMI-Islamic University Student Association) and *Pelajar Islam Indonesia* (PII-Islamic Student Association), this intellectual current presented a vision of Islam that was quite different from that articulated by the old Masyumi leadership or the *Darul Islam* movement.

Neo-Modernist Islam

Arguing that, although Islam contained a set of socio-political principles, it was not an ideology *per se*, neither was it clear that the *Qur'an* and the *Sunna* obliged Muslims to establish an "Islamic" state. Moreover, since man was a fallible being

---

[180] *Indonesia: A Country Study*, 241.

[181] Bahtiar Effendy, *Islam and the State in Indonesia*. Research in International Studies. Southeast Asia Series No. 109 (Singapore: Institute of Southeast Asian Studies, 2003), 45–46.

incapable of grasping the absolute reality of Islam, the religion was necessarily subject to a variety of interpretations, and Muslims therefore were enjoined to be tolerant, both of other Muslims as well as non-Muslims, for the benefit of the community.[182] Desirous of ending the historic hostility between the partisans of an "Islamic" state and the established political order, this emerging school of thought argued that Muslims should accept *Pancasila* as the overarching ideology of the state, because it permitted Muslims to practice their religion freely, as it did other religions in Indonesia.

Being Muslim, however, did not make a man apolitical. Rather, hostility to *Pancasila* prevented the Muslim from being engaged politically, whereas acceptance of *Pancasila*, which was deemed by the partisans of the movement to be in accordance with Islam, enabled them to be engaged politically and to struggle to "uphold and implement the basic principles of Islam within the framework of the *Pancasila* state."[183]

The doyen of this movement was the scholar Nurcholish Madjid, who for two consecutive periods (1966–1969 and 1969–1971) held the position of national chairman of the HMI. His views were echoed and supported in a variety of ways, however, by a number of scholars in a variety of fields, including Dahlan Ranuwihardjo, Djohan Effendi, Mansur Hamid, Abdul Wahib, M. Dawam Rahardjo, A. Mukti Ali, Harun Nasution, Munawir Syadzani, Ahmad Syafii Maarif, Amien Rais, and Abdurrahman Wahid (later director of *Nahdlatul `Ulama* (from 1984) and finally President of Indonesia (1999–2001)).[184] In many ways, the movement paralleled a similar one led by Anwar Ibrahim and the ABIM in neighboring Malaysia during this same period, although in this case ABIM (established in 1971) was probably modeled after its Indonesian counterpart, HMI (established in 1947). Like ABIM, HMI and other similar groups in Indonesia placed an emphasis on study groups, seminars, conferences, and other educational venues as a means of raising their and others' Islamic consciousness and thinking about how Islamic values could best be promoted in a modernizing Indonesia.

Called by many scholars a "neo-modernist" movement[185] whose primary goal was to reconcile the values, ethics, and requirements of Islam with the realities of modern life by means of vigorous reasoning (*ijtihad*), its effluorescence coincided with the general trend toward Islamic revival at the societal level throughout the world, including Indonesia, during the years following the late 1960s. This was particularly true among the country's growing urban middle class that was expanding rapidly as a result of Suharto's massive economic development schemes. By the mid-1980s, observers universally took note of what they called the growing *santri*fication of Indonesian society, particularly among the urban middle class for whom pious

---

[182] Effendy, *Islam and the State in Indonesia*, 70.

[183] Effendy, *Islam and the State in Indonesia*, 82.

[184] For a brief sketch of the thoughts of many of these individuals, see Effendy, *Islam and the State in Indonesia*, 71–80.

[185] See, for example, Malcolm Cone, "Neo Modern Islam in Suharto's Indonesia," in *New Zealand Journal of Asian Studies 4*, 2 (December 2002), 52–67.

observance of religion had become increasingly fashionable.[186] Suharto increasingly managed this trend by empowering the neo-modernist movement, appointing its most articulate spokesmen to high-level government offices and leadership positions in Indonesian society. Affiliation with the ruling party, Golkar, and collaboration with the ruling regime in support of its objectives were, of course, part of this synergy.[187]

Increased Centrality of Islam under the New Order

Toward the end of the 1980s and early 1990s, the Suharto government undertook a number of steps that had the appearance of strengthening the centrality of Islamic values in Indonesian political life. Among the steps taken were:[188]

- A new law (March 1989) requiring religious instruction at all levels of state-supported educational institutions.
- Enhancing the authority of `ulama-controlled Islamic courts operated by the Ministry of Religious Affairs (December 1989), restoring their autonomy from the civil courts operated by the Ministry of Justice since the Dutch colonial era, and placing both court systems on an equal footing.
- The establishment of an Islamic bank (*Bank Muamalet Indonesia*/BMI) (1991)
- Lifting the previous ban on wearing of the veil (known as *jilbab* in Indonesia) by women in schools (1991)
- Strengthened regulations concerning state management of *zakat* (obligatory alms) (1991)
- The founding of an Islamic newspaper, *Republika* (1992)
- Increased Islamic TV programing, including educational programs to teach Arabic
- Increased state funding for Islamic schools
- Termination of the state lottery (1993)

It is impossible to measure the degree to which these steps were adopted as concessions to the Muslim majority community of Indonesia or reflected the growing impact of the neo-modernist school on government policymaking or the apparently successful model of neighboring Malaysia, where reforms of a similar nature reflecting Islamic values had also been implemented a few years earlier. What is clear, however, is that Suharto believed he, like Mahathir Mohammed in neighboring Malaysia, could manage this increasing Islamization of Indonesian institutions by relying on the leadership provided by the neo-modernist school of Indonesian intellectuals who

---

[186] See Greg Barton, "The Prospects for Islam," in *Indonesia Today: Challenges of History*, ed. by Grayson Lloyd and Shannon Smith (Lanham, MD: Rowman & Littlefield Publishers, Inc., 2001), 245.

[187] Effendy, *Islam and the State in Indonesia*, 151–154.

[188] Abuza, *Militant Islam in Southeast Asia*, 64–65. Effendy, *Islam and the State in Indonesia*, 154–167.

strongly believed in the possibility of combining traditional Islamic values with modern modes of life within the context of the state ideology of *Pancasila*.

To this end Suharto in 1990 created a new state-controlled organization, the Association of Muslim Intellectuals (ICMI), to serve as a central focal point, research center, and distributor of information for neo-modernist ideas about Islam and its relation to the Indonesian state. Headed by his close associate, B. J. Habibie, whom Suharto later designated his Vice President and who succeeded him briefly as President following his fall from power in May 1998, the ICMI was designed to be a center for authoritative interpretation of Islam as well as a venue for discussion about an Islam that was perceived to be deeply imbedded as part of the cultural fabric of Indonesia but irrelevant politically in a depoliticized *Pancasila*-based state. Although some have argued that Surharto's "turn toward Islam" during this period, highlighted by his own well-publicized pilgrimage to Mecca in 1991, was designed to balance weakening support for him within the military, his traditional base of political support, it also seems true that he was seeking to implant permanently a vision of Islam that recognized the religion's salience in Indonesian society, yet which also could not be construed as offensive by the Christian, Hindu, and Buddhist minorities of Indonesia. The synergy achieved led some outside observers to view Indonesia in the last years of Suharto's New Order as one of the "most vibrant centers for new Muslim political thinking the modern world has seen."[189]

Conservative Reactions to Neo-Modernism

The growing ascendancy of "neo-modernist" Islam in Suharto's Indonesia did not go unchallenged, however. The leading opposition movement to the neo-modernists, as well as Suharto, was the *Dewan Dakwah Islamiyah Indonesia* (DDII). Established as early as February 1967 by former *Masyumi* party leaders who were disgruntled by Suharto's opposition to them, despite their support for his *coup d'état* against Sukarno and liquidation of Indonesia's communist movement, its most prominent spokesman was Mohammed Natsir (d. 1993), whom one writer has characterized as "the most charismatic puritan Muslim leader there ever was."[190] Ostensibly devoted to Islamic proseletyzing rather than politics, Natsir and his colleagues expressed the view that recent history indicated that Indonesians were not yet ready to constitute an Islamic state. Impressed, but also gravely concerned, by the apparent success of Christian, especially Catholic missionaries, at gaining converts, particularly in former Communist stronghold areas, they decided to devote their organization to *dakwah*

---

[189] Robert Hefner, "Indonesian Islam in a World Contest," paper presented at a joint conference sponsored by the United States-Indonesia Society and the Asia Society, Washington, DC, February 7, 2002, 4. Available at URL: *http://www.usindo.org/miscellaneous/into-us_conf.pdf*. Accessed April 7, 2005.

[190] Martin van Bruinessen, "Genealogies of Islamic Radicalism in post-Suharto Indonesia," online article posted by the author on the University of Utrecht website. URL *http://www.let.uu.nl/~martin. vanbruinessen/personal/publications/genealogies_islamic_radicalism.html*.

Close-up view of Borobuder Buddhist Temple in Yogyakarta, Java, Indonesia, September 2000.
Source: NGA Research Center—Ground Photography Collection.

(*du'a*—Islamic evangelism) in order to encourage Indonesia's Muslims to be "better" Muslims and also to combat Christian evangelism. Another feature of *Dewan Dakwah*, particularly in light of the 1967 Arab-Israeli war, was a strong orientation toward the Middle East, and Saudi Arabia in particular. In 1962, the Saudis had established the Islamic World League (*Rabitat al-'Alam al-Islami*), and Natsir, who eventually became one of its vice presidents, was able to gain recognition for his organization as the principal operating arm of the League in Indonesia. This status, of course, brought with it significant sources of funding and broad international connections with like-minded groups elsewhere in the Islamic world.[191]

Regardless of its overtly apolitical stance, the DDII remained a principal focal point of opposition to the Suharto regime and most of its policies. Although most of its leaders had their roots in the modernist Muhammadiyah movement and the old Masyumi party, in their new form they adopted a more conservative and even paranoid outlook, holding that the end result of the Suharto government would be the destruction of Islam in Indonesia. Reflecting the support it received from Saudi Arabia and allied oil-rich states, such as Kuwait, the DDII fiercely opposed Shi'a teachings as it also did those of the neo-modernists who were finding favor with the Suharto regime. Both were perceived as threats to Islam, as were also the alleged activities of

---

[191] Van Bruinessen, "Genealogies," 4. Also Peter Symonds, "Political Origins and Outlook of Jemaah Islamiyah," Part 2, 2. *World Socialist Web Site.* URL *http://www.wsws.org/articles/2003/ nov2003/ji2_n13. shtml.* Accessed 6 May 2005. Also Barton, "Islam and Politics in the New Indonesia," 50.

View from the base of Borobuder Temple in Yogyakarta, Java, Indonesia, September 2000.
Source: NGA Research Center—Ground Photography Collection.

Jews and both foreign and domestic Christians, tolerance of whom was the primary basis for upholding the doctrine of *Pancasila*.[192] Unable to act politically, the DDII remained primarily a preaching and educational movement, but it kept alive a climate of hostility to the Suharto government that would eventually bear fruit in the collapse of the regime in May 1998.

SURVIVAL AND REVIVAL OF *DARUL ISLAM*

The degree of collaboration between the DDII and continuing militant groups remains unclear, but groups more militant than the DDII continued to make their presence felt throughout the Suharto years, despite fierce efforts of the government's security organs to contain them. Although it was militarily crushed in 1962, with its top leadership either executed or imprisoned, the *Darul Islam* movement, which had challenged the legitimacy of Sukarno's nationalist, republican movement from the beginning, survived, albeit underground, and continues to be active today.[193] Indeed, although aware of its existence and determined to crush it once and for all, the Suharto government unwittingly played a role in breathing new life into the movement almost from the beginning. In the wake of the failed, so-called communist-led *Gestapu* coup that brought Suharto to power, the new leader through his intelligence chief, General Ali Murtopo, provided arms to a number of former *Darul Islam* cadres in exchange for their help in attacking communists in the areas where they lived. For their part, some *Darul Islam* leaders saw it to their advantage to collaborate with

---

[192] Van Bruinessen, "Genealogies," 7.

[193] A detailed examination of the underground *Darul Islam* movement after 1962 is provided by the International Crisis Group (ICG), *Recycling Militants in Indonesia: Darul Islam and the Australian Embassy Bombing*. ICG Asia Report No. 92, February 22, 2005. Available at *http://www.crisisgroup.org/ library/documents/asia/indonesia/092_recycl_militants_indon_darul-islam_austr_embassy_bombing.pdf*. Unless otherwise noted, the discussion here follows this ICG report.

the government both to weaken the communist movement in Indonesia and to relieve pressure on themselves.

Murtopo, who had been an original member of *Hizbollah*, but had joined the PETA following the 1947 split between the two organizations, was in fact engaged in a double game. Gradually he encouraged the revival of *Darul Islam*, but mainly to gain information about its membership and to direct its activities to support of government purposes.[194] The *Darul Islam* leaders, however, were collaborating with the government in order to bide time until they could reestablish their organization. In 1974, the up-to-now highly fragmented *Darul Islam* managed to reforge a unified organization, and in 1976 began to undertake military (terrorist) operations under the name of a newly formed operations group, *Komando Jihad*. From this time until the mid-1980s, Indonesia was beset by repeated instances of "Islamic" terrorism-arson and bombing of churches, nightclubs, and cinemas-that usually were attributed in the press to an unknown group called *Komando Jihad*. The violence associated with *Komando Jihad*, however, tended to coincide with election campaigns, as if violence would persuade voters to vote for the single Muslim party, the PPP. It, of course, had the opposite effect.[195]

Government collaboration with the *Komando Jihad* was in fact a "sting" operation, and in mid-1977 the Suharto regime arrested 185 people, mostly individuals with long-time *Darul Islam* connections, whom it accused of constituting the *Komando Jihad* organization. The government action did not halt the pattern of violence, however. What government officials had failed to recognize was that the revival of *Darul Islam* tapped into the emerging Islamic "intellectual ferment that was particularly pronounced in university-based mosques. That ferment was only beginning when *Komando Jihad* was created, but through the late 1970s and early 1980s it was fueled by the Iranian revolution, the availability of Indonesian translations of writings on political Islam from the Middle East and Pakistan; and anger over...government policies."[196] Among the sources of this anger was the government sting operation itself. One of those arrested in the 1977 dragnet was the father of Fathur Rahman al-Ghozi, later a key *Jemaah Islamiyah* operative, active in the Philippines.[197] To some in the younger generation, the *Komando Jihad* proved to be a source of inspiration, strengthening the movement with new recruits, as well as providing evidence of the perfidious nature of the ruling regime.

---

[194] Some have argued that Murtopo's real agenda was to build a force that would enable him to "neutralize Suharto and raise himself to the presidency. In return, he had promised support to the goals of *Darul Islam* in the event he became President." International Crisis Group, *Recycling Militants*, 6, fn 24. If this was the case, he was outmaneuvered by Suharto, who used the inside knowledge gained of the organization and structure of the revived *Darul Islam* in a determined effort to crush the movement permanently.

[195] Van Bruinessen, "Genealogies," 7.

[196] International Crisis Group (ICG), *Al-Qaeda in Southeast Asia: The Case of the Ngruki Network in Indonesia*, ISG Indonesia Briefing, Jakarta/Brussels, August 8, 2002, 8–9. Available at URL: *http://www. crisisgroup.org/library/documents/report_archive/A400733_08082002.pdf*. Accessed April 13, 2005.

[197] International Crisis Group, Ngruki Network, 9.

Among those caught up in the follow-up arrests of the *Komando Jihad* liquidation operation were two Islamic scholars, Abdullah Sungkar and Abu Bakar Ba'asyir, founders of the religious school Pondok Ngruki, near Solo (Surakarta) in central Java, and who later would establish the *Jemaah Islamiyah* organization in Malaysia. Accused, tried, and convicted of being initiated members of *Darul Islam*, despite their protestations to the contrary, the charges against these two men do indeed appear to have been fabricated, although the two men were supportive of the goals of *Darul Islam* and were acquainted with its leaders.[198] Rather they were active leaders of the DDII and were closely associated with DDII leader, Muhammad Natsir. This was especially true of Sungkar, who had been an active figure in the now defunct *Masyumi* party and a close associate of Natsir. Some have argued that the charges against Sungkar and Ba'asyir at this time were aimed at associating the DDII with the violence of *Komando Jihad* and the *Darul Islam* movement. Whatever the case, Natsir and the DDII remained strong supporters of Sungkar and Ba'asyir, even during their period of exile in Malaysia, when after 1985 the DDII and the *Rabitat al`Alam al-Islami*, of which Natsir was a vice president in Indonesia, were the principal sources of funding for the several hundred Indonesian fighters that were sent through Malaysia to Pakistan to receive military training and to provide support to the Afghan resistance to the Soviet occupation of Afghanistan.[199]

As active leaders of the DDII—Sungkar was chairman of the DDII Central Java Branch—Sungkar and Ba'asyir, together with another, Hasan Basri, in 1967 established a radio station called *Radio Dakwah Islamiyah Surakarta* (Islamic Proselytization Radio Surakarta/Solo) that remained on the air until closed down by the government in 1975 because of its anti-government tone. Meanwhile, in 1971 the two men also established Pesantren al-Mu'min, which in 1973 they moved to the village of Ngruki, outside of Solo, after which time it gradually came to be called Pondok Ngruki.[200] In later years, this school would gain fame as a principal recruiting ground for young recruits being sent to Afghanistan and in the 1990s for being the *alma mater* of many associated with the militant *Jemaah Islamiyah* movement.

Arrested on November 10, 1978, for alleged involvement with *Komando Jihad* and the *Darul Islam* movement, Sungkar and Ba'asyir were finally tried and found

---

[198] In its 2005 report on *Darul Islam*, the International Crisis Group stated that "Achmad Hussein, from Kudus, Central Java, and Hispran [Haji Ismail Pranoto] from Surabaya...formally inducted Abu Bakar Ba'asyir and Abdullah Sungkar into DI in 1976." International Crisis Group, *Recycling Militants*, 11. In its earlier 2002 *Ngruki Network* study, 7, the same authors had noted that "while Sangkar and Ba'asyir were never part of the original *Darul Islam*, they were deeply sympathetic to its aims," but that "the government charged [during their trial] that in 1976, Hispran inducted them into *Darul Islam* by having them swear an oath used in 1948 by Kartosuwirjo." The earlier charge is well-documented by the authors, whereas the latter is not. Whether formally "inducted" or not, the very least one can say is that they were implicated by association because of the moral support they lent to *Darul Islam* and the close relationship they had with some of its members.

[199] International Crisis Group (ICG), *Jemaah Islamiyah in South East Asia: Damaged but Still Dangerous*, ICG Asia Report No. 63, August 26, 2003, 3. Available at URL: *http://www.crisisgroup.org/ library/documents/report_archive/A401104_26082003.pdf*. Accessed April 13, 2005.

[200] International Crisis Group, *Ngruki Network*, 6–7.

guilty of many anti-government activities in 1982 and sentenced to nine years in prison. Released on appeal in late 1982, they returned to Pondok Ngruki for the next two years until, learning of their imminent rearrest in February 1985, they secretly fled to Malaysia. The rearrest order for Sungkar and Ba'asyir was part of yet another crackdown that had followed heightened Islamic opposition across the country to Suharto's May 1984 requirement that all organizations adopt *Pancasila* as their "sole ideological basis." Although the main Muslim organizations, Muhammadiyah and *Nahdlatul Ulama*, formally accepted this requirement, many other smaller Islamic organizations did not and engaged in protest demonstrations against the new law.

A particularly bloody confrontation occurred in September 1984 in the Tanjung Priok port area of Jakarta, in which government forces fired on and killed dozens of Muslim protesters (rioters). The Tanjung Priok "massacre," as it came to be remembered, signaled the beginning of an even more intense period of conflict between the government and militant Muslim groups that included several bombings and other acts of violence in which a number of figures associated with Pondok Ngruki were implicated. Among these were a Christmas Eve 1984 church bombing in Malang and another major bombing of the recently restored Borobodar Buddhist temple on January 21, 1985.[201] Also hit were several branches of a major bank owned by one of President Suharto's Chinese business partners.[202]

The flight of Sungkar and Ba'asyir along with others[203] to Malaysia did not mean an end to conflict in Indonesia, however. A 1989 bloody shootout at a Muslim school in Way Jepara, Lampang, like Tanjung Priok, became yet another in a growing list of Muslim grievances against the Suharto government.[204] Still, massive arrests and rigged trials of virtually anyone who could be associated with dissent against the regime had a certain quieting effect in the early 1990s.[205] This was also the period when Suharto began to adopt the variety of measures, noted above, that tended to recognize the centrality of Islamic values for most Indonesians, albeit only within the context of the "neo-modernist" understanding of Islam that supported the doctrine of *Pancasila* upon which the state was based.

Islamists in Disarray

For its part, the Islamic opponents of the regime were entering a period of disarray that reflected leadership struggles as well as differences concerning long- and short-term goals and objectives. Although the goal of all remained the establishment of

---

[201] International Crisis Group, *Ngruki Network*, 8–9, 15.

[202] Van Bruinessen, "Genealogies," 8.

[203] Among those who traveled with the two leaders were Fikiruddin, Agus Sunarto, Ahmad Fallah, Rusli Aryas, Mubin Bustami, Fajar Sidaq, and Agung Riyadi. ICG, *Ngruki Network*, 11.

[204] International Crisis Group, *Ngruki Network*, 15.

[205] Van Bruinessen, "Genealogies," 8.

Indonesia as an Islamic state in which the *shari`a*, administered by the `*ulama*, would prevail as the characteristic law of the state, there were differences in approach about how to achieve this end. Put most simply, the split was between those called *fillah* (with God) and those called *fisabilillah* (in the way/path of God). To the latter, *jihad* (struggle in the way/path of God — *fisabilillah* — including military actions) was a continuing requirement of God and the *shari`a* that was incumbent on every Muslim and could not be set aside or postponed for a later time. For the former, Indonesia was simply a society that was not yet ready for a military struggle to be successfully waged in the short term. What was necessary was to work through *dakwah* (proselytization) to build up a stronger Islamic society (*jemaah islamiyah*) that would eventually become the basis of a mass movement that the secular, nationalist, and authoritarian *Pancasila* regime could no longer resist. The approach of the *fillah* reflected the influence of Natsir's DDII, yet much to the consternation of the *fisabilillah*, the *fillah* considered themselves part of *Darul Islam*, while refusing to accept the *fisabilillah* leadership.[206]

The *fillah* movement within *Darul Islam* also reflected the model of the Muslim Brotherhood (*al-Ikhwan al-Muslimin*) in Egypt and the teachings of its founder, Hasan al-Banna. Although both the Egyptian Muslim Brotherhood and the Indonesian Muhammadiyah organization had grown out of the Islamic modernist reform movement articulated in the late 19th and early 20th centuries by the modernist thinkers, Jamal al-Din al-Afghani, Muhammad Abduh, and Rashid Rida, the Muhammadiyah, much more effectively than the Muslim Brotherhood, had retained the modernist spirit advocated by the reformers, funding schools that trained students in modern technical subjects as well as providing them with a strong *santri*-oriented religious education. As a result, Muhammadiyah graduates were generally more effectively prepared to obtain employment in the modern sector of Indonesia's government and economy than graduates of schools operated by the *Nahdlatul `Ulama*, who received a more traditional *abhangen*-oriented religious education. Although Indonesia, therefore, remained dominated politically by the *abhangen* Islamic religious tradition, its mid-level professional sector tended to be filled with *santri* Muslims from the Muhammadiyah schools.

In Egypt, by contrast, the Muslim Brotherhood had rapidly lost its original modernist character and evolved into an organization championing a more orthodox form of traditional Islam.[207] It nevertheless had been successful in growing into a large mass organization. One of the apparent secrets of its success, adopted by the promoters of the *fillah* movement within *Darul Islam*, was al-Banna's recruitment method known as *usroh* (literally family). The concept was to gather together small groups of ten to fifteen people who committed themselves to live together in accordance with the requirements of Islamic law. Such groups were fundamentally study groups that together undertook a directed program of instruction that culminated in the group's induction into *Darul Islam* at a graduation ceremony.[208]

---

[206] International Crisis Group, *Recycling Militants*, 10–11.

[207] For an interesting comparative analysis of the two movements, see Giora Eliraz, *Islam in Indonesia: Modernism, Radicalism, and the Middle East* (Portland, OR: Sussex Academic Press, 2004), 1–25.

[208] International Crisis Group, *Recycling Militants*, 12.

Although the *fisabilillah* sector of *Darul Islam* strongly disparaged the "passive" activities of the *fillah* group, the *usroh* proselytization activity gave new energy and a sense of purpose to those activists engaged in it, and the *usroh* movement flourished in the 1980s and 1990s, whereas those associated with the *fisabilillah* group were increasingly driven underground in the face of government efforts to liquidate the movement. The *fillah* activists were no less fervent in their opposition to the Suharto regime, however, than their *fisabilillah* counterparts. Strongly influenced by the example of the 1979 Islamic revolution in Iran, they viewed Suharto as Indonesia's Shah. At some point, due to mass pressure resulting from his autocracy, he would fall. At such a time, it was necessary for Indonesian society to be structured as a true *jemaah islamiyah*. As in Iran, under an effective leader like Khomeini, a strong *jemaah islamiyah* would enable an Islamic state to be proclaimed.[209]

Preparation at Pondok Ngruki

Although the *usroh* movement had a number of centers, one of the important ones was the Ngruki school of Abdullah Sungkar and Abu Bakar Ba'asyir.[210] Al-Banna's manual, translated into *bahasa Indonesia*, was a standard text in Pondok Ngruki.[211] So also was another work by a Ngruki faculty member, Abd al-Qadir Baraja. His work, *Jihad and Hijrah*, was considered subversive by the Suharto regime, and use of it in Pondok Ngruki was one of the charges brought against Sungkar and Ba'asyir at their 1982 trial.[212] Again drawing on the example of militant elements of the Egyptian Muslim Brotherhood, Baraja argued that successful *jihad* had to be preceded by a *hijrah* (migration), following the Prophet's example of first migrating from Mecca to Madina, where he was able to create a strong *jemaah islamiyah* prior to successfully confronting his enemies in Mecca. Such a migration could be an internal, spiritual one in which the believer separated himself from the corrupt society surrounding him[213] and associated himself with an *usroh* group, where a pure Islamic life based on the *shari`a* could be lived. It could also be a literal migration, such as Muhammad's *hijrah* to Madina, or Ayatollah Khomeini's more recent exile from Iran. Both Sungkar and Ba'asyir interpreted their decision to evade arrest in February 1985 and escape to Malaysia as just such a *hijrah*.[214] There was much work to be done, however. Both clearly expected to return to Indonesia one day-if God willed it-as Khomeini had in Iran and Muhammad in Mecca, as the leaders of a movement that would finally achieve the objective of *Darul Islam*—the transformation of Indonesia into an Islamic state.

---

[209] For the full discussion of the "Iran model," see International Crisis Group, *Recycling Militants*, 13–14.

[210] International Crisis Group, *Ngruki Network*, 9–10.

[211] *Usroh serta Pedoman Penyelenggaraan Grup Studi dan Diskusi Usroh* [Usroh and a Guide for Implementing Usroh Study and Discussion Groups]. International Crisis Group, *Recycling Militants*, 12.

[212] International Crisis Group, *Ngruki Network*, 15.

[213] In Islamic terminology, such a separation is called *takfir* (declaration of the corrupt, surrounding society as infidel — *kafir*), even though most of its members are ostensibly Muslims. Sometimes translated into English as "repentance," *takfir* is a stronger word that implies more than just turning oneself away from the corrupt society in which one lives, but actually condemning that society.

[214] International Crisis Group, *Ngruki Network*, 11.

Soon after arriving in Malaysia, both Sungkar and Ba'asyir travelled to Saudi Arabia to solicit financial support, and at the same time "decided to strengthen the *jemaah* militarily by sending volunteers from Jakarta to train in Afghanistan."[215] Saudi agreement to provide such funding was obtained, but apparently only through the *Rabitat al-`Alam al-Islami* office in Jakarta and Natsir's DDII. For local support, Sungkar found sympathetic Malaysian businessmen who agreed to employ a number of Indonesian workers brought over in return for agreement to provide twenty percent of their salaries to support the organization he was building. Donors in Indonesia also remained important sources of income for Sungkar and Ba'asyir.

Although in exile in Malaysia, Sungkar continued to maintain close contact with colleagues in Indonesia, primarily through couriers, and as an institutional base he and Ba'asyir established a new school in Johor called *Pondok/Pesantren Luqmanul Hakiem*.[216] This school, presumably a clone of Pondok Ngruki in Solo, became a halfway house for young recruits prior to their being sent on to Pakistan/Afghanistan, or simply as a place of refuge for Islamic opponents of the Suharto regime.[217] The gradual preparation of a well-trained network of supporters to serve eventually as the vanguard of an Iranian-style Islamic revolution in Indonesia following the fall of Suharto was the primary aim of Sungkar's and Ba'asyir's organizational efforts in Malaysia, however. For this purpose, the program of sending young recruits to Pakistan and Afghanistan to receive *mujahidin* training was central.

The Role of Afghanistan

In its August 2003 study, *Jemaah Islamiyah in Southeast Asia: Damaged but Still Dangerous*, the International Crisis Group, relying on police reports and personal interviews with arrested *Jemaah Islamiyah* operatives, accomplished the remarkable feat of detailing who many of the Indonesian recruits sent to Pakistan, beginning in 1985, were.[218] That more Indonesians went to Pakistan/Afghanistan than just those sent by Sungkar is also apparent from the observation that when the first cadres of Filipino Moro Islamic Liberation Front (MILF) fighters arrived at Afghan resistance leader Abd al-Rasul Sayyaf's Camp Saadah in Parachinar, Khurram Agency, Pakistan,

---

[215] International Crisis Group, *Ngruki Network*, 12.

[216] International Crisis Group (ICG), *Indonesia Backgrounder: How the Jemaah Islamiyah Terrorist Network Operates*. ICG Asia Report No. 43, December 11, 2002, 3. URL: *http://www. crisisgroup.org/ home/index.cfmid=6686516&CFTOKEN=17890206*. Accessed April 20, 2005.

[217] One example of an attendee of *Luqmanul Hakiem* who was not among those sent on to Pakistan was Amrozi, arrested in November 2002 for involvement in the October 2002 bombing of the Sari nightclub in Bali. One of those workers brought over from Indonesia in late 1985 to work for six months with a Malaysian employer, he returned to Malaysia in 1992 to study at Sungkar's school in Johor, where he remained until 1997. International Crisis Group, *How Jemaah Islamiyah Operates*, 3, 31.

[218] International Crisis Group (ICG), *Jemaah Islamiyah in Southeast Asia: Damaged but Still Dangerous*. ICG Asia Report No. 63, August 26, 2003, 4–10. URL: *http://www.crisisgroup.org/home/ index.cfmid=1452&l=1. Accessed April 20, 2005.*

for training in 1985, they found Indonesian instructors among their trainers.[219] Indeed, according to Pakistani journalist Ahmed Rashid, Southeast Asians had been training in Pakistan and Afghanistan at least as early as 1982.[220] With the arrival of Sungkar and Ba'asyir in Malaysia, however, this program of recruitment and training took on clearer form and organization.

Little specific evidence exists detailing the degree to which Sungkar and Ba'asyir also took over the recruitment and travel arrangements of volunteers for Afghanistan from elsewhere in Southeast Asia, specifically Malaysia itself, southern Thailand, and the southern Philippines. In light of subsequent developments, it is clear that they became a key node for this trafficking. In Pakistan as well, all Southeast Asians were grouped as one *qabilah* (Arabic for tribe) at Camp Saadah. Another *qabilah* grouped Arabs from Saudi Arabia, Egypt, and Jordan, while yet a third *qabilah* grouped volunteers from North Africa, largely Algerians and Tunisians. There reportedly was little contact or interaction among the separate *qaba'il* (plural of *qabilah*).[221]

FORMAL ESTABLISHMENT OF *JEMAAH ISLAMIYAH*

The involvement of Sungkar and Ba'asyir in this larger effort led to an evolution in their own sense of mission. Evidence of this change became apparent in a 1988 meeting in Pakistan in which Sungkar and Ba'asyir had arranged for the *Darul Islam* leader, Ajengan Masduki, to observe *mujahidin* training at Camp Saadah and to meet Abd al-Rasul Sayyaf as well as the *Maktab al-Khidmat* director, Abdullah Azzam. Fluent in Arabic, which Masduki was not,[222] Sungkar conducted the meeting as if he rather than Masduki was the true spiritual leader of *Darul Islam* and that *Darul Islam* was now a movement throughout Southeast Asia and not solely confined to Indonesia. A growing split between the two men became increasingly evident, as Masduki and those loyal to him raised complaints about Sungkar's alleged misappropriation of funds for Afghanistan training and his insistence that new recruits swear loyalty (*bai`a*) to himself rather than to the *Darul Islam* organization and remain under his control after returning from Afghanistan, whether settling in Malaysia or Indonesia. The split became final when, on January 1, 1993, Sungkar and Ba'asyir formally established the *Jemaah Islamiyah* organization. One manifestation of this "split was that all the students at Pondok Ngruki whose parents were Masduki loyalists moved to another *pesantren*, Nurul Salam in Ciamis."[223]

---

[219] International Crisis Group, "Southern Philippines Backgrounder: Terrorism and the Peace Process" (Singapore/Brussels: ICG Asia Report No. 80, July 13, 2004), 14. URL: *http://www.crisisgroup. org/home/ index.cfm?id=2863&l=1*. Accessed April 13, 2005.

[220] International Crisis Group, *Damaged but Still Dangerous*, 3, fn. 13.

[221] International Crisis Group, *Damaged but Still Dangerous*, 5.

[222] Both Sungkar and Ba'asyir were Indonesians of Hadramati (South Yemeni) origins for whom Arabic was a native language. They were part of a large Hadramati immigrant community in Indonesia. On their historic role as cross-cultural brokers between Indonesia and the Muslim Arab world, see Eliraz, *Islam in Indonesia*, 48–52.

[223] International Crisis Group, *Recycling Militants*, 22.

As detailed elsewhere in this study,[224] the formal establishment of *Jemaah Islamiyah* followed another meeting in Pakistan in late 1991 between Sungkar and *al-Qa'ida* leader Usama bin Ladin, following the latter's break with the royal family of Saudi Arabia over its decision to request U.S. troops to enter Saudi Arabia to confront Iraq's August 2, 1990, invasion and occupation of Kuwait. In light of subsequent events, it is clear that at this meeting bin Ladin agreed to take over the financing of further *mujahidin* training of Southeast Asians in Afghanistan. The decision to establish a formally structured *Jemaah Islamiyah* organization in Southeast Asia, closely paralleling bin Ladin's own *al-Qa'ida*, also appears to have dated from this meeting. So also did the establishment of the group in the Philippines that soon would be called the Abu Sayyaf Group (ASG).[225]

Yet another decision appears to have been *Jemaah Islamiyah* agreement to provide safe haven and logistical support to *al-Qa'ida* operatives planning and/or executing military (terrorist) operations against Western interests in the Southeast Asia region. On this basis the groundwork was laid for OPLAN Bojinka, the *al-Qa'ida* operation accidentally foiled by Philippine security forces in January 1995 that had had as its aim the potential assassinations of Pope John Paul II, U.S. President Bill Clinton, and the blowing up over the Pacific Ocean of up to eleven U.S. commercial aircraft planned for sometime in early 1995. Supported by *Jemaah Islamiyah* operatives in Malaysia, OPLAN Bojinka was an entirely *al-Qa'ida* operation, despite a telephone call from operation leader Ramzi Yousef to the Associated Press claiming credit for the Abu Sayyaf Group.[226]

Goals of *Jemaah Islamiyah*

Little actually is known about the formative years of *Jemaah Islamiyah*, although new information constantly comes to light as various members of the organization are apprehended, interrogated, and tried. The organization, officially established on January 1, 1993, operated with the utmost secrecy, and it was not until the December 2001 arrests of 15 individuals in Singapore and another 15 in Malaysia that knowledge of *Jemaah Islamiyah*'s existence became known. The arrests, moreover, only occurred as the result of a tip-off from U.S. authorities who had discovered a surveillance videotape in Afghanistan that indicated planning for terrorist attacks against the U.S. presence and personnel in Singapore. Found in the rubble of a house in Kabul that had been inhabited by *al-Qa'ida* leader Muhammad Atef, the videotape indicated surveillance of potential U.S. military, commercial, and diplomatic targets in Singapore and a clear linkage between the *al-Qa'ida* leadership in Kabul and individuals in Singapore and

---

[224] See above, Chapter 2, 45.

[225] See below, Chapter 6, 202-203.

[226] Simon Reeve, *The New Jackals: Ramzi Yousef, Osama bin Ladin and the Future of Terrorism* (Boston: Northeastern University Press, 1999), 80.

Malaysia. Interrogation of those arrested in Singapore and Malaysia revealed the existence of *Jemaah Islamiyah*.[227]

By the time of these arrests, however, Sungkar, Ba'asyir, and other elements of the organization had returned to Indonesia following the fall of the Suharto regime in May 1998. In the chaotic political environment that emerged after Suharto's fall from power, the *Jemaah Islamiyah* leadership clearly hoped to lead the long hoped for Islamic revolution in Indonesia, as had Ruhollah Khomeini in Iran two decades earlier. As a result, the portrait drawn of *Jemaah Islamiyah* as it was developing in the 1990s was significantly altered, as the attention of its leadership shifted back primarily to Indonesia rather than the Malay-Muslim Southeast Asia region as a whole. Key *Jemaah Islamiyah* operatives remained in Malaysia and the Philippines, however, and remained active there for a period. Hence, the portrait drawn from arrested operatives and captured documents was not entirely obsolete.

A document produced by the *Jemaah Islamiyah* leadership in Malaysia in May 1996—*Pedoman Umum Perjuangan al-Jamaah al-Islamiyah* [General Guideline for the *Jemaah Islamiyah* Struggle], or PUPJI, as Indonesian authorities came to call it—served as a virtual constitution, or by-laws, of the organization.[228] Written in Arabic, one of the first things a reader notes is that the document makes no mention of Indonesia or Southeast Asia, or any other country. Rather, it is conceptualized wholly in Islamic terms and probably bears close resemblance to parallel *al-Qa'ida* and later Taliban documents in Afghanistan. Arguing as a first principle that the establishment of religion requires the establishment of an Islamic state, it begins by outlining the goal of *Jemaah Islamiyah*, which it sketches in seven stages:[229]

1. Formation and development of a *Jemaah Islamiyah* (which within the document it more clearly defines as a *jemaah min al-Muslimin*—a *jemaah* within the larger Islamic world)
2. Developing the strength of *Jemaah Islamiyah*
3. Using the strength of the *Jemaah Islamiyah* (through *dakwah* and *jihad*)
4. Establishing the Islamic State
5. Organizing the Islamic State
6. Strengthening the Islamic State
7. Coordinating and collaborating with other Islamic states to reestablish the Caliphate

---

[227] Zachary Abuza, *Militant Islam in Southeast Asia: Crucible of Terror* (Boulder, CO: Lynn Reinner Publishers, 2003), 157. For details on the Singapore cell, 138–140.

[228] The PUPJI document was first discovered on the computer of *Jemaah Islamiyah* operative Imam Samudra, a key organizer of the October 12, 2002, bombing in Bali, Indonesia, who was arrested by Indonesian authorities on November 21, 2002. Translated into English by Dr. Rohan Gunaratna of the Singapore-based Institute for Defence and Strategic Studies, the document came into the author's hands from a source that asked to remain anonymous. A copy of Dr. Gunaratna's initial analysis of the document was provided with it. A search by the author suggests that the PUPJI document has not yet been posted on the Internet.

[229] PUPJI, 4–5.

Presumably the first Islamic state envisioned by the PUPJI need not be a regional one encompassing all the Malay Muslims of Southeast Asia nor even the whole of Indonesia. It might be a series of states within the region where Islamic sentiment was strong, such as Patani in southern Thailand, Kelantan and/or Terengganu in northern Malaysia, the Muslim islands of the southern Philippines, Aceh in northwestern Sumatra, and/or southern Sulawesi in eastern Indonesia. Once these were established as Islamic states, each would work to strengthen itself and collaborate with the others under the overall supervision of the *amir* of *Jemaah Islamiyah* to encourage the emergence of similar Islamic states, ultimately culminating in the emergence of a unified Islamic state in southeast Asia that would in the longer run submerge itself under the authority of a reestablished Caliph of the entire Islamic world.

Return to Southeast Asia

Training as a means of developing a strong organization is given central emphasis in the document, and such training was the primary task of the new organization during its formative years in the late 1990s. Although Abd al-Rasul Sayyaf's Camp Sadah in western Pakistan, and after 1992 his new camp at Torkham, was the major source of this training, the training effort was increasingly organized within the region as trained individuals returned. The full scope of this effort is not fully known. At least one *Jemaah Islamiyah* training camp was established in Malaysia itself, at Negri Sembilan.[230] Other training centers were established in southern Thailand as well.[231] By far the largest training effort was centered in the southern Philippines, however. By agreement with the Moro Islamic Liberation Front (MILF) in Mindanao, a *Jemaah Islamiyah* training camp, Camp Hudaibiyah, was opened up beginning in October 1994 in a remote section of the MILF's large Camp Abu Bakar.[232] At the beginning, *al-Qa'ida* leader Abu Zubayda sent several Arabs, including Kuwaiti Omar al-Farouk[233] and Algerian al-Mughira al-Gaza'iri, the commander of Camp Khaldun in Afghanistan, to oversee this effort.[234] The role of Arab and other foreign *al-Qa'ida* trainers was a temporary one, however, as mainly Indonesian instructors soon took over most of this training. Some MILF personnel are also reported to have served as both instructors and trainees at Camp Hudaibiyah.

The arrangement lasted until July 2000, when Philippine Army forces took over Camp Abu Bakar, and then Camp Hudaibiyah in 2001. By this time, with the fall of the Suharto government in May 1998, Indonesian members of *Jemaah Islamiyah* began to return home, and various training camps began to be established there, especially in the eastern Indonesian islands, the Malukus and Sulawesi in particular. Collaboration between *Jemaah Islamiyah* and the MILF reportedly continued, however, with some

---

[230] See Chapter 2, 48.

[231] See Chapter 3, 73.

[232] See Chapter 6, 209. Also ICG. *Damaged but Still Dangerous*, 16–17.

[233] The Government of Kuwait has denied he is a Kuwaiti national.

[234] Abuza, *Militant Islam in Southeast Asia*, 137.

MILF fighters receiving training in the new Indonesian *Jemaah Islamiyah* camps, and some Indonesians continuing to be seen in MILF areas of Mindanao.[235]

Secrecy of *Jemaah Islamiyah*

The need to maintain secrecy and discipline are two other themes that pervade the PUPJI document. *Jemaah Islamiyah* is conceptualized as an elite military organization, each of whose members has been carefully vetted during his recruitment process in accordance with these two criteria as well as for his "solid base" (*al-qa'ida al-shulabah*) in religion. Each is required to give an oath of allegiance (*bai'a*) to the `amir (Abdullah Sungkar), to listen carefully to the `amir's instructions, and to obey them unwaveringly to the best of his abilities. The ability and desire to work together collectively, as well as to be mutually protective of other members of the group, are other key criteria for membership. At least a portion of the organization is defined as *Tanzim Sirri* (secret organization). The document is not clear whether this means all or a portion of *Jemaah Islamiyah*. Until the uncovering of the organization in December 2001, it succeeded in maintaining its clandestine nature, including its first terrorist operations in 2000 (e.g., the Christmas Eve church bombings in Indonesia in December 2000) that occurred without attribution. Both of the known planned operations, the 1995 OPLAN Bojinka in the Philippines and the probable 2002 planned operations against U.S. facilities in Singapore, were meant to have been carried out by *al-Qa'ida* personnel with *Jemaah Islamiyah* support.[236] They were not to have compromised the clandestine character of the organization until it had garnered the strength to be able to reveal its existence.

Structure of *Jemaah Islamiyah*

The remainder of the PUPJI document is organizational in nature. At the head of *Jemaah Islamiyah* was the `amir (Abdullah Sungkar), said to have been chosen by the seven-man *Syuro* (*shura*) Council appointed by himself. Sungkar is alleged to have given *bai`a* to *al-Qa'ida* leader Usama bin Ladin,[237] but this was not the basis of his authority in *Jemaah Islamiyah*. The `amir, in turn, was to be supported by four councils:

1. The *Qiyadah* (Leadership) Council, consisting of the leadership of three other councils:
   a. The *Qiyadah Markaziyah* (Central Leadership) Council
   b. The *Qiyadah Mantiqiyah* (Territorial Leadership) Council
   c. The *Qiyadah Wakalah* (Representative Leadership) Council

2. The *Syuro* (Consultative) Council (seven members)

3. The *Fetwa* (Legal Advice) Council

4. The *Hisbah* (Internal Judiciary) Council

---

[235] International Crisis Group, *Damaged but Still Dangerous*, 23.

[236] Abuza, *Militant Islam in Southeast Asia*, 139.

[237] Abuza, *Militant Islam in Southeast Asia*, 127.

Not all of this structure may have been brought into being before the uncovering of *Jemaah Islamiyah*. Article 43, the final article of the PUPJI, states, "This Constitution will be implemented in stages depending on available conditions." One element that was established was the *Qiyadah* Council, which consisted of four *mantiqi* councils and a number of *wakalah* councils. The four *mantiqi* councils had purview over four territorial regions into which Southeast Asia was divided:

1. *Mantiqi* 1: Covered southern Thailand, the Malay peninsula, and Singapore. Headed by *al-Qa'ida*-trained (1987-1989) Indonesian, Riduan Isamuddin, better known as Hambali, until early 2002, when he was reportedly replaced by Ali Gufron (Muklas),[238] this region was less a theater of operations than a headquarters organization engaged primarily in fundraising, planning, and logistical support for training in Afghanistan and later the southern Philippines. It was Hambali and others that established business operations in Malaysia that provided logistical support for *al-Qa'ida* operative Ramzi Yousef's OPLAN Bojinka in late 1994-early 1995.

2. *Mantiqi* 2: Covered the main islands of Java, Sumatra, and Maluku in Indonesia, except for Sulawesi and Kalimantan. Headed by Mindanao-trained Abdullah Anshori, also known as Abu Fatih, region was considered the primary operational region of *Jemaah Islamiyah*.

3. *Mantiqi* 3: Covered the southern Philippines and all of Borneo, including Kalimantan (Indonesia), Sabah and Sarawak (Malaysia), and Brunei and Sulawesi (Indonesia). Headed by Pranato Yudha, more commonly called Mustopa, and also known as Abu Thalout, until his arrest in July 2003, this mantiqi was formed in 1997 as a means of more effectively administering the logistical requirements of *Jemaah Islamiyah* recruits receiving training at Camp Hudaibiyah in the southern Philippines. In military terms, it was a training command rather than an operations command.

4. *Mantiqi* 4: Covered cells in Australia and Papua (formerly Irian Jaya), although not Papua New Guinea. Headed by an unidentified individual called Abdul Rohim, this mantiqi was formed sometime before December 2001, primarily for the purpose of fundraising and recruiting Indonesian and other southeast Asian Muslims residing in these areas for *Jemaah Islamiyah* training, providing organizational structure, and possibly future operational planning.

Each of these regions was further subdivided into *wakalah*, which in turn were further divided into *khatibah*, *qirdas*, and *fiah*. Although these were territorial divisions, the terms also reflected the hierarchical military structure of *Jemaah Islamiyah* into: *mantiqi* (brigades), *wakalah* (battalions), *khatibah* (companies), *qirdas* (platoons), and *fiah* (squads).[239] A number of *walalah* were established. Those so far known include, in Malaysia: Kuala Lumpur/Selangor, Johor, Kuantan, Perak, Kelantan, and

---

[238] International Crisis Group, *Damaged but Still Dangerous*, 11. Gufron was headmaster of *Pondok/Pesantren Luqmanul Hakiem*, which he helped Sungkar and Ba'asyir establish in Johor in 1991.

[239] International Crisis Group, *Damaged but Still Dangerous*, 11.

Negri Sembilan; the *wakalah* of Singapore[240]; *Wakalah* Hudaibiyah in the southern Philippines[241]; and in Indonesia: Jakarta, Medan, Pakanbaru, Lampung, Solo, Surabaya, Nenado, Makassar, Poso/Palu, East Kalimantan, and Nosa Tengara.[242]

During *Jemaah Islamiyah*'s period of development in the late 1990s, each of these divisions was focused primarily on recruitment and training, developing effective communications throughout the hierarchy, collecting information, and presumably planning. Aside from supporting OPLAN Bojinka in 1994–95, no operational (terrorist) activity is known to have occurred[243] until the year 2000. By this time, however, a new era had dawned with the May 1998 fall of the Suharto regime in Indonesia, and the whole perspective of the *Jemaah Islamiyah* leadership changed from one of preparation into one of action.

FALL OF THE SUHARTO REGIME

As throughout the rest of Southeast Asia, the sudden devaluation of Thai currency in July 1997 produced a financial crisis that soon reached Indonesia as well. Immediately, the value of the Indonesian *rupiah* began to fall. By August, when it had declined by nine percent, the government abandoned further efforts to sustain its value by injecting cash into the economy. As the *rupiah* went into freefall, reaching RP 4,000 to U.S. $1.00 in October, RP 5,000 to U.S. $1.00 in December, and RP 17,000 to U.S. $1.00 by January 1998, interest rates soared.[244] Foreign capital, which for so long had fueled the Indonesian economy at an annual growth rate of nearly eight percent for nearly three decades, now suddenly began to flee the country, and "so too did billions of dollars of local capital."[245] Inflation became rampant, debt-ridden businesses and banks collapsed, and nearly 14 million Indonesians had been made unemployed during the first eleven months of the crisis[246] that, in the case of Indonesia, has not been overcome even today.

Efforts of the International Monetary Fund (IMF) to restore confidence in the *rupiah* (with a U.S. $38 billion loan package) also floundered, due in part to political

---

[240] Reported on in detail in Republic of Singapore, *White Paper: The Jemaah Islamiyah Arrests and the Threat of Terrorism* (Singapore: Ministry of Home Affairs, January 7, 2003). URL: *http://www. channelnewsasia.com/cna/arrests/whitepaper.pdf*. Accessed October 22, 2005.

[241] International Crisis Group, *Southern Philippines Backgrounder*, 16. The initial head of this wakalah was Fathur Rahman al-Ghozi.

[242] International Crisis Group, *Damaged but Still Dangerous*, 12.

[243] The assumption here is that terrorist activities of the Abu Sayyaf Group (ASG) in Basilan, Mindanao, and Sulu in the southern Philippines during this period were independent of *Jemaah Islamiyah* involvement. Although clear linkages existed between *al-Qa'ida* and the ASG, there is little evidence of connection between *Jemaah Islamiyah* and the ASG aside from a limited degree of joint training in MILF camps in Mindanao.

[244] Judith Bird, "Indonesia in 1997: The Tinderbox Year," *Asian Survey*, 38, 2 (February 1998), 173.

[245] Greg Barton, "Islam and Politics in the New Indonesia," in *Islam in Asia: Changing Politcal Realities*, ed. by Jason F. Isaacson and Colin Rubenstein (New Brunswick, NJ: Transaction Publishers, 2002), 14.

[246] Ressa, *Seeds of Terror*, 54.

uncertainty about Suharto's age (70) and health, but also because of the President's evident reluctance to implement the package of economic reforms imposed upon him by the IMF.[247] The crisis also exposed the well-known but heretofore impossible-to-publicly-discuss cronyism and corruption of the ruling regime. Particularly involved were members of Suharto's immediate family and a number of wealthy Chinese businessmen whose economic stakes in the country could be seriously undermined by strict compliance with the IMF-mandated reforms. As long as the Indonesian economy had remained strong, and investments could be made in improved health services as well as in providing educational and employment opportunities, the Army-dominated Suharto regime was able to maintain its firm and sometimes brutal stranglehold on Indonesia's political life. Opposition had remained marginalized and had been forcibly suppressed whenever it appeared threatening. With the sudden transformation of Indonesia from a "miracle" economy into a "melt-down" economy dependent on the charity of the international aid community and donor countries for its continued survival, opposition to Suharto's continued rule grew rapidly and became general. Put in traditional Indonesian terms, the Sultan appeared to have lost his *wayhu*, the ability to create order in the universe.[248]

Broad societal opposition to Suharto coalesced following his announcement on January 20, 1998, that he intended to run again for his seventh five-year term as President of Indonesia, when the Parliament convened in March.[249] Although he had governed with dictatorial authority since assuming power in 1965, Suharto had never abandoned the appearance of a republican form of government, nor a capitalist image of the Indonesian economy, although most of it was state-owned and operated by the military. Instead, he had driven all political activity into three political parties, one of which was his own government-based Golkar Party. Requiring all political office-seekers to be approved by his government as a condition for running for office, he then relied on police-state tactics to ensure a significantly large enough vote (usually 65–70 percent) for Golkar. In such a manner, the May 1997 parliamentary elections had proceeded, and Suharto once again in March 1998 found himself unanimously reelected President of the Republic, despite abundant evidence of massive opposition to his continued rule throughout the country.

With the mandate of a new election behind him, Suharto began to implement the more than 100 IMF economic policy reforms required of him to stabilize the Indonesian economy. Among these was the abolition or reduction of government subsidies for a variety of basic commodities. One, announced on May 4, was a fuel subsidy reduction that meant a 70 percent increase in gasoline prices. Anti-government demonstrations had already emerged on university campuses, but spread across the country with

---

[247] Howard Dick, "Brief Reflections on Indonesia's Economic History," in *Indonesia Today: Challenges of History*, ed. by Grayson Lloyd and Shannon Smith (New York: Rowman and Littlefield Publishers, 2001), 164.

[248] Ressa, *Seeds of Terror*, 55.

[249] Indonesian Presidents are chosen by the Parliament. The last parliamentary elections had been held in May 1997, just before the outbreak of the Asian financial crisis. Bird, "Indonesia in 1997," 60.

this announcement. No violence had yet erupted, but did so after May 12 when four students from the prestigious, upper-middle class Catholic Trisakti University were shot dead by snipers, believed to be loyal to Suharto's son-in-law, Lieutenant General Prabowo, while returning to their campus from a peaceful demonstration.[250] Ten days later, Suharto was gone.

What followed was an upheaval in Jakarta that saw days of savage rioting in the Chinese and commercial sections, including an undetermined number of rapes of Sino-Indonesia girls and women; a death toll from mob violence that mounted to over a thousand souls; and an orgy of looting, plundering, and torching of malls and the houses of ethnic Chinese. By May 14, foreign embassies were evacuating personnel and President Soeharto was winging his way back from the G-15 summit in Cairo. The military-after some bizarre absences from the districts of conflict-seemed to regain control of the situation the next day. The students massed and marched to Parliament, vowing to oust Soeharto, and the elite began to turn against him. On the 19th, Soeharto spoke on national television, vowing to leave office in due time after new elections and the setting up of a reform committee in a phased process. But again it was too late. By that evening he discovered that the Muslim hierarchy wanted him to go, with ABRI chief General Wiranto saying he would protect Soeharto if he stepped down. Harmoko, Soeharto's most trusted flack and head of the ruling GOLKAR organization, said the party and Parliament wanted him out, and most of his cabinet resigned. The grand chessmaster who had ruled for 32 years had been checkmated. On the morning of May 21, Soeharto resigned in a simple ceremony while a hesitant and tense Vice President Habibie took the oath of office, followed by a short declaration from Wiranto of ABRI's fealty to the Constitution and the new President.[251]

The collapse of the Suharto regime left the country in a long period of political turmoil characterized by a gravely weakened central government. The widespread popular upheaval of 1998 appeared to signify a societal rejection of the tradition of authoritarian rule that had long characterized Indonesia-first under the Dutch and then under both Sukarno and Suharto. The need for *reformasi* that served as the battle cry of the demonstrators demanding an end to the Suharto regime reflected a widespread vision of the early years of the new Indonesian republic before 1957 as a "golden age," when democratic institutions, however anarchic, had flourished.[252] As it turned out, the Constitution and its republican institutions have thus far prevailed, although at the cost of considerable political turmoil.

---

[250] Barton, "Islam and Politics," 15.

[251] Judith Bird, "Indonesia in 1998: The Pot Boils Over," *Asian Survey*, 39, 1 (January/February 1999), 29.

[252] Jean Gelman Taylor, *Indonesia: Peoples and History* (New Haven, CT: Yale University Press, 2003), 339.

After Suharto

B.J. Habibie, who replaced Suharto as President, had been chosen as the latter's Vice President in January 1998, many asserted, because Suharto had judged that few in the Indonesian political spectrum would want Habibie to replace him.[253] A diminutive, eccentric figure, with peculiar mannerisms that led many to consider him a man lacking presidential stature,[254] Habibie nevertheless had been patronized by Suharto since his youth, and in turn was one of the former President's staunchest allies. A West German-trained aeronautical engineer, he had returned to Indonesia in the 1970s to become director of the state-controlled aircraft industry, prior to being made Minister of Research and Technology, in charge of Indonesia's "strategic industries," which included the manufacture and procurement of armaments for the Indonesian Armed Forces.[255] Known primarily for his overriding passion for the manufacturing of aircraft, he nevertheless was picked by Suharto in 1990 to serve as the director of the newly established Association of Muslim Intellectuals (ICMI).[256] Not particularly known for his religious piety, Habibie nevertheless was a close associate of the President, and his appointment as director of ICMI communicated the importance Suharto attributed to the new institution. The symbolism of associating Islam with modern science, technology and industrial development was yet another factor behind the choice of Habibie.

CNN corespondent Maria Ressa suggests that historians will be kinder to Habibie than his contemporaries were "to this enthusiastic man with boundless energy, who accomplished more in his sixteen months in office than anyone could have expected-passing more than twelve hundred laws, releasing political prisoners, and strengthening political institutions."[257] Unable to maintain the confidence of the Parliament, however, Habibie agreed to authorize new national elections in June 1999, although there was no Constitutional requirement for him to do so. The elections, held on June 7, 1999, were the first free and fair elections conducted in Indonesia since 1955. Habibie himself had removed the ban on political parties (besides the three the Suharto government had sanctioned), and more than 140 had formally registered with the government by the end of 1998. Of these, 46 were judged by the Interior Ministry as having the minimum requirements to be included on the ballot, and 21 of these parties gained seats in the new Parliament elected in June 1999.[258]

---

[253] Bird, "Indonesia in 1998," 28.

[254] Ressa, *Seeds of Terror*, 55.

[255] Greg Barton, "Assessing the Threat of Radical Islamism in Indonesia," 15, fn. 26. Draft paper published on the Internet. URL: *http://www.sisr.net/apo/Islamism_in_Indonesia.rtf*. Accessed April 15, 2005.

[256] See above, 91.

[257] Ressa, *Seeds of Terror*, 55.

[258] Greg Fealy, "Parties and Parliaments: Serving Whose Interests?" in *Indonesia Today: Challenges of History*, ed. by Grayson Lloyd and Shannon Smith (Lanham, MD: Rowman and Littlefield Publishers, 2001), 100.

Table 6.1
The 1999 General Election Results and Parliamentary Seats for Major Parties

Party	Votes %	No. of Seats
1 PDI-P (Indonesian Democratic Party of Struggle)	33.76	153
2 Golkar (Functional Groups Party)	22.46	120
3 PKB (National Awakening Party)	12.62	51
4 PPP (United Development Party)	10.62	58
5 PAN (National Mandate Party)	7.12	34
6 PBB (Crescent Moon and Star Party)	1.94	13
7 PK (Justice Party)	1.36	7
8 PKP (Justice and Unity Party)	1.01	4
9 PNU (Muslim Community Awakening Party)	0.64	5
10 PDKB (Love the Nation Democratic Party)	0.52	5
Eleven other parties	7.85	15

Source: Greg Fealy, "Parties and Parliaments: Serving Whose Interests?" in Indonesia Today: Challenges of History, ed. by Grayson Lloyd and Shannon Smith (Lanham, MD: Rowman and Littlefield Publishers, 2001), 101.

Generally considered by international observers to have been "free and fair" elections, the outcome was believed to be reasonably reflective of the complex political landscape that Indonesia constituted. Five parties gained 85 percent of the votes. The major winner was the PDI-P, headed by the daughter of former President Sukarno, Mrs. Megawati Sukarnoputri. Observers noted that, despite the increased *santrification* (Islamization) that had characterized Indonesian society over the last two decades, the combined Islamic parties favoring a *shari`a*-based state — as opposed to one based on *Pancasila* — gained only 18 percent of the vote, significantly less than the approximately 40 percent a parallel grouping had won in the 1955 elections.[259] Nevertheless, partly because of a lingering bias against choosing a woman as President, Megawati was unable to muster sufficient support among the members of the Parliament to win the election.[260] Instead, after a complex political process, the choice fell upon third-place PKB leader Abdurrahman Wahid. Megawati was in turn elected as Vice President, and both were installed in office, replacing Habibie, on October 20, 1999.

---

[259] Theodore Friend, *Indonesian Destinies* (Cambridge, MA: The Belknap Press of Harvard University Press, 2003), 391. It should be noted that Muhammadiyah had accepted *Pancasila*, when required to do so in 1984, and its 1999 political manifestation, PAN, under the leadership of Amien Rais, continued to do so as a matter of principle. Friend, *Indonesian Destinies*, 389.

[260] Friend, *Indonesian Destinies*, 392.

Presidency of Gus Dur

The grandson of two founders of the 40 million-strong, *abhangen*-based mass organization, *Nahdlatul Ulama*, Wahid (or Gus Dur, as he was more popularly known) had assumed leadership of the *Nahdlatul Ulama* in 1984. Although deeply rooted in Indonesia's rural-based, syncretic *abhangen* Islamic religious tradition, Wahid was also a liberal modernist, closely associated with the "neo-modernist" school of Nurcholish Madjid that President Suharto had empowered through the creation of the ICMI in 1990.

An enigmatic figure whose strengths (articulate idealism combined with bewildering tactical maneuvering) as an opposition figure became weaknesses in the office of the Presidency, Wahid also had the misfortunate to have suffered a stroke in January 1998. Although he made a reasonably good recovery, the stroke greatly reduced his stamina and also caused him to become legally blind.[261] His "middle way" approach to handling the country's manifold political, economic, and social problems failed to satisfy more radical elements on both sides of Indonesia's political spectrum, particularly the Army whose support he could never gain.[262] His key dilemma was how to serve as a strong President when he himself, as well as a majority in the Parliament that had elected him, wanted to curtail the powers of the Presidency in the interests of a stronger democracy. Without a sufficiently strong political base within the Parliament, and increasingly perceived as lacking the leadership qualities needed to guide the country, he was impeached by the Parliament in a unanimous 591 to 0 vote in July 2001. His Vice President, Megawati Sukarnoputri, took over as President for the remainer of his five-year term. Hamza Haz, leader of the Suharto-era Islamic party, the PPP, and one of Wahid's fiercest critics, as well as of Megawati, was chosen as the replacement Vice President.[263]

Megawati, Indonesia, and September 11, 2001

Long a firm opponent of Suharto, in part because of his "non-person" treatment of her father, Megawati too had suffered the brutality of the former President's regime, when in July 1996, fully a year before the scheduled national elections of May 1997, government forces had attacked the headquarters of her increasingly popular

---

[261] Barton, "Islam and Politics in the New Indonesia," 29.

[262] For capsule views of Wahid's personality and character, see John L. Esposito and John Voll, *Makers of Contemporary Islam* (New York: Oxford University Press, 2001), Chapter 9, "Abdurrahman Wahid," 199–216. Also Greg Barton, "Indonesia's Nurcholish Madjid and Abdurrahman Wahid as Intellectual *Ulama*: The Meeting of Islamic Traditionalism and Modernism in Neo-Modern Thought," *Islam and Christian-Muslim Relations*, 8, 3 (October 1997), 323–350. Also Barton, "Islam and Politics in the New Indonesia," 76–84.

[263] Michael S. Malley, "Indonesia in 2001: Restoring Stability in Jakarta," *Asian Survey*, 41, 1 (January–February 2002), 124.

PDI-P political party, resulting in a number of deaths.[264] Megawati's strength was that she was the bearer of her father's legacy that was increasingly being perceived nostalgically during the latter years of the Suharto era. Otherwise, she did not prove to be an effective politician, as was demonstrated by her failure to be elected President, despite her party's victory in the 1999 elections. Now made President almost by default following the July 2001 impeachment of Abdurrahman Wahid, she owed much politically to the Islamic parties in the Parliament that had turned against Wahid. This was particularly true of PPP leader Hamza Haz, the virtual "kingmaker" of her Presidency who now served as her Vice President. No longer bound by Suharto's 1984 "sole ideological principle" requiring all organizations, including political parties, to support *Pancasila* as the "civil religion" of the state, the contest between those, like Megawati and the PDI-P, who continued to champion *Pancasila*, and those like Haz and the PPP, who favored replacement of *Pancasila* by the *shari`a*, resumed. Although the 1999 elections suggested overwhelming public support for *Pancasila*, the political dependence of Megawati on the support of the Islamic parties made the contest a more even one than the 1999 elections implied.

The United States' response to the September 11, 2001, attacks on the World Trade Center and the Pentagon at first appeared to strengthen Megawati's hand politically. The December 2001 Singapore discovery of *Jemaah Islamiyah*, its linkages to the *al-Qa'ida* sponsors of the September 11 attacks on the United States, and knowledge that the *Jemaah Islamiyah* leaders had returned to Indonesia in early 1999 following the collapse of the Suharto regime, placed a spotlight on Indonesia in U.S. President George W. Bush's global war on terrorism. Whereas U.S.-Indonesian relations had been very strained since the Indonesian Army-supported militia violence in East Timor following the August 30, 1999, UN-sponsored referendum on East Timorese independence (79.5 percent in favor), the United States now sought improved relations with the Megawati government and support for the war against terrorism. Although Megawati was keen to restore good relations with the United States, she was constrained by the Islamic parties who feared that the war against terrorism could in fact become a war on Islam, particularly in Indonesia.[265]

Accordingly, despite lip-service support for U.S. opposition to terrorism,[266] until the October 2002 *Jemaah Islamiyah*-sponsored bombing of the Sari nightclub in Denpasar, Bali, Indonesian authorities tended to deny the existence of any significant terrorist threat in Indonesia-this despite several pre-9/11 terrorist attacks on Indonesian soil. These included the attempted assassination of the Philippine

---

[264] Ressa, *Seeds of Terror*, 52–53. The aim of the attack was to "encourage" the party to choose someone other than Megawati as its leader. The effort failed and probably only strengthened the party's and her appeal among the Indonesian public.

[265] Ann Marie Murphy, "Indonesia and the World," in *Indonesia: The Great Transition*, ed. by John Bresnan (Lanham, MD: Rowman and Littlefield Publishers, 2005), 271.

[266] Officially, Megawati, reflecting widespread popular opinion in Indonesia, expressed grave reservations about U.S. military operations in Afghanistan, stating that "international regulations and conventions should be followed to ensure that the war on terrorism did not become a new form of terrorism itself." Murphy, "Indonesia and the World," 276.

Table 6.2 The 2004 General Election Results	
Party	Votes %
Golkar (Functional Groups Party)	21.6
PDI-P (Indonesian Democratic Party for Struggle)	18.5
PKB (National Awakening Party)	10.6
PPP (United Development Party)	8.2
PD (Democratic Party)	7.5
PKS (Prosperous Justice Party)	7.2
PAN (National Mandate Party)	6.4
PBB (Crescent Moon and Star Party)	2.6
Other parties	17.3

Source: R. William Liddle and Saiful Mujani, "Indonesia in 2004: The Rise of Susilo Bambang Yudhoyono" in *Asian Survey*, 45, 1 (January/February 2004), 120.

Local police post in Bali in 2000. This was the site of the Jemaah Islamiyah-sponsored bombing of a nightclub in October 2002, which killed scores of tourists.
Source:

115

Ambassador to Indonesia in Jakarta (August 2000); the bombing of the Jakarta Stock Exchange (August 2000); the Christmas eve bombing of 30 churches throughout Indonesia (December 2000); and the bombing of the Atrium Shopping Center in Jakarta (August 2001). The later March 2003 U.S. invasion of Iraq totally undercut her relationship with the United States, however, as popular support for U.S. President Bush sank to a low of 15 percent in Indonesia.[267]

Although Megawati managed to remain in office for the remainder of her constitutional term, her effort to be reelected in 2004 failed. Instead, former President Suharto's official party, Golkar, reemerged as the strongest party electorally, perhaps suggesting a degree of nostalgia for the more orderly Suharto years. For President, the electorate, now voting across the country for the first time, chose a relatively unknown retired general, Susilo Bambang Yudhoyono, who previously had been coordinating minister for political and security affairs in Megawati's cabinet. Yudhoyono had taken the precaution of forming his own political party (PD) in 2001 as a vehicle to support his Presidential candidacy. His overwhelming victory over Megawati should perhaps be seen more as a rejection of her rather than a positive affirmation of Yudhoyono. Nevertheless, the process signaled the continued, successful operation of Indonesia's restored constitutional democracy-the desire for which appears uppermost in the minds of most Indonesians in the post-Suharto era, despite the myriad problems that continue to beset the country during the *reformasi* period.

---

[267] Murphy, "Indonesia and the World," 176.

CHAPTER 5

SEPARATISM: THREAT TO INDONESIAN UNITY?

REVIVAL OF SEPARATISM IN INDONESIA

Problems facing the *reformasi* era included a failure of the Indonesian economy to rebound effectively following the 1997 Asian financial crisis, but perhaps the most serious problem was the revival of long dormant separatist movements that threatened the unity of the Indonesian state. Among these were the conflicts that emerged in East Timor, the Maluku Islands, Sulawesi, Irian Jaya (Papua), Kalimantan, and Aceh, where elements of the native population took advantage of a weakened central government following the fall of Suharto to revive historic claims to independence. Except for Aceh, whose population is Muslim, and where the quest for independence is based on different foundations, each of the other areas is characterized by a significant Christian population, so that struggles to achieve freedom from Indonesian rule tend to have the appearance of Christian-Muslim conflict. It was primarily in these conflicts that *Jemaah Islamiyah* and other related militant Islamic groups found scope for action in the post-Suharto era.

Dutch policy during the colonial era generally forbade Christian missionaries from teaching or establishing schools or hospitals in Muslim communities. Rather they were directed to areas where the local population had not yet accepted Islam.[268] These populations also were generally in the peripheral areas of the colonial state and consisted of different tribal groups so that what sometimes appeared as Christian/Muslim religious conflict was also, in fact, ethnic conflict. Examples of largely Christian ethnic groups are the Dyacks of Kalimantan, the Minahasa of northern Sulawesi, the Ambonese of Ambon (Maluku), and the Irianese of Papua. As Christians, these groups typically received favorable treatment by the Dutch authorities.[269] The Ambonese, for example, served as the backbone of Dutch police and security forces throughout the archipelago. As a result, when the Dutch sought to reestablish their rule after World War II, these groups generally fought alongside the Dutch against the Indonesian nationalists and favored a continuation of Dutch rule and/or recognition as independent Christian states. For this reason, a group of Christian Ambonese declared the birth of the independent Republic of the South Moluccas in 1950.[270] The separatist movements were rapidly crushed by the new Indonesian Republic, however, that was determined to lay claim to all the lands that had been brought under control by the Dutch. Successfully suppressed by the young Indonesian Republic, they remained dormant until an opportune time, when a weakened central government that followed the end of the Suharto regime in 1998 opened the door to renewed separatist tendencies.

---

[268] Taylor, *Indonesia*, 259.

[269] Taylor, *Indonesia*, 268–270.

[270] Taylor, *Indonesia*, 342.

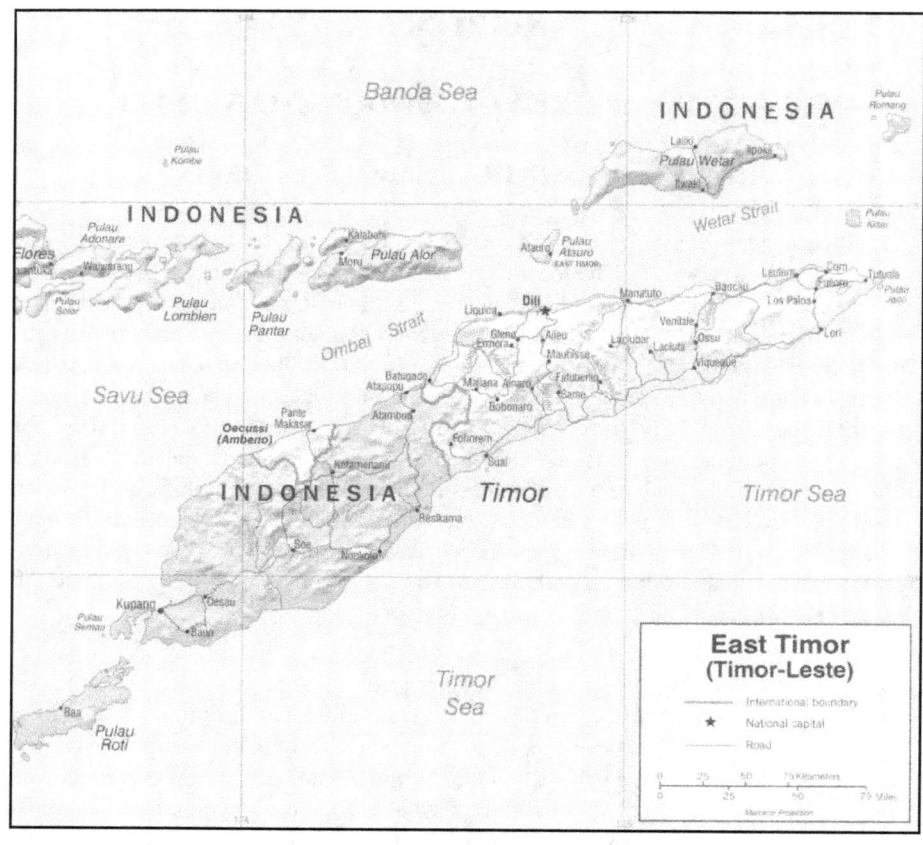

Map of East Timor, long claimed by Indonesia and now a UN protectorate.
Source: CIA.

EAST TIMOR

East Timor was a special case. Never part of the Dutch East Indies (as was West Timor), it had remained, like East Papua (formerly a colony of Australia; today Papua New Guinea), a colonial possession of Portugal. With Portuguese rule came Christianity. When Portugal made its decision to withdraw from East Timor (in 1975), although only 30 percent of the native population was Christian, these constituted the "ruling elite" of the half-island that was both Portuguese-speaking and Roman Catholic.[271] Among this elite, three parties emerged to compete with one another for control of post-colonial East Timor. The Timorese Democratic Union preferred union with Portugal and wanted Portuguese to remain the official language of administration. Fretilin also wanted Portuguese to be the official language of East Timor, but favored independence in a commonwealth relationship with Portugal. The Timorese Popular Democratic

---

[271] Taylor, *Indonesia*, 379. The remaining 70 percent were animist in religion, venerating local spirits of the land and the sky. There were virtually no Muslims among the indigenous Timorese population.

Association, on the other hand, favored union with West Timor, incorporation into Indonesia, and the adoption of Bahasa Indonesia as the official language.[272]

This last party had the support of the government of Indonesia, whose President Suharto viewed incorporation of East Timor into Indonesia as the only acceptable option. Accordingly, it provided arms, military training, and funds to pro-Indonesian forces that provoked clashes with pro-independence forces, especially Fretilin, which nevertheless succeeded in taking control of East Timorese government institutions as the last Portuguese troops departed the island in August 1975. Undeterred, the Suharto government succeeded in portraying Fretilin as a communist-inspired movement that in the wake of the fall of Vietnam, Cambodia, and Laos to communist forces in this period threatened yet further expansion of communism in Southeast Asia. Accordingly, the Western powers, particularly the United States and Australia, acquiesced in Suharto's decision to invade East Timor in December 1975 and to annex it the following year as Indonesia's 27th province.[273] The United Nations, however, never recognized Indonesian sovereignty over East Timor and continued annually until 1982 to call for a "self-determination" referendum to decide the political fate of East Timor.[274]

Although Fretilin was defeated, its forces retreated to the rugged mountainous interior and continued to wage guerrilla warfare against Indonesia's "occupation forces." Indonesian counterinsurgency efforts proved especially brutal, as most native Timorese were eventually uprooted and moved into designated "strategic hamlets" that usually were ill-suited for agricultural production. Estimates of 100,000 to 200,000 deaths among a pre-war population of 650,000 highlighted the brutality of Indonesian rule and kept the East Timor question alive at the international level.[275]

Indonesian Rule in East Timor

Another Suharto strategy common to all the "Christian" areas of Indonesia that were seen as areas of potential separatist sentiment was to encourage internal Muslim transmigration. In East Timor, use of the Portuguese language was banned, and only Bahasa Indonesia could be used in government offices, schools, and public business. Only the Indonesian state school curriculum could be taught in schools, and appointed government positions were restricted to Indonesian speakers who possessed certificates denoting official *Pancasila* training. In due time, the former Portuguese-speaking Roman Catholic elite had been replaced by an Indonesian-speaking Muslim

---

[272] Taylor, *Indonesia*, 380.

[273] Virtual Information Center, East Timor Primer, updated 29 November 2004, 7–8. URL: *http://www. vic-info.org/RegionsTop.nsf/0/140323653b451c978a256aabb0002a3dc?OpenDocument*. Accessed April 4, 2005.

[274] Murphy, "Indonesia and the World," 253.

[275] Murphy, "Indonesia and the World," 253.

elite, mostly immigrants from elsewhere in the country who increasingly controlled the economic as well as the political life of East Timor.[276]

The imposition of Indonesian rule, however, had a contrary consequence. In order to meet the state's *Pancasila* requirement that all citizens subscribe to a monotheistic religion, the large majority, at least 80–85 percent, of East Timor's animists chose to register as Roman Catholics, a development the Catholic Church, through its Indonesian priesthood, aggressively sought to consolidate.[277] An impact of this change was that continuing government efforts to suppress the Fretilin-led insurgency was increasingly perceived internationally in religious terms, as Muslim persecution of Christians.

A particularly egregious event occurred in November 1991, when government troops pursued and fired upon a Christian funeral procession in the East Timor capital of Dili, killing more than 200 and injuring many more. Later called the "Santa Cruz Massacre," after the name of the cemetery toward which the mourners were marching, the incident was caught on film by international journalists and smuggled out of the country. The deceased had been a well-known pro-independence activist, and during the procession banners had appeared calling for independence and celebrating the Fretilin guerilla leader Xanana.[278] Government efforts to explain the episode as dealing with "an unacceptable infraction of public order" were belied, however, by the film images of Indonesian troops firing on unarmed, fleeing civilians, some trying unsuccessfully to save their lives by hiding behind gravestones.[279]

The Santa Cruz massacre brought the East Timor question back into the international spotlight. "The European Community condemned the event and within weeks the Dutch, Canadians and Danish governments had suspended aid programs to Indonesia. The facilitating role that U.S. weapons played in Indonesia's actions received great publicity, and Congress responded in 1992 by severely restricting Indonesia's access to American military education and training."[280] Leading the effort to publicize internationally the "hell" in which most East Timorese lived under Indonesian rule was Bishop Carlos Felipe Ximenes Belo of East Timor and Fretelin publicist (living in exile) Jose Ramos Horta, both of whom found themselves fêted for their courage by award of the Nobel Prize for Peace in 1996. Despite mounting international pressure to permit the long-demanded, UN-supervised referendum on self-determination in East Timor, Suharto remained firm in his determination to establish effective control of the "province." In 1997 the Army labeled its counterinsurgency campaign in East Timor "Operation Eradicate," and in 1998 "Operation Clean Sweep."[281]

---

[276] Taylor, *Indonesia*, 381.

[277] Taylor, *Indonesia*, 381.

[278] Later President of independent Timor Leste, José Alexeandre Gusmao.

[279] Friend, *Indonesian Destinies*, 275–276.

[280] Murphy, "Indonesia and the World," 256.

[281] Friend, *Indonesian Destinies*, 433–434.

A False Illusion

The 1997 Asian financial crisis and the consequent May 1998 collapse of the Suharto regime, however, posed many problems for Indonesia, including a grave weakening of central government authority. Under strong international pressure, successor President B.J. Hababie, "in a moment of inspiration" in January 1999, suddenly decided to relieve himself of the East Timor problem by agreeing to permit the UN-sponsored referendum. Arguing that the East Timorese would likely vote for autonomy under Indonesian sovereignty rather than independence, he sought to make the case domestically that such a referendum would resolve the East Timor question once and for all. In the unlikely event they did vote for independence, Indonesia would be rid of a problem that had drained its resources for far too long. In either case, the country would be better positioned to restore its relations with the international community that had become strained over the East Timor question. Privately, Habibie also seemed to believe that final resolution of the East Timor problem would enhance his stature politically and help to strengthen the likelihood of his being reelected President later in the year. How wrong he was became clear at the time of the October presidential elections, when his East Timor policy emerged as the major complaint of those parliamentarians voting against him.[282]

In accordance with Habibie's agreement, the first elements of the UN's International Force in East Timor (INTERFET) moved into its capital, Dili, on June 4, 1999, and the referendum took place on August 30. Despite efforts of the Army's Eastern Division Command, under Major General Zacky Anwar Makaram, to sabotage the referendum and eliminate leaders of the independence movement, both before and after the vote, an astonishing 98.5 percent of registered voters participated in the referendum, and 78.5 percent of them voted against autonomy, thereby beginning a process leading to independence for East Timor by the terms of the referendum.[283]

The overwhelming vote in favor of independence did not immediately ameliorate conditions in East Timor, however. Pro-Indonesian militia, acting in concert with army and police officials in the country, embarked on a reign of terror, burning towns and villages and displacing hundreds of thousands of East Timorese, forcing most to take refuge in West Timor. The continued efforts of hardline elements of the Indonesian armed forces and their East Timorese supporters to challenge the outcome of the referendum, despite the formal policy of the government, led the international community to force Indonesia to acquiesce in permitting a larger international force, the United Nations Transitional Administration for East Timor (UNTAET), to take charge of the administration of the country. This force took over from INTERFET in November 1999, enforced law and order, and administered East Timor until its transfer of sovereignty to an independent East Timor (Timor Leste) on May 20, 2002.

---

[282] B. William Liddle, "Indonesia in 1999: Democracy Restored," *Asian Affairs*, 40, 1 (January/February 2000), 37.
[283] Virtual Information Center, *East Timor Primer*, 9.

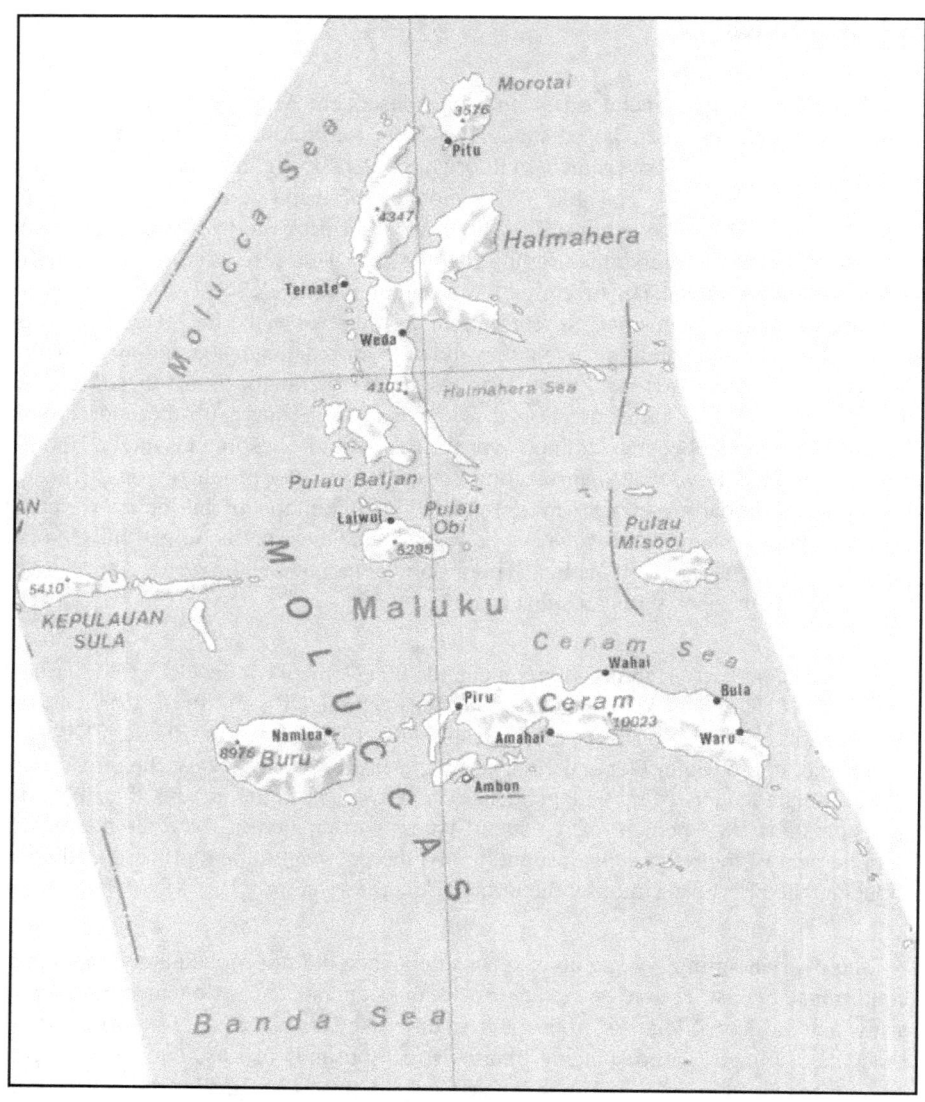

Map of the group of Indonesian islands known as Maluku.
Source: CIA.

Despite the official acquiescence of the Indonesian government to the loss of East Timor, the loss was perceived domestically as a national humiliation. That Timor was an integral part of Indonesia was the firm view of both the nationalist and Islamist wings of the Indonesian political spectrum. In the view of most, international determination to secure the independence of East Timor raised fears that the very unity of the Indonesian state was threatened. Similar movements in other parts of the country posed potential threats to this unity, or so many Indonesians believed.

MALUKU AND *LASKAR JIHAD*

The Indonesian province of Maluku in the far east of the archipelago consists of approximately 1,000 islands scattered over about 1.5 million sq. km. of area that constitutes the province. Called by the early European explorers and traders the "Spice Islands" because of the cloves, nutmeg, and mace that at the time were grown only there and were much in demand in Europe and elsewhere, they nonetheless are remote from the central government authority in Jakarta. Moreover, the province's relatively small population of two million constitutes less than one percent of Indonesia's total population. Economically, particularly the northern islands of Maluku together with neighboring Sulawesi to the west, are as much in the trading orbit of the southern Philippines, just to the north, as they are to the main Indonesian island of Java that holds 50 percent of Indonesia's population. Nevertheless, it was the Dutch rather than the Spanish who established monopoly control over trade with the Spice Islands, and Maluku was part of the Dutch empire that in 1950 was inherited by the newly established Indonesian government.

Culturally, Maluku also is highly diverse ethnically, inhabited by peoples speaking 129 languages.[284] Religiously, although Islam came first to the islands, which were and remain the site of several sultanates (Ternate, Tidore, Banda), the *sultans* ruled an ethnically diverse population, most of whose non-Muslim inhabitants became Christians during the period of Dutch rule. Prior to the violence that erupted in Maluku in 1999, Christians constituted approximately 40 percent of the total Maluku population, whereas Muslims made up about 59 percent.[285]

During the Suharto years, a government policy of encouraging Muslim transmigration, particularly from overpopulated Java to Maluku, strengthened the percentage of Muslims in the province, but the total number of approximately 100,000 Muslim transmigrants who settled there between 1969 and 1995 only strengthened the Muslim majority in the islands; it did not create it.[286] What did change during this period, however, was the relative status of Maluku's Christians. Ever fearful of the separatist tendencies demonstrated by the Christians of Maluku since the formation of the Republic, highlighted by the continued existence of a Republic of South Moluccas (RSM) government-in-exile in Holland, Suharto sought gradually to strengthen the Muslim demographic character of Maluku. He provided favorable economic and trade advantages to Muslim businessmen operating in Maluku and, with his shift in the early 1990s to mobilizing Muslim support for his regime, for the first time he appointed a

---

[284] Ethnologue.com, "Languages of Indonesia (Maluku)," URL: *http://www.ethnologue.com/ show_ country.asp?name=IDM.* Accessed November 8, 2005.

[285] Ambon Information Website, "Population and Religious Breakdown of Maluku," URL: *http:// www.websitesrcg.com/ambon/Malukupop.htm.* Accessed November 8, 2005. The data are from the 1995 Republic of Indonesia census. Data include a caveat that any person not claiming to belong to one of the five recognized religions (Muslim, Protestant, Catholic, Hindu, or Buddhist) is classified as Muslim. Seven-eighths of Maluku's Christians are Protestants, and about one-eighth are Roman Catholics.

[286] Ambon Information Website, "Transmigration into Maluku," URL: *http://www.websitesrcg. com/ ambon/Transmig.htm.* Accessed November 8, 2005.

local Muslim governor (Saleh Latuconsina) in Maluku's provincial capital, Ambon,[287] and through a kind of affirmative action program enabled more Muslims to obtain positions in the heretofore largely Christian-dominated provincial administration.[288]

These factors, along with the May 1998 collapse of the Suharto regime and the post-Suharto focus on the revival of democratic processes in Indonesia, perhaps also combined with the increasingly aggressive mood of many Indonesian Muslims, seem to have led many Maluku Christians to conclude that they were being marginalized in Indonesian society, even in their own Maluku homeland. Although historic communal tensions had tended to be local and associated with specific ethnic or village rivalries, general Muslim-Christian tension became apparent in the last months of 1998 and finally erupted into violence in January 1999. Sparked by a minor quarrel between a Christian bus driver and a Muslim immigrant passenger in the Maluku capital of Ambon on January 19, 1999, a holiday marking the end of Ramadhan, the Muslim month of fasting, the incident escalated into a major street brawl that quickly spread to other towns and villages throughout the province. Although no specific cause-and-effect relationship can be established, the outbreak of violence in Maluku coincided precisely with President B.J. Hababie's decision to permit a national self-determination referendum in East Timor-a decision that upset Muslim opinion in Indonesia but may have raised hopes among Christians for similar international intervention on their behalf in Maluku.

Evolution of the Crisis

Although at first perceived as a conflict between indigenous Ambonese and migrants, the conflict rapidly became a general one between Christians and Muslims in which attacks and counterattacks led to the burning of both churches and mosques. It was the burning of mosques by Christian gangs that especially outraged Muslim opinion and led others to join the Muslim transmigrant communities that were the initial victims of the Christian attacks.[289] Most sources agree that in the early stages of the conflict it was Christian groups that were on the offensive, with Muslim groups acting in retaliation or to defend their communities. Although a lull in the fighting occurred in June at the time of the national elections,[290] it quickly resumed and continued through the end of

---

[287] Previous appointments had been military officers. International Crisis Group (ICG), *Indonesia: Overcoming Murder and Chaos in Maluku*. ICG Asia Report No. 10, December 19, 2000, 2. URL: *http:// www.crisisgroup.org/library/documents/report_archive/A400320_19121999.pdf*. Accessed August 25, 2005.

[288] International Crisis Group (ICG), *Indonesia: The Search for Peace in Maluku*, ICG Asia Report No. 31, February 8, 2002, 2. URL: *http://www.crisisgroup.org/library/documents/report_archive/ A400544_08022002.pdf*. Accessed August 15, 2005.

[289] International Crisis Group, *Indonesia: The Search for Peace in Maluku*, 2. In a note the ICG reports that when similar attacks broke out on exactly the same day in West Kalimantan (Borneo), Muslim Malays had joined with the non-Muslim (Christian) Dayaks in attacks on Muslim Madurese transmigrants. Such conflicts were not inherently Christian-Muslim, therefore, but became so in Maluku.

[290] International Crisis Group, *Indonesia: Overcoming Murder and Chaos in Maluku*, 5.

the year, at which time official government data indicated that 775 people had been killed and 1,108 seriously wounded, while 8,665 houses, 115 churches and mosques, and 9,212 shops had been destroyed.[291]

More significant than these figures, however, was the flight (in 1999) of 276,446 (400-500,000 by the end of 2000) refugees, nearly all Muslim transmigrants, many returning to the home islands from which they had originated and others into hastily erected refugee camps on "safe" islands away from Maluku.[292] The aim of the hastily organized Christian militias was clearly "ethnic cleansing," ridding Maluku of as many Muslims as possible and staking out areas of territory that could be Christian strongholds, as opposed to Muslim stronghold areas that the latter were able to defend and cleanse of their Christian inhabitants.

Although vicious attacks were made by both sides, over time the Christian groups appeared to have gained the upper hand. Particularly high levels of violence erupted in the last week of December 1999, when Muslims burned the largest Protestant (Silo) church in Ambon, and partially in retaliation Christians in northern Halmahera island "cleansed" the Muslim Tobelo district of 10,000 inhabitants, killing an estimated 400 or more in the process.[293]

Until this point, the fighting in Maluku was confined primarily to the inhabitants of the province. The Tobelo massacre, however, coming as it did in the wake of the humiliating loss of East Timor in late 1999, stirred emotions throughout the country. On January 7, 2000, over 100,000 Muslims in Jakarta held an angry demonstration calling for a *jihad* for the purpose of saving the Muslims of Maluku. Many senior Indonesian political figures, including Amien Rais, Speaker of the Parliament and leader of the Muhammadiyah-based PAN political party, spoke and expressed support for the demands of the demonstrators. By the end of the month, various fighters labeling themselves *Laskar Mujahidin* began arriving in northern Maluku in direct response to the Tobelo Massacre. These fighters were having little impact on the situation, however.[294]

Arrival of *Laskar Jihad*

In April 2000, a dramatic development was the sudden public appearance of a newly organized Muslim militia calling itself *Laskar Jihad*. Organized and led by an ascetic Indonesian cleric of Yemeni (Hadramati) origin, Jaffar Umar Thalib, yet

---

[291] International Crisis Group, *Indonesia: The Search for Peace in Maluku*, 2.

[292] International Crisis Group, *Indonesia: Overcoming Murder and Chaos in Maluku*, 26.

[293] International Crisis Group, *Indonesia: Overcoming Murder and Chaos in Maluku*, 8.

[294] International Crisis Group, *Indonesia: Overcoming Murder and Chaos in Maluku*, 8.

another veteran of the war in Afghanistan,[295] *Laskar Jihad* received support from wealthy Indonesian benefactors, including elements of the Indonesian military.[296] Opening recruiting centers in each of Indonesia's 26 provinces, the new militia rapidly emerged as a vehicle for mobilizing popular support for a "peoples' war" in defense of the Muslims of Maluku that the armed forces of the country seemed incapable of doing. Training camps were organized at Jogjakarta and on Bogor Island, and on April 6, 2000, a massive rally was conducted at a large sports stadium in Jakarta, in which thousands of *Laskar Jihad* members participated. The culmination of the rally was a march from the stadium to the presidential palace, where Thalib, accompanied by thousands of supporters carrying rifles and machetes and dressed in flowing white, Arab-style *thobes*, demanded a meeting with President Abdurrahman Wahid. Agreeing to see the militia leader, Wahid reportedly exchanged angry words with him in a five-minute meeting that ended with the President abruptly dismissing him from his office and issuing an order for the army to close down the Bogor Island training camp.[297] Thalib responded by publicly announcing that 3,000 *Laskar Jihad* fighters would be departing Surabaya (East Java) for Maluku on April 29 and 30, in effect challenging the government to stop him. Despite the President's order that Indonesian security forces prevent the militia from embarking for Maluku, his order was ignored, and the first elements of *Laskar Jihad* departed Surabaya as scheduled.[298] More followed in subsequent weeks.

The arrival of the *Laskar Jihad* in Ambon had the effect of quickly changing the balance of power in Maluku. By mid-June they had joined local Muslim groups in offensives against Christian positions and reportedly were receiving the support of certain military units.[299] One reason Indonesia's formal security institutions heretofore had been unable to contain the violence in Maluku was that they were not large, most were locally recruited, and units were confessionally mixed. Christians constituted

---

[295] International Crisis Group, *Indonesia: Overcoming Murder and Chaos in Maluku*, 9. Although most reports, including this one, identify Thalib as an Afghan war veteran, the International Crisis Group in its later 2003 study of the Indonesian veterans (*Jemaah Islamiyah: Damaged but Still Dangerous*) does not include him among its list of those who received training in the Pakistani/Afghan training camps. Certainly he claimed to have done so, and also that he had personal relations with Usama bin Ladin. Given that *Laskar Jihad* later emerged as a rival organization of *Jemaah Islamiyah*, and that Thalib often referred to bin Ladin as a "bad" Muslim who did not have a true understanding of Islam, his experience as an "Afghan" jihadi certainly led him on a different path than those associated with *Jemaah Islamiyah*.

[296] Elements of Indonesian military reportedly provided Thalib with at least $9.3 million to help him start up and organize *Laskar Jihad*. Ressa, *Seeds of Terror*, 91, 93.

[297] International Crisis Group (ICG), *Indonesia's Maluku Crisis: The Issues*, ICG Indonesia Briefing Paper. Jakarta/Brussels, July 19, 2000, 2–3. URL: *http://www.crisisgroup.org/library/documents/report_archive/A400113_19072000.pdf*. Accessed September 3, 2005.

[298] International Crisis Group, *Indonesia: The Search for Peace in Maluku*, 6. By chance, an American journalist, Tracy Dahlby of *Newsweek International*, on May 22, 2000, boarded the inter-island passenger liner *M.V. Bukit Siguntang* that was carrying Thalib and several hundred of the *Laskar Jihad* fighters as it stopped to take on new passengers for Ambon at Makassar, Sulawesi. For an account of his observations, see his *Allah's Torch: A Report from Behind the Scenes in Asia's War on Terror* (New York: Harper-Collins Publishers, 2005), 11–61.

[299] International Crisis Group, *Indonesia: The Search for Peace in Maluku*, 7.

approximately 70 percent of the local police forces, whereas military units were nearly evenly divided between Muslims and Christians. Both tended to be emotionally involved in the conflict, and their officers tended to remain aloof from the conflict in order to avoid a breakdown of discipline and authority in the security services.[300] Notably, among the first attacks by the new *Laskar Jihad* forces was one on the elite Police Mobile Brigade in downtown Ambon, designed to go directly at the heart of Christian strength in Maluku.[301]

The Government Reasserts Ascendancy

By late June 2000, the tide had turned, and it was now Christian groups that were on the defensive and being made refugees. At this point, on June 26, President Wahid who, up to this time had resisted calls to establish martial law-primarily to keep the army from regaining lost political influence-placed Maluku (which in 1999 had been divided into two provinces[302]) under a state of "civil emergency."[303] The declaration had no immediate impact on the situation, however, as the *Laskar Jihad* offensive against Christian enclaves continued.[304] Only after the arrival on August 9 of a specially created 450-man Joint Battalion (*Yon Gab*) consisting of special forces personnel from the army, navy, and marines did government forces gradually take control of the situation. They did so, however, by clashing primarily with *Laskar Jihad* and other Muslim elements, thus opening up the government to charges that it, and particularly President Wahid, was aligned with the Christian side of the conflict.

Despite relative government success in imposing security in Maluku by the end of 2000, tensions remained high and sporadic attacks by *Laskar Jihad* on Christian enclaves in and around Ambon continued during 2001.[305] A result of the violence of the previous two years was a clear division of especially southern Maluku into mutually hostile enclaves, where inhabitants of each were unable to travel safely through the other. Under such circumstances, despite an overall diminution of violence, the temporary civil emergency government was unable to take legal action against individuals on either side well known to be responsible for various atrocities during the previous two years. Without such action, efforts to arrange even an informal cease-fire, much less reconciliation talks, foundered. Meanwhile, Thalib and other *Laskar Jihad* leaders traveled freely throughout various parts of Indonesia, giving press and television interviews and addressing mosque congregations. Taking credit for rescuing the Muslims of Maluku from massacre by Christians and for saving Maluku from the

---

[300] International Crisis Group, *Indonesia: The Search for Peace in Maluku*, 4.

[301] Ressa, *Seeds of Terror*, 92.

[302] A more Muslim northern province called North Maluku, and a more Christian southern province called South Maluku. International Crisis Group, *Indonesia: The Search for Peace in Maluku*, 1.

[303] A state of civil emergency, which placed military forces in the provinces under the authority of the provincial governors, was a step just short of martial law, which Wahid was loath to declare. International Crisis Group, *Indonesia: The Search for Peace in Maluku*, 8.

[304] For details, see International Crisis Group, *Indonesia: The Search for Peace in Maluku*, 8–10.

[305] For details, see International Crisis Group, *Indonesia: The Search for Peace in Maluku*, 12–13.

fate of East Timor, they were sharply critical of the government both for its relative inaction as well as its protection of the Christians of Maluku.[306]

In an effort to break the impasse, the civil emergency government on April 30, 2001, arrested Alexander Manuputty, the Christian leader of the Maluku Sovereignty Front (FKM — *Front Kedanlatan Maluku*). The arrest was in response to an April 25 FKM ceremony recognizing the anniversary of the 1950 declaration of Moluccan independence by the Republic of South Moluccas (RSM). In a clear effort to capture international attention, both the United Nations and RSM flags had been raised, the latter still being an illegal act in Indonesia. Although there was no suggestion that the Christian leader had been involved in violent action against Muslims in Maluku, Manuputty was subsequently sentenced to four months in prison for his offense. Most observers agreed, however, that the arrest of Maluku's most prominent Christian leader was in fact done as a prelude to the arrest of *Laskar Jihad* leader Jaffar Umar Thalib, which it did a few days later, on May 4.[307]

The arrest of Thalib had the impact of transforming him into a controversial, but nevertheless national, hero, further undercutting President Wahid's hold on political power. The Muslim political parties-PPP, PBB, PAN, and PK (Justice Party)-all issued formal protests of his arrest, as did most of the leading Muslim organizations, such as the DDII and KISDI (Committee for Islamic Global Solidarity). Under intense political pressure, the government released Thalib from prison on May 15, and on June 12 he was released from house arrest, although the charges against him were not lifted. Thalib immediately became a prominent television celebrity, denouncing the government for its weakness in the face of the "international Christian-Jewish conspiracy" against Islam in general and Indonesia in particular. Without the intervention of *Laskar Jihad*, he argued, the fate of Maluku would have been the same as for East Timor.[308] The very success of *Laskar Jihad* highlighted the relative impotence of the government and contributed to the impeachment process against President Abdurrahman Wahid, led by PPP leader Hamzah Haz, that reached its conclusion on July 23. Named Vice President in the successor government of President Megawati Sukarnoputri, Haz demonstrated the new government's support for *Laskar Jihad* by officially receiving Thalib in his vice presidential office on August 8.

Close-down of *Laskar Jihad*

The July 2001 change of government in Jakarta did not greatly ameliorate the situation in Maluku that continues to remain tense until today. The intensity of the fighting that had characterized the region since early 1999, however, markedly declined. Feeling confident of its "victory," *Laskar Jihad* increasingly focused on

---

[306] International Crisis Group, *Indonesia: The Search for Peace in Maluku*, 14.
[307] International Crisis Group, *Indonesia: The Search for Peace in Maluku*, 15.
[308] International Crisis Group, Indonesia: The Search for Peace in Maluku, 16

religious, educational, and social welfare activities that it claimed had always been the central aspect of its mission. Its members continued to be prepared for military conflict, however, and the continuing presence of *Laskar Jihad*, particularly in the southern Maluku capital of Ambon, remained a primary source of continuing tension in the islands.[309]

Following the September 2001 *al-Qa'ida* attacks in the United States, the question immediately arose, particularly in the United States, concerning the possible connections between *al-Qa'ida* and *Laskar Jihad*. Thalib's history as a veteran of the war in Afghanistan and evidence of visits by "Middle Eastern-looking men" to *Laskar Jihad* locations in Maluku raised natural suspicions. Although Thalib admitted he had been offered financial assistance by *al-Qa'ida*, he adamantly asserted that he had not accepted such assistance and took pains to dissociate himself from *al-Qa'ida* leader Usama bin Ladin, whom he labeled as being "very empty about the knowledge of religion."[310] At the same time, he made use of his television celebrity to sharply condemn U.S. military actions in Afghanistan, a stance guaranteed to make him perceived by the U.S. administration as a supporter of Usama bin Ladin.

Laskar Jihad remained a highly visible militant Islamic organization operating primarily in Maluku, but also in Papua and Sulawesi, until the October 12, 2002, *Jemaah Islamiyah*-sponsored terrorist bomb attack in Bali. Four days later, Thalib announced the disbanding of the organization and of his intent to return to teaching and writing. A highly publicized withdrawal of 300 *Laskar Jihad* fighters from Ambon followed, but it was widely understood that many had elected to stay behind. A new outbreak of Christian-Muslim violence in Ambon in April 2004 revealed that these had morphed into at least two local organizations—*Forum Pemuda Muslim Baguala* and *Pemuda Reformasi Maluku*.[311] The parent organization of *Laskar Jihad, Forum Kommunikasi wal Sunnah wal Jummah*, moreover, continued to exist and operate with offices in at least 70 cities throughout Indonesia.[312] As a formal, centrally organized militia, however, *Laskar Jihad* had ceased to exist.

SULAWESI AND *JEMAAH ISLAMIYAH*

Even before the May 2000 arrival of *Laskar Jihad* fighters in Maluku, other fighters labeling themselves *Laskar Mujahidin* had made their appearance. Unlike the *Laskar Jihad* organization that numbered at least 3,000 almost from the beginning and operated with great publicity, the *Laskar Mujahidin* in Maluku never numbered

---

[309] International Crisis Group, Indonesia: The Search for Peace in Maluku, 18.

[310] International Crisis Group, Indonesia: The Search for Peace in Maluku, 19. Cf. Abuza, Militant Islam in Southeast Asia, 71, and Ressa, Seeds of Terror, 94.

[311] International Crisis Groups, *Violence Erupts Again in Maluku*, ISG Asia Briefing, Jakarta/Brussels, May 17, 2004, 2. URL: *http://www.crisisgroup.org/library/documents/asia/indonesia/ 040517_indonesia_ violence_erupts_again_in_ambon.pdf*. Accessed July 15, 2005.

[312] Abuza, *Militant Islam in Southeast Asia*, 72.

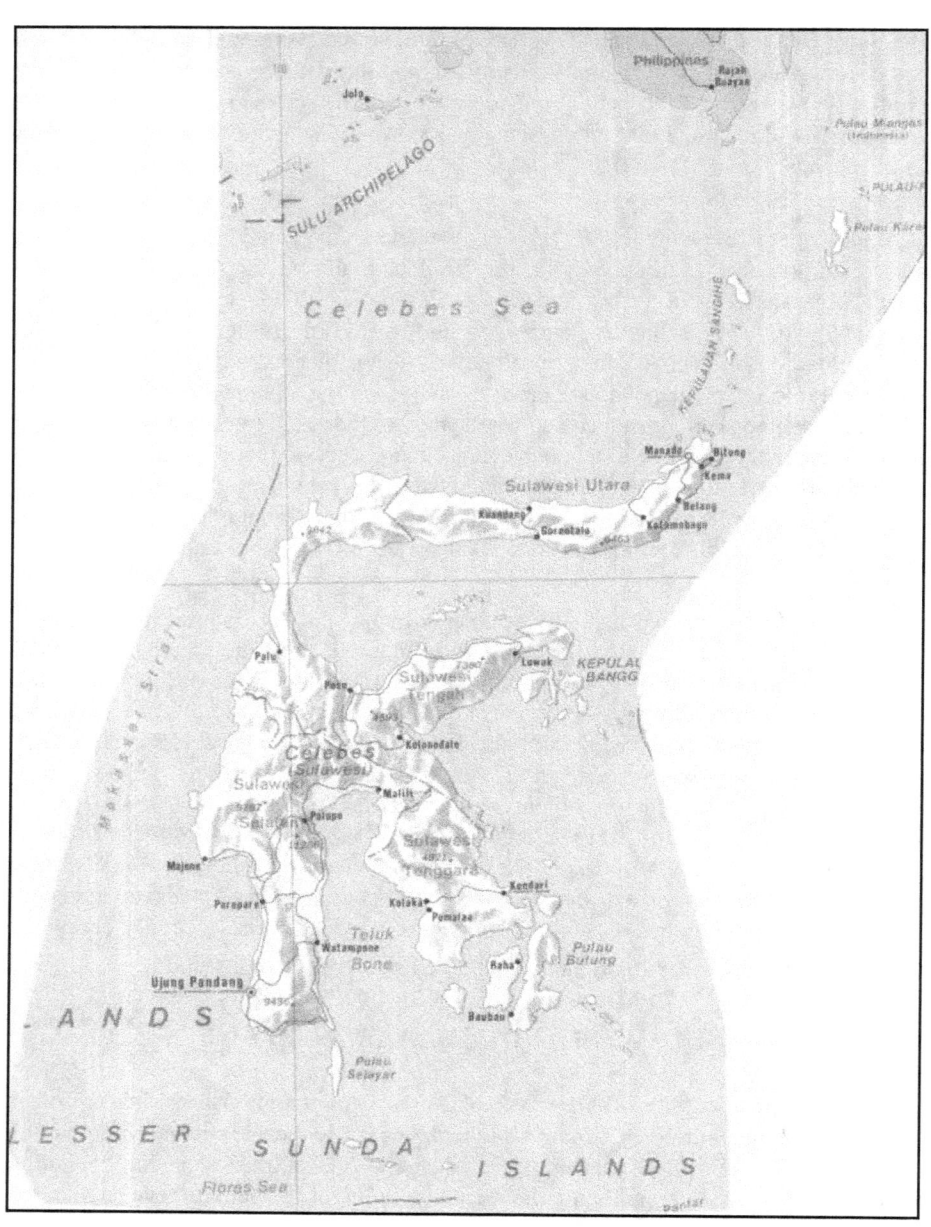

Map of Sulawesi.
Source: CIA.

more than 200 and operated in great secrecy.[313] Dressed in black and often wearing masks, they were popularly called "ninjas" in contrast to the *Laskar Jihad* fighters who wore flowing white, Saudi-like *thobes*. Moreover, whereas *Laskar Jihad* engaged in sometimes well-organized direct and indirect attacks on Christian positions, the *Laskar Mujahidin* engaged solely in guerrilla operations-bombings, assassinations, and sabotage. Despite assertions by some observers that the *mujahidin* were mainly absorbed by the *Laskar Jihad* after its arrival in Malaku, the two groups were in fact rival organizations that, although they may have had parallel goals, pursued different strategy and tactics.[314]

The *Laskar Mujahidin*, it later became clear, was in part the creation of Abdullah Sungkar's *Jemaah Islamiyah*, and more particularly of a collaborating individual, Abu Dzar (Haris Fadillah-killed in battle on October 26, 2000 in Siri-Sori Islam, Saparua [Maluku]).[315] Still a clandestine organization (until revelation of its existence as a result of the December 2001 arrests of some of its members in Singapore), *Jemaah Islamiyah*, unlike *Laskar Jihad*, continued to conceal its existence. The *Laskar Mujahidin*, therefore, remained a very mysterious group until more knowledge about it emerged at a later date.

Return of *Jemaah Islamiyah*

Following the May 1998 fall of the Suharto regime, *Jemaah Islamiyah* leaders Abdullah Sungkar and Abu Bakar Ba'asyir, taking note of the increasingly chaotic political conditions in Indonesia, decided to return to Pondok Ngruki, which they did apparently in early 1999. Sometime after his return, Sungkar, believing that the time was ripe for a commitment to armed struggle (*jihad*), met with Achmed Roihan, one of the Mantiqi II leaders, and reportedly queried him why such an armed struggle had not yet begun. The meeting revealed a fracture in *Jemaah Islamiyah* between the

---

[313] International Crisis Group, *Indonesia: The Search for Peace in Maluku*, 20.

[314] International Crisis Group (ICG), *Indonesia Backgrounder: How the Jemaah Islamiyah Terrorist Newtork Operates*, IGC Asia Report No. 43, Jakarta/Brussels, December 11, 2002, 20. URL:*http://www.crisisgroup.org/library/documents/report_archive/A400845_11122002.pdf*. Accessed October 11, 2005.

[315] Not a member of *Jemaah Islamiyah*, but of the also underground *Darul Islam* movement, Fadillah is now best known as the father of Mira Augustine, the wife of the alleged Kuwaiti-born *al-Qa'ida* member, Omar al-Farouk (Mahmud bin Ahmad Assegaf). International Crisis Group, *Jihad in Central Sulawesi*, 5–6. Arrested by Indonesian authorities in Bogor on June 5, 2002, and immediately deported to the newly established U.S.-controlled air base in Bagram, Afghanistan, Farouk was a key *al-Qa'ida* operative who had been dispatched with others from Afghanistan in October 1994 by *al-Qa'ida* leader Abu Zubayda to establish a *Jemaah Islamiyah* training camp, Camp Hudaybiyah, within the confines of the Moro Islamic Liberation Front (MILF) Camp Abu Bakar. See Romesh Ratnesar, "Confessions of an Al-Qaeda Terrorist," *Time*, September 3, 2002, 35–37, and below, Chapter 6, 209. Later, in 1998, Farouk was transferred to Indonesia, where he married the daughter of Abu Dzar. In July 2005, Farouk and others made a daring escape from the prison in Bagram. Farouk was believed killed by British forces in Basra (Iraq) on September 25, 2006. Amit R. Paley, "Al-Qaeda Figure Killed in Raid in Basra, British Military Says," in *The Washington Post*, September 26, 2006, A16.

more idealistic stance of those who had been in exile in Malaysia (Mantiqi I) and the more pragmatic realism of those who had remained home in Indonesia (Mantiqi II). Roihan replied that human resources were insufficient and that further recruitment, education, and training were required for *Jemaah Islamiyah* to move into a phase of armed struggle. Sungkar allegedly replied that the time was currently ripe, and it was necessary to act now.[316]

Soon after this encounter, in June 1999, an operational meeting of about 20 *Jemaah Islamiyah* leaders was convened in Solo to discuss the developing crisis in Maluku. The meeting was conducted by *Jemaah Islamiyah* chief of military operations Zulkarnaen. A number of those present reportedly criticized Mantiqi II leader Abu Fatih for his slowness and bureaucratic approach to taking action. A key result of the meeting was the dispatch of Zulkarnaen and several other Afghan veterans, all associated with Mantiqi I, to Maluku. The *Jemaah Islamiyah* group did not conceptualize its mission as fighting, however, but rather as training. Calling down a number of *Jemaah Islamiyah* fighters posted in the Moro Islamic Liberation Front (MILF) training camps on the Philippine island of Mindanao, the first *Jemaah Islamiyah* action was to establish a three-month training course on Buru Island for local men and other volunteers desirous of confronting the more effectively organized local Christian militias.[317]

Most of this eclectic group of fighters was grouped under the name of another organization, Mujahidin KOMPAK (*Komite Aksi Penanggulangan Akibat Krisis*/Action Committee for Crisis Response). KOMPAK was a Muslim charitable organization established in 1998 by the DDII "to assist Muslims affected by natural disasters, conflict, and poverty."[318] With the development of the crisis in Maluku, and possibly that in East Timor as well, one KOMPAK branch leader in Solo, Arismanandar, a 1989 graduate of Pondok Ngruki, organized Mujahidin KOMPAK, a subordinate militia group initially composed of impatient *Jemaah Islamiyah* members dissatisfied with the inaction of the Mantiqi II leadership. Technically separate from *Jemaah Islamiyah*, the distinction was at first more artificial than real, probably reflecting the continuing clandestine nature of *Jemaah Islamiyah* and its policy of not revealing its existence. The confusion is compounded by the fact that in training the militia was called *Mujahidin* KOMPAK under the leadership of Arismandar, whereas when fighting it was known as *Laskar Mujahidin* under the leadership of Abu Dzar.

In the serious battles in Maluku during the summer and fall of 2000, however, the *Laskar Mujahidin* forces were totally overshadowed by those of *Laskar Jihad*, and by the autumn the two groups had fallen into conflict, a conflict that reflected struggles

---

[316] International Crisis Group, *Jihad* in Central Sulawesi, 3. Citing the May 9, 2003, interrogation disposition of Roihan, ICG Asia Report No. 74. February 3, 2004. URL: *http://www.crisisgroup.org/ library/documents/asia/indonesia/074_jihad_in_central_sulawesi_mod.pdf*. Accessed October 14, 2005.
[317] International Crisis Group, *Jihad in Central Sulawesi*, 4–5.
[318] International Crisis Group, *Jihad in Central Sulawesi*, 4.

over turf and leadership as well as ideological differences.[319] The hegemony of *Laskar Jihad* appears to have led *Jemaah Islamiyah/Laskar Mujahidin* to fall back on Poso in neighboring Central Sulawesi as its main base of operations. Another reason for this focus on Poso was the fall in July 2000 of the MILF Camp Abu Bakar in Mindanao to the Philippine Armed Forces. The fall of Camp Abu Bakar, which for several years had hosted *Jemaah Islamiyah* Camp Hudaibiyah and *al-Qa'ida* Camps Palestine and Vietnam, meant that Mindanao no longer provided a safe haven for Indonesian and other foreign *mujahidin*. Significant numbers of *Jemaah Islamiyah* and also *al-Qa'ida* trainees began to flow back to Indonesia in the summer and fall of 2002, many of them flowing to a new safe haven (*al-Qa'ida al-'aminah*) in the rapidly growing *Jemaah Islamiyah/Laskar Mujahidin* camp in the mountainous jungles near Poso.[320]

Strategic Importance of Sulawesi

Geographically, the island of Sulawesi is the natural logistical, supply, and trading route between the southern Philippines and Indonesia, either indirectly via ports in East Kalimantan or directly through ports in northern Sulawesi.[321] Probably for this reason the *Jemaah Islamiyah* had included Sulawesi as well as all of Borneo along with the southern Philippines in Mantiqi III, which it had created in 1997. Northern Sulawesi, however, is a largely Christian area, whereas Southern Sulawesi is primarily Muslim, while Central Sulawesi-the Palu-Poso corridor that cuts through the middle of the island-is a mixed Muslim-Christian region, and Poso, on the east coast of Sulawesi, is a natural jumping-off point for supporting military operations in Maluku. Like Maluku, although Christians and Muslims in Sulawesi had lived harmoniously for centuries, following the collapse of the Suharto regime in May 1998, outbreaks of Christian-Muslim violence in central Sulawesi had become increasingly common. Unlike Maluku, however, there was no discernible separatist movement among the Christians of Sulawesi. The central issues centered around land disputes and competition among the militias of various contending political strongmen, but also resentment toward the large number of recent transmigrants from other parts of Indonesia, especially Java, that had settled in Sulawesi with the encouragement of the Suharto regime.[322]

---

[319] International Crisis Group, *Jihad in Central Sulawesi*, 6. The IGC report notes that the primary difference was that, whereas the *Jemaah Islamiyah*-affiliated militia rejected the legitimacy of the Indonesian state, *Laskar Jihad* saw the purpose of *jihad*, particularly in Malaku, was solely to defend the state against Christian separatists.

[320] International Crisis Group, *Damaged but Still Dangerous*, 23.

[321] On the regional transportation networks, see International Crisis Group, *How the Jemaah Islamiyah Terrorist Network Works*, 18–19.

[322] Human Rights Watch, *Indonesia: Breakdown: Four Years of Communal Violence in Sulawesi*, III, Part One: Context, Causes and Laskar Jihad, 14, 9 (December 2002). URL: *http://www.hrw.org/ reports/2002/ indonesia/indonesia1102–03#TopOfPage*. Accessed November 30, 2005.

Splits Within *Jemaah Islamiyah*

The *Jemaah Islamiyah* buildup in the Poso district in late 2000 coincided with yet another outbreak of Christian-Muslim conflict in which *Jemaah Islamiyah/Laskar Mujahidin* fighters gradually involved themselves, rapidly translating the conflict into a more purely religious one (*jihad*). The escalating conflict in Central Sulawesi at this time also exposed significant divisions within *Jemaah Islamiyah* ranks. The split was basically between *Jemaah Islamiyah*'s trainers and the locally raised *Mujahidin* KOMPAC and other trainees. The former insisted on a relatively long training period (at least three months) that involved large amounts of religious (ideological) instruction designed to produce "educated mujahidin" (*mujahadin tertarbiyah*) with sound understanding of the religious basis of *jihad* as well as the military skills to wage it. The local recruits wanted only military training. Their general attitude was expressed by one source as "Enough Quran reading, where's the war?"[323]

The situation was made even more complex by the appearance of other separate groups that emerged at this time to engage in the conflict in Central Sulawesi. In its report, the International Crisis Group identified at least ten different groups, in addition to *Jemaah Islamiyah*, that were active, sometimes in cooperation and at other times in competition and even conflict with one another.[324] The successful example of *Laskar Jihad* in Maluku, which also appeared in Sulawesi in July 2001, clearly had an impact on the popular imagination of others who sought to be part of the action. The total impact of this complex situation on *Jemaah Islamiyah* was to limit its recruiting efforts and to marginalize it as only one of a number of Islamist groups operating in Central Sulawesi.

Transformation of *Jemaah Islamiyah*

Jemaah Islamiyah was also impacted by another split within its ranks at this time. In November 1999, *Jemaah Islamiyah* leader Abdullah Sungkar died soon after his return from Malaysia to Pondok Ngruki in Solo. He was immediately succeeded by his lifelong friend and colleague, Abu Bakar Ba'asyir. Ba'asyir's assumption of the leadership was opposed, however, by some of the younger, more militant leaders of the group who viewed Ba'asyir as "too weak, too accommodating, and too easily influenced by others" and not suitable to continue the legacy of Sungkar.[325] Among those opposing Ba'asyir included *Jemaah Islamiyah* operations chief Riduan Isamuddin (Hambali), Abdul Aziz (Imam Samudra), Ali Gufron (Mukhlas), and others, all soon to be involved in the planning and conduct of significant terrorist operations in Indonesia. The split was only aggravated in August 2000, when Ba'asyir and other Islamist leaders convened the first meeting of a new organization, the *Majelis Mujahidin Indonesia* (MMI-

---

[323] International Crisis Group, *Jihad* in Central Sulawesi, 8.
[324] International Crisis Group, *Jihad in Central Sulawesi*, 11.
[325] International Crisis Group, *How the Jemaah Islamiyah Terrorist Network Works*, 3.

Congress of Indonesian *Mujahidin*), in Jogjakarta that was attended by approximately 1,500 individuals.[326] Clearly an attempt by Ba'asyir and the other Islamist leaders to forge a measure of unity among the proliferating number of radical Islamic groups that were springing up in the country in the post-Suharto era, the *Jemaah Islamiyah* radicals opposed Ba'asyir's leadership role in this new organization on the grounds that it betrayed Sungkar's position that the movement should remain underground "until the time was ripe to move toward an Islamic state." Ba'asyir's view, on the other hand, was that the post-Suharto political environment made it necessary for Islamic leaders to participate in the political process to achieve this same end.[327]

Jemaah Islamiyah Launches Operations

It was just at this time, on August 1, 2000, that the *Jemaah Islamiyah* radicals carried out their first terrorist operation in Indonesia, a bombing of the residence of the Philippine ambassador in Jakarta. Done in apparent retaliation for the Philippine government's closure of MILF Camp Abu Bakar in Mindanao in July, the operation was clearly put together on short notice. Although ordered by Hambali, still in Malaysia, it was carried out under the supervision of Fathur Rahman al-Ghozi, Indonesian head of *Jemaah Islamiyah*'s Camp Hudaybiyah within Camp Abu Bakar, who travelled to Jakarta in late July for this purpose.[328] At the time a totally unattributed event, it appeared possibly to have been a Philippine MILF action. Mysteriousness was to remain a characteristic of *Jemaah Islamiyah* terrorist operations until the uncovering of the organization in Singapore in December 2001.

The attack on the Philippine ambassador was just a warm-up for the major *Jemaah Islamiyah* terrorist operation yet to come-the Christmas Eve 2000, nearly simultaneous, bombings of 38 churches or parsonages in 11 Indonesian cities across the country, resulting in 19 deaths and 120 wounded.[329] Again, at the time a wholly unattributed event, given the continuing Muslim-Christian violence in Maluku and Central Sulawesi, the attacks had the appearance of widening the conflict to include all Christians in Indonesia. In fact, the attacks probably were more motivated by an effort to demonstrate the presence in Indonesia of a large, well-organized underground organization capable of taking actions that no other Islamist group could do.

---

[326] Peter Symonds, "The Political Origins and Outlook of Jemaah Islamiyah," *World Socialist Web Site*, November 12, 2003,.Part 3, 3. URL: *http://www.wsws.org/articles/2003/nov2003/ji3-n14_prn.shtml*. Accessed February 20, 2005. Also International Crisis Group, Ngruki Network, 17.

[327] International Crisis Group, *How the Jemaah Islamiyah Terrorist Network Works*, 3.

[328] For details, see International Crisis Group, *Southern Philippines Backgrounder*, 18. The report notes that there had been an earlier, failed effort to bomb churches in Medan (Sumatra) in May 2000. Ghozi returned to the Philippines in October and began organizing a second operation-five nearly simultaneous explosions in Manila on December 30, 2000, the so-called Rizal Day bombings. See Chapter 6, ...65....

[329] The Christmas Eve bombings are the primary subject of the entire study of the International Crisis Group, *How the Jemaah Islamiyah Terrorist Network Works*.

Formation of *Laskar Jundallah*

Despite the efforts of the *Jemaah Islamiyah* radicals to expand the conflict and to assert their own leadership of the Islamist movement in Indonesia, for most the attention remained focused on Maluku and Central Sulawesi. In an apparent effort to counter the influence of the *Jemaah Islamiyah* radicals, in September 2000 yet another militia, the *Laskar Jundallah,* was established with headquarters in the southern Sulawesi city of Makassar (Ujung Pandang). Raised primarily from among the Muslims of southern Sulawesi, its founder was Agus Dwikarna, who recently had been chosen general secretary of the *Majelis Mujahidin Indonesia* (MMI) at its founding meeting in August. Not a known member of *Jemaah Islamiyah,* Dwikarna was nevertheless a close associate of Abu Bakar Ba'asyir and served at this time as head of the Makassar branch of the charitable organization KOMPAK.[330] Seen in hindsight, the establishment of *Laskar Jundallah* appears to have been an effort by Ba'asyir, working through Dwikarna, to assert his own authority over the *Jemaah Islamiyah* radicals who opposed his leadership.[331] Originally conceptualized as a kind of religious police that would enforce Islamic law among the Muslims of Sulawesi rather than to fight against Christians,[332] it soon emerged as yet another militia engaged in the conflict in Central Sulawesi.

Laskar Jundallah's role in the fighting would be postponed until mid-2001, however. Following the government's arrest in late July 2000 of Christian militia leader Fabianus Tibo,[333] and the arrival of augmented government security forces, violence in Central Sulawesi diminished significantly over the next year, until a new outbreak of fighting in June 2001.[334] In the meantime, *Laskar Jundallah* recruits engaged in training with *Laskar Mujahadin* and *Mujahidin* KOMPAK at their joint training camp located at

---

[330] For details on Dwikarna, see International Crisis Group, *How the Jemaah Islamiyah Terrorist Network Works*, 31.

[331] Dwikarna appears to have used funds from *al-Qa'ida,* distributed to him through Omar al-Farouk, to establish *Laskar Jundallah,* but soon came to distrust the Arabs who sought to impose a model for *jihad* that was "inappropriate" for Indonesia. International Crisis Group, *Damaged but Still Dangerous*, 15.

[332] International Crisis Group, *How the Jemaah Islamiyah Terrorist Network Works*, 21.

[333] Tibo (age 57 in 2001) was a Catholic immigrant from Flores who emerged as a leader of a particularly violent, largely Protestant, Christian militia. On May 28, 2000, he allegedly led a bloody attack on the Muslim Wali Songo Pesantren (school) in Poso in which, Muslim sources said, 191 students were killed (although only 39 bodies were ever discovered). It was for his leadership of this massacre that he and two others were finally arrested on July 25. His trial in the early months of 2001 stirred passions on both sides and was a contributing factor to renewed Christian-Muslim fighting that erupted again in Central Sulawesi in June 2001. For details, see Human Rights Watch, *Indonesia: Breakdown: Four Years of Communal Violence in Sulawesi, IV, Part Two: Chronology of the Conflict.* Study edited by the staff of Human Rights Watch, 14, 9 (December 2002), 4–9. URL: *http://www.hrw.org/reports/indonesia/ indonesia1102-04.htmTopOfPage.* Accessed November 30, 2005.

[334] International Crisis Group, *Jihad in Central Sulawesi,* 13–14.

Pendola, Pamona Selatan, Poso,[335] apparently with the aim of asserting Dwikarna's (and Ba'asyir's) authority over the *mujahidin* effort.

Enter *Laskar Jihad*

Following the sentencing of Tibo and two of his associates to death in April 2001 and the failure of their appeal in May, violence again erupted in June. A particularly inflammatory event was the brutal murder of 14 Muslims, mostly women and children, by Christian militiamen in the hamlet of Buyung Katedo during the early morning of July 3. This led to general fighting which even government forces were unable to quell. The volatile situation led Jafar Umar Thalib to order about 150 of his *Laskar Jihad* from Maluku to "save the situation" in Poso, who arrived in late July. Although small in number, they were well-armed with automatic weapons and, as had been the case in Maluku a year before, government security forces did nothing to prevent their activities. Arriving publicly with great fanfare, the *Laskar Jihad* presence "reinvigorated the conflict and the sporadic attacks increasingly took the form of organized assaults that leveled entire villages."[336]

Laskar Jihad's effort to take command of the situation quickly brought it into conflict with both the *Jemaah Islamiyah* forces[337] as well as government security forces.[338] Although the conflict with the former did not result in fighting, *Laskar Jihad* efforts to demonstrate the incompetence of the *Jemaah Islamiyah* parties led to confrontations and name-calling. Conflict with the security forces beginning in October 2001 did lead to bloodshed, casualties, and arrests, apparently due to heightened government efforts to assert its authority following the September 11 *al-Qa'ida* attacks in the United States. Government efforts to contain *Laskar Jihad*, however, led the Islamic militia to engage in even fiercer offensives in November and December.[339] Increased international criticism of Indonesia, particularly from the United States, which worried that the chaotic conditions in Central Sulawesi were precisely those that *al-Qa'ida* was seeking, finally led the new Megawati government to take high-level interest in the conflict.

Government Intervention—The Malino Accords

In early December, additional police and army units were sent to Sulawesi "to protect vulnerable areas, separate the two sides, conduct mobile patrols, and secure

---

[335] For a thumbnail sketch of this camp, see International Crisis Group, *Jihad in Central Sulawesi*, 11–12. The report notes the existence of several camps in the Poso area, but the one at Pendolo was the major camp with the most rigorous training program.

[336] Human Rights Watch, *Chronology of the Conflict*, 14.

[337] International Crisis Group, *Jihad in Central Sulawesi*, 14.

[338] Human Rights Watch, *Chronology of the Conflict*, 15.

[339] Human Rights Watch, *Chronology of the Conflict*, 15–21.

roads."[340] At the same time, a high-level delegation was appointed to open negotiations with the conflicting parties in an effort to end the fighting. The delegation was headed by Coordinating Minister for Political and Security Affairs, retired General Susilo Bambang Yudhoyono (later elected President of Indonesia in September 2004), and Coordinating Minister for Public Welfare, Yusef Kalla (later elected Vice President of Indonesia in 2004). A particularly key role was played by Kalla, a native of Makassar in southern Sulawesi, where he was the owner of a large Toyota auto dealership that would become the target of a *Laskar Jundallah* retaliation bombing one year later on December 5, 2002.[341]

The result of this effort was the so-called Malino Declaration,[342] signed by various leaders involved in the Central Sulawesi conflict on December 20, 2001, in the South Sulawesi resort town of Malino. Satisfied with this process, the two ministers went on to apply it in Maluku, reaching the so-called Malino II Agreement on February 12, 2002.[343] Although the two very parallel agreements succeeded in reducing the level of violence in both conflict areas, they did not eliminate it altogether. A feature of the negotiation process was the inclusion of only local leaders of both sides and the exclusion of the outside groups whom all agreed should be disarmed but permitted to continue residing in the conflict zones. This last provision was sufficient to gain the acquiescence of *Laskar Jihad* and *Jemaah Islamiyah* leaders, the latter having come to see Poso as fertile ground for the building of a new *qa'ida `aminah* (secure base), "a refuge much like that which Medina became for the Prophet" in early Islamic history and as called for in the PUPJI document. A period of peace would facilitate this development.[344]

Post-Malino Sulawesi

A source of continuing dissatisfaction with the agreement was its failure to assign blame for the atrocities committed by both sides. Rather, both agreements promised government support and substantial resources for a restoration of the *status quo ante*, the return of all displaced persons to their former places of residence, and government funding to replace destroyed homes. Although these provisions as well as the enhanced government role in both security and rebuilding activities were sufficient to end general hostilities, a pattern of "mysterious shootings" and "bomb explosions," primarily against non-Muslim victims, continued.[345] As a result, the situation in both Central Sulawesi and Maluku remained tense and volatile, despite the agreements. Although

---

[340] Human Rights Watch, *Chronology of the Conflict*, 21.

[341] International Crisis Group, *Damaged but Still Dangerous*, 13.

[342] Text at Human Rights Watch, *Chronology of the Conflict*, 25–26.

[343] Text at Ambon Information Website, "Mailino II Agreement," February 12, 2002. URL: *http://www.websitesrcg.com/ambon/documents/Mailino-II-agreement.htm*. Accessed November 6, 2005.

[344] International Crisis Group, *Jihad in Central Sulawesi*, 14.

[345] International Crisis Group, *Jihad in Central Sulawesi*, 16. Appendix C of this report, "Post-Malino Accord Violence in Poso," 28–33, provides a full list of these incidents and their perpetrators, if known.

Traditional Tongkanan rice barns in southern Sulawesi.
Source: NGA Research Center—Ground Photography Collection.

government security forces investigated these incidents, they made few arrests until after the *Jemaah Islamiyah*-organized bombing of the Sari nightclub in Denpasar, Bali, in October 2002. Naming names, the government apparently reasoned, would only undermine the Malino Accord. The Bali bombing, however, demonstrated that a more forceful approach was needed.[346]

Survival of *Jemaah Islamiyah*

The general cessation of hostilities in Central Sulawesi achieved by the Malino Agreement indeed proved to be a boon for the *Jemaah Islamiyah* in Poso. Permitted to remain in the area by the agreement as long as they did not engage in hostilities, the organization began to build up its numbers in the Palu-Poso corridor. Already in 2001 the headquarters of Mantiqi III had been moved from Camp Hudaibiyah in Mindanao to Sandakan (in Sabah, Malaysia) in response to the closure of the former camp by the Philippine Armed Forces. Sandakan remained primarily a logistics transit point, however, facilitating the movement of arms and men from the Philippines to Sulawesi. Throughout 2002, the camp at Pendola, on the shore of Lake Poso in the mountains south of Poso City, increasingly became the principal *Jemaah Islamiyah* training camp,[347] gradually replacing Camp Hudaibiyah in the Philippines. Toward

---

[346] International Crisis Group, *Jihad in Central Sulawesi*, 17.

[347] International Crisis Group, *Jihad in Central Sulawesi*, 17–20.

this development Indonesian authorities appear to have cast a blind eye. By the terms of the Malino Agreement, as long as it did not engage in hostilities in the two conflict regions, *Jemaah Islamiyah* was free to build up its organization.

This attitude radically changed following the Bali bombing on October 12, 2002, which was quickly attributed to the radical elements of *Jemaah Islamiyah*.[348] Over the next year, more than 90 *Jemaah Islamiyah* operatives, nearly all affiliated with Mantiqi I, were arrested throughout Indonesia for alleged involvement in the Bali bombing.[349] These included 12 residing in Central Sulawesi, arrested in Palu in April 2003.[350] An impact of the increased government pressure was the total end of violence in Central Sulawesi until May 2003. The gradual revival of "mysterious killings" and bombings, beginning at that time, was attributed to local inhabitants rather than the non-local *mujahidin* groups that continued to maintain a low profile as well as to disperse to other parts of Indonesia.[351] Some, such as *Laskar Jihad*, officially disbanded, in part to separate themselves from the tactics demonstrated by the *Jemaah Islamiyah* radicals.

Like Maluku, Central Sulawesi continues to remain tense and volatile. Mysterious assassinations and bombings have continued to remain a feature of life in both regions in 2004 and 2005,[352] creating the odd situation in which violence continues to occur despite the general cessation of hostilities that was achieved by the two Malino Accords

---

[348] Most of the individuals involved in the Bali bombing, it turned out, were associated with Mantiqi I, still headquartered in Malaysia, but with many now residing in Indonesia. Almost all were found to have been the same men who had carried out the Christmas Eve bombings in 2000. Among them were Hambali (who ordered the operation, but was not on the scene); Mukhlis (coordinator of financial and logistical requirements); Imam Samudra (field commander on the ground); Dr. Azahari Husin, Dulmatin, and Ali Imron (who constructed the bombs and triggered them); Amrozi (purchaser of the explosives); Jimi (suicide bomber, driver of the van carrying the explosives detonated outside the Sari nightclub); Iqbal (suicide bomber, wearer of an explosive vest who first entered the club and blew himself up before the explosion of the van outside); and Idris (detonated a nearly simultaneous, small package bomb outside the U.S. consulate in Bali). A total of about 20 individuals were said to have been involved in the Bali bombing. For the full story of the Bali bombing, disclosed after the arrest of some of the above individuals, see Ressa, *Seeds of Terror*, 164–189.

[349] Ressa, *Seeds of Terror*, 208. The first was Amrosi (arrested November 5, 2002), soon followed by *Imam* Samudra (November 21, 2002) and Mukhlis (December 3, 2002), and finally Ali Imron (January 13, 2003). Others eluded escape, such as Dr. Azahari Husin (killed in a confrontation with police in East Java on November 5, 2005) and Dulmatin (believed to still be eluding capture in Mindanao). Hambali was arrested by Thai police in Thailand on August 13, 2003. The actual first arrest was MMI and *Jemaah Islamiyah* leader Abu Bakar Ba'asyir (October 19, 2002), who denied any knowledge or connection with the bombing event. It was Amrozi, owner of the van used in the bombing, who confessed his role and named the others involved in the attack.

[350] International Crisis Group, *Jihad in Central Sulawesi*, 20.

[351] International Crisis Group, *Jihad in Central Sulawesi*, 20, 22–23.

[352] For a list of such incidents in both regions, see Appendix F, "Violence in Poso and Maluku, 2004–2005," in International Crisis Group, *Weakening Indonesia's Mujahidin Networks: Lessons from Maluku and Poso*, ICG Asia Report No. 103, Jakarta/Brussels (October 13, 2005), 27–29. URL: *http:// www.crisisgroup.org/library/documents/asia/indonesia/103_weakening_indonesia_mujahidin_networks_ lessons_fr_maluku_poso.pdf*. Accessed December 3, 2005.

of late 2001 and early 2002.[353] Analysis of this pattern of violence suggests that it is largely the product of local *mujahidin* networks that continue to find Poso and areas of Maluku safe havens (*qa'ida `amina*) in which to live and operate.[354] They remain engaged in *jihad* with the Christians of the local areas, thus assisting the government in containing potential separatist activity that might emerge from local Christian groups. Meanwhile, the higher profile of government security forces is sufficient to prevent incidents of violence from escalating into wider hostilities. Government actions to move against the *mujahidin* groups have been insufficient to bring these perpetrators of violence to justice. Nor is such action expected, at least in the short term. In Poso and Maluku, at least, the *mujahidin* groups remain useful adjuncts for maintaining Indonesian sovereignty over these potential separatist areas.

PAPUA

When Indonesia gained its independence from Dutch rule in December 1949, Netherlands New Guinea (today Papua) was not part of it. Indeed, the remote half-island remained under Dutch rule until 1963, when as a result of the August 1962 United Nations-sponsored Dutch-Indonesian "New York" Agreement, it was transferred to Indonesian control. Until 1969 Indonesia governed the future province as a United Nations Mandate, at which time it was required by the treaty to permit a vote on self-determination. In fulfillment of this requirement, the Suharto government "brought 1025 traditional leaders to Jakarta where, under great pressure, they voted unanimously on behalf of the people of Papua to join the Republic of Indonesia."[355] The new province was immediately renamed West Irian (*Irian Jaya*) and, like East Timor six years later, incorporated as a province of the Republic.[356]

From the viewpoint of Indonesian nationalists, such as President Sukarno, who considered even Brunei, the Malay peninsula, and southern Thailand as potential Indonesian territories and at a minimum all those lands that had been ruled by the Dutch, there was no question but that the new province was an integral part of Indonesia. Moreover, having abolished voting as un-Indonesian in 1958, when he adopted his Guided Democracy concept, Sukarno considered the United Nations-required plebiscite a challenge to be finessed rather than implemented literally.[357] The so-called Act of Free Choice of 1969, conducted under United Nations supervision, provided sufficient legitimacy to turn nationalist aspirations into reality, and troops originally sent under the command of then Lieutenant General Suharto in 1963 to take control of the province ensured that Jakarta commanded the outcome that the nationalist leadership desired.

---

[353] International Crisis Group, *Lessons from Maluku and Poso*, 1.

[354] International Crisis Group, *Lessons from Maluku and Poso*, 3.

[355] International Crisis Group, *Indonesia: Ending Repression in Irian Jaya*, ICG Asia Report No. 23, Jakarta/Brussels (September 20, 2001), 3. URL: *http://www.crisisgroup.org/library/documents/report_archive/A400414_20092001.pdf*. Accessed November 15, 2005.

[356] International Crisis Group, *Dividing Papua: How Not to Do It*, ICG Indonesia Briefing, Jakarta/Brussels (April 9, 2003), 2. URL: *http://www.crisisgroup.org/library/documents/report_archive/A400941_09042003.pdf*. Accessed November 15, 2005.

[357] Taylor, *Indonesia*, 350–351.

Early Resistance to Indonesian Rule

From the beginning, however, there was resistance. In October 1961, prior to the New York Agreement, a committee of leading Papuan members of the New Guinea Council had adopted a flag (Morning Star) and an anthem (*Hai Tanahku Papua*), together with a political manifesto requesting Dutch recognition of West Papua as an independent state.[358] In 1964, moreover, following the establishment of the Indonesian Mandate, a Free Papua Organization (OPM) had come into being, and the first major insurrection against Indonesian rule erupted in Manokwari in 1965. Although the OPM never emerged as a sustained insurgent movement as did Fretilin in East Timor, it remained a troublesome problem along the border of Papua New Guinea, where its fighters were able to maintain sanctuary.[359]

Despite the weakness of the OPM, popular opposition to Indonesian rule was general among the native, non-Malay, Melanesian population of the province that as late as 1998 constituted about 70 percent of its 1.5 million inhabitants. This percentage was significantly reduced from the nearly 98 percent non-Malay population that had constituted the province in 1965 because of large-scale government-sponsored transmigration from other Islands to Irian Jaya.[360] Nevertheless, there long had been a small established Malay population, mainly from the eastern islands of Maluku and Sulawesi, in the coastal trading towns of West New Guinea. These had remained connected to their homes of origin and favored incorporation into Indonesia.[361] Their numbers augmented by the new transmigrants, these emerged as the new dominant economic and political elite of Irian Jaya under Indonesian rule. Generally perceiving themselves as part of a higher civilization than the generally more primitive native inhabitants, they remained a faithful block of support for Irian Jaya as a part of Indonesia. Over a century of Dutch rule, however, had produced a native Papuan, largely Protestant Christian, counter-elite that had preferred a continuation of Dutch rule or, in its absence, political independence. Although this counter-elite tended to collaborate with Dutch rule, serving as members of parliament or in bureaucratic positions in Irian Jaya, but especially as church leaders, it continued to symbolize Papuan separatist aspirations, particularly in the face of often brutal military efforts by the Indonesian government to suppress manifestations of Papuan nationalism.[362]

The stakes became even higher following the discovery of major copper and gold deposits in Papua in the late 1960s. From 1973 on, this meant that Freeport-McMoRan Copper and Gold, Inc., the New Orleans-based American company contracted to mine these resources, was the largest taxpayer in Indonesia and a major source of revenue

---

[358] International Crisis Group, *Ending Repression in Irian Jaya*, 4.

[359] International Crisis Group, *Ending Repression in Irian Jaya*, 2.

[360] International Crisis Group, *Ending Repression in Irian Jaya*, 4–5.

[361] Taylor, *Indonesia*, 351.

[362] One local human rights activist alleged "921 deaths in Irian Jaya from military operations in the period 1965–1999." Friend, *Indonesian Destinies*, 273.

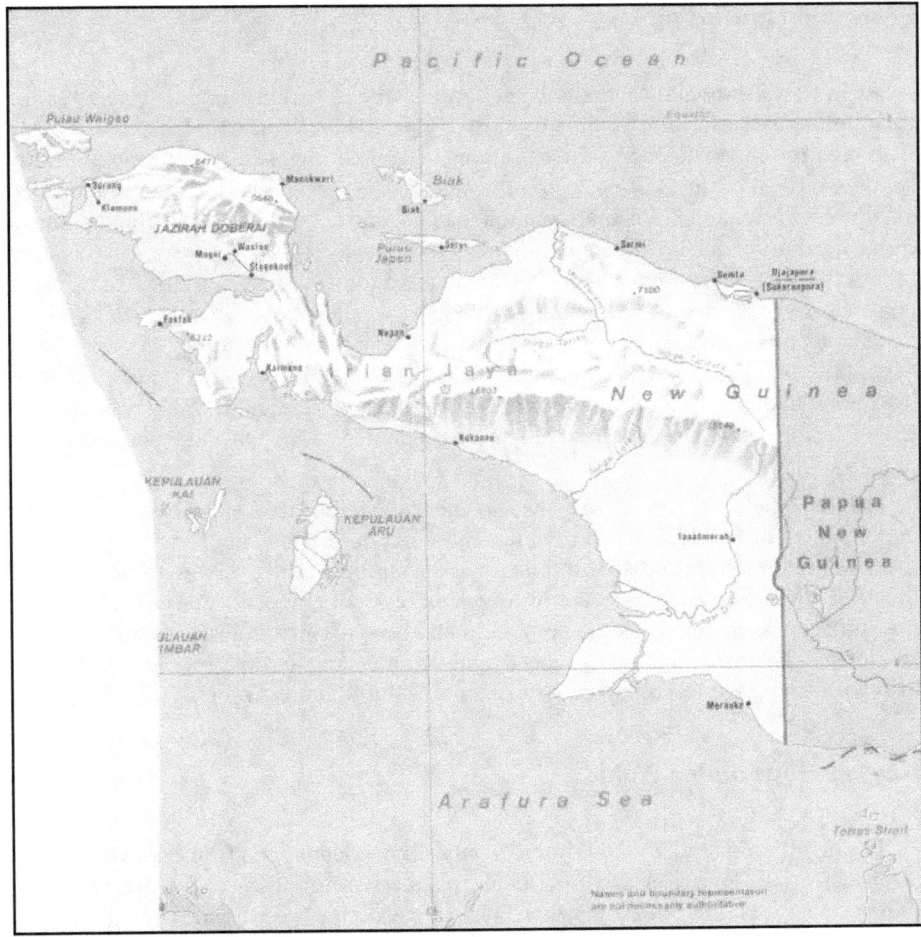

Map of Irian Jaya.
Source: CIA.

for the Jakarta government. The growing importance of Freeport-McMoRan in Irian Jaya and in Indonesian economic life, especially as close Suharto family members and friends became major investors, and also the flourishing forestry industry of the province, raised other issues-especially environmental and economic-that fueled a Papuan national movement while at the same time making the Suharto government determined to maintain Irian Jaya as an integral part of Indonesia.[363]

---

[363] International Crisis Group, *Indonesia: Resources and Conflict in Papua*, ICG Asia Report No. 39, Jakarta/Brussels (September 13, 2002), 17–20. URL: *http://www.crisisgroup.org/library/documents/ report_archive/A400774_13092002.pdf*. Accessed November 15, 2005.

Post-Suharto Revival

As in East Timor and Maluku, the collapse of the Suharto regime in May 1998 led to an immediate revival of long-suppressed separatist sentiment in Irian Jaya/Papua. Although pro-independence demonstrations in several towns in August were brutally suppressed by the army, killing 26, the new *reformasi* spirit sweeping Indonesia soon led a number of Papuan intellectuals, church leaders, and activists to form a new political front, the Forum for the Reconciliation of Irian Jaya Society (Foreri). Dissociating themselves from the OPM, which they condemned for its violent activities, their stated goal was to seek greater autonomy for Papuans to manage their own affairs, either through a federal system of government or independence.[364] Agreeing to meet with a "Team of 100" Papuan leaders designated by Foreri in February 1999, just days after his "moment of inspiration" regarding East Timor, new President Habibie was shocked to hear that the delegation carried only a single demand—Papua's independence.[365]

Habibie made no formal response to the delegation, then or subsequently. The unpopularity of his decision to permit a referendum in East Timor virtually ensured the adoption of a wait-and-see attitude toward Irian Jaya. The overwhelming rejection of autonomy by the East Timorese in August in favor of independence guaranteed that no similar experiment would be applied to another province in response to separatist sentiments. In any event, by October Habibie was gone, and the problem of how to deal with Irian Jaya fell to the new President, Abdul Rahman Wahid.

Rays of Hope under Wahid

The liberal, modernist Wahid immediately acknowledged the former government's errors in Irian Jaya, released political prisoners, and affirmed the right of all Indonesians, including those of Irian Jaya, to freedom of expression, including pro-independence demonstrations, as long as they remained peaceful. At the same time, however, he made it clear that his government would not accede to Papuan demands for political independence.[366] A key date was December 1, 1999, the anniversary of the 1961 formal declaration of Papuan independence. On this day, Papuan nationalists led by Theys Hiyo Eluay raised "both the 'Morning Star' flag in the same place [Jayapura] as in 1961, outside the building that had housed the Dutch-established New Guinea Council,"[367] an act that in previous years would surely have guaranteed arrest on charges of rebellion and hero status for those so arrested. On this day, Indonesian security forces were absent from the event, a circumstance Eluay described as a "miracle." Efforts the following day by the inhabitants of Timika to raise the flag

---

[364] International Crisis Group, *Ending Repression in Irian Jaya*, 10.

[365] Human Rights Watch, "Violence and Political Impasse in Papua," *A Human Rights Watch Short Report*, 20, 10(x), (July 2001), 9–10. URL: *http://www.hrw.org/reports/2001/papers/PAPUA0701.pdf#*. Accessed December 5, 2005.

[366] Human Rights Watch, "Violence and Political Impasse in Papua," 10.

[367] International Crisis Group, *Ending Repression in Irian Jaya*, 11.

again, however, provoked a clash with security forces in which many of the pro-independence demonstrators were shot and wounded. The incident and others like them led Wahid to pay a personal visit to Jayapura on December 31, 1999, where he again assured Papuan leaders "that flag-raising and other peaceful expressions of pro-independence views would be considered protected acts of free speech," but emphasized that greater autonomy rather than independence was the best Papuans could expect from his government.[368]

Wahid also agreed to the use of state funds to help finance a Papuan congress "at which, for the first time, Papuan representatives could gather to air their concerns."[369] Two such congresses actually met during 2000. The first, held February 23–26, which chose a Papuan Presidium Council headed by Theys Eluas, was preparatory to the second and main congress, which met between May 29 and June 4. Attended by thousands from throughout the province, including many exiles from abroad, but only 500 official delegates, the second Congress concluded with a resolution stating that West Papua (as they called it) had always been a sovereign state since its declaration of independence on December 1, 1961; that its incorporation into Indonesia in 1969 was "legally flawed," and that Jakarta should move quickly to recognize the sovereignty and independence of West Papua.[370]

Swing of the Pendulum

Despite the peaceful political process by which these developments were playing out in Irian Jaya, the outbreak of Christian separatist violence in Maluku and Christian-Muslim hostilities in Central Sulawesi during same period, as well as the even more powerful separatist movement struggling for independence in Aceh, the apparent inability of established security forces to contain the violence, and the emergence of popular militia groups such as *Laskar Jihad* (probably with covert support from elements of the armed forces) all contributed to a sense of popular alarm in Jakarta and growing disenchantment with the liberal (weak) policies of President Wahid. This disenchantment was finally reflected in the Indonesian Parliament (MPR), which in August strongly criticized the President's "accommodative attitude" and ordered him to take "decisive actions against separatism and to implement "special autonomy" for Irian Jaya and Aceh.[371] The action of the Parliament severely undercut Wahid's efforts to reach an accommodating agreement with Papuan leaders and empowered the military to resume its traditional hardline policy of suppressing all manifestations of Papuan separatism by force.

---

[368] Human Rights Watch, "Violence and Political Impasse in Papua," 10.

[369] Human Rights Watch, "Violence and Political Impasse in Papua," 10.

[370] R. William Liddle, "Indonesia in 2000: A Shaky Start for Democracy," *Asian Affairs*, 41, 1 (January–February 2001), 214.

[371] International Crisis Group, *Ending Repression in Irian Jaya*, 18.

Unlike the earlier part of the year, the latter months of 2000 witnessed a number of bloody clashes between pro-independence supporters and security forces. In most cases, the incident sparking the violence was the simple raising of the Morning Star flag. The International Crisis Group detailed the main clashes:

> Three people were killed in Sorong on 22 August; 34 in Wamena, many of them non-Papuan immigrants, on 6 October; five in Marauke on 5 November; seven more in a clash there on 2 December; three, including a policeman, in Abepara on 7 December, with seventeen arrested and later tortured.[372]

As a result of this increased tension, Papuan independence day celebrations on the 1st of December took place in an entirely different atmosphere from the year before. As a precaution, on the day before the observances, police arrested Theys Eluay and four other members of the Papuan Presidium Council, charging them with subversion because of the role they had played in the congresses earlier in the year. In addition, martial law was declared, but organizers of the independence day activities were permitted to fly the Morning Star flag-for one day only. The clashes that followed represented military efforts to enforce this one-day rule.

Megawati Takes Charge

Meanwhile, a "Crash Program" was set in motion under the leadership of Vice President Megawati Sukarnoputri to win Papuans back to support for remaining part of Indonesia. The three stated goals of the program were:

1. Doubling the budget of Irian Jaya to facilitate the development of social and economic programs for the benefit of the native inhabitants.
2. Removal of all symbols of Papuan nationalism, including vocal leaders, from the public arena.
3. Promoting a Special Autonomy status for Irian Jaya.[373]

Accordingly, in the tense atmosphere of late 2000 and early 2001, an appointed joint committee began work drafting a special autonomy law. "Eleven drafts went back and forth between a Papuan team and a parliamentary team" before a final version consisting of 79 articles was produced and finally adopted by the Indonesian Parliament on October 22, 2001.[374]

Unlike in Aceh, where security forces were less able to assert government authority, they were in general able to suppress the pro-independence forces in Irian Jaya that

---

[372] International Crisis Group, *Dividing Papua: How Not To Do It*, 5. Human Rights Watch, "Violence and Impasse in Papua," provides a detailed analysis of the incidents in Wamena and Abepura, 11–22.

[373] International Crisis Group, *Ending Repression in Irian Jaya*, 18.

[374] International Crisis Group, *Dividing Papua: How Not To Do It*, 6–7.

had been active in 2000. With the silencing of the generally non-violent independence movement represented by Foreri, however, that represented by the OPM (*Organisasi Papua Merdeka*/Free Papua Organization) began to make itself felt again during 2001. The kidnapping of three Indonesian transmigrants, employees of a timber company, on March 31; the kidnapping of two Belgian film-makers in early June 2001; and the killing of five policemen on June 13 were all indicators of this trend. Fierce counter-reactions by Indonesian security forces, which included mass arrests, torture, and the burning of villages, had the impact of producing nearly 5,000 civilian refugees and the complete disruption of economic life in some parts of the province.[375]

Autonomy for Papua

It was in this atmosphere that Law No. 21 on Special Autonomy for Papua was passed by the Indonesian Parliament in October. Megawati, now President of Indonesia since the July impeachment of Abdul Rahman Wahid, had planned to attend the implementation ceremony for the new law in Jayapura on November 21, but cancelled her plans after the November 11 assassination of Papuan independence leader Theys Eluays by elements of the army's special forces (*Kopassus*). At his trial later, one of the *Kopassus* officers affirmed that he had ordered Eluays' killing on the basis of intelligence that the independence leader, who had denounced the autonomy law from the beginning, was planning to make a declaration of independence on December 1.[376]

The death of Eluays produced a profound shock throughout Irian Jaya and reinforced Papuan hatred of the Jakarta regime, while making it clear that the government would go to any length to retain control of the province. The new law on Special Autonomy, in which Papuan leaders had had significant imput, was sufficiently far-reaching, however, to gain at least the tacit support of a number of previously pro-independence leaders. Realizing the determination even of the current administration to retain possession of their province, the consensus of many was that the success of the new law depended on how effectively it was implemented, not in its specific provisions. Still others argued that the law could be accepted as a stepping stone toward independence-providing practice in self-government that Indonesian authorities previously had never tolerated.

The central feature of the law was the establishment of a bicameral legislative structure, the upper house (*Majlis Rakyat Papua*/MRP—Papuan People's Council) being composed only of native Papuans.[377] Although only advisory bodies, both houses could veto laws or decrees emanating from Jakarta. Now elected rather than appointed from Jakarta, but still reporting to the Ministry of Interior, both the governor and

---

[375] International Crisis Group, *Ending Repression in Irian Jaya*, 21–22.

[376] International Crisis Group, *Dividing Papua: How Not To Do It*, 6.

[377] Appointed rather than elected, the MRP was to be composed of one-third community leaders, one-third religious leaders, and one-third women. International Crisis Group, *Resources and Conflict in Papua*, 7.

deputy governor were now supposed to be native Papuans rather than appointees from elsewhere in Indonesia. The law also renamed the province Papua (not West Papua) in deference to Papuan sensibilities, but continued to forbid display of the Morning Star flag or use of the anthem as instruments of political mobilization. Most importantly, 80 percent of revenues earned from mining and forestry, and 70 percent from oil and gas, were to remain in Papua rather than go to the central government treasury.[378] The new law also provided for a locally raised constabulary, reporting to the governor, that was responsible for security within the province. Army, navy, and air force units of the central government could only be deployed in consultation with the provincial governor and then only against an external threat, not for domestic security. Control of migration in and out of the province was also assigned to "autonomous" provincial government. National defense, foreign affairs, and the coinage and regulation of money, of course, remained in the hands of the central government.

All these provisions responded to concrete grievances that Papuan natives had been articulating for years. Whether they could be effectively administered by a local provincial bureaucracy composed overwhelmingly of non-Papuan Indonesian transmigrants remained to be seen. Nevertheless, adoption of the autonomy law had the effect of significantly reducing tension during early 2002, as elected (in 2000) Papuan governor Jacobus (Japp) Solossa (d. December 2005), a strong supporter of the autonomy law, gained increasing popularity throughtout the province because of his efforts to increase Papuan involvement in governance and to develop the province economically.[379]

Breakdown of Progress

Several developments toward the end of the year, however, shattered the brief interlude of improved Indonesian-Papuan relations brought on by the autonomy law. On August 31, 2002, gunmen attacked a convoy of school teachers from the Freeport-MacMoRan Company, resulting in the deaths of two U.S. citizens and one Indonesian. Made to appear an OPM-type operation, police investigations later implicated members of *Kopassus*, the Indonesian army special forces unit.[380] The incident served as a pretext, however, for intensive military operations against alleged OPM havens

---

[378] According to the first Papuan governor, Japp Solossa, these percentages represented an increase in the amount of revenues historically available to the provincial government by a factor of about three. International Crisis Group, *Resources and Conflict in Papua*, 8.

[379] Roy Tupai, "Papua Governor Dies, Supporters Suspect Foul Play," *Paras Indonesia*, December 20, 2005. URL: *http://www.laksamana.net/read.php?gid=148*.

[380] Michael S. Malley, "Indonesia in 2002: The Rising Cost of Inaction," *Asian Survey*, 42, 1 (January/February 2003), 141.

in Papua.[381] Totally in violation of the Law on Special Autonomy, the offensive nevertheless was justified as being part of the global war on terrorism.[382]

A second development was the widely reported appearance of *Laskar Jihad* fighters from Maluku in the mainly transmigrant-inhabited coastal towns of Papua. Although reports of *Laskar Jihad* presence occurred as early as 2000, the militia began arousing local concern only in December 2001, when its leader, Jafar Umar Thalib, visited the newly opened office of its parent organization, the *Forum Kummunikasi Ahlus Sunna wal Jamaah* in Sorong.[383] The large influx of *Laskar Jihad* fighters, consisting of as many as several thousand men, came only in 2002, however.[384] They allegedly infiltrated along with a large influx of mainly Muslim refugees from the conflict in Maluku. The *Laskar Jihad* presence in Papua may have been more illusory than real, however. Great publicity attended the fighters' arrival in both Maluku in May 2000 and Poso in July 2001. Such publicity did not accompany their alleged arrival in Papua. Rumor and innuendo seemed to be the primary basis of knowledge about their presence. Such rumors were perhaps part of a government-sponsored information campaign designed to intimidate remaining pro-independence Papuans. On the other hand, Papuans themselves, fearful of the cost of rebelling against Indonesian authority, may have tended to project their own collective fears onto the reality of the situation. According to one *Laskar Jihad* member interviewed in Papua interviewed in May 2002, the organization had only seven members in Papua, in contrast to the several thousand popularly believed to be there.[385]

No evidence of *Jemaah Islamiyah* presence in Papua has been found, although Papua was included in the geographical region-along with Australia-as part of the recently formed Mantiqi 4. Mantiqi 4 was the last of the four regional structures established by *Jemaah Islamiyah*, although the date of its creation is not yet known. Little is known about Mantiqi 4. Most reporting about it comes from Australian sources and refers to its activities in Australia, where recruiting, fundraising, and the operation of at least

---

[381] International Crisis Group, *Resources and Conflict in Papua*, 6.

[382] In late June 2004, U.S. Attorney General John Ashcroft succeeded in obtaining a federal grand jury indictment against Anthonius Wamang, a commander in the Free Papua Movement (OPM), for leading the August 31 attack. The indictment contradicted the findings of Papua police chief General Made Pastika that elements of the Indonesian military (*Kopassus*) had in fact carried out the attack. Conn Halliman, "Indonesia: U.S. Underwiting Terrorism?" *Foreign Policy in Focus (FPIF)*, September 15, 2004, 1. URL: www.fpif. org/fpiftext/547. Accessed September 16, 2004. Indonesian authorities, with apparent U.S. FBI assistance, finally arrested Wamang on January 11, 2006, along with eleven of his associates. Ellen Nakashima and Alan Sipress, "Indonesian Arrested in 2002 Slaying of American Teachers," *The Washington Post*, January 12, 2006, A17. Also Ellen Nakashima, "FBI Said Involved in Arrest of 8 Indonesians," *The Washington Post*, January 14, 2006, A17.

[383] International Crisis Group, *Resources and Conflict in Papua*, 10.

[384] Michael S. Malley, "Indonesia in 2002," 140–141.

[385] International Crisis Group, *Resources and Conflict in Papua*, 10.

two remote training camps appear to have been its primary responsibilities.[386] No known sources refer to any activities in Papua.

The third development contributing to a new unraveling of Indonesian-Papuan relations was a presidential instruction (*Inpres*) issued by President Megawati Sukarnoputri in January 2003 calling for immediate implementation of Law No. 45, adopted by the Indonesian parliament in September 1999, which divided Irian Jaya into three provinces. In the words of one observer, the instruction did "more to create tension and turmoil [in Papua] than any government action in years."[387] The original 1999 law had been adopted in reaction to the Papuan demand for independence stated by the "Team of 100" to President Habibie in January of that year. Clearly aimed at countering the Papuan independence drive by means of a "divide and rule" strategy, the law nevertheless had not been implemented due primarily to strong Papuan opposition and the bias of President Abdul Rahman Wahid to encourage an autonomy process rather than measures that would provoke dissent and therefore a more determined independence movement. As Megawati, while Vice President, had been the virtual architect of the October 2001 autonomy law and had become President by the time of its passage and implementation, her action in January 2003 seemed an inexplicable reversal of her previous policy.

In any event, Megawati's instruction also was not implemented. In 2004, Indonesia's Constitutional Court overturned the controversial 1999 law and upheld the Law on Autonomy as being in line with the country's constitution.[388] In issuing the instruction, Megawati was clearly responding to political pressures from more hawkish elements in Indonesia's government establishment that feared Papuan autonomy, if successful, would only be a stepping stone to Papuan independence, a vision that some Papuan pro-independence leaders had espoused as well. The *KopassU.S.*-sponsored terrorist incident in August 2002 and the widely believed rumor of significant *Laskar Jihad* forces in the province when in fact they probably were few gave evidence of a kind of paranoia on the part of some elements of the Indonesian ruling elite that had been dismayed by the Law on Autonomy. It was to these elements that Megawati was responding in issuing the instruction, despite abundant evidence that such a policy would only increase Papuan resentment against Indonesian rule and tended to fuel aspirations toward independence.

Papua continues to be a part of Indonesia and will likely continue to remain so for the foreseeable future. As has been the case since 1961, however, Indonesia will

---

[386] Wayne Turnbull, "Mantiqi IV: Australia, Irian Jaya," in *A Tangled Web of Southeast Asian Islamic Terrorism: The Jemaah Islamiyah Terrorist Network.* Paper written for a graduate study program in Southeast Asian Terrorism at the Monterey Institute of International Studies, Monterey, CA, 31 July 2003. URL: *http://www.terrorismcentral.com/Library/terroristgroups/JemaahIslamiyah/JITerror/Mantiqi4.html.* Accessed November 14, 2005.

[387] International Crisis Group, *Dividing Papua: How Not To Do It*, 1. This entire article is devoted to an analysis of President Megawati's instruction, its motivation, and its implications. The discussion here is based largely on the ICG report.

[388] Tupai, "Papua Governor Dies."

continue to face stiff opposition to its rule. Such opposition has endured for more than forty years and will not likely be silenced over the short term, except by brute force that was characteristic of the Suharto era. Papua will likely remain a problem for Jakarta for many years to come.

ACEH AND GAM

By far the fiercest and most bitter separatist conflict in Indonesia has been that in Aceh, in the far west of the archipelago. Unlike the separatist movements in Maluku, Papua and East Timor, which have a Christian-Muslim religious as well as an ethnic dimension, however, Aceh is a profoundly Muslim region. Part of its rationale for independence, or at least an autonomous status, has been that Indonesia, with its *Pancasila* ideological basis, is widely perceived to be insufficiently Islamic for Aceh to be a part of it. For this reason, the Acehnese leadership during the early independence period, headed by Daud Beureueh, associated themselves with the *Darul Islam*

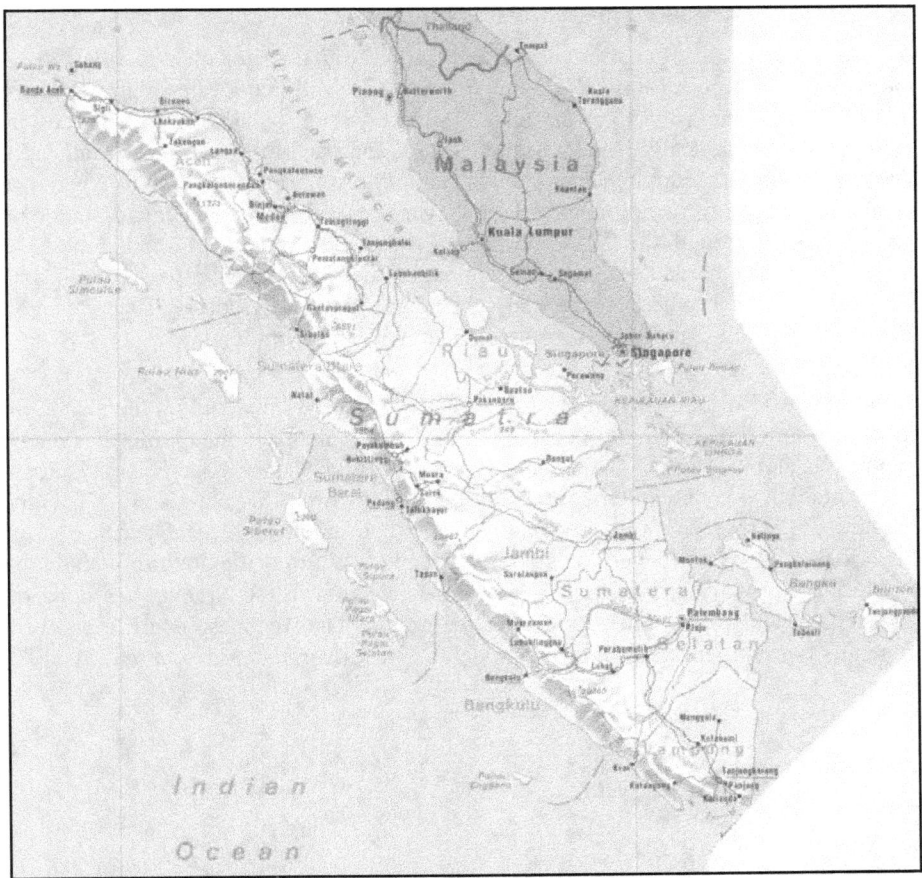

Map of Sumatra indicating the Aceh reigion of Indonesia.
Source: CIA.

movement, fighting to establish Indonesia as an "Islamic state" against the Republican forces headed by Ahmad Sukarno. The failure of the *Darul Islam* movement left many Acehnese preferring non-inclusion in Indonesia rather than incorporation within it.

Roots of Acehnese Separatism

An even stronger factor animating Acehnese desires for independence was associated with the province's long history as an independent sultanate. Aceh was the last region of the Indonesian archipelago to be brought forcibly under Dutch rule, beginning in 1873, and its sultanate was abolished only in 1907.[389] Acehnese resistance to Dutch rule in fact never ended, and Dutch personnel were being assassinated in broad daylight up through the 1930s in Aceh, just prior to the Japanese occupation in 1942.[390] Until conquest by the Dutch, Aceh had never been a taxpaying vassal to any of the *raja*s or *sultans* of Java. Indeed it was a competing state vying with the rulers of Java for suzerain authority over the *raja*s and *sultans* of the rest of Sumatra.

Aceh's geopolitical horizons were also different from those of Java. Its rulers were more closely associated through trading relationships and marital ties with the states of the Malay penninsula than those of the more distant islands of the Indonesian archipelago. Strategically located at the western approach to the Strait of Malaka, it was able to threaten shipping lanes to and from India and Arabia and therefore was in a position to forge strong diplomatic relations with external powers wishing to maintain secure passage through the Straits. With the Portuguese conquest of Malaka in 1511, moreover, Aceh emerged as the primary threat to this bastion of European presence in the East Indies, and whereas other parts of the Malay world gradually succumbed to British, Dutch, and Spanish control, Aceh held out longest among them.

Aceh was also the first region of the East Indies to be impacted by the arrival of Islam. Although it eventually became one of many sultanates inhabiting the Malay penninsula and Indonesian archipelago, it had pride of precedence and emerged, along with Pattani in today's southern Thailand, as one of the two principal centers of Islamic learning in the region. Known regionally as the "threshhold to Mecca" because of its historic role as the key departure and return point for pilgrims making the annual *hajj* to Mecca, Acehnese in general felt a closer connection to the Arabian heartland of the Islamic world than other peoples of the region. The Acehnese court, moreover, generally conceptualized itself as the model Islamic government in Southeast Asia.[391]

---

[389] Taylor, *Indonesia*, 258.

[390] Michael Vatikiotis, "Dissenting History," *Far Eastern Economic Review*, 162, 30 (July 29, 1999), 17.

[391] Taylor, *Indonesia*, 210–214.

Indonesia Prevails

Given its long independent history, it was perhaps not unnatural that as Holland abandoned its imperial claims in the Dutch East Indies in December 1949, Acehnese, like many in Maluku and Papua, tended to favor the revival of an independent Acehnese state rather than continued subordination to Jakarta. The Indonesian nationalists under the leadership of Sukarno and the Sumatran Muhammad Hatta, however, were determined to hold Indonesia together as a unitary, centralized state and proved able to do so. Under these circumstances, Daud Beureueh, leader of the Acehnese separatist movement at the time, threw his lot with the *Darul Islam* movement. If Aceh were to be a part of a greater Indonesia, then it should be on Acehnese terms, an Islamic state governed by the *shari`a* for which Aceh would serve as a model.[392]

As a result of its rebellion as part of the *Darul Islam* struggle against the Sukarno regime in the early 1950s, however, Aceh was once again subordinated to rule from Jakarta by force, a circumstance that ever since has affected its relations with the central government. Had Sukarno at this time afforded Aceh with some type of special status, as he was later forced to do, many subsequent problems might have been avoided. Instead, however, in order to "control" Aceh, he chose to graft it onto a larger, newly created province of North Sumatra that relegated historic Aceh to the status of a subordinate residency in the bureaucratic structure of the new state. Such a humiliation produced continuing resentment in Aceh and contributed to its participation in the brief, U.S.-supported North Sumatra rebellion, led by Indonesian Colonel Maludin Simholon against the Sukarno regime in 1957.[393]

Under the able command of the Indonesian army's Chief of Staff, Abdul Haris Nasution, the U.S.-supported rebellions of 1957–58 were gradually suppressed,[394] and in 1959 Sukarno designated Aceh as a "special region," where Acehnese "could substitute their own laws on religion, custom, and education for rulings from Jakarta's ministries."[395] This status was never confirmed in law, however, and although Aceh

---

[392] Richard Chauvel, "The Changing Dynamics of Regional Resistance in Indonesia," in *Indonesia Today: Challenges of History*, ed. by Grayson Lloyd and Shannon Smith (Lanham, MD: Rowman and Littlefield, 2001), 152.

[393] This rebellion along with others in other parts of Indonesia received U.S. support because of Eisenhower administration perceptions that Sukarno's leadership of the Non-Aligned Movement (NAM) was in fact a cover for strengthening Communist world interests in Indonesia. See Friend, *Indonesian Destinies*, 56–63.

[394] During the period 1952 to 1955, when he was out of favor with Sukarno, Nasution, who had commanded Indonesian forces on Java during the revolutionary war against the Dutch as well as against the *Darul Islam* movement, then served as the army's first chief of staff, wrote *Pokok-Pokok Gerilya: Dan Pertahanan Indonesia Dimasa Jang Lalu Dan Jang Akan Datang* [Fundamentals of Guerrilla Warfare: And the Defense of Indonesia, Past and Future] (Jakarta: Pembinbing, 1953). A product of his own experience as well as of his studies of the strategies of Mao-Tse Dung and Ho Chi Minh, Nasution's work has come to be considered a classic study of guerrilla warfare and counterinsurgency operations. Friend, *Indonesian Destinies*, 68–69.

[395] Taylor, *Indonesia*, 365.

remained relatively quiescent during the remainder of Sukarno's term of office, separatist sentiments rapidly reemerged during the Suharto era.[396]

Aceh Under the "New Order"

Although Acehnese participated enthusiastically in the killing of communists following the *Gestapu* coup against Sukarno, especially those communists of Javanese origin in Aceh, and at first appeared supportive of the new Suharto regime, they soon became disillusioned with his efforts to forge a Java-centric unitary state. His forcing all political activity into two, then later three, official political parties with headquarters in Jakarta had the effect of banning all parties having an "Aceh first" platform. From 1974, all candidates for government positions down to the district level had to be approved by the Ministry of Interior in Jakarta and were accountable to that ministry rather than to Aceh's consultative assembly. From 1975, moreover, all government officials in Aceh were required to be members of Golkar and loyal servants of the ruling regime as a condition of employment. Although Suharto placed emphasis on regional development, all planning and funding for the building of roads, bridges, schools, and industrial infrastructure was accomplished in Jakarta. Technical experts involved in regional development, moreover, were employed by the central government and were responsible only to it. Industrial zones, conceived of as instruments of national security, were controlled either by the military or the Ministry of Interior. `Ulama` were required to be members of the Aceh branch of the national Council of Indonesian `Ulama` and tasked with using their influence, through *fatwas*, to explain and justify, not criticize, the wisdom of Jakarta's policies in Aceh.[397]

Suharto's Java-centric policies in Aceh were nowhere more evident than in Indonesia's oil and gas industry, a large portion of which happened to be centered in Aceh. Particularly after the 1973–74 oil crisis provoked by the October 1973 Arab-Israeli war, the nearly four-fold increase in petroleum prices helped fuel rapid economic growth in Indonesia that continued until the Asian financial crisis of 1997. However, the benefits of the economic boom flowed mainly to Jakarta, which returned only an estimated five to seven percent of the wealth generated by Aceh's oil and liquefied natural gas (LNG) back to Aceh.[398] Some saw Aceh's wealth in natural resources as having the potential to transform the province into another Brunei, one of the world's richest states that had retained its independence from Malaysia solely by a referendum. As it was, Aceh's wealth provided more jobs to Javanese and foreign workers than to Acehnese. The industrial zones created in Aceh for national development, meanwhile, served as modern enclaves for foreign workers and Indonesian technocrats who lived a world apart from the impoverished Acehnese peasantry living just outside their gates.[399]

---

[396] Vatikiotis, "Dissenting History," 17.

[397] Taylor, *Indonesia*, 365.

[398] Samantha F. Ravich, "Eyeing Indonesia through the Lens of Aceh," *The Washington Quarterly*, 23, 3 (Summer 2000), 13.

[399] Taylor, *Indonesia*, 365.

Revival of Acehnese Separatism and the Formation of GAM

By the early 1970s growing dissatisfaction with Javanese exploitation of Aceh became increasingly apparent in two local developments. From the late 1960s, efforts led by former Acehnese governor Daud Beureueh to reconsitute the defeated *Darul Islam* were underway. These efforts finally bore fruit in 1974 in a formal reestablishment of the movement, with Daud Beureueh recognized as *imam*, or leader, of the reconsituted organization.[400] Although his role may have been more that of a figurehead, the real center of the movement being in Java, his readiness to accept the leadership role reflected reborn non-acceptance of Jakarta's rule in Aceh as it was currently constituted.

The reestablishment of *Darul Islam* was a secret, underground development, however. Far more public and dramatic was the announcement two years later, in October 1976, of the formation of the Free Aceh Movement (*Gerakan Aceh Merdaka*), or GAM. Much more a classic "national liberation movement," akin to the PULO in southern Thailand or the MNLF in the southern Philippines, GAM was animated more by Acehnese ethno-nationalism than by religious ideology, although its founder, Hasan di Tiro, openly stated that the Constitution of independent Aceh would be the *Qur'an*.[401]

Although GAM was an apparently rival movement of *Darul Islam* and initially drew many of its recruits from the families of former *Darul Islam* fighters, it is perhaps noteworthy that it emerged at precisely the same time that *Komando Jihad* operations were getting underway in various parts of Indonesia. As noted earlier, *Komando Jihad* was the shadowy operations arm of *Darul Islam* that had been put together with the assistance of Suharto's intelligence chief, General Ali Murtopu. Murtopu's support, however, had been part of a sting operation that became clear in mid-1977, when he ordered the arrest of those *Komando Jihad* operatives that had become known to him.[402] Despite the crackdown and witch hunt for *Darul Islam* members that followed, however, Indonesia continued to be bedeviled by *Darul Islam*-related violence through at least the late 1980s.

For the short run, the Suharto government appeared to have dealt more effectively with the GAM, which initially was not a deeply rooted movement. Di Tiro (b. 1930), who long has made much of his genealogical background as a descendant of the *sultans* of Aceh, including its golden age *sultan*, Iskandar Muda (r. 1607–1636), but more significantly of Teungu Chik Maat di Tiro, one of the martyred heroes of the Acehnese resistance to the Dutch in the late 19th century, had in fact been absent from Aceh for

---

[400] International Crisis Group, *Recycling Militants*, 3–5.

[401] Taylor, *Indonesia*, 366. Indeed, the formal name of di Tiro's organization is the Acheh Sumatra National Liberation Front (ASNLF), for which the GAM was its military arm. On the ASNLF, see its website at URL: *https://www.asnlf.net*. Accessed January 2, 2006.

[402] See above, Chapter 4, 93.

many years. Educated in the United States, where he graduated from Columbia and Fordham Universities, he became a businessman in New York City until his return to Aceh in 1976.

Announcing the formation of GAM, he embarked on his return in October 1976, traveling to Bangkok. On October 30, he was smuggled into Aceh and went into hiding in the mountains along with a few hundred fighters who rallied to his cause. On December 4, 1976, a day after the anniversary of the death of his martyred uncle, he issued a formal "redeclaration" of Acehnese independence, noting that "Aceh has always been a separate country."[403] His revolt posed no grave threat to Indonesian authorities, however, which defined him as a criminal wanted "dead or alive" and conducted a manhunt across the country searching for him. On March 29, 1977, just five months after his arrival, di Tiro secretly fled Aceh across the Molocca Strait to a "neighboring country," eventually reaching Sweden, where he continues to reside today in the southern Stockholm suburb of Nordsborg.[404]

The Endurance of GAM

The independence movement launched by Hasan di Tiro proved to have more staying power than the brief revolt of 1976 tended to indicate, however. In large part, this was because of the failure of the Suharto regime to make adjustments to the exploitative character of its rule in Aceh. Rather, "Jakarta responded by stationing large numbers of troops in the Acehnese province. The result of this throughout the Suharto regime was a series of human rights abuses and ongoing political repression by violent means through intimidation and organized terrorism which...left deep scars on the psyche of the Acehenese people."[405] The policy of subsidizing the out-migration of Javanese from overpopulated Java to provincial areas gained particular emphasis in Aceh. As it did in Maluku, Papua, and Kalimatan, the transmigration policy, as it was intended to do, tended to marginalize native Acehnese and contributed to increasing discontent with what was increasingly seen as Javanese imperial rule.

Although GAM remained an ineffectual guerrilla movement throughout the 1970s and 1980s, it endured and continued to be a nuisance to government security forces. Periodically, di Tiro made surreptitious visits to GAM fighters in remote locations in Aceh, presumably to bring money and provide moral support. By and large, however, he and others focused on international activities, particularly in Europe, publicizing the plight of the Acehnese people under Indonesian rule. In the mid-1980s, he achieved

---

[403] Biographical information drawn mainly from di Tiro's *The Price of Freedom: The Unfinished Diary of Tengku Hasan di Tiro*, 1984. Exerpts found at URL: *http://www.library.ohiou.edu/indopubs/ 1990/ 12/19/0012.html*. Accessed January 4, 2006. Also Bertil Lintner, "Giving No Quarter: Guerrilla Leader Runs Separatist Campaign from Stockholm Flat," *Far Eastern Economic Review*, 162, 30 (July 29, 1999), 19.

[404] Lintner, "Giving No Quarter," 19.

[405] Barton, "Islam and Politics in the New Indonesia," 53.

a breakthrough, when he gained the support of Libyan leader Mu'ammar Qadhafi to provide military training and support to several hundred Acehnese fighters. The return of these estimated 500–750 fighters to Aceh in 1989 sparked new life in the GAM revolt. "Armed in part by the Pattani United Liberation organization" (PULO), whose own movement in southern Thailand was in a quiescent phase,[406] "and in part through raids on military outposts, GAM began a series of attacks on local military posts and non-Acehnese migrants."[407]

The DOM Period, 1990–1998

The Indonesian government reacted fiercely against the new wave of rebellion. In May 1990, all of Aceh was declared an area of military operations (*daerah operasi militer*, or DOM), a status it continued to hold until after the fall of the Suharto regime, the DOM being officially lifted in August 1998 by the new Habibie government. Determined to end the insurgency once and for all, the Indonesian military embarked on a campaign of violence that made little distinction between members of GAM and other Acehnese. Hundreds were killed and buried in mass graves. Many more Acehnese were arrested, tortured, and arbitrarily detained for months, sometimes for years. Women whose husbands or sons were suspected of involvement or providing support to the guerrillas were often raped. The army also burned down houses of suspected rebels or sympathizers, sometimes razing entire villages.[408]

Throughtout 1991, the military conducted public executions of alleged rebels, causing many fearful Acehnese to flee to Malaysia. Somewhat sympathetic to the plight of the Acehnese, the Malaysian government of Mahathir Mohamad refused to return these refugees back to Indonesia, when requested to do so by the Suharto regime. Despite strong international condemnation of alleged Indonesian military brutalities in 1991–1992, Indonesia refused to permit journalists or the International Red Cross access to the province to investigate and report on the alleged atrocities. In 1992, the military affirmed that the GAM had been totally crushed.[409] And so it seemed when in the 1992 parliamentary elections Suharto's official Golkar party won 57 percent of the vote in Aceh, up from the typically 40 percent it usually had received in previous years.[410] By the mid-1990s, support for the GAM appeared to be at an all-time low. The continued economic boom, *coupl*ed with the repressive measures adopted by the government in Aceh, appeared to have eliminated any lingering resistance among the inhabitants of Aceh as well as willingness to assist the insurgents.

---

[406] See above, Chapter 3, 70.

[407] Ravich, "Eyeing Indonesia Through the Lens of Aceh," 13.

[408] Human Rights Watch, *Indonesia: Why Aceh is Exploding*. A Human Rights Watch Press Backgrounder, August 27, 1999. URL: *http://www.hrw.org/campaigns/indonesia/aceh0827.htm*. Accessed November 13, 2005.

[409] Andrew Tan, "Armed Muslim Separatist Rebellion in Southeast Asia," *Studies in Conflict and Terrorism*, 23 (October/December 2000), 278.

[410] *Indonesia: A Country Study*, 227.

After Suharto

How wrong this assessment was became evident immediately after the fall of the Suharto regime in May 1998. The new thrust toward democratic change was accompanied by a liberalization of the press that previously had been a mouthpiece of the Suharto regime. Throughout the summer of 1998, newspapers and nightly television broadcasts were filled with revelations of atrocities committed by the military forces in Aceh as well as East Timor and other parts of the country. A strong mood emerged that the DOM should be lifted, military forces withdrawn from Aceh, the perpetrators of crimes persecuted, and victims compensated.

Accordingly, on August 8, 1998, following a formal apology to the people of Aceh for all they had endured at the hands of the military, General Wiranto, Chief of Staff of the Indonesian Armed Forces, officially lifted the DOM and stated that all combat forces would be withdrawn from Aceh by the end of the month. At the formal ceremony on August 31 marking the final troop pullout, however, cheering Acehnese jeered and pelted the withdrawing troops with stones. The violence quickly turned into a full-scale riot in the oil and gas center of Lhokseume. Although many Acehnese believed the troubles had been initiated "by departing troops unhappy at being taken away from their lucrative sources of income from illegal logging and marijuana cultivation in Aceh," charges that were never investigated, the riot caused the troop withdrawal to be promptly reversed. In justifying his new decision, General Wiranto stated that withdrawal depended upon the good behavior of the people of the province.[411]

It quickly became apparent, however, that in the new post-Suharto political environment GAM, which originally had lacked deep popular support, had now become a grassroots movement, largely because of "deep-seated resentment and growing hostility toward the military's abuse of power."[412] As instances of violence multiplied, many Acehnese flocked to the GAM, as the military began to return to Aceh and to renew its brutal campaign to contain the revived insurgency. Despite the apparent good will of August, the year ended in a paroxysm of violence, as GAM forces renewed their attacks on government installations and Javanese migrants, and the army responded with indiscriminate attacks on villages thought to harbor GAM "terrorists" or to be sympathetic to the GAM.

Impact of the East Timor Referendum

Yet another critical shift occurred following the January 27, 1999, announcement by President B.J. Habibie that East Timor would be permitted to have a referendum on the question of autonomy or independence. Almost immediately an all-Aceh student

---

[411] Human Rights Watch, *Indonesia: The War in Aceh*, A Human Rights Watch Report, 13, 4 (August 2001), 8. URL: *http://www.hrw.org/reports/2001/aceh/indacheh0801.pdf*. Accessed November 13, 2005.
[412] Ravich, "Eyeing Indonesia Through the Lens of Aceh," 13.

congress called for a similar referendum in Aceh. This was followed by the formation of a province-wide, student-led Information Center for a Referendum on Aceh (*Sentral Informasi Referendum Aceh*, or SIRA). SIRA presented itself as an alternative to GAM, arguing that a referendum would be a peaceful way to end the conflict rather than the violent path followed by GAM.[413]

Although there were at first no known links between SIRA and GAM, their objectives were closely parallel, and both movements experienced great success during 1999 mobilizing popular support, despite brutal efforts of Indonesian security forces to disperse pro-independence demonstrators and track down GAM fighters. While SIRA demonstrated in November 1999 that it could organize a peaceful gathering of more than 500,000 Acehnese in support of a referendum, GAM began in various districts where it could to organize village councils loyal to its leadership, rather than that of the central government, and to collect taxes that enabled it to buy arms from various markets.[414] According to one observer, by mid-2000 GAM controlled as many as half the villages in the province.[415]

Part of the reason for the growing success of the Acehnese independence movement at this time was clearly the large discrepancy between the policy orientations toward Aceh of Jakarta's new political leadership and the military which retained the strong support of the Parliament. Whereas President Habibie in a March 1999 visit to the Acehnese capitol, Banda Aceh, had formally apologized for past abuses by the military and in June appointed an Independent Commission to Investigate Violence in Aceh, he was not able to deliver any positive result prior to his electoral defeat and replacement by President Abdurrahman Wahid in October. Wahid, meanwhile, when campaigning in Aceh, had stated that he favored the desired referendum, leading many to believe that it would be forthcoming following his election.[416] Wahid too proved unable to deliver on his promise, due primarily to parliamentary as well as military opposition. For a brief moment, though, the fragmented politics of Jakarta gave hope to pro-independence forces in Aceh that their movement contained the promise of success.

Wahid's Opening to GAM

Unable to risk his limited political capital by permitting a referendum in Aceh, particularly after the overwhelming rejection of Jakarta's rule by the August 1999 referendum in East Timor, Wahid instead toward the end of 1999 sent an envoy to Stockholm to open a dialogue with GAM leader Hasan di Tiro. Although di Tiro rejected this overture after Wahid announced it publicly, he did authorize GAM representatives to meet with Indonesia's ambassador to Switzerland and the United Nations, Dr. Hasan

---

[413] Human Rights Watch, *Indonesia: The War in Aceh*, 9.

[414] Human Rights Watch, *Indonesia: The War in Aceh*, 10.

[415] R. William Liddle, "Indonesia in 2000: A Shaky Start for Democracy," *Asian Survey*, 41, 1 (January/ February 2001), 213.

[416] Friend, *Indonesian Destinies*, 477.

Wirajuda, under the auspices of the Henry Dunant Center for Humanitarian Dialogue in Geneva.[417] This meeting initiated a negotiation process that finally led to a three-month "humanitarian pause" agreement between GAM and the Indonesian military in May 2000 that continued to be extended until it finally broke down in July 2001.[418]

Not quite a complete cease-fire, the agreement did produce a significant decline in violence for several months. The lull in the fighting, whose purpose was to permit a flow of humanitarian aid to the people, nevertheless, provided an environment in which the GAM was able to expand its control in the countryside.[419] These advances Indonesian forces tended to counter violently, while GAM responded with counterattacks. As outbreaks of fighting soon resumed, monitoring teams operating under the agreement tended to keep the fighting in check. Nevertheless, total deaths from fighting escalated from an estimated 400 in 1999 to nearly 800 in 2000.[420]

A particular strategy adopted by GAM at this time was to target ExxonMobil's oil and gas production and refinery facilities at Lhokseume, on Aceh's northern coast. These facilities, located in an area where the fiercest insurgency activity was occurring, produced about 32 percent of the total value of Indonesia's oil and gas production and generated about $1.43 billion per year (in 2000) in foreign currency. Sniping, kidnapping, murder, arson, trespassing, and robbery, mainly against individual employees of the company, were all techniques used to increase the level of insecurity experienced by ExxonMobil employees. The strategy had its desired effect, when in March 2001 the company announced the closing down of its operations in Aceh. The shutdown, which

---

[417] Rohan Gunaratna, "Aceh Rebels Agree to Extend Ceasefire," *Jane's Intelligence Review*, 13, 3 (March 2001), 4.

[418] The texts of all the agreements between the Indonesian government and the GAM can be found on the Dunant Center (now called the Humanitarian Dialogue Center) web site at URL: *http://www. Hdcentre. org/?aid=153*. Accessed January 16, 2006.

[419] United States-Indonesia Society (USINDO), "National Integration in Indonesia: The Cases of Aceh and Papua." Remarks by Ambassador Wiryono Sastrohandoyo. *USINDO—East-West Center Washington Joint Forum.* (October 1, 2002). URL: *http://www.usindo.org/Briefs/Joint%20USINDO-EWC%20on%20 Aceh%20and%20Papua.htm*. Accessed January 16, 2006. It was at this time, in June 2002, just after the May "humanitarian pause" agreement under which two *al-Qa'ida* leaders, Muhammad Atef and Ayman al-Zawahiri, visited Indonesia, stopping first in Aceh and then moving on to Maluku. They were escorted during their visit by *al-Qa'ida* representative in Indonesia Omar al-Farouk and South Sulawesi Islamic leader Agus Dwikarna, who later in the year would participate in the establishment of the *Majelis Mujahidin Indonesia* with *Jemaah Islamiyah* leader Abubakar Ba'asyir and others and also of *Laskar Jundallah*, a new militia aimed at enforcing Islamic law in Southern Sulawesi. According to Abuza, the purpose of the *al-Qa'ida* visit was "to establish a base area and training facilities in Indonesia, to complement Afghanistan." Abuza goes on to say that although Zawahiri and Atef were favorably impressed by the situation in Aceh, "GAM resisted their overtures and al-Qaeda did not establish a base in Aceh." Abuza, *Militant Islam in Southeast Asia*, 149, 160, 176. A more likely interpretation of the meaning of this visit was to see how *al-Qa'ida* could assist the GAM rebels. The move to expand control of the countryside, establish an improved tax base, and purchase more weapons, most of which seemed to come from arms markets in Thailand and Cambodia through Malaysia, in which *Jemaah Islamiyah* may have played an important intermediary role, seems to have dated from this visit.

[420] CNN, "Aceh: A Timeline of Insurgency," *CNN.com* web site. URL: *http://www.cnn.com/2003/ WORLD/asiapcf/southeast/05/19/acehtimeline/*. Accessed September 19, 2005.

lasted until July, had a devastating economic impact on Indonesia, still reeling from the 1997 Asian financial crisis, when it forced the company's biggest customers-especially Japan and South Korea-to seek other sources for their oil and gas supplies.[421]

Although GAM's strategy seemed counterproductive to many, a key grievance of pro-independence Acehnese was Jakarta's expropriation of nearly 95 percent of the revenues earned from Aceh's oil and gas production for use elsewhere in the country rather than Aceh. The forced closure of ExxonMobil, therefore, harmed the government far more than it did the local Acehnese economy. Moreover, it demonstrated the inability of Indonesian security forces to provide the security necessary for the company to maintain operations without local Acehnese cooperation.

Resumption of the Conflict

Despite President Wahid's preference for a negotiated settlement, he found himself with no choice but to authorize a renewed military campaign in Aceh, which he did in April.[422] At the same time, in July, he obtained from the parliament a new law that granted Aceh's provincial government 70 percent of revenues from natural gas exports, the right to hold direct elections for local officials, to raise its own police force, and authority to implement Islamic law. This basic grant of autonomy was considered insufficient by most Acehnese, however, for whom independence had now become a deeply rooted demand. As a result, the new law failed to receive a positive response and fighting continued, 2001 being the bloodiest year to date in the history of the conflict, with nearly 1,500 recorded deaths by year's end.[423] In July, as ExxonMobil resumed operations in Lhokseume, the government withdrew from its dialogue with GAM in Geneva as well as participation in the joint monitoring teams tasked with investigating outbreaks of violence. Government forces also started arresting Acehnese members of the monitoring teams, setting off a flurry of GAM retaliatory actions through the rest of the year.[424]

Even this reversal of his former conciliatory policy did not save the presidency of Abdurrahman Wahid, however, who was impeached on July 23 on grounds of incompetence and corruption. His successor, Megawati Sukarnoputri, although she too suffered from limited support in both the parliament and the military, nevertheless was very hardline on maintaining the unity of Indonesia, which she saw as a legacy of her father. In the interest of maintaining this unity, she strongly supported the autonomy law for Aceh, which she signed into effect on August 11, 2001, and which immediately

---

[421] John McBeth, "Too Hot to Handle: Why ExxonMobil Closed Down Onshore Gas Fields in Aceh," *Far Eastern Economic Review*, 164, 12 (March 29, 2001), 16. Also Paul Harris, "No Solution in Sight in Anarchic Aceh," *Jane's Intelligence Review*, 13, 5 (May 2001), 30.

[422] Malley, "Indonesia in 2001," 128.

[423] Malley, "Indonesia in 2001," 128.

[424] Human Rights Watch, "Indonesia," *Human Rights Watch World Report 2002*, 6–7. URL: *http://www.hrw.org/wr2k2/asia7.html*. Accessed December 12, 2005.

became the centerpiece of her policy in Aceh.[425] Correctly perceived as an "imposed" policy from Jakarta by pro-independence elements in Aceh, it gained little support in the province, where the struggle for independence continued. The intensity of military action increased accordingly as the official position of the government hardened into a stance of "autonomy or nothing."[426]

Impact of 9/11

At this juncture, the *al-Qa'ida*-sponsored, September 11, 2001, attacks in the United States intervened to change the international climate in which the conflict with Aceh was taking place. United States efforts to improve relations with Indonesia and to solicit its support in the global war on terrorism led Megawati to link publicly GAM with Islamic terrorism, despite the lack of strong evidence that could be marshaled to demonstrate such a linkage. U.S. policymakers, however, although they urged a peaceful resolution of the Aceh conflict through negotiations, also continued to express support for the continued "territorial integrity of the Republic of Indonesia."[427] In contrast to the earlier East Timor conflict, the international climate favored the position of the Indonesian government in Aceh rather than that of the pro-independence forces.

"Cessation of Hostilities"

Realizing that the negotiating process it had been mediating was disintegrating, in early 2002 the Henry Dunant Center (HDC) in Geneva sought to revive it by involving three particularly influential international "wise men." The three were retired American Marine General Anthony Zinni, known to have a personal relationship with U.S. President George W. Bush as well as State Department sanctions for working with the HDC; Dr. Surin Pitsuwan, former Muslim foreign minister of Thailand and currently active as Thai representative in ASEAN; and former Yugoslav foreign minister Budimir Loncar, who had been Yugoslavia's ambassador to Indonesia during the Sukarno regime and remained close to the Sukarno family. Traveling extensively during 2002, meeting GAM and Indonesian government representatives, and working with their respective constituencies-Zinni with the U.S. government, Pitsuwan with the ASEAN foreign ministers, and Loncar particularly with President Megawati-the team ultimately succeeded in leading the two parties into signing a "Cessation of Hostilities Framework Agreement" in Geneva on December 9, 2002.[428]

---

[425] Human Rights Watch, "Indonesia," *Human Rights Watch World Report 2002*, 7.

[426] Kira Kay, "The 'New Humanitarianism': The Henry Dunant Center and the Aceh Peace Negotiations," *WWS Case Study 2/03*, Princeton University, Woodrow Wilson School of Public and International Affairs (February 2003), 7. URL: *http://www.wws.princeton.edu/cases/papers/newhumanit. html*. Accessed January 17, 2006.

[427] Kira Kay, "The 'New Humanitarianism,'" 7.

[428] Text at HDC website, URL: *http://www.Hdcentre.org/?aid-153*. Accessed January 16, 2006.

The task of the three "wise men" was not an easy one because, after the signing of the autonomy law on Aceh in August, the policy of the Megawati government was to forego continued negotiations with the GAM in favor of imposing the law by force, although it remained open to discussions with GAM if the rebel organization formally accepted the autonomy law, rather than independence, as the "end point" of the negotiating process.[429] Unable to obtain such a commitment from GAM spokesmen, fighting continued throughout the year, as the military, whose forces amounted to nearly 30,000 as opposed to 4,000 GAM rebels, intensified its pressure in Aceh. Over the course of the year, the GAM forces were gradually driven back into mountain and jungle retreats where they remained effectively surrounded by elements of the Indonesian military, thereby losing control over the territories and districts GAM had come to dominate during the previous year.[430] Meanwhile, estimated deaths for the fighting during 2000 were 1,230 persons, mainly civilians rather than combatants from either side.[431] Within this context, the mediated settlement of December 9 appears to have been reached on the basis of three principles laid down by the mediating team: (1) International community respect for the territorial integrity of Indonesia and non-support for the independence of Aceh; (2) Indonesian acceptance of international monitors to oversee implementation of the agreement; and (3) restoration of U.S. military and economic assistance to Indonesia, severed since the East Timor crisis of 1999, only in response to a satisfactory settlement of the Aceh conflict.[432] Although the term "autonomy" did not appear in the cease-fire agreement, a provision mandating early elections (independently set for April 2003) in terms of the autonomy law of August 2002 implied its acceptance by GAM. Moreover, a central role for a reconstituted Joint Security Committee, comprised equally of GAM, Indonesian, and international (mainly Thai) members to report on violations of the cease-fire, was meant to ensure adherence by both parties to the terms of the cease-fire agreement.

Fighting Resumes

The ink was barely dry on the new agreement when fighting erupted again. As had been true after the May 2000 "humanitarian pause," GAM was perceived to be taking advantage of the lull in fighting to rearm and recover its strength,[433] and Indonesia responded by renewing the fighting. In April 2003, Megawati cancelled the scheduled election mandated by both the cease-fire agreement and the autonomy law and also broke off further talks with the GAM. On May 19, the government once again declared martial law in Aceh. Troop strength in the province was raised to approximately 45,000, and a full-scale offensive was ordered to eliminate the 3,000–5,000 GAM fighters

---

[429] Malley, "Indonesia in 2002," 140.

[430] Tom Farrell, "Hopes for Aceh Ceasefire," *Jane's Intelligence Review*, 14, 8 (August 2002), 47.

[431] Human Rights Watch, "Asia: Indonesia," *Human Rights Watch World Report 2003*, 4. URL: *http://www.hrw.org/wr2k3.asia7.html*. Accessed December 5, 2005.

[432] Kira Kay, "The New Humanitarianism," 8.

[433] Jamie Miyazaki, "Aceh Talks Raise Hopes for Settlement," *Jane's Intelligence Review*, 17, 4 (April 2005), 23.

once and for all.[434] Although army offensives pushed GAM forces into the mountains and eastern portions of Aceh, greatly weakening their operational capabilities, they remained far from defeated after two more years of war. Meanwhile, hostilities resulted during the period May 2003 to December 2004 in an estimated 2,300 deaths and upward of 125,000–150,000 internally displaced refugees living in deplorable conditions.[435] Most external observers doubted that the GAM could ever be totally defeated. At best, it could be keep in an isolated condition, but only at a prohibitive cost to the government.

Impact of the Tsunami

The devastating tsunami that hit Aceh's western coastline and destroyed most of the capital, Banda Aceh, on December 26, 2004, totally altered the context in which the conflict was perceived by all parties. Of a total population of about four million people in Aceh, the tsunami resulted in approximately 200,000 deaths and more than 800,000 displaced persons.[436] The requirements for international humanitarian assistance were overwhelming, and the international community was quick to respond with massive infusions of humanitarian relief. The Indonesian government, meanwhile, unable to cope with the crisis alone, opened the region to international aid and human rights workers who previously had not been permitted access to the province because of the exigencies of the war. For its part, GAM, from its headquarters in Stockholm, called for an immediate cease-fire so that relief supplies and aid personnel would not be hampered by insecurity.[437] For a few weeks, the large Indonesian military presence in Aceh did scale back operations against the GAM as it sought to cope with the immensity of the humanitarian crisis (many Indonesian soldiers also lost their lives in the tsunami) and also to assert control over the international relief effort. Soon, however, skirmishes resumed, with the military claiming to have killed as many as 200 GAM rebels in January 2005.[438]

Yudhoyono's Preference for Negotiations

New political leadership in Jakarta also had a significant impact on the post-tsunami political environment in Aceh. In October 2004, Susilo Bambang Yudhoyono had replaced Megawati Sukarnoputri as President of Indonesia and had brought with him as his vice presidential running mate Yusef Kalla, a wealthy South Sulawesi businessman

---

[434] Rita Smith Kipp, "Indonesia in 2003: Terror's Aftermath," *Asian Survey*, 44, 1 (January/February 2004), 67.

[435] Brad Adams, "Aceh's Forgotten Victums," *Jakarta Post*, May 27, 2005. URL: http://www.hrw.org/english/docs/2005/27/indo11069. Accessed January 17, 2006.

[436] Edward Aspinall, "Indonesia after the Tsunami," *Current History*, 104, 680 (March 2005), 105.

[437] Centre for Humanitarian Dialogue, "Acahe, Indonesia-Latest Update," *HD Centre for Humanitarian Dialogue* Website, undated. URL: http://www.Hdcentre.org/?aid=44. Accessed January 17, 2006.

[438] Anthony L. Smith, "Aid Efforts in Aceh Encourage Peace Talks," *Jane's Intelligence Review*, 17, 3 (March 2005), 40.

and important member of Golkar.[439] As former ministers in Megawati's government, the two had been key facilitators of the two Malino Agreements of December 2001 and February 2002 that had gone far to defuse separatist sentiment and sectarian conflict in Sulawesi and Maluku respectively. They would soon do so in Aceh as well.

A retired military officer, who subsequently had served in several cabinet positions, Yudhoyono cultivated the image of a strong leader interested only in effective and efficient government. During his first year in office, moreover, he gained much popular credit for cultivating Indonesia's democratic institutions-fair local elections, a free press, respect for the parliament, and a concerted effort to crack down on corruption.[440] Regarding Aceh, the new President early on indicated that only a negotiated rather than an imposed settlement could end turmoil in the province. The lead in this effort, however, was undertaken by Kalla who, following the tsunami "was the first senior official to visit Aceh, flying over the devastated coastal fringe in his private jet."[441] Kalla's assumption of leadership in the Aceh crisis and in subsequent negotiations with the Acehnese led to speculation that he rather than the President was "actually running the show," rumors that Yudhoyono sought to set aside by saying, "Nothing that is done by the vice president is unknown to me."[442] Others speculated that the hard-headed businessman from Makassar was motivated primarily by securing contracts for housing and infrastructure reconstruction in Aceh for his own companies as well as those of his key political allies.[443] Nevertheless, the sincerity of the new administration's policy toward a negotiated settlement was probably best expressed by the replacement in early 2005 of Army chief of staff General Ryamizard Ryncuda, who openly opposed the reopening of negotiations with the GAM just at the moment the armed forces were on the edge of victory and a total capitulation of the GAM.[444]

GAM's positive response to the overtures of the government was probably due less to the effects of the tsunami on Aceh than to the new international spotlight that had been placed on Aceh as a result of the tsunami. With the influx of international media, thousands of international aid workers, and hundreds of foreign officials monitoring the relief effort, the plight of the inhabitants of Aceh had in fact become internationalized, long a strategic goal of GAM. With Aceh finally having international visibility, GAM

---

[439] Making use of his new office as Vice President, Kalla won control of Golkar at its national congress in December 2004, shortly before the tsunami disaster. By assuming leadership of the party, he transformed the opposition party it had become since the fall of Suharto back into a party that was part of the ruling coalition. Aspinall, "Indonesia after the Tsunami," 107.

[440] Michael Vatikiotis, "Yudhoyono's First Year: Striking the Right Balance," *The Straits Times*, October 4, 2005. URL: *http://www.worldsecuritynetwork.com/printArticle3.cfm?article_id=11989*. Accessed November 6, 2005.

[441] Aspinall, "Indonesia after the Tsunami," 107.

[442] Michael Vitikiotis, "Yudhoyono: Indonesia's Man in Charge," *International Herald Tribune*, February 17, 2005. URL: *http://www.worldsecuritynetwork.com/printArticle3.cfm?article_id=10981*. Accessed November 6, 2005.

[443] Aspinall, "Indonesia after the Tsunami." 108.

[444] Jamie Miyazaki, "Aceh Talks Raise Hopes for Settlement," 23.

negotiators could enter new talks with hope that international concern for Aceh could be translated into a more evenhanded negotiation process.

Settlement in Helsinki

Talks reopened in Helsinki on January 27, 2005, just one month after the devastating tsunami. The Crisis Management Initiative (CMI), a Finland-based crisis-intervention NGO under the leadership of former Finnish President Martti Ahtisaari (1994–2000), served as the international mediator rather than the former Geneva-based Henry Dunant Center, although representatives of the latter organization were present to give advice. There were five rounds of talks before a final settlement was reached and officially signed on August 15, 2005.[445]

Officially titled a "Memorandum of Understanding between The Government of the Republic of Indonesia and The Free Aceh Movement,"[446] the agreement became possible only after GAM, after thirty years of determined insistence, finally abandoned its demand for full independence and agreed to disarm. In return, the Government of Indonesia granted amnesty to all GAM fighters who laid down arms and agreed to implement a new law of autonomy for Aceh by March 31, 2006, in which a democratically elected government of Aceh would exercise authority in "all sectors of public affairs...except in the fields of foreign affairs, external defence, national security, monetary and fiscal matters, justice and freedom of religion, the policies of which belong to the Government of the Republic of Indonesia in conformity with the Constitution." Aceh was "entitled to retain seventy (70) percent of the revenues from all current and future hydrocarbon deposits and other natural resources in the territory of Aceh as well as in the territorial sea surrounding Aceh," and the government agreed to reduce its troop presence on Aceh to no more than 14,700 soldiers (from 35,000) and 9,100 police (from 14,000) by the end of 2005.

To supervise implementation of the agreement, the Memorandum of Understanding also established an Aceh Monitoring Mission (AMM) comprised of personnel contributed by the European Union and five ASEAN nations. Although it was granted no coercive authority, both GAM and the Indonesian government committed themselves to accept the decisions of the Head of the AMM (Dutch diplomat Pieter Feith was the first individual selected for this role[447]) and binding on them both.

---

[445] All key documentation concerning the five rounds of Helsinki talks, including the text of the final settlement, is found on the CMI website, URL: *http://www.cmi.fi.* Accessed January 10, 2006.

[446] Text of the agreement at URL: *http://www.cmi.fi/files/Aceh_MoU.pdf.* Accessed January 10, 2006.

[447] Associated Press, "Indonesia, Aceh Rebels Sign Peace Treaty," *The New York Times*, August 15, 2005.

Peace in Aceh at Last?

Although considerable skepticism remained on both sides, by the end of 2005 implementation of the agreement was proceeding on schedule. The last of 840 arms required to be turned in by the GAM had been deposited with the AMM and destroyed by December 21, and on December 27, the *Gerakan Aceh Merdaka* formally dissolved itself. Indonesian troop movements out of Aceh also proceeded apace, with the final 3,353 troops boarding five warships and a C-130 transport plane and departing the province on December 29. Much remained to be done to implement the political and economic phases of the agreement, but a further meeting in Helsinki between Vice President Kalla and former GAM leader Malik Mahmud (signer of the MOU for GAM) on January 21, 2006, continued to indicate positive progress on both sides.

On the darker side, both western and Acehnese observers took note of the arrival in Aceh soon after the December 2004 tsunami of several hundred *Laskar Muhahadin* personnel and other Islamist groups-such as the *Front Pembela Islam* (FPI/Islamic Defenders Front)-many of whom had come on military transports.[448] Ostensibly present to provide humanitarian relief like many other relief organizations arriving on the scene, they established command posts and set about distributing aid, burying the dead, and tending to the injured. Unlike their secretive presence in Maluku and Sulawesi three years earlier, they were now blatantly overt in Aceh, as *Laskar Jihad* had been before. In the four command posts established by *Laskar Mujahidin*, signs were posted that read, "Islamic Law Enforcement." Despite protests by western aid officials and also GAM leaders about the presence of these groups, Indonesian military officials generally defended their presence, arguing that their humanitarian support was needed and that they should not be discriminated against unfairly.[449]

GAM leader Malik Mahmud protested bitterly about the presence of these non-Acehnese militia groups. He argued that once GAM was disarmed these groups would be used to hunt down and kill former GAM members, since under terms of the amnesty government forces could not do this. He added, "If GAM defends itself against these militias, this will be the excuse the [military] is looking for to relaunch military operations."[450] Mahmud's concern was undoubtedly well-founded. A key concern of Indonesian policy-makers throughout was the continuing suspicion that Acehnese nationalists perceived autonomy only as a first step toward independence rather than the end of the process. Regarding this issue, the government and the Islamist groups were of one mind; Indonesia should remain a single, unified state. The issue separating them was whether *Pancasila* or the *shari`a* should be the guiding ideology of the

---

[448] Zachary Abuza, "Out of the Woodworks: Islamic Militants in Aceh," *The Jamestown Foundation*, January 28, 2005. URL: *http://www.jamestown.org/news_details.php?news_id=88*. Accessed November 14, 2005.

[449] Yang Razali Kassim, "GAM, Islam and the Future of Aceh," IDDS Commentaries, February 8, 2005, 1. Published in *The Straits Times*, February 12, 2005. URL: http://www.infid.be/tsunami_gam_aceh. htm. Accessed December 23, 2005.

[450] Associated Press, "Indonesia, Aceh Rebels Sign Peace Treaty," *The New York Times*, August 5, 2005. URL: http://www.nytimes.com/aponline/international/AP.Aceh-Peace.html. Accessed August 15, 2005.

state. Regarding the role of the *shari`a*, on the other hand, the GAM and the Islamists were not at odds. In March 2002, following the adoption of the autonomy law by the Indonesian parliament in August 2001, the provincial government had been permitted to implement *shari`a* as the prevailing law of Aceh province.[451] Through autonomy, therefore, Aceh held the potential for emerging as precisely that type of *jemaah islamiyah* Indonesian Islamists long had been seeking to create. Although, under the terms of the Helsinki settlement, some elements of the Indonesian government may have perceived a coincidence of interests between the government and the *mujahidin* groups, they undoubtedly were also laying the groundwork for further conflict in Aceh at some future date.

OUTLOOK

Eight years after the fall of the Suharto regime in 1998, the centrifugal forces unleashed by the collapse of the strong, centralized, and dictatorial "new order" seem to have been largely contained. The anarchic politics of *reformasi* that followed opened the door to many possibilities. Aside from the loss of East Timor, the potential Yugoslavia-like breakup of Indonesia appears to have been averted, largely because of the adoption of reasonably liberal legal reforms permitting a higher degree of provincial autonomy and control of indigenous resources, plus the wealth derived from those resources in restive provinces like Aceh and Papua.

The terrorist threat posed by militant Islamist groups such as *Darul Islam* and *Jemaah Islamiyah*, although it continues, appears also to be in the process of being neutralized. Three major terrorist bombings after the Bali explosions in October 2002 — of the J.W. Marriott Hotel in Jakarta in August 2003, the Australian Embassy in September 2005, and Bali again in October 2005 — communicate the continuing existence of fugitive elements, but the Indonesian dragnet launched after the first Bali bombing also continues. The death in a police shoot-out in November 2005 of Dr. Azhari bin Husin, one of the men involved in all of the bombings, was yet another tightening of the noose around the militant movement, although Husin's principal colleague, Noordin Mohamed Top, remains at large.

The violent character of the Islamist movements in Indonesia was at least in part a reaction to the violent methods of the Suharto regime in particular to suppress radical opposition to it. As the democratic institutions laid down in the original republican constitution seem finally to have begun to take root in the post-Suharto era, it can be expected that the views of those committed to the establishment of a *shari`a*-based political order can be more effectively articulated. Therefore the perceived need to retreat to violent action is likely reduced.

---

[451] Human Rights Watch, "Asia, Indonesia," *Human Rights Watch World Report 2003*, 5. URL: http://www.hrw.org/wr2k3/asia7.html. Accessed December 5, 2005.

Thus far, Indonesian voters have rejected the Islamic alternative for the political organization of the state. The successful preservation of a democratic political process after years of dictatorial rule appears to be the central preoccupation of the Indonesian political establishment. To some degree, the firm Islamic opposition to Suharto's rule, for which many paid a heavy price, can claim some credit for the ultimate demise of the regime and the reopening of the country to more democratic processes. The argument between those who champion Indonesia's prevailing *Pancasila* ideology and those who seek change to a *shari`a*-centered political order has not ended, however. The struggle will likely divide Indonesia for the foreseeable future.

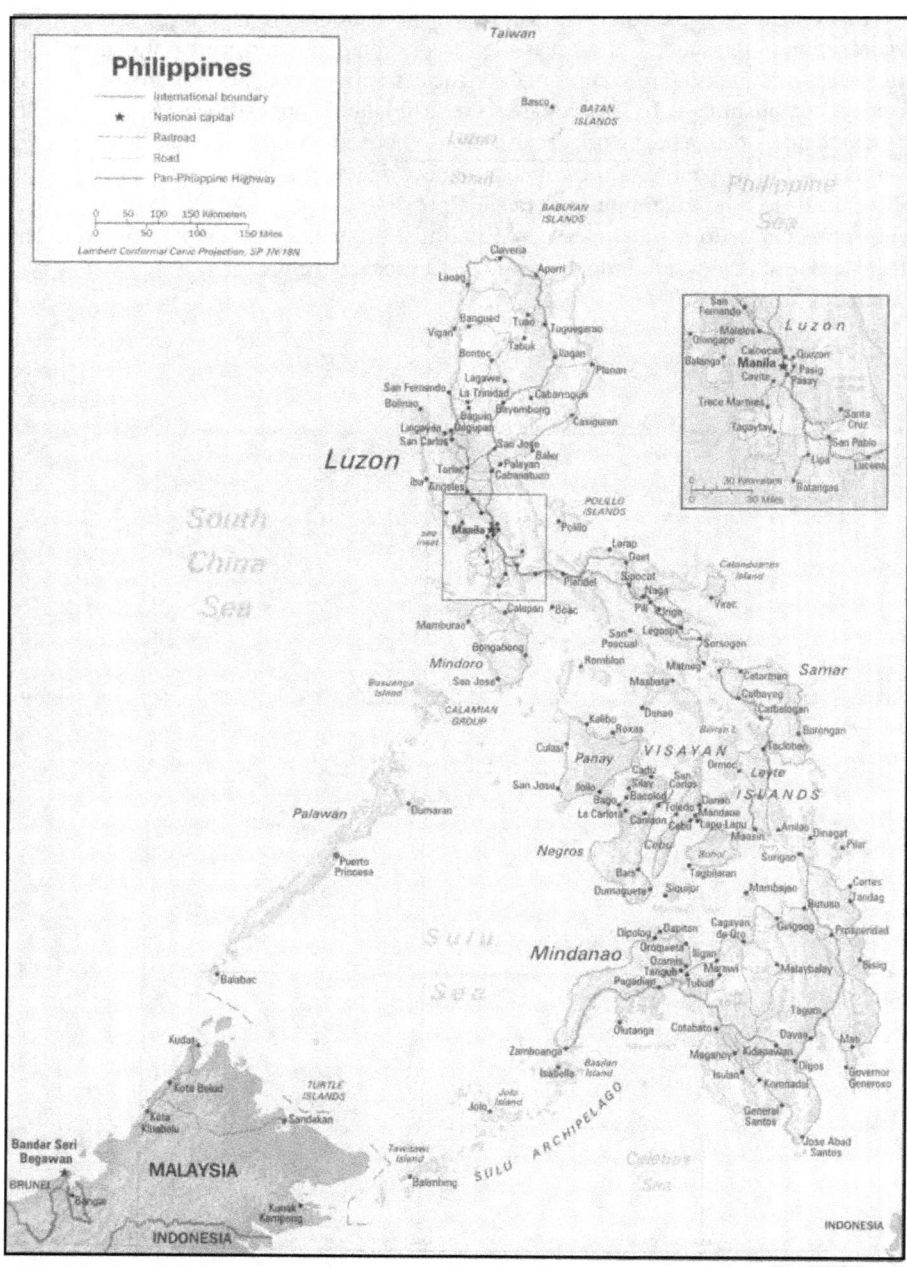

Map of the Philippines.
Source: CIA.

CHAPTER 6

ISLAM IN THE PHILIPPINES

If Filipinos will acknowledge the advantages of pluralism, if they will accept rather than reject it, then the various cultural groups can share a common loyalty to the national community while proudly retaining their distinctiveness.

—Cesar Adib Majul

Despite relative Spanish success over a 300-year period at consolidating rule over the Philippine Islands, Christianizing the great majority of their population, and evoking by the late 19th century a growing sense of Filipino cultural identity among the disparate tribes and peoples that inhabited the archipelago, two areas that had continued to resist and elude firm Spanish control were the Igorot highland tribal people of northern Luzon and the Moros of Mindanao and the Sulu Archipelago in the southern region of the country. By 1898, when Spain was forced to transfer control of the Philippines to the United States as a result of losing the Spanish-American War, the sultanates of Maguindanao and Maranao on Mindanao, and Sulu in the Sulu Archipelago remained intact.[452] From the standpoint of the *sultans*, they remained independent of Spanish control, although, of course, Spain claimed their territories as a part of its colonial holdings, as it had the territory of Sabah on Borneo until 1885, when in exchange for British recognition of Spanish control of Sulu it dropped its claims to Sabah.[453]

---

[452] The predominately Tausug-inhabited Sulu archipelago had only one sultanate, based in Jolo. In Mindanao, two and sometimes three sultanates had existed among the predominately Maguindanao peoples that inhabited the Pulangi river valley that emptied into Ilana Bay on the west coast of the island. Further north, around Lake Lanao, the various tribes that constituted the Maranao people counted as many as 43 sultanates (village states actually). In the Philippines, a *sultan* was a sovereign ruler who paid no tribute (taxes) to another. Subordinate rulers who paid such tribute to a *sultan* were called *datus*. Peter G. Gowing, *Muslim Filipinos: Heritage and Horizon* (Quezon City: New Day Publishers, 1979), 50.

[453] Notably, although Spain may have dropped its claim to Sabah in 1885, the independent government of the Philippines after 1946 resurrected the issue, and it became a matter of fervent dispute between Malaysia and the Philippines in 1963, when Sabah was formally incorporated into Malaysia and again under the Marcos regime in the late 1960s. Not until after the fall of the Marcos regime did successor Philippine President Corazon Aquino attempt to rush a bill renouncing the Philippine claim to Sulu through the Philippine Congress in November 1987, just prior to a visit by Malaysian Prime Minister Mahathir Mohammad to attend an ASEAN summit in Manila. The Philippine Congress failed to act, however, leaving the issue technically unresolved. Ronald E. Dolan, *Philippines: A Country Study* (Washington, DC: U.S. Government Printing Office, 1993), 237.

THE PHILIPPINES UNDER AMERICAN RULE

The Philippine Insurrection

Filipino independence leaders, headed by Emilio Aguinaldo, collaborated with the Americans during the brief war against the Spanish with the aim of achieving Philippine independence, issued a declaration of independence on June 12, 1898, and began forming an independent government in preparation for international recognition. Nevertheless, their hopes were betrayed by the Treaty of Paris, signed between Spain and the United States on December 10, 1898, in which the former colonial power ceded the Philippines, Guam, and Puerto Rico to the U.S. government, while granting Cuba its independence. The treaty provoked outrage throughout the Philippines and, as a result, U.S. occupation forces that grew to 76,000 soldiers before they finally prevailed in 1903 and found themselves engaged in major counterinsurgency operations aimed at preventing the U.S. from taking control of the country.[454]

Suspicious of both the Christian Filipino insurgents and the Americans, the Moro *sultans* did not join the insurrection, hoping to gain recognition as separate from the rest of the Philippines, while at the same time desiring American protection against Christian Filipino efforts to maintain the unity of the former Spanish colony. Accordingly, in August 1898 the Sultan of Sulu, Jamal al-Kiram II, signed an agreement with U.S. General John C. Bates pledging Muslim neutrality in the U.S.-Philippines conflict in return for a U.S. pledge of non-interference in the affairs of the Muslim populations of Mindanao and the Sulu archipelago.[455]

While U.S. military efforts to quell the Philippines independence movement continued, at the political level efforts were underway by a series of U.S.-led commissions to establish an American-guided governance structure for the whole of the Philippines that would "eventually" lead the Filipinos toward "self-rule." The culmination of these efforts was the Philippine Organic Act of July 1902 that, with later changes, became the basis of the constitution governing the Philippines after its grant of independence by the United States in 1946. A part of this Organic Act was a division of the Philippines into provinces, one of which was a Moro province that encompassed both Mindanao and the Sulu archipelago.[456]

---

[454] For a well-documented account of this struggle, see Stuart Creighton Miller, *Benevolent Assimilation: The American Conquest of the Philippines, 1899–1903* (New Haven, CT: Yale University Press, 1982).

[455] Gowing, *Muslim Filipinos*, 34.

[456] *The Philippines: A Country Study*, 28–29.

The Moro Insurrection

Almost immediately, in 1903, efforts were begun to implement the provisions of the Organic Act. For the Moro province, like the others, these provisions meant an abolition of slavery; the establishment of new schools in which a new non-Muslim curriculum was provided; the construction of a new provincial government headed by a governor appointed from Manila, whose authority totally bypassed and undercut that of the historic *sultans*; and the traditional *datus*,[457] who viewed themselves as sovereign rulers and substituted a new legal system that replaced and totally ignored the *shari`a*. From the standpoint of the Moros, but especially their traditional *datus*, American policy in the Philippines was quickly perceived as more destructive and subversive to traditional culture than Spanish rule had ever been. Accordingly, U.S. authorities governing the Philippines soon found themselves faced with a second insurrection against their presence in the southern Philippines, one even more fierce than the first. The Moro insurrection that got underway just as the first insurrection was being quelled continued until 1914, when U.S. forces finally were able to conclude that the

Photo of the Sultan of Sulu, Jamal al-Karim II, who signed an agreement with U.S. forces in 1898 pledging neutrality in the U.S. — Philippines conflict in return for a U.S. pledge of non-interference in the affairs of the Muslim population of Mindanao and the Sulu archipelago.

Source: Peter G. Gowring, *Muslim Filipinos: Heritage and Horizon* (Quezon City: New Day Publishers, 1979). Used with permission.

---

[457] The term *datu*, literally "ruler," or "one entitled to rule," is a complex term that generally refers to the leading male members and descendents of the ruling *sultans'* families since the establishment of Islam in the Philippines in the mid-15th century. Referred to by one author as a myth of "sanctified inequality," the "myth" held that the men who first brought Islam to the southern Philippines and became the first *sultans* of Sulu and Mindanao were both of Arab origin and descendants of the Prophet Muhammad. According to the myth, only the descendants might carry the title of *datu* who formed a ruling class from which the *sultans* were drawn. The *datus*, therefore, constituted an aristocratic class, who were honored whether or not they held a formal position of leadership and authority. Thomas M. McKenna, *Muslim Rulers and Rebels: Everyday Politics and Armed Separatism in the Southern Philippines* (Berkeley, CA: University of California Press, 1998), 45–68. The term *datu* corresponds to the term *tunku* in Malaysia. Gowing, 48, notes that every *datu* was served by a *pandita*, a personal advisor in religious matters. The *panditas* and others, such as *imams* who had charge of mosques, constituted the Philippine `ulama class, but there was less sense of their acting as a collectivity in the traditional Philippines as in most Muslim countries. The *datus* more closely resembled the `ulama class found elsewhere in the Islamic world. McKenna later notes that it was only in the 1980s that the religious authority (but not necessarily the political authority) of the *datus* began to be successfully challenged by a new class of `ulama, the products of scholarship educations in Egypt and Saudi Arabia in the 1950s and 1960s and known locally as *ustadz* (teacher), who stressed the egalitarianism of Islam and the religion's stress on social justice. McKenna, 200–207. It was around this new class of non-*datu* `ulama that the Moro Islamic Liberation Front (MILF) was formed by a minor *datu*, Salamat Hashim, in 1984.

major Muslim resistance groups had been subjugated and the Moro province could be released from military rule.[458]

Failure to Curry American Favor

American success in subduing the Moro insurrection led some Moro leaders to adopt a more positive attitude toward U.S. administrators of the Philippines. Whereas U.S. policy was formally aimed at achieving eventual Philippine independence, and U.S. administrators adopted a "policy of attraction" toward the *ilustrado* leadership class[459] throughout the country, some Moro *datus* curried favor with the U.S. administration in the hope that through cooperation and goodwill they might eventually obtain support for a separate and independent Moro state. American policymakers, desirous of maintaining the goodwill of the large Christian majority in the Philippines, remained committed to the idea of Philippine unity, and in 1920 disestablished the American governor of the "Department of Mindanao and Sulu," turning over responsibility for governance of the Moro region to the Bureau of Non-Christian Tribes of the recently established Philippine Department of Interior that reported to the Philippine Legislature (created in 1906). In response, a few months later, in June 1921, a group of 57 prominent *datus* in Sulu presented a petition both in Manila and Washington requesting that the United States either grant the Moros a separate independent state or retain their lands as "permanent American territory."[460]

Later, in 1935, reacting to the U.S. decision to grant the Philippines Commonwealth status for a 10-year transition period prior to becoming independent, a group of 120 Lanao *datus* (Mindanao) addressed a letter to President Franklin Roosevelt that read in part:

Because we have learned that the United States is going to give the Philippines independence, we want to tell you that the Philippines is populated by two different peoples with different religious practices and traditions. The Christian Filipinos occupy the islands of Luzon and the Visayas. The Moros (Muslims) predominate

---

[458] On the Moro insurrection, the major study is that of Samuel K. Tan, *The Filipino Muslim Armed Struggle, 1900–1972* (Manila: Filipinas Foundation, 1977). For a brief account, see W.K. Che Man, *Muslim Separatism: The Moros of Southern Philippines and the Malays of Southern Thailand* (Quezon City: Ateneo de Manila University Press, 1990), 46–51.

[459] The *ilustrado* or "oligarchy of intelligence" was a wealthy Filipino landowning, business, and professional elite that had emerged in the Christianized Philippines in the latter half of the 19th century, typically as a result of close collaboration with the Spanish colonial authorities. Often educated in European schools and universities, it was around this class that ideas of Philippine nationalism, as opposed to local ethnic identity, began to coalesce as well as among some, ideas of securing independence from Spanish rule. *The Philippines: A Country Study*, 16–22, 29. U.S. administrators cultivated this class during the colonial period, and its descendants have tended to dominate Philippine life until now. The Moro *datu* class were not technically a part of this class, but their role in the Moro areas was similar, and some responded by cooperating with American colonial rule and the independent Philippine state after 1946. For a detailed examination of this collaboration, see McKenna, *Muslim Rulers and Rebels*, 88–112.

[460] Gowing, *Muslim Filipinos*, 168.

in the islands of Mindanao and Sulu. With regard to the forthcoming independence, we foresee what condition we and our children who shall come after us will be in. This condition will be characterized by unrest, suffering, and misery and because of this we do not desire to be independent. It is by living under the Stars and Stripes that those hardships would not bear down against us. The Americans have ever respected our religion, customs, traditions and practices. They have also recognized our rights to our property. The Americans have directed most of their efforts for the welfare of our people.[461]

Regardless of the relative accuracy of the prediction made in this letter, various U.S. administrations remained committed to maintaining the integrity of the Philippine state that had been ceded to the United States by Spain in 1898 and won by hard-fought battle.[462] Most U.S. administrators, committed to a "civilizing mission" of promoting education, improved health care, economic development, rule by [American-derived] law and democratic principles of governance, and originating in a society that took religious tolerance and freedom of religion for granted, simply could not see that their well-intended efforts might fail to achieve the civilizing goal toward which they were directed, especially in "Moroland," as they tended to call it. American administrators were also strongly influenced by the adamant opposition of Philippine Christian leaders, who represented 95 percent of the country's population, to any diminution of the Philippine state. Moreover, although

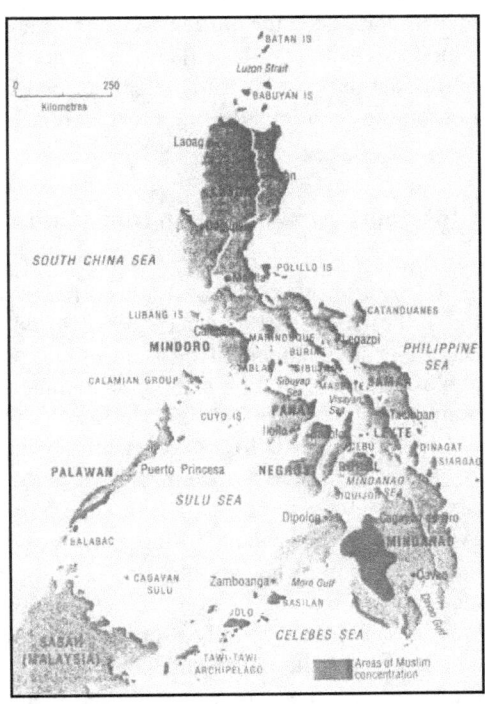

Map of the Philippines showing areas of Muslim concentration.

Source: Author.

the largely Protestant orientation of most U.S. administrators led many of them to view the historically dominant role of the Catholic Church in the Philippines with

---

[461] Cited in Gowing, *Muslim Filipinos*, 169.

[462] The ultimate rationale for this position was that failure to maintain the unity of the Philippine state might open the door to competing imperial powers — England, the Netherlands, Germany, Japan — to inherit parts of the Philippines left unclaimed by the United States. At the beginning, some, including Admiral Dewey, argued that the U.S. should lay claim only to Manila as an American naval base in the far Pacific and perhaps one or two other places as coaling stations. After the hard-fought battles to defeat the Philippine insurgency, however, it was politically difficult to challenge those who argued that the Philippines was America's by right because of the blood and sacrifice expended by its soldiers and sailors during a more than decade-long military campaign. See Miller, *Benevolent Assimilation*, 13–30.

some suspicion, their general view of the Moro lands, which they shared with most Christian Filipinos, was that they were inhabited by a backward and stubbornly unprogressive people who needed association with the more economically developed Christian-dominated Philippine state in order to share the benefits of the modern, more "civilized" world.[463]

During the period of direct American rule over the Philippines (until 1920 in the Moro province), American administrators did pay special attention to the Moro province. Its first and only U.S. civilian governor, Frank Carpenter, was an educator who placed great emphasis on the building of schools and promoting universal education based on a modern [American-based] curriculum of instruction. The provision of health clinics, new roads and port facilities, telephone and telegraph networks and other infrastructure to promote economic development were also parts of the American program.

Christian Transmigration into Mindanao

The establishment of a number of Christian Filipino agricultural settlements on the still sparsely populated island of Mindanao also had as its aim the more rapid economic development of the island as well as facilitating Christian-Muslim interaction and eventual integration of both as members of a united Philippine society. This last policy, which became a flood during the Commonwealth period (1935–1946) and continued unabated in the years after independence in 1946, became the primary issue that finally led to the emergence of the Moro separatist movement in the 1970s. The Moros were not pleased with all U.S. policies in their region, however, and were even less pleased when, in the years after 1920, administration of Moroland was increasingly in the hands of Christian Filipino rather than American administrators. Outbreaks of resistance were common, usually over specific issues and in specific locations, but were rapidly suppressed, at first by U.S. forces, and later increasingly by elements of the Philippine Constabulary. The overall defeat of the Moros by U.S. forces by 1913 had gravely weakened them and prevented any immediate revival of a common struggle. Specific issues such as the *cedula* (a government-imposed head tax on all inhabitants) that the *datus* opposed because it eliminated their traditional role as revenue collectors; the requirement to turn in arms; opposition to compulsory education in the new government schools that did not teach *shari`a*; exactions for road construction; efforts to enforce monogamy; and maltreatment by the Philippine Constabulary[464] were the usual sources of dissatisfaction.

---

[463] Gowing, *Muslim Filipinos*, 38–42.

[464] For details concerning many of the resistance movements, see Tan, *Filipino Muslim Armed Struggle*, 32–42, and Che Man, *Muslim Separatism*, 51–56.

	Table 3			
	Estimated Moro and Non-Moro Populations in Mindanao, 1903–1980			
	Moro Population		**Non-Moro Population**	
Year	**Number**	**Percent**	**Number**	**Percent**
1903	250,000	76	77,741	24
1913	324,816	63	193,882	37
1918	358,968	50	364,687	50
1939	755,189	34	1,489,232	66
1948	933,101	32	2,0101,223	68
1960	1,321,060	23	4,364,967	77
1970	1,669,708	21	6,294,224	79
1975	1,798,911	20	7,348,084	80
1980	2,504,332	23	8,400,911	77

Source: W.K. Che Man, *Muslim Separatism: The Moros of Southern Philippines and the Malays of Southern Thailand* (Quezon City: Ateneo de Manila University Press, 1990), 25. Citing Philippines, *National Economic and Development Authority* (1980a).

Transmigration: Source of Growing Alienation

By far the most irritating issue related to conflicts associated with land resettlement by Christian Filipinos on Mindanao. Historically, although there long had been small settlements of Christians on the island, they lived on lands claimed by the *sultans* and paid taxes to them. The political authority of the *sultans* and *datus* was no longer recognized by the government created by U.S. administrators and was gradually turned over to Filipino administrators, having no clear title to most of these lands as new Filipino law required. Hence, it was not a difficult matter for Philippine officials to lay claim on behalf of the government to unsettled tracts of land for purposes of Christian settlement, particularly with the Philippine Constabulary available to enforce government policy. Matters became more critical during the Commonwealth period after 1935, when resettlement became part of an overall economic development plan for Mindanao (a reaction to the Great Depression of 1929). This plan, which foresaw aggressive settlement and economic development of Mindanao as a project beneficial for the entire Philippine state and involved confiscation of settled lands for purposes of economic development, virtually ignored the original Muslim inhabitants of the land and was designed almost entirely around the new settlers whose numbers were growing rapidly. Significant corruption in the National Land Settlement Administration (NLSA) that administered this plan also enabled a number of wealthy Christian speculators with advance knowledge of government plans to obtain title to lands that placed them in a position to exploit both Christian settlers and Muslim inhabitants of the island.[465]

Cooperation During World War II

Despite continuing and growing alienation between the Muslim inhabitants of the South and the emerging Philippine government, Moros generally joined in with Christian Filipinos and American forces in resisting the Japanese forces that occupied the Philippine islands between 1942 and 1945. Unlike their policy in Malaysia and Indonesia, where the Japanese had sought to empower the existing Malay Muslim national movements against the former colonial powers—Britain and Holland—they were equally harsh with both Muslims and Christians in the Philippines. Although a number of *ilustrados* and *datus* collaborated with the Japanese occupation forces in order to protect their private interests—a collaboration that became an important issue in Philippine politics after the war-a number of them also led resistance forces against the Japanese during the occupation.

The vast majority of Moros in fact were quite active in the resistance against the Japanese, as they had been against all forces trying to occupy their soil, be it the Spanish, the Americans, the Christian Filipinos, or the Japanese. Somewhat empowered by funds and large quantities of arms and ammunition provided by American submarines based in Australia, some Moros took advantage of the fall of the Commonwealth government to the Japanese to drive Christian settlers from their recently occupied farms into the cities of Mindanao, where the bulk of Japanese occupation forces were located. At the same time, they also collaborated closely with Christian Filipino resistance groups against the occupation.[466]

THE MOROS UNDER PHILIPPINE RULE

Early Benefits

The role played by the Moros during the war in resisting the Japanese produced several outcomes in the post-war period. In gratitude for their service, the restored Commonwealth government appointed a number of former Muslim guerrilla leaders (mostly *datus*) to high political office (including governorships of the Moro provinces), and a number of Muslim leaders ran successfully for Congress. This policy continued under the independent Republican government after 1946, giving the Moros a sense of self-government they had not known for half a century.[467]

---

[465] An excellent analysis of the settlement process is provided by McKenna, *Muslim Rulers and Rebels*, 114–119. See also Cesar Adib Majul, *The Contemporary Muslim Movement in the Philippines* (Berkeley, CA: Mizan Press, 1985), 26–27, and Che Man, *Muslim Separatism*, 24–29.

[466] Gowing, *Muslim Filipinos*, 181–182.

[467] Majul, *Contemporary Muslim Movement*, 27–28.

Secondly, back pay awarded to those who could demonstrate their participation in the resistance and Japanese reparations payments to families for destroyed properties poured monies into the local economy, fueling a period of relative Moro prosperity. The impact of this new wealth cut two ways, however. On one hand, it tended to transform the Moro areas from a traditional barter economy into one based more on cash transactions, leading many to aspire to salaried jobs and professional and business careers, rather than traditional farming. As the economic bubble gradually receded by the late 1950s, however, the Moros increasingly became conscious of how relatively disadvantaged they were in relation to the rest of the country. On the other hand, the period of prosperity also facilitated a growing sense of Moro nationhood, a pride in being Moro that expressed itself in stronger commitment to Islamic activities. Hundreds now could afford to make the annual *hajj* (pilgrimage) to Mecca and began doing so. There was also an emphasis on the construction of new mosques and *madrasas* and a revival of numerous and often impressive, as well as costly, religious festivals.[468]

Finally, a third outcome stemmed from the large quantities of arms and ammunition that had come into Moro hands during the war. Determined not to be disarmed again, as they had been after the American suppression of the Moro resistance in the early part of the century, some Moros adamantly refused to turn in their weapons, while others simply proclaimed they had "lost" them. At least the Moros now possessed a stronger deterrent against government efforts to impose policies in the Moro areas they didn't like.[469]

Acceleration of Transmigration

While the Moro region remained increasingly self-assured and relatively quiescent during the immediate post-war period, the major problem faced by the central government in Manila was the Hukbalahap (Huk) rebellion in central Luzon, the main northernmost island of the Philippines. Fundamentally a rural peasant uprising against rich landowners who dominated the Philippines both politically and economically, the movement was also a continuation of resistance against the Japanese occupation,[470] with which so many of the wealthy landowners had collaborated. Although government forces ultimately prevailed by 1954, the Huk rebellion preoccupied the government for nearly a decade. One mechanism finally used by the government to defuse the rebellion was resettlement of some 950 families of former Huks on lands purchased for them by the government on Mindanao.[471]

---

[468] Majul, *Contemporary Muslim Movement*, 28. McKenna, *Muslim Rulers and Rebels*, 136.

[469] Gowing, *Muslim Filipinos*, 183.

[470] The Hukbalahap, or People's Anti-Japanese Army, had been organized in 1942 by Luis Taruc, a member of the Philippines communist party. An estimated 30,000 strong during the war, it was the leading resistance movement against the Japanese occupation in Luzon, but it was also opposed to any restoration of U.S. authority in the Philippines after the war, and also to the wealthy Filipino landowning class that exploited the peasants making up the Huk movement. *Philippines: A Country Study*, 41.

[471] *Philippines: A Country Study*, 48.

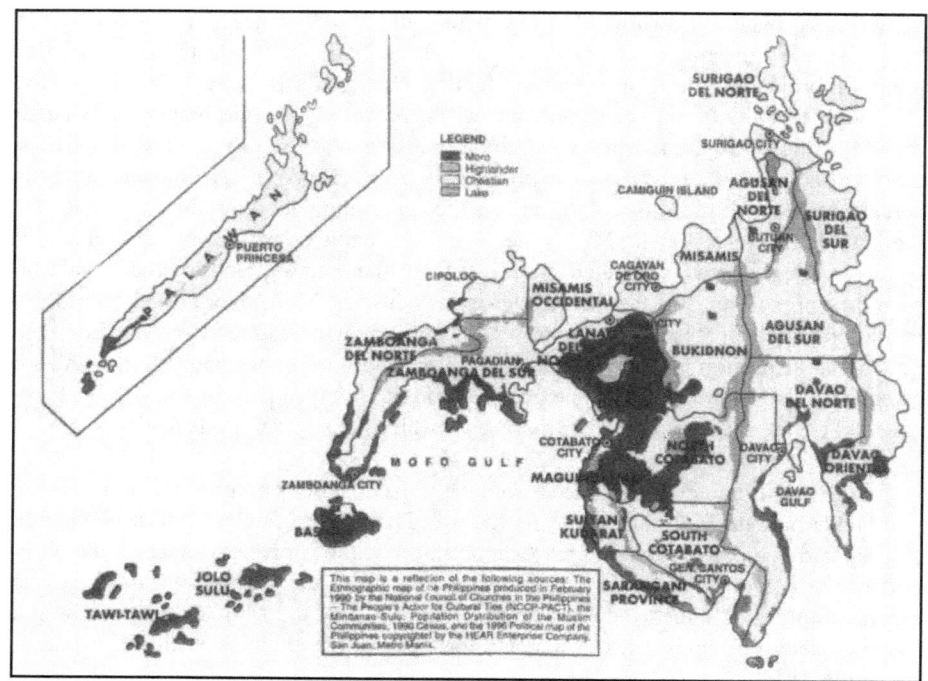

Map of the southern portion of the Philippines, indicating predominantly Muslim areas of Mindanao, Sulu, and Palawan islands.

Source: HEAR Enterprise Company, San Juan, Metro Manila, Philippines. Provided to the author by Eugene Martin, United States Institute of Peace. Used with permission.

The resettlement of the Huk rebels, who previously had held the status of criminal terrorists in the eyes of the government, and their families on Mindanao was only part of a much larger resettlement program that had resumed after the hiatus period of World War II. Now managed by the Army-administered Economic Development Corps (EDCOR), the program had as its goals not only relief of overpopulated areas in the northern Philippines by resettlement in the relatively underpopulated south but also the economic development of Mindanao as a means of more effectively integrating the southern islands into the Philippine economy. A part of this program was provision of low-interest loans and other forms of government assistance, such as new varieties of seeds, fertilizers, herbicides, tractors and farm machinery, as well as the building of new roads, irrigation networks, and swamp-draining projects. The recipients of the benefits of these programs were mainly the new settlers who happened to be Christian rather than the indigenous inhabitants who happened to be Muslims.[472]

The long-term result of these efforts was a major demographic shift in the population of Mindanao. Whereas in 1903 Muslims had constituted approximately 75 percent of the population of the island, by the 1960s they constituted no more than 25 percent,

---

[472] McKenna, *Muslim Rulers and Rebels*, 116–117.

and significant numbers of them had been driven off their farm lands and into villages or growing urban slums in the increasingly Christian major towns of Mindanao. More important perhaps than the demographic shift was the gradual "marginalization" of the Moros in their own lands, both economically and socially, if not entirely politically.

In a purely technical sense, such marginalization need not have happened, for government policy officially provided equal access to state resources for both Christians and Muslims.[473] The Moros, however, generally remained aloof from dealings with the government as much as possible, and they deeply resented official efforts to forge Philippine unity by application of national laws that contradicted or did not take into account the requirements of Muslims under the *shari`a*. They also resented a nationally-run education program and curriculum designed to forge a strong sense of Philippine identity but that also seemingly designed to alienate their children from Islam.[474] Then too, Philippine government administrators-mostly Christian-identified more closely with the needs and aspirations of the settlers and tended to be oblivious to the needs and aspirations of the Moros, who preferred to minimize their contacts with Filipino administrators in any case. As the leading Muslim historian of the Philippines put it:

> The increase of the non-Muslim population in [Mindanao] led many Muslims to conclude that there was a deliberate government scheme either to disperse them or to ensure that they remain a permanent minority in their own territories. They noted with frustration, if not envy, that the areas where the Christians had settled now had better roads and more effective irrigation projects, civic centers, and schools in comparison with their own backward facilities. So they believed that they were the victims of government discrimination and of neglect by their own leaders. In turn, Muslim leaders blamed all the ills on the so-called Christian government in Manila.[475]

Continued Moro Quiescence

Although perhaps it was only a matter of time before the situation reached some type of crisis, no organized opposition to the central government or its policies in the south emerged until the late 1960s and early 1970s. In part, this was due to the continuing role played by leading Muslim political figures as elected representatives to the Congress-often with the help of votes from Christian settlers who linked their own sense of security with voting for Muslim candidates-and the continued appointment of Muslim governors and mayors in Muslim majority areas. Usually these figures were members of the traditional *datu* class who had thrown in their lot with cooperation and collaboration with the central government, were still honored and remembered as

---

[473] McKenna, *Muslim Rulers and Rebels*, 118.

[474] Majul, *Contemporary Muslim Movement*, 29–30.

[475] Majul, *Contemporary Muslim Movement*, 32.

guerrilla leaders against the Japanese occupation, and continued to reap the benefits of participation in Philippine politics. Although the Moro population was in general alienated from the larger Filipino society, its members continued to respect their *datus*, a legacy of traditional Moro society that remained helpful in containing mounting Moro resentment.

Yet another mechanism used by the Philippine government as an effort to facilitate the integration of young Moros into mainstream society was education. In 1957, in response to a study of Moro needs, the government established a Committee on National Integration (CNI), the chief focus of which came to be the granting of scholarships to Muslims and other minority groups. Over the next 20 years, several thousand young Muslims were provided with free higher education at academic institutions in Manila, especially in law, which provided them entry into government and professional positions.[476] Such educations, however, tended to promote cynicism about the old political order among the Moros, especially the *datus* and those political figures whom the students tended to define as collaborators.[477] Many became involved in a host of new activist organizations-the Muslim Association of the Philippines, the Muslim Progress Movement, the Agama Islam Society, the Sulu Islamic Congress, the Muslim Youth National Assembly, the Union of Islamic Forces, the Muslim Lawyers' League, the Supreme Islamic Council, and others[478]—that had as their aim the raising of Moro consciousness as Muslim Filipinos and advocating programs to benefit their less fortunate countrymen. Although not originally intended as opposition groups, they did have the impact of giving voice to a new "articulately literate class" capable of analyzing and defining the plight of the Moros in new and more modern ways.[479]

Simultaneous with this trend was another set of scholarships that were made available during the same era for Muslim students from the Philippines to study in various universities in the Middle East. Several hundred Filipino Muslims studied in these years at universities in Egypt, Saudi Arabia, Syria, Algeria and Libya. Although some focused on professional studies, such as engineering or medicine, a great many devoted themselves to Islamic studies at Cairo's al-Azhar University or the Islamic University of Medina, Saudi Arabia.[480] The experience of these students had the impact of broadening their horizons and raising their consciousness of being connected to a larger Islamic world beyond their small provincial region in the southern Philippines. Many others also established contacts with fellow students from many parts of the Islamic world that later would be useful in soliciting international Islamic support for the Moros of the Philippines.

---

[476] McKenna, *Muslim Rulers and Rebels*, 140.

[477] Abuza, *Militant Islam in Southeast Asia*, 36.

[478] Gowing, *Muslim Filipinos*, 186.

[479] The term "articulately literate class" is that of McKenna, *Muslim Rulers and Rebels*, 136.

[480] Che Man, *Muslim Separatism*, 57.

THE MORO REVOLT

The Moro National Liberation Front

The revolt, when it finally erupted in the early 1970s, was due to a variety of factors, in addition to those already mentioned. Centered on a new movement among the Moros, the Moro National Liberation Front (MNLF), the revolt was led by the new generation of university-educated Muslims from the south who conceptualized the Moros, not as Tausugs or Samals of Sulu, Maguindanao of Cotabato [Mindanao], Maranao or Iranun of Lannao [Mindanao], or Palawani or Molbog of Palawan, all owing loyalty to their respective *datus* or *sultans*, but as a single Muslim nation (*Bangsa Moro*), inherently separate from the rest of the Philippines, and more closely attached to the larger Islamic world of which the Moros were a part, especially the Malay Muslims of Indonesia and Malaysia.[481]

Established clandestinely in late 1968 or early 1969, the MNLF was a nationalist movement modeled after other anti-colonial resistance organizations that were common in many parts of the Third World in the 1960s, such as the FLN in Algeria, the PLO among the Palestinian Arabs, or the PULO among the Malays of nearby Thailand. Having as its aims the mobilization of general Moro support; the recruitment, training, and equipping of armed cadres to resist Philippine "imperialism"; and obtaining international backing for the justness of its cause, the MNLF unambiguously organized itself with the ultimate aim of achieving Moro political independence from the Philippines.

The Jabida Incident. The event that sparked the formation of the MNLF was the so-called Jabidah massacre of Muslim conscript soldiers on the island of Corregidor in Manila Bay in March 1968. President Ferdinand Marcos, elected President of the Philippine Republic in 1965, was widely perceived as engaging in a cover-up of the incident in order to dissociate his Presidency from it. Allegedly being trained for military operations in Sabah, a province of Malaysia since 1963, in support of the Philippines' historic claim to that region, the Moro soldiers were said to have mutinied upon learning the purpose of their training and were killed in cold blood to ensure their silence.

---

[481] McKenna presents the interesting argument that the historic tendency of the Spanish, then the Americans, and finally the Filipinos themselves to conceptualize the Muslims of the southern Philippines as a more or less collective entity — the Moros — despite the vast ethnic diversity and inter — as well as intra-ethnic rivalries that characterized traditional "Moro" society and contributed to its weakness politically was finally absorbed by a critical mass of Moro students studying in Philippine schools and universities. In other words, the idea that the Moros constituted a single people was fundamentally a Western idea that was finally absorbed by those Filipino Muslims who had been drawn into the Philippine educational system with the purpose of facilitating their integration into Philippine society. The unintended consequence was to facilitate an idea of Moro nationalism, based on new and modern premises, that contributed to the formation of the MNLF. McKenna, *Muslim Rulers and Rebels*, 86–88, 110–112.

Although probably more rumor than fact-the government position was that the mutiny was over back pay issues and living conditions-the story was widely believed among the Moros and also in Malaysia, whose government lent its support to the newly established MNLF.[482] The final acquittal of those Philippine officers and soldiers associated with the killings sparked massive anti-government demonstrations in Manila and produced the resolve among many Moros to align themselves with the idea of an independent *Bangsa Moro*.

Christian Transmigrants React. Almost immediately, on May 1, 1968, *Datu* Udtog Matalam, the former influential governor of Cotabato [Mindanao], announced the formation of the Muslim Independence Movement (MIM) out of which the MNLF grew as its "student branch." Its stated purpose was to "work toward gaining independence for Mindanao and Sulu."[483] Despite the apparent inactivity of the new organization, the growing popularity of the movement and of *Datu* Matalam caused concern among the Christian settlers of Mindanao, and various Christian militia groups began to emerge to defend Christian rights on the island. Although open conflict did not emerge until 1970, the atmosphere on Mindanao became increasingly tense, leading *Datu* Matalam at one point to change the name of his organization to the Mindanao Independence Movement (still MIM) in an effort to reassure Christian settlers, among whom the *datu* had been historically popular.[484]

The MIM was in fact a cover organization for the MNLF, the student branch of MIM that was being organized clandestinely, primarily in Sabah, under the leadership of Nur Misuari, a former professor of politics at the University of the Philippines. What Datu Matalam and other *datus* associated with him did not realize at this point was that Misuari's vision of the organization he was forming was that of a modern nationalist movement in which the traditional "feudalist" position of *datu* in Moro society would eventually have to be overturned. Conflict between Misuari and the traditional *datus* would in the end emerge as a source of grave weakness for the MNLF, when many *datus* turned back to collaboration with the Marcos government, as Misuari and the MNLF increasingly gained Islamic world recognition as the official representative of the Moro cause in the southern Philippines.

For the moment, however, the MNLF and the MIM worked in close collaboration. Key figures in the development of the MNLF were Matalam colleague Datu Rashid

---

[482] Che Man, *Muslim Separatism*, 139–140.

[483] Majul, *Contemporary Muslim Movement*, 45.

[484] McKenna argues that Datu Matalam, long a proponent of Christian-Muslim harmony in Mindanao, formed the MIM, not out of ideological reasons, but for personal political motives. A member of the Liberalista party, he was defeated in the 1967 elections for governor of Cotabato by a younger Muslim *datu* who was aligned with President Marcos' Nationalista Party. His personal interest, therefore, was less to achieve Moro political independence, despite his public stance, than to advance his own personal political standing among the Muslims of the Cotabato region. McKenna, *Muslim Rulers and Rebels*, 144–146.

Lucman of Lanao, Misuari, and Tun Mustafa, the elected governor of Sabah.[485] In 1969 a first batch of 90 young Muslim recruits, mostly Maranaos provided by Lucman, but including Misuari, a Tausug from Sulu, quietly departed for Sabah to receive military training provided by professional Malaysian instructors under the overall guidance of Tun Mustafa. Additional groups were sent for training in the following years.[486] On their return to the southern Philippines to train other recruits for the MNLF, they also smuggled in weapons provided by Tun Mustafa and the Malaysian government, and after 1972 by Libyan leader Muammar Qadhafi who became a major external supporter of the MNLF.

Outbreak of Violence. Growing sectarian tension in Mindanao erupted into violence in mid-1970. This was not a matter of Christian militias fighting Muslim militias, but rather of one militia attacking and burning the undefended village of the other sect and then being retaliated against by the destruction of a village associated with the offending militia—a strategy designed to inflame tensions rather than to achieve victory. Such tit-for-tat violence continued through 1971, when by the end of the year it was estimated that more than 100,000 inhabitants of Mindanao from both sides had been made homeless refugees and 800 lives had been lost.[487]

Escalation of the Conflict

Two events in 1971 and 1972 rapidly transformed the escalating conflict into a full-scale civil war between the MNLF and the Government of the Philippines. The first was congressional elections held in November 1971 in which Muslim candidates, for the first time since the establishment of the Republic in 1946, were swept from office. The growing insecurity in Mindanao led many Christians who previously had voted for Muslim candidates as a guarantee of their security now expressed their lack of confidence in the Muslim *datus* by voting for Christian candidates. As a result, "political power in areas that historically had been part of the sultanates shifted from Muslims to Christians."[488] Some of the violence during 1971 had been politically motivated and designed to secure precisely the political results that occurred. Ironically, following the election, sectarian violence subsided and the security situation in Mindanao under the new political order became increasingly benign until the end of 1972, although the psychological shock of what had happened proved transformative.

---

[485] Tun Mustafa was a Tausug Muslim with many close relatives living in Sulu and also a close associate of *Datu* Rashid Lucman. McKenna, *Muslim Rulers and Rebels*, 147–148.

[486] Included in the second group in 1970 was Haj Ali Murad, later Chief of Military Operations of the Moro Islamic Liberation Front (MILF), a breakaway organization from the MNLF, and later head of the the MILF after the death of its founder and leader, Hashim Salamat, in July 2003. International Crisis Group, "Southern Philippines Backgrounder: Terrorism and the Peace Process" (Singapore/Brussels: ICG Asia Report No. 80, July 13, 2004),4. URL: *http://www.crisisgroup.org/home/index.cfm?id=2863&l=1.* Accessed April 13, 2005.

[487] For a detailed analysis of this pattern of violence, see McKenna, *Muslim Rulers and Rebels*, 149–156. Also Majul, *Contemporary Muslim Movement*, 47–58, and Gowing, *Muslim Filipinos*, 192–196.

[488] Majul, *Contemporary Muslim Movement*, 56.

Declaration of Martial Law

The second shock arrived on September 21, 1972, when President Ferdinand Marcos declared martial law throughout the Philippines. Although the communist-inspired New People's Army (NPA), established in 1968, was a growing threat, it did not yet constitute the challenge to government authority posed by the Huk rebellion, its predecessor movement in the 1950s, and the proclamation of martial law only strengthened the appeal of the NPA within the country.[489] The primary reason for Marcos' action appears to have been to lay the basis for arresting and detaining about 30,000 individuals whom he considered part of his political opposition, including rival politician Benigno Aquino.[490] In publicly stating his rationale, however, he gave the principal reasons for the declaration of martial law the existence of armed conflict between Muslims and Christians and a Muslim "secessionist movement" in the southern Philippines.[491] From the perspective of the Moros, the declaration was the final straw. It was a declaration of war against a defeated people who now had no option except that of resistance.

Ferdinand Marcos, controversial long-time President of the Philippines from 1965 to 1986.

Source: URL: *http://www.encarta.com.*

Internationalization of the Moro Issue

Marcos may have been influenced in his decision to declare martial law by pressures coming from a number of Islamic countries expressing grave concern about the welfare of the Moros in southern Philippines. International reporting on the violence, especially with regard to those few cases where Philippine government forces seemed to be in league with the Christian militias, spurred charges of genocide and pressure on the Marcos government to be more active in preventing it. Malaysia and Kuwait were particularly vocal, but the most indignant was Libyan leader Muammar Qadhafi, who on October 7, 1971, made a bitter speech accusing the Philippine government of genocide. He also announced that he was sending a personal mission to the Philippines to study the situation and to provide aid to the refugees.[492] Later, in January 1972, another delegation consisting of the ambassadors to the Philippines of eight different Islamic countries[493] toured the south at the request of President Marcos to investigate

---

[489] *Philippines: A Country Study*, 280–290.

[490] *Philippines: A Country Study*, 52.

[491] Ferdinand Marcos, "Proclamation of Martial Law," *Philippine Sunday Express*, 1, 141 (September 24, 1972), 7.

[492] Majul, *Contemporary Islamic Movement*, 55.

[493] Egypt, Indonesia, Malaysia, Singapore, Pakistan, Iran, Iraq, and Saudi Arabia. Singapore, though technically not a Muslim country, nevertheless has a 15 percent Malay Muslim population, is a significant regional entity, and is perforce closely tied to the affairs of its predominately Islamic region.

186

the situation. Although their report absolved the government of charges of genocide, its description of the wretched plight of especially the Muslim refugees in Mindanao garnered widespread attention in the Islamic world.

The issue of the southern Philippines was raised at the Third Islamic Conference of Foreign Ministers (ICFM) that met in Jiddah, Saudi Arabia, between February 29 and March 4, 1972. The Conference referred the issue to the Seventh Conference of the Research Academy of al-Azhar University (Egypt), scheduled to meet in Cairo on September 9, 1972. There on behalf of the Islamic Conference Organization (OIC) that would remain engaged with the situation in the southern Philippines until today, "the Conference passed a resolution expressing grave concern over the situation of Muslim Filipinos."[494] Two weeks later, despite the fact that violence in the south had virtually ended, at least for the moment, President Marcos made his decision to impose martial law, disestablish the Philippine Congress, and assume dictatorial authority.

Under the circumstances, "the imposition of martial law was, in fact the proximate cause, not the consequence, of [the] armed Muslim insurgency against the Philippine state,"[495] that likely would at least have been delayed had there been no martial law. As it was, the Army moved immediately to collect all unauthorized weapons in the Philippines and a ban was placed on all political organizations. The moment was an existential one for the Moros of the Philippines. The choice was to submit or resist. Most Moros chose the course of resistance.

The MNLF Takes Charge

The ban on political organizations brought the clandestine MNLF to the forefront of the gathering confrontation. The previously above-ground organizations, such as the MIM or Salamat Hashim's *Nurul Islam*, were immediately dissolved, with many of their members rallying to the MNLF. Salamat, later leader of the Moro Islamic Liberation Front (MILF) after his break with Misauri, became vice-chairman of the MNLF. Throughout the conflict, the MNLF remained a loose-knit organization, which at best could only coordinate and support various groups of fighters operating independently in different sectors. The primary reason for its ascendancy derived in large part "from its access to critical resources, particularly weapons, from outside the Philippines."[496] These came primarily by boat from Sabah, having been delivered there from Libya and a number of other Muslim states.[497]

[494] Majul, *Contemporary Islamic Movement*, 59.

[495] McKenna, *Muslim Rulers and Rebels*, 156.

[496] McKenna, *Muslim Rulers and Rebels*, 157.

[497] Che Man, *Muslim Separatism*, 148.

Yet another reason for the MNLF ascendancy was the fact that it had gained the attention of the external Islamic world, which was a vital source of support for the Moro struggle. From fairly early in the conflict, most of the top leadership of the MNLF, including Misuari and Hashim-wanted men in the Philippines-were in exile in Tripoli, Libya, where, with the support of Libyan leader Qadhafi, they constituted the "political front" of the MNLF, as opposed to its fighting arm in the Philippines, known as the *Bangsa Moro* Army. There, *Datu* Abulkhayr Alonto, a member of a prominent Maranao family in northern Mindanao, served as overall commander of military operations.

Civil War

Fighting erupted on October 24, 1972, the day before the deadline President Marcos had set for the turning in of all weapons. It quickly spread to most Muslim-populated areas of Mindanao and then Sulu, as Moro fighters, in accordance with an apparently well-coordinated plan, attacked government outposts and sought to take control of strategic positions vital for dominating the region. The government, somewhat surprised by the intensity of the uprising, sent thousands of troops south, and by late November fierce clashes were taking place throughout the south between government forces and the Moro separatists.[498]

With the advantage of aircraft, helicopters, troop carriers, superior troop strength and mobility, as well as heavy weapons, the Philippine Armed Forces (AFP) were able to beat back most rebel attacks that were increasingly coordinated by the MNLF and to wreak devastating damage on towns and villages believed to harbor rebel fighters. Despite the advantages of the AFP, it could not end the rebellion, which only escalated over the next three years before finally abating in 1976. At its peak between 1973 and 1975, the MNLF was estimated to be able to field 30,000 fighters, while the Philippine military deployed 70 to 80 percent of its strength to contain the rebellion.[499] The destruction caused in the Moro areas by both sides, but especially by the AFP, was massive. The war was estimated to have produced 50,000 deaths and a refugee population of over one million.[500]

Philippine government determination to crush the rebellion and to preempt the MNLF-led effort to establish an independent *Bangsa Moro* produced many outrages, such as the virtual destruction of the city of Jolo, the capital of Sulu and former seat of the

---

[498] McKenna, *Muslim Rulers and Rebels*, 156.

[499] General Fortunato U. Abat, *The Day We Nearly Lost Mindanao: The CEM-CON Story*, 3rd ed. (Manila: FCA Publishers, 1999), 165–166.

[500] *Philippines: A Country Study*, 291; Abuza, *Militant Islam in Southeast Asia*, 38.

Sultanate of Sulu, in February 1974.[501] With each new report of even greater suffering of the Philippine Muslims, international Islamic world pressure, which previously had been exerted on the Marcos government to be more active in ameliorating the conflict, now began to be exerted even more forcibly to achieve a diplomatic settlement. The Marcos government was highly subject to this pressure, because 40 percent of its oil imports came from these countries, especially Saudi Arabia and Iran, whose influence in international affairs after the 1974 oil crisis had been substantially augmented.[502]

International Intervention

The Islamic Conference Organization (OIC) and more particularly its Islamic Conference of Foreign Ministers (ICFM) were the principal agents for exerting this pressure. An important difficulty was that the MNLF, whose leaders were perceived as wanted criminals by the Philippine government, was increasingly gaining the support of member countries of the OIC as the only representative with whom the Marcos regime could negotiate an end to the conflict. Complicating this difficulty was the demand of MNLF leader Nur Misauri that total Moro independence, which he was unable to win by force, was the only possible outcome of such a diplomatic settlement. For the Philippine government, much more able to effect its will on the ground militarily, the MNLF position was totally unacceptable, and no recognition of the MNLF was possible until it abandoned it.

---

[501] On February 6, 1974, about 1,000 MNLF fighters attacked the Jolo airport and various army positions in the area of Jolo in an effort to retake control of the town. Government forces retaliated the following day, making use of tanks, aircraft and heavy offshore naval shelling, as well as a large number of ground troops. The city center was virtually destroyed before government forces could reclaim control over it several days later. The battle exacted heavy casualties on all sides, but especially among the civilian population of Jolo, while surviving MNLF fighters retreated and dispersed back into the countryside surrounding the town. Occurring just before a meeting of the OIC in Lahore, the Jolo "massacre" had a strong effect on the Conference delegates who supported a Conference resolution condemning the Philippine Army. Majul, *Contemporary Muslim Movement*, 66; Che Man, *Muslim Separatism*, 150. The Sulu archipelago emerged to be a critical theater of the Moro insurgency. Never as heavily impacted by Christian Filipino migration, its overwhelming Muslim majority (80 percent) was more strongly positioned to resist efforts of the government to maintain control. In addition, as a crossroads in the MNLF arms trafficking program from Sabah, control of Sulu was of vital importance to both sides. The Tausug inhabitants of Sulu did little to diminish their historic reputation as the fiercest warriors in the Philippines. Gowing, *Muslim Filipinos*, 188.

[502] One important country that abstained from such interference was Suharto's Indonesia, which never lent support to the MNLF and remained consistently as a voice within OIC councils recommending caution about intervening in the internal affairs of other states. Che Man, *Muslim Separatism*, 141–142.

189

The Tripoli Agreement

Negotiations between OIC representatives and Philippine government officials during 1973-74 proved tortuous and unproductive. A breakthrough was finally achieved when Marcos agreed to permit a Philippine delegation to meet representatives of the MNLF in Jiddah, Saudi Arabia, in January 1975. Such a meeting was possible, however, only after Misauri had agreed to negotiate on the basis of "autonomy" for the Moro areas instead of "independence."[503] Although the Philippine government did not at this time agree to the concept of autonomy, it nevertheless had finally recognized the MNLF as an interlocutor with whom it had to deal, and this step made further negotiations possible. Delaying tactics by Marcos and the glacial pace of the OIC deliberative process, however, meant that progress was slow, and it was not until December 23, 1976, that a final "autonomy" agreement and general cease-fire were reached between the government and MNLF representatives in Tripoli, Libya.[504]

Reaching an autonomy agreement was one thing; successfully implementing it was another. Continuing conflict between the government and Muslim rebels since has been primarily over differences of interpretation of the Tripoli Agreement or perceptions of non-compliance by one party or the other. By the time the agreement was struck, the Marcos government had gained the upper hand over the MNLF, and the President appears to have been determined to implement its terms by fiat rather than by further negotiations between the two signing parties.

Weakening of the MNLF

In the years prior to the Tripoli Agreement, the MNLF, despite the continuing general support of the OIC, had found its position deteriorating. In 1974, due in part to a vigorous Philippine diplomatic campaign, the government of Malaysia officially changed its policy from support of Moro independence to that of supporting autonomy.[505] Such a shift of policy made it difficult for Misuari to sustain the MNLF's insistence that independence was the only solution for the Moro problem. Then, the electoral defeat in April 1976 of Sabah governor Tun Mustafa deprived the MNLF of the transit facility through which it had been able to maintain a supply of arms and

---

[503] Majul, *Contemporary Muslim Movement*, 68–69.

[504] Text of the Tripoli Agreement is found in Majul, *Contemporary Muslim Movement*, 120–125. A major offshore earthquake and *tsunami* tidal wave that caused terrible destruction in western Mindanao in August 1976 brought a temporary end to the fighting, as Muslims, Christians, government troops and humanitarian organizations cooperated to bring assistance to the victims of the disaster. The occurrence of the *tsunami* may have contributed to the finally successful negotiations in Tripoli in December. The conjunction of events is eerily similar to the potential connection between the December 2004 *tsunami* off the coast of Sumatra and the August 2005 settlement between Aceh and Indonesia in Helsinki, Finland. Majul, *Contemporary Muslim Movement*, 72.

[505] Abuza, *Militant Islam in Southeast Asia*, 38.

ammunition to the fighters in Moroland.[506] The high civilian casualty rate also had a negative impact on popular support for the war, a trend Marcos sought to exploit by emphasizing the "communist" nature of the MNLF from whom all "good" Muslims ought to dissociate themselves. At the same time, he announced a general amnesty for rebel commanders who surrendered with their men, offering them cash or business incentives and positions in the government or the army if they did so. Many, especially those associated with *datu* families, did so.[507] In July 1975, Marcos invited about two hundred former rebel leaders to a conference in Zamboanga that was billed as "peace talks" between the government and the "true voice" of the Moro people. Although this effort to discredit the MNLF did not succeed in altering OIC support for it and for Misuari's leadership, it did highlight a deterioration of the organization's authority, particularly in Mindanao.[508]

Meanwhile, even while pursuing a robust military campaign, President Marcos embarked on "a two-pronged campaign to convince Muslims in the Philippines and, more importantly, heads of Muslim states abroad, of his sincere desire to solve the "Moro problem."[509] On one hand, he inaugurated a major reconstruction campaign to rebuild the economic infrastructure in the south that was being destroyed by the war. Although most of the projects undertaken-airports, roads, and harbor improvements-actually served the needs of the military more than the general population of the region, the impression of commitment had a certain impact. On the other hand, he sought to demonstrate increased sensitivity to Islam by providing funds to build a large mosque in the center of Manila, permitting the establishment of an Islamic bank (Amanah Bank), establishing an Islamic Studies Institute at the University of the Philippines, officially recognizing Muslim holy days as government holidays, building statues and memorials to historic Moro cultural heroes, and encouraging the writing of a code of Muslim personal laws to be applied specifically for Muslims.[510]

Revival of the Traditional *Sultans*

A part of this strategy was to revive and reinvigorate the old *datu* system that the MNLF was seeking to undermine. In July 1974, a few months after the destruction of Jolo, Marcos formally recognized Datu Mahakutta Kiram as Sultan of Sulu.[511] Although other members of the royal family contested this decision, the new *sultan*

---

[506] Che Man, *Muslim Separatism*, 140.

[507] McKenna, *Muslim Rulers and Rebels*, 167.

[508] Majul, *Contemporary Muslim Movement*, 71.

[509] McKenna, *Muslim Rulers and Rebels*, 166.

[510] Cf. Majul, *Contemporary Muslim Movement*, 78–80.

[511] When Sultan Jamal al-Kiram II, who had surrendered all claims to temporal authority to the United States (Gowing, *Filipino Muslims*, 50), finally died in 1936, the Commonwealth government declared that the office ceased to exist. Although the inhabitants of Sulu failed to recognize this government decision and continued to choose one or several members of the royal family as rival claimants to the office, the function remained only ceremonial and in fact continued to remain so after being revived by Marcos. Gowing, *Filipino Muslims*, 56.

was the man with whom the government would henceforth deal. About the same time, Marcos also gave formal recognition to fifteen *sultans* among the Maranaos and three among the Magindanaons of Mindanao. Above them all he recognized former Congressman Rashid Lucman of Bayang as "Paramount *Sultan* of the Nineteen Royal Houses of Mindanao and Sulu."[512] Such was the reward to this *datu* cofounder with Nur Misuari of the MNLF, when he chose to break with the resistance and return to cooperation with the government.

The impact of all these actions was that by the time of the signing of the Tripoli Agreement in December 1976, the MNLF had been significantly split and weakened. It remained primarily the continued support of external Islamic countries, embodied in the OIC, that enabled Misuari and the MNLF to remain a party to the agreement. But the agreement had a significant benefit to the MNLF leadership, in that they were no longer criminal elements in the eyes of the government and technically were able to return to the Philippines and play political roles in the new autonomous structure of the thirteen provinces identified as having this status in the Tripoli Agreement.[513]

The MNLF was even further weakened as a result of the peace agreement with the government. If the threat of martial law and the perceived assault on the last vestiges of Moro independence was the great unifying factor enabling the MNLF as the dominant force leading the Moro revolt, peace proved to be an even greater threat to the continuing unity and solidarity of the organization. The split that emerged constituted basically a three-way break-(1) the original MNLF that remained loyal to Misuari, centered increasingly on his fellow Tausugs of Sulu, and largely led by secularly educated Muslims like himself with a fundamentally secular, nationalist agenda for the autonomous region defined by the Tripoli Agreement; (2) the MILF, a more religiously oriented organization, led (until 2003) by Salamat Hashim, formerly deputy leader of the MNLF until his break with Misuari in 1977, centered mainly on his fellow Maguindanaos of Cotabato and Maguindanao, and largely led by an emerging non-*datu*-connected `ulama class educated mainly abroad at various colleges and universities in the wider Islamic world; and (3) the BMLO (*Bangsa Moro Liberation Organization*-later the MNLF-Reformed Group (RG)), headed at first by Rashid Lucman, now "Paramount *Sultan* of the Nineteen Royal Houses of Mindanao and Sulu," and led mainly by *datus* among the Maranaos of northern Mindanao, also Islamist in orientation, but more in tune with the traditional *datu*-dominated Islam of the past and positive about reconciliation with the government.[514] The split represented geographical and regional as well as ideological differences within

---

[512] Gowing, *Filipino Muslims*, 56–57. See also Che Man, *Muslim Separatism*, 125.

[513] Namely Lanao del Norte, Lanao del Sur, North Cotabato, South Cotabato, Maguindanao, Sultan Kudarat, Davao del Sur, Zamboanga del Norte, Zambuanga del Sur, Basilan, Sulu, Tawi Tawi, and Palawan. Majul, *Contemporary Muslim Movement*, 73.

[514] Che Man, *Muslim Separatism*, 84–90. The author notes the existence of two other minor factions that split from the MNLF—the BMILO that stressed the need to spread Islam to all of the Philippines, but by *dawa* (proselytizing) rather than by violence; and the MORO, a Muslim revolutionary party associated with the Communist Party of the Philippines.

the MNLF and became apparent almost immediately after the cease-fire mandated by the Tripoli Agreement that came into effect on January 20, 1977. When MNLF-Philippine government talks resumed in Tripoli in early March to refine the details of the Agreement, the BMLO, supported by Marcos, presented itself as the "true voice" of the MNLF. The OIC continued to recognize the leadership of Nur Misuari, however.[515]

Implementation of the Tripoli Agreement

The primary issue at stake in the follow-up talks in Tripoli was the definition of "autonomy." The Tripoli Agreement had stated only that autonomy would be established in the thirteen provinces so designated. As he made clear in the second round of talks, Misauri's vision of autonomy was the designation of the thirteen provinces as a single, autonomous region, presumably under the leadership of the MNLF. Government representatives resisted this demand, however, on the grounds that the Philippine Constitution required any such change to be subject to a local plebiscite in all thirteen provinces affected. There being a significant majority of Christians in several of these provinces, and a slight majority of Christians in all of them combined, as well as clearly growing opposition to Misuari's leadership of the MNLF, a number of the provinces would likely vote against unification, and a single autonomous region would not come into being. Misauri, accordingly, opposed the idea of the plebiscite on the grounds that the Tripoli Agreement made no provision for it. The disagreement provoked an impasse that caused the talks to break down, never to be resumed until Corazon Aquino replaced Marcos as President in 1986. MNLF-sponsored insurgent activity soon resumed in the southern Philippines, although never again at the levels that the region had known between 1973 and 1975.

Despite the breakdown of the talks and the cease-fire, Marcos pressed ahead with his own unilateral vision of autonomy. On March 25, 1977, he issued Proclamation Number 1628,[516] in which he announced the formation of four regions into which the thirteen provinces were to be grouped.[517] Although under martial law he perhaps did not need to do so, Marcos insisted that his proclamation be subject to a plebiscite in the thirteen provinces, which was held on April 17, 1977. The MNLF demand for a unified autonomous province was included in the referendum. As expected, the MNLF program was rejected in favor of that expressed in the Presidential proclamation, and Marcos was able to assert that he had met the terms of the Tripoli Agreement.

---

[515] Majul, *Contemporary Muslim Movement*, 85–90.

[516] Text in Majul, *Contemporary Muslim Movement*, 126–128.

[517] Region 4 (Palawan) Region 9 (Tawi Tawi, Sulu, Basilan, Zamboanga del Sur, Zamboanga del Norte) Region 11 (Davao del Sur, South Cotabato) Region 12 (Lanao del Norte, Lanao del Sur, Maguindanao, North Cotabato, Sultan Kudarat) Majul, *Contemporary Muslim Movement*, 127.

SPLIT IN THE MNLF

Emergence of the Moro Islamic Liberation Front

Misuari rejected this effort by Marcos to "dictate" the terms of autonomy in the Tripoli Agreement, called it instead a violation of the Agreement, and resumed his campaign for full Moro independence and secession.[518] His intransigence, however, provoked an even deeper split with the MNLF, which became public and apparent later in the year at a meeting of the MNLF Central Committee in Mecca, Saudi Arabia, in December. There, his deputy, Salamat Hashim, arguing that Misuari was wrong to abandon the Tripoli Agreement and revive the campaign for independence, challenged his leadership of the MNLF. When the OIC and World Muslim League (*Rabit al-Islami al-Alami*), meeting in Mecca at the same time, refused to accept his leadership challenge, Misuari expelled Hashim and 57 of his supporters from the organization. Hashim accordingly removed himself and his supporters from MNLF headquarters in Tripoli to Cairo and then later to Lahore, Pakistan.[519] Salamat did not formally announce the formation of his rival Moro Islamic Liberation Front (MILF) until 1984. Nevertheless, the core of his new organization went with him, and his loss gravely weakened the MNLF, especially in the Cotabato region of western Mindanao.[520]

Rise of Salamat Hashim

Born in 1942 in Pagalungan, near Cotabato, Mindanao (Maguindanao Province), Salamat Hashim was to emerge, like many of those who followed his leadership, as a member of a new `ulama in the southern Philippines, trained and educated abroad. Although a minor *datu* himself, and related to some of Mindanao's most distinguished Muslim political figures, he found on his return from Cairo in 1967 that these connections were of no personal use to him.[521] Accordingly, he was drawn to the more radical separatist cause represented by the MNLF. A member of the fourth cohort of

---

[518] In October 1977, Misuari gave a blistering speech before the International Congress on Cultural Imperialism at the Palais des Nations in Algiers, in which he again accused the Philippine government of "cultural genocide" because of its brutal resistance to Moro efforts to achieve independence. Regardless of the merits of the analysis presented in the speech, it represents a profound articulation of the challenge faced by the Muslims of the Philippines to retain their identity as Muslims in the face of a non-Muslim government's determination to control their cultural destiny. Full text of the speech in Majul, *Contemporary Muslim Movement*, 134–142.

[519] *Philippines: A Country Study*, 292. Abuza, *Militant Islam in Southeast Asia*, 39. McKenna, *Muslim Rulers and Rebels*, 207. International Crisis Group, "Southern Philippines Backgrounder," 4.

[520] Even more serious was the defection in early 1980 of Salamat's regional commander, Amelil Malaguoik (aka Commander Ronnie), with a number of his field commanders to the government in exchange for being appointed the first governor of the newly created autonomous region XII, which encompassed western Mindanao. Although this was a blow to the MNLF, it was a blow to Hashim as well, although he was able to slowly rebuild his position in the region, thanks largely to the loyalty and effectiveness of Commander Ronnie's successor, Haj Ali Murad. McKenna, *Muslim Rulers and Rebels*, 208.

[521] McKenna, *Muslim Rulers and Rebels*, 144.

Muslim students from Cotabato to receive scholarships to attend al-Azhar University, he departed for Cairo in 1959 and returned to the Philippines only after graduating in 1967 to assume a minor position as a provincial librarian.

His years in Cairo coincided with those of certain Afghan students-Burhanuddin Rabbani, Gulbuddin Hekmatyar, and probably others-later to emerge as leaders of the Afghan resistance to the Soviet occupation of their country, who were also studying at al-Azhar at that time.[522] Although no evidence exists to confirm interaction during their student years in Cairo, Salamat's decision to settle in Pakistan after his split with Misuari and his rapid involvement with the Afghan resistance suggests that his decision may have been influenced by going to a place where he knew he would be welcome.

A noted figure in any case as deputy leader of the MNLF to which he had rallied after the declaration of martial law by President Marcos in 1972, he, like most other leaders of the MNLF Central Committee, spent the years of the civil war residing in Tripoli, Libya, having personal recognizance over military operations in his native area of western Mindanao. A Philippine government document listing all ten meetings between various government representatives and the MNLF from June 1975 to April 1979 demonstrates that Salamat was often the chief negotiator for the MNLF in lower-level meetings and was usually present when Misuari was leading the MNLF delegation.[523]

Hashim's Islamic Vision

As the 1977 split between Salamat and Misuari made clear, however, the two had different visions on the role of the MNLF and how it should deal with the government. Whereas Misuari insisted on independence and the formation of a secular, nationalist state in which the traditional "feudal" *datu* order would have no place, Salamat, a religious scholar and a minor *datu* himself who nevertheless considered the *datu* system antiquated, saw the movement more in religious terms. The quality that distinguished the Moros from other Filipinos was religious; they were Muslims, and other Filipinos were not. Whether Muslims achieved an independent state or only an autonomous region, where they were "free" to be Muslims, was not the point. What was necessary was for the Muslims of the southern Philippines to claim their rights as Muslims, and for this they required an Islamic political order that likely might be more possible under the autonomy agreement reached in Tripoli than under the political order envisioned by Misuari.

---

[522] Olivier Roy, *Islam and Resistance in Afghanistan* (New York: Cambridge University Press, 1985), 70.

[523] Majul, *Contemporary Muslim Movement*, 143–144.

The Role of the Afghanistan Jihad

Salamat's Islamic vision was strengthened and given greater clarity as a result of his experiences in Pakistan between 1982 and 1987. He quickly became involved with the Pakistani ISI's (Inter-Service Intelligence Directorate) and Saudi-funded effort to recruit Muslims from around the world to assist the Afghan *mujahidin* in their struggle against the Soviet occupation of Afghanistan. Administered in large part by Usama bin Ladin, a son of the wealthy and powerfully connected bin Ladin family in Saudi Arabia, the program is said to have brought 35,000 potential fighters from different Muslim countries during the years 1982 –1992, 17,000 from Saudi Arabia alone.[524] The Philippine contribution to this effort, organized and coordinated by Hashim Salamat, is estimated to have been 500-700.[525] These generally arrived in small groups, either directly from the Philippines, generally Mindanao, where they had been recruited by Salamat's local commanders, or indirectly from the large Filipino expatriate community living as workers abroad, especially in the Persian Gulf region.[526] Among those who arrived in 1986 was Abdurajak Janjalani from Basilan, later head of the Abu Sayyaf terrorist group that became active in the Philippines in the 1990s. He reportedly had been engaged in studies in the Middle East, when he was drawn to participate in the *jihad* in Afghanistan.[527]

Unbeknownst to, or perhaps just not understood at the time by, Western supporters of the Afghan resistance, whose focus was on the U.S.-Soviet Cold War, Pakistani President Zia ul-Haq's long-term policy for Afghanistan was to replace the Soviet-supported Communist government in Kabul with a regime that would constitute an "Islamic" government. For this reason, of the six resistance groups supported by the Pakistani ISI during the conflict, only those three with clear Islamic political agendas received the bulk of Pakistani and U.S. support.[528] Perhaps the Pakistani President was also engaged in a divide-and-rule strategy. For its part, Saudi Arabia preferred to distribute nearly all of its support through a group called *Ittihad-i Islami* (Islamic Union), headed by Abd al-Rasul Sayyaf, whose studies had been in Saudi Arabia, who spoke Arabic fluently, and whose views on Islam closely paralleled those of the Saudi Wahhabi clerics among whom he had studied.[529] Sayyaf, therefore, formed a seventh resistance faction supporting military resistance in Afghanistan, and it was primarily from his organization that the foreign fighters joining the resistance, including those

---

[524] Abuza, *Militant Islam in Southeast Asia*, 10.

[525] Abuza, *Militant Islam in Southeast Asia*, 91.

[526] International Crisis Group, "Southern Philippines Backgrounder," 4.

[527] Graham H. Turbiville, Jr., "Bearers of the Sword: Radical Islam, Philippines Insurgency, and Regional Stability," *Military Review* (March–April 2002). URL:_http://www.leavenworth.srmy.mil/milrev/ English/ MarApr02/turbiville.htm. Accessed June 6, 2005.

[528] These groups were Gulbuddin Hekmatyar's *Hizb-i Islami*, Burhanuddin Rabbani's *Jamiyat-i Islami*, and Younes Khales's faction of *Hizb-i Islami*. Supported, but at a much lower level, were Muhammad Nabi Muhammadi's *Harakat-e Inqelab Islami*, Sibghatullah Mojadeddi's *Jebh-i Nejat-i Milli*, and Pir Sayyid Gilani's *Mahaz-e Milli Islami*. Roy, *Islam and Resistance in Afghanistan*, 119–121.

[529] Roy, *Islam and Resistance in Afghanistan*, 123, 135–137, 212.

from the Philippines, received their training, lodging, and sustenance, primarily at Sayyaf's *mujahidin* training school at Camp Saddah in Parachinar, Kurram Agency, Pakistan.[530] For this reason, too, later Philippine terrorist leader Abdurazak Janjalani called his group Abu Sayyaf, after his former mentor in Afghanistan.

Establishment of the MILF

For Salamat Hashim, his role in Pakistan produced a new opportunity; he was now able to replace the MNLF training center in Sabah that had been closed in 1976, but now for the purpose of his own organization, the MILF, which he formally established in 1984. Many of the Philippine fighters receiving training in Pakistan, such as Janjalani, stayed on to fight with the Afghan *mujahidin*. Others, however, filtered back home to join the resistance there and to become trainers for new recruits being raised locally. A feature of the 1976 Tripoli Agreement and cease-fire had been the designation of several bivouac areas in remote locations as safe areas for MNLF fighters. In Mindanao, at least seven of these areas had been transformed into regular military camps — Camps Abu Bakar, Basrah, Ali, Omar, Khalid, Othman, and Salman-by 1985, now belonging to the MILF, under the leadership of Hashim's local commander, Haj Ali Murad.[531] To these camps the Filipino trainees returned, as did Hashim himself in 1987, following the fall of the Marcos government.

Another feature of the Pakistani experience for all those involved was association with Muslim resistance fighters from other parts of the Islamic world. In the case of Salamat and other MILF fighters, this meant not only a link with bin Ladin, but also compatriots from neighboring Indonesia, Malaysia, and Thailand. Much of the training at Sayyaf's Camp Saddeh in Pakistan, the Filipinos learned, was carried out by Indonesians claiming to be part of the *Darul Islam* movement in their country.[532] All these contacts would have later significance when, after the formation of the *Jemaah Islamiyah* in 1992, *al-Qa'ida* training of MILF personnnel moved from Pakistan to Mindanao.

Continuing Resistance in Moroland

Although Moro resistance to Philippine government authority continued after the breakdown of the cease-fire in 1977, it never again reached the levels of violence of the early 1970s, prior to the Tripoli Agreement. Sporadic attacks on Army posts or government facilities kept the Army on alert, periodically retaliating with massive dragnets aimed at capturing and/or killing wanted fugitives and/or terrorists, often with significant "collateral damage."[533] The omnipresence of the Army in Muslim

---

[530] International Crisis Group, "Southern Philippines Backgrounder," 14.

[531] International Crisis Group, "Southern Philippines Backgrounder," 5.

[532] International Crisis Group, "Southern Philippines Backgrounder," 14.

[533] McKenna, *Muslim Rulers and Rebels*, 180–181.

areas made it clear that the new Autonomous Muslim Regions were still under military occupation.

Nevertheless, Marcos persisted in implementing the autonomy scheme he had proclaimed and which had been approved by the plebiscite of April 1977. In January 1981 the new Autonomous Regions were formally established; Muslims, mostly *datus* and former MNLF commanders who had defected back to the government, were appointed to newly established regional government offices; and martial law was repealed, restoring constitutional government and paving the way for the restoration of electoral politics.[534] The illusion of a cease-fire was also maintained, for as long as MNLF/MILF fighters remained in their remote camps (MILF Liberated Zones, as they later came to be called), the government did not bother them; only outside of the camps did they become wanted fugitives and terrorists.

The hollowness of the "autonomous" regional governments was apparent to all. They had no legislative or tax collection authority, nor any independent operating budget. All decisions continued to be made in Manila, and although the new regional governments soon employed a number of college-educated Muslims, the terror produced by the Philippine Army as it tried to master the continuing insurgency against its presence was the stark reality for most Filipino Muslims.[535]

In a letter to the OIC announcing his establishment of the MILF in 1984, Salamat Hashim noted that "The MILF operates as a parallel government vis-à-vis the enemy government within its area of responsibility and exercises influence extensively among the Bangsamoro masses in a degree more effective and binding than that of the enemy administration."[536] American anthropologist Thomas McKenna, in his field research conducted in Mindanao in 1985–86, observed that such a "shadow government" did in fact exist in the particular areas that he studied. Although he noted that its impact was difficult to measure with any precision, his conclusion was that the MILF was more influential in most matters than the "enemy administration."[537]

The MILF as the "Shadow Government" of Mindanao

A characteristic of the new "shadow government" gradually coming into being in the Cotabato area of Mindanao in the early 1980s, of which the MILF was to emerge as the symbolic authority, was the key role played by a new `ulama (called ustadzes[538] in Mindanao) establishment that had not been apparent in earlier years. Most members

---

[534] Majul, *Contemporary Muslim Movement*, 99–100.

[535] McKenna, *Muslim Rulers and Rebels*, 195.

[536] Datu Michael O. Mastura, *The Crisis in the MNLF Leadership and the Dilemma of the Muslim Autonomy Movement*, Collected Papers of the Conference on the Tripoli Agreement: Problems and Prospects, September 13–14, 1985 (Manila: International Studies Institute, University of the Philippines, 1985), 18.

[537] McKenna, *Muslim Rulers and Rebels*, 209.

[538] In Arabic, *ustadh*—professor, teacher.

of this new `ulama, like Salamat Hashim himself, were products of the scholarship educations many Mindanao Muslims had received in various Middle Eastern countries, particularly Egypt, beginning in the 1950s. As McKenna notes, however, "while their origins may be traced to the early 1950s, it is not accurate to speak of the *ulama* as a significant religious force before 1980."[539] By 1980 their numbers appear to have reached a critical mass. The impact of the 1979 `ulama-led Islamic revolution in Iran had an inspirational impact, as did also the growing jihadist campaign against the Soviet occupation of Afghanistan, in which several hundred Muslim Filipinos would ultimately be engaged. Most importantly, however, the new *ustadzes* were increasingly supported by salaries paid by various Islamic world donors as part of the humanitarian assistance and reconstruction financing provided to relieve the plight of the dispossessed and suffering Muslim refugees of the Philippines.[540] Unlike the clandestine MILF, the new *ustadzes* were public figures who stressed the egalitarianian nature of Islam, the necessity of political leadership to represent the rights of the poor and oppressed, the need to live pure Islamic lives, and the importance of achieving Islamic unity in the face of the threats posed to their community. During the 1980s, the *ustadzes* rapidly emerged as a "counter-elite" that challenged the authority of the historic *datus* that were tending to collaborate with the "enemy administration," and were influential in mobilizing popular support for the MILF.[541]

THE POST-MARCOS ERA

Fall of the Marcos Regime

The cronyism, corruption, high-handed authoritarianism, militarism, and brutality of the Marcos regime finally came to an abrupt end in February 1986, as a result of the popular People's Power movement that garnered the support of millions of Filipinos to demand the ouster of the President and his replacement by Corazon Aquino. She was the widow of the assassinated Benigno Aquino, Marcos' leading political opponent and critic who had strongly disagreed with Marcos about policy toward the southern Philippines. Beset by an even greater threat posed to the government by the communist-inspired New People's Army (NPA) that controlled large remote areas in the northern Philippines, the new President moved quickly in an effort to resolve the long-festering conflict with the Philippine Moros.

The Jiddah Accord

In an unprecedented move, President Aquino in September 1986 paid an official visit to MNLF leader Nur Misuari in his hometown of Maimbung on Sulu Island. There the two leaders agreed in principle to hold further talks that would result in

---

[539] McKenna, *Muslim Rulers and Rebels*, 205.
[540] McKenna, *Muslim Rulers and Rebels*, 204–205.
[541] McKenna, *Muslim Rulers and Rebels*, 213–214.

an end to hostilities, Aquino accepting Misuari's demand for a single Autonomous Region rather than four, and Misuari accepting the government's demand for autonomy rather than secession.[542] Such an agreement was struck on January 4, 1987, in Jiddah, Saudi Arabia, during final talks between Misuari and the Philippine government, represented by the President's brother-in-law, Agapito Aquino.[543] The promised unified Autonomous Region would have its own elected governor and unicameral legislature and would have full control over its internal affairs, except for foreign affairs and national security.

Although the Jiddah Accord amounted to the first diplomatic breakthrough since the Tripoli Accord of December 1976, it immediately ran into trouble on two counts. First, because it was negotiated only by Misuari as the sole spokesman of the Muslim peoples of the Philippines, the agreement was rejected by the MILF and was not well received by the traditional *datu* class that had been drawn into collaboration with the Marcos government. Within a week of its signing, MILF fighters on January 13, 1987, launched a series of attacks on government facilities and infrastructure in Cotabato City and other parts of southwestern Mindanao.[544] Non-plused, Aquino immediately made plans to meet MILF military chief Haj Ali Murad in Cotabato City, which she did on January 18. Although the meeting resulted in a temporary cease-fire, it did not result in MILF acceptance of Misuari's leadership of the new Autonomous Region.

Secondly, the perceived softness of the new President toward the Moro rebels, as well as the NPA with whom she was also negotiating, added to her alleged general "incompetence," led a number in the Army leadership that she had inherited from the Marcos era to attempt a *coup d'état* against her in late January 1987.[545] Although the *coup* failed, as did subsequent rebellions culminating in the large and well-organized *coup* attempt in December 1989 that required U.S. air support to save the regime, the turmoil highlighted the weakness of her government and the chaotic politics that characterized the Philippines in the immediate post-Marcos period. Such weakness emboldened Moros still committed to independence rather than autonomy to reopen their struggle.

Return of Salamat Hashim to the Philippines

The new political situation in the Philippines led Salamat Hashim to return to Mindanao from Pakistan in 1987 along with a number of his Philippine Afghan veterans.[546] Although Janjalani and a number of others are reported to have remained in Pakistan/Afghanistan until after the Soviet withdrawal from Afghanistan in February 1989, Filipino support to the Afghan resistance basically ended in 1987, when Salamat

---

[542] McAmis, *Malay Muslims*, 98.

[543] *Philippines: A Country Study*, 217.

[544] McKenna, *Muslim Rulers and Rebels*, 246.

[545] *Philippines: A Country Study*, 212.

[546] International Crisis Group, "Southern Philippines Backgrounder," 4.

decided that the changed political circumstances in the Philippines required his presence there. Upon his return, he established himself at Camp Abu Bakar, located in remote mountainous and jungle terrain north of Cotabato City, which was now MILF headquarters on Mindanao. Among his first tasks was to establish in Camp Abu Bakar a military training "academy," probably modeled on Sayyaf's Camp Saddah in Pakistan, which was given the name Abdul-Rahman Badis Memorial Academy. Making use of his "Afghan alumni" to transmit the lessons they had learned on the Afghan frontier, a reported 122,000 MILF supporters received some sort of military training at Camp Abu Bakar, and a permanent force of some 10,000-15,000 armed regulars had been raised by 1990.[547]

Connections with *al-Qa'ida*

A role in supporting this effort financially appears to have been played by Usama bin Ladin and perhaps also the government of Saudi Arabia.[548] In 1988, bin Ladin had established his *al-Qa'ida* organization, and in the same year he dispatched his brother-in-law, Muhammad Jamal Khalifa, to Manila to take charge of the International Islamic Relief Organization (IIRO) office there. The IIRO, a Saudi-based charitable organization, had been established in 1978 as a mechanism for providing humanitarian assistance to distressed Muslim populations, including those in the Philippines. Following the Soviet invasion of Afghanistan, it had been transformed into a major conduit for providing Saudi, U.S., and Gulf state funding to the *mujahidin* in Afghanistan.

Prior to being dispatched to Manila, Khalifa, a Lebanese Muslim, had from 1985 to 1987 been director of the Muslim World League (*Rabit al-Alam al-Islami*) office in Peshawar, where he no doubt had been active in cooperation with bin Ladin in coordinating the activities of the various Islamic world *mujahidin* that had descended on Pakistan. The IIRO office in Manila was a regional office with subordinate offices in Indonesia, Thailand, and Taiwan, as well as other subordinate offices in the southern Philippines.[549] Although no specific evidence demonstrates that Khalifa's IIRO was instrumental in helping to finance the growing strength of the MILF in the late 1980s,

---

[547] International Crisis Group, "Southern Philippines Backgrounder," 4. Abdul-Rahman Ben Badis, for whom the Academy was named, was a notable leader of the Algerian `ulama during the 1930s who led a powerful movement opposing French control of Algeria, suggesting that Hashim perceived the situation of the Moros in the Philippines as analogous to that of the Algerians under the French.

[548] It should be recalled that bin Ladin was not at this time the notorious figure he later became. In 1989, following the Soviet withdrawal from Afghanistan, bin Ladin returned home to a hero's welcome in Saudi Arabia. It was only after Iraq's invasion of Kuwait in August 1990 and the royal family's decision to admit U.S. and other Western forces into the Kingdom to counter the Iraqi action that he broke with the regime and began his independent campaign to oppose Saudi rule and facilitate *jihad* against Western influence throughout the Islamic world. See Adam Robinson, *Bin Ladin: Behind the Mask of the Terrorist* (New York: Arcade Publishing, 2001), 123–130. Also Anonymous [Michael Scheuer], *Through Our Enemies' Eyes: Osama Bin Ladin, Radical Islam and the Future of America* (Washington, DC: Brassey's, Inc., 2002), 112–115.

[549] Abuza, *Militant Islam in Southeast Asia*, 92–93.

its subsequent role in underwriting the establishment and training of the Abu Sayyaf Group after 1992 suggests an earlier role in providing financial support to the MILF as well.

MILF Assumes Leadership of the Resistance

With the signing of the Jiddah Accord in January 1987, it was now Misuari's MNLF, based in Sulu, that was working in collaboration with the government and Hashim's MILF, based in Camp Abu Bakar, that had become the principal opposition. Despite the opposition, President Aquino, like Marcos before her, pressed on in implementing the Jiddah Accord as she understood it. On November 19, 1989, in accordance with the Philippine Constitution, voters in the thirteen provinces designated in the Tripoli Accord participated in another plebiscite to decide whether to join a new united Autonomous Region formally titled the "Autonomous Region of Muslim Mindanao" (ARMM). As Misuari had feared in 1977, but now accepted, only four provinces—Tawi Tawi, Sulu, Maguindanao, and Lanao del Sur—elected to join the new Region. Even Cotabato City, the pre-designated capital of the united Region, voted not to join, requiring the designation of another capital city instead.[550] Nevertheless, President Aquino, moving forward to fully implement the Jiddah Accord, traveled south on November 6, 1990, to formally inaugurate the ARMM.

As sincere an effort as it may have been to create a fully autonomous ARMM, it left many problems unresolved. Many Muslims in the nine provinces that had voted not to join the ARMM, mainly because Christian voters carried the day, now found themselves vulnerable minorities in these provinces. The MILF camps were now both inside and outside the ARMM in relatively remote jungle locations. Left alone, beyond government control, they represented an even more autonomous, even independent, Muslim presence in the Philippines that seemed to mock the autonomy achieved in the four provinces of the ARMM. More Islamically-oriented than the secularly-oriented, MNLF-dominated ARMM, the MILF represented the continuing struggle of the Moros to achieve independence rather than the acquiescence of the MNLF. The continuing threat posed by the MILF, moreover, kept sizable numbers of the Philippine Army deployed in the south, especially Mindanao. Despite the Jiddah Accord and the ARMM, the Muslim areas of Mindanao in particular remained lands under military occupation, making something of a mockery of the concept of autonomy.

EMERGENCE OF ABU SAYYAF

As noted previously, sometime between April and December 1991, following his break with the Saudi royal family, Usama bin Ladin spent time in Pakistan/Afghanistan, where he recalled certain of his former associates to meet with him. Among those who joined him at this time included the Indonesians (though based in Malaysia) Abdullah

---

[550] *Philippines: A Country Study*, 211.

Sungkar, Abu Bakar Ba'asyır, and Hambali, who returned to Malaysia to establish the *Jemaah Islamiyah* organization in 1992/93. Yet another who came was the Filipino Muslim Abdurazak Janjalani. When Janjalani returned to the Philippines in late 1991, he was accompanied by Ramzi Yousef, who later would be involved as principal organizer of the first World Trade Center bombing in New York in February 1993.

Part of the agreement struck at this time was use of the MILF camps in Mindanao to train *Jemaah Islamiyah* recruits from southeast Asia, rather than to continue bringing them to the Pakistan/Afghanistan border area. For his part, bin Ladin appears to have agreed to provide financial support and *al-Qa'ida* trainers. His brother-in-law, Muhammad Jamal Khalifa, and the IIRO, and perhaps other humanitarian assistance groups would serve as the conduit for financial support. Ramzi Yousef and perhaps others accompanied Janjalani back to the Philippines to assist in training. Whether Salamat Hashim and Haj Ali Murad were party to this initial agreement or their cooperation was assumed is not certain. A final part of the agreement seems to have been a commitment by Janjalani to establish an independent organization, the Abu Sayyaf Group, (ASG)[551] which he began to do immediately upon his return to the Philippines.

Early Steps

Janjalani's home was Basilan Island, one of the nine provinces that had not voted to join the ARMM, and it was here, in a remote jungle area on Mount Kapayawan they called Camp Madina, that the ASG was established and headquartered. Other *al-Qa'ida* associates who joined Yousef at this time were Abdul-Hakim Murad and Wali Khan Amin Shah.[552] Apparently with the concurrence of the MILF leadership, another camp for Abu Sayyaf recruits, Camp Shafi'ie, was established on Mindanao near the northern city of Marawi, which trained both ASG and MILF trainees in equal numbers-about 50 per year over a three-year period before 1995. Among those who matriculated through this program was Janjalani's younger brother, Kadaffy Janjalani, who later replaced his elder brother as leader of the ASG after the former's death in a shoot-out with police in 1998. Salamat's cooperation with this program may have been due to its funding support being entirely from Khalifa's IIRO.[553]

---

[551] The Abu Sayyaf Group is an offshoot of another group, *al-Harakat al-Islamiyah* (The Islamic Movement), established on Basilan Island by a local Egyptian-trained (al-Azhar) *ustadz*, Wahab Akbar, in the late 1980s after Nur Misuari's Jiddah Agreement with Philippine President Corazon Aquino. The two are often conflated, and the distinction between the two is not clear. Fe B. Zaman, "Al Harakatul al-Islamiya: The Beginnings of Abu Sayyaf," *INQ7 Specials/Inside the Abu Sayyaf*. URL: *http://www.inq7.net/specials/inside_abusayyaf/2001/features/formative_years.htm*. Accessed September 3, 2005.

[552] It was at this time that Yousef was given the nickname "The Chemist," because of his knowledge and ability to construct a wide variety of bombs. Gunaratna, *Inside al-Qaeda*, 178.

[553] International Crisis Group. "Southern Philippines Backgrounder," 22.

Janjalani quickly announced the presence of the ASG by taking credit for two bomb attacks in Zamboanga City and Davao City in early 1992, also demonstrating that the new group's scope of operations included the whole of Mindanao and not just Basilan Island.[554] From these first attacks until 1996, the ASG was credited with "67 terrorist attacks, more than half of which were indiscriminant bombings. All led to the death of fifty-eight people and 398 injuries."[555] Whereas MILF targets were typically Philippine Army outposts or government infrastructure facilities, what characterized the ASG attacks was that they generally aimed at the Christian presence on Basilan or Mindanao-either Christian symbols (e.g., churches), foreign or Filipino missionaries, or Christian towns, such as the southern Mindanaon town of Ipil, which the ASG attacked and burned on April 4, 1995, leaving 53 people dead and many others wounded.

Kidnapping for ransom also became an important method of operation of the ASG. Although demands for money later became a major motive for such kidnappings, it does not appear to have been necessarily so at first. In April 1993, the ASG kidnapped a young five-year-old Christian boy, Luis "Ton-Ton" Biel, on Basilan Island. The demands for his release included three requirements: (1) removal of all Catholic symbols in Muslim communities, (2) banning of all foreign fishing vessels in the Sulu and Basilan seas, and (3) bringing the `ulama into the peace negotiation process with the Philippine government.[556]

Following the Biel kidnapping, the Philippine Armed Forces mounted a major operation to close down the ASG Camp Madina. They succeeded temporarily, but Janjalani and most of his followers managed to escape to Sulu Island, where they found refuge in jungle camps there. The flight to Sulu in fact resulted in a strengthening of the ASG, for the group soon was able to find new recruits and to continue its operations without interruption.[557]

Abu Sayyaf Linked to *Al-Qa'ida*

The appearance of the ASG and the violence associated with it gravely compromised President Corazon Aquino's efforts to implement the 1987 Jiddah Accord and the fully autonomous ARMM it had brought into being. After the settlement, the violence associated with the "Moro problem" was greater than before and was now characterized by pure acts of terrorism. At the time it was not clear if the ASG had an affiliation

---

[554] Many sources date the first ASG attack as occurring in 1991, when a military checkpoint on Basilan Island was attacked by *al-Harakat al-Islamiya* supporters, led by Wahab Akbar, who subsequently fled to Malaysia. Zamora, "The Beginnings of Abu Sayyaf." Although it may be an exercise in splitting hairs, this first attack appears to have been a pre-ASG operation undertaken while Janjalani was in Pakistan/Afghanistan meeting with bin Ladin.

[555] Abuza, *Militant Islam in Southeast Asia*, 101.

[556] Zamora, "The Beginnings of Abu Sayyaf."

[557] Zamora, "The Beginnings of Abu Sayyaf."

with the MILF, was a secret arm of the MNLF, or was simply acting alone.[558] What was known of Janjalani from those who had observed him was that "in his white flowing robe, [he] was a vision of serenity [and] like a human magnet, attracting young Muslim scholars newly returned from studies in Saudi Arabia, Libya, Pakistan and Egypt, and local Muslims disillusioned with Misuari's change of heart."[559] One affiliation became clear to Philippine authorities in December 1994, however, when after a bomb explosion on a Philippines Airline flight from Cebu to Tokyo, al-Qa'ida operative Ramzi Yousef, the actual planter of the bomb, called the Associated Press in Manila and claimed responsibility for the explosion on behalf of the ASG.[560]

The subsequent arrest in early January 1995 of Yousef associate Abdul-Hakim Murad, in Manila, the discovery of Yousef's laptop computer containing plans to blow up eleven U.S. airliners over the Pacific, and finally the arrest in February 1995 of Yousef himself by authorities in Pakistan, led the Philippine government to draw a clear connection-for the first time-between the ASG and bin Ladin's emerging al-Qa'ida organization. Although it probably was not directly connected with the al-Qa'ida conspiracy in Manila known as Operation Bojinka, the alleged association of the ASG with an act of international terrorism forced Philippine government authorities to begin thinking about it in an entirely different light.

RAMOS AND THE MORO PROBLEM

Retired General Fidel Ramos had replaced Corazon Aquino as President of the Philippines in June 1992, and it was he who faced the new challenge seemingly posed by the ASG. Throughout the years of martial law until the overthrow of Marcos (1972-1986), Ramos, a graduate of the U.S. Military Academy at West Point, had been chief of the Philippine Constabulary, the bureau of the government having primary responsibility for law and order throughout the country, including the south. Long a Marcos loyalist, he switched sides to join the People's Power movement in 1986, bringing significant military support with him. Upon Ramos assuming the Presidency, a grateful Aquino appointed him Chief of Staff of the Armed Forces during the first two years of her six-year term, and then Secretary of National Defense during her final

---

[558] There later even arose suspicions that the ASG may have been a clandestine Philippine Army operation aimed at discrediting the Moro insurgency. In February 1995, Ibrahim Yakub, one of the original ASG cadre of 30, "came in from the cold," and it was subsequently learned that his real name was Edwin Angeles and he had been working as a government agent within the ASG. As operations officer for the ASG, he had been in charge of every ASG operation, including the Biel kidnapping, the concept for which was said to have originated with him. After his return to government service, he continued to assist by identifying his former ASG colleagues as they were caught by government authorities. In January 1999, he was assassinated outside a mosque in Basilan. Whether the ASG or Philippine government services were behind the assassination is not clear. Where his true loyalties lay was also unclear. "Edwin Angeles: The Spy Who Came in from the Cold," *INQ7 Exclusive.* URL: *http://www.inq7.net/specials/inside_abusayyaf/2001/features/spy-turns-bandit.htm.* Accessed September 3, 2005.

[559] Zamora, "The Beginnings of Abu Sayyaf."

[560] Simon Reeve, *The New Jackals: Ramzi Yousef, Osama bin Ladin and the Future of Terrorism* (Boston: Northeastern University Press, 1999), 80.

four years in office. Now the twelfth President of the Philippine Republic and with great experience with the long Moro rebellion, Ramos sought to move decisively to reach a final resolution of the problem of the Moro south.[561]

Animated, like most Filipino leaders, by the view that economic deprivation was the primary factor underlying Moro dissatisfaction rather than cultural uniqueness and a strong sense on the part of the Moros, although articulated many times, that they were not Filipinos, Ramos placed great stress on economic development programs and a policy of reaching a formal peace agreement between his government and that of the ARMM. In 1993, strongly supported by the governments of Malaysia and Indonesia, he opened talks with MNLF leader Nur Misuari, who was still recognized by the OIC as the official representative of the Bangsamoro people, despite the fact that the first elected governor of the ARMM had been Linding Pangandangan. Gradually, Jakarta emerged as the principal venue for continuing talks and the site of the final agreement reached between the Ramos government and the MNLF on August 30, 1996.

The Jakarta Agreement

Formally called the "Final Agreement on the Implementation of the 1976 Tripoli Agreement between the Government of the Republic of the Philippines and the Moro National Liberation Front with the Participation of the Organization of the Islamic Conference Ministerial Committee of Six and the Secretary-General of the Organization of the Islamic Conference," or more simply the "Jakarta Agreement," it was officially signed by President Ramos and MNLF leader Misuari in the Malacanang Presidential Palace in Manila on September 2, 1996.[562]

Among other things, although the 1989 plebiscite had resulted in the grouping of only four Muslim provinces into the ARMM, the new Agreement recognized 14 provinces (13 plus a newly created province of Saranggani) and nine cities as part of the Autonomous Region. Although another plebiscite would have to be held to confirm this part of the Agreement, such language was not part of the Agreement, and Ramos made no effort to hold one during the course of his administration. Another provision of the Agreement was for MNLF fighters to be integrated into the Philippine Constabulary and the Armed Forces, with primary responsibility for enforcing law and order in the ARMM.[563] Within a week of signing the Agreement, on September 9, 1996, new elections resulted in Nur Misuari, with the full backing of the Ramos administration, being chosen as the new governor of the ARMM as well as Chairman of a newly formed Southern Philippines Council for Peace and Development (SPCPD)

---

[561] Data on Ramos drawn largely from "President Fidel Ramos," *Neofinoy.Info*. URL: *http://www. neofinoy.info/The%20RP%20Presidents/ramos.htm*. Accessed September 5, 2005.

[562] McAmis, *Malay Muslims*, 99.

[563] As a result of the Jakarta Agreement, 5,070 MNLF fighters laid down their arms, and 2,200 were integrated into the Philippine Army or police. Others, however, rallied to the MILF or ASG or simply remained outlaws. Abuza, *Militant Islam in Southeast Asia*, 42.

that was also created by the Jakarta Agreement. Yet another provision of the Agreement was the establishment of an Office of Muslim Affairs, a central Philippine government agency tasked with assessing and responding to the needs of the Philippine Muslim community.

Misuari Again in Charge

Under the terms of the Jakarta Agreement, and following his election as Governor of the ARMM, Nur Misuari assumed the role of principal peace broker in the southern Philippines on behalf of the government, with primary responsibility for dealing with and neutralizing the continuing opposition of the MILF and the ASG. With funds made available to him as Chairman of the SPCPD and still maintaining significant moral authority over MNLF fighters being integrated into the Army and police, Misuari finally was being vested with significant powers to resolve the long-festering problem of the southern Philippines. The only price was acceptance of autonomy rather than independence for the Bangsamoro people, which Misuari now seemed committed to doing.

For President Ramos, the linchpin of his policy was the SPCPD, through which he proposed to channel much needed government funds to promote the economic development especially of the resource-rich, but war-ravaged, island of Mindanao.[564] Moreover, through the Jakarta Agreement, he had gained OIC promises of support for the economic development of the ARMM, Malaysia and Indonesia being especially enthusiastic to play a positive role in promoting investments in the region.

During the Ramos years, at least until the Asian financial crisis that hit all of southeast Asia in July 1997, the Philippine economy that had languished during the latter Marcos years and remained hostage to the political instability that marked the years of the Aquino administration finally began to experience the "Asian miracle" of rapid economic growth that characterized the entire southeast Asian region during the 1980s and 1990s until the 1997 collapse. In part, this was due to the President's own strong hand in implementing reforms designed to open up the once closed national economy, to encourage private investment, and to reduce corruption.[565] Moreover, this economic growth was being felt in the south. Although per capita income in the southern Philippines was estimated to be only two-thirds of that in the rest of the country, it was growing at a more rapid rate than elsewhere in the country during the Ramos years.[566]

---

[564] For a listing of proposed economic projects for the ARMM after the Jakarta Agreement, see the ARMM website. URL: *http://park.org/Philippines/government/armm.htm*. Accessed September 5, 2005.

[565] "President Fidel Ramos."

[566] See "The Autonomous Region in Mindanao." URL: *http://www.mindanao.org/mindanao/overview/muslim1.htm*. Accessed September 5, 2005.

General Success of the Ramos Policy

The Ramos policy and the Jakarta Agreement did have a positive short-term impact on conditions in the south, as MILF- and ASG-sponsored violence diminished significantly over the next several years.[567] Possibly the uncovering of the *al-Qa'ida* Operation Bojinka plot in early 1995 led Filipino militants associated with the perpetrators to lay low for a period of time. An absence of violent resistance did not mean acceptance of the provisions of the Jakarta Agreement by either the MILF or Abu Sayyaf, however. In late 1996, Salamat Hashim convened a Bangsamoro Consultative Assembly at Camp Abu Bakar in which 200,000 people from throughout Mindanao were reported to have attended. There, the Assembly strongly expressed its opposition to the Jakarta Agreement, calling instead for an independent state.[568]

Cease-fire with the MILF

Undaunted, the Ramos administration pressed its agenda of low-profile meetings with MILF representatives in provincial towns around Mindanao, finally reaching a 3-year cease-fire agreement between the government and the MILF on July 18, 1997.[569] A part of this agreement was government acceptance of the various MILF camps in Mindanao, or "liberated zones," as Hashim preferred to call them, as secure areas that the Army would not attack if not provoked. Ramos' clear strategy was to buy time for economic development projects to improve the living conditions of the inhabitants of the region, which he believed was a precondition to a peaceful settlement. Accordingly, "in addition to projects in the ARMM, the government began to implant other projects in MILF-held territories, including the Narcisso Ramos Highway linking Cotabato to Marawi, including a 15-km road to the MILF headquarters at Camp Abu Bakar; a water system for 10,000 people; an irrigation system for 2,500 people; and the Malmar Dam."[570]

The "Shadow Government" Emerges

The new circumstances seemed to embolden Salamat Hashim's confidence. "In December 1997, the MILF held its 15th general assembly, and was so assured of his hold [on its territories] that the assembly was all but public knowledge." And Salamat closed the assembly by holding a public press conference for the first time.[571] "Like all unjust, oppressive and corrupt governments," he said, "the Manila government will collapse...when this happens, the Bangsamoro Islamic government will automatically

---

[567] Larry Niksch, *Abu Sayyaf: Target of Philippines — U.S. Anti-Terrorism Cooperation*, CRS Report for Congress RL31265 (Washington, DC: Congressional Research Service, January 25, 2002), 3.

[568] Rigoberto Tiglio, "Moro Reprise," *Far Eastern Economic Review*, December 26, 1996.

[569] International Crisis Group, "Southern Philippines Backgrounder," 6.

[570] Abuza, *Militant Islam in Southeast Asia*, 45.

[571] Abuza, *Militant Islam in Southeast Asia*, 45.

arise."[572] His confidence was perhaps based on the idea that, under the terms of the cease- fire, he was in fact operating a government in the "liberated zones" under his control as a virtually independent state, certainly more independent than the ARMM. And in his view, it was an Islamic government, operated and supported by the `ulama throughout Mindanao, and governed by the shari`a administered by Islamic courts.[573] The authority of the MILF's "shadow government" in the rest of Mindanao also engendered confidence. Time, in his view, was on the side of the MILF, not the Philippine government.

Connections Between MILF and al-Qa'ida

Hashim's confidence was also no doubt bolstered by the secret relationship that was emerging between the MILF and bin Ladin's al-Qa'ida organization. In 1994, after having agreed a year earlier to establish Camp Shafi`i for the training of Abu Sayyaf and his own MILF fighters, he made an agreement to host a new Jemaah Islamiyah training facility at Camp Hudaibayah, a remote location within the larger Camp Abu Bakar. To supervise this effort, al-Qa'ida leader Abu Zubayda in October of that year appointed from Afghanistan Omar al-Farouk whom, with several other al-Qa'ida and Jemaah Islamiyah operatives, he sent to the Philippines to establish and oversee the new camp.[574] Funded by al-Qa'ida, the primary mission of Camp Hudaibayah was "to conduct jihadist training" for Jemaah Islamiyah recruits, primarily Indonesians, of whom more than one thousand were reported to have received training in Mindanao during the years 1996-98.[575] Initially, the al-Qa'ida trainers appear to have been mainly Arabs from camps in Afghanistan, but soon Indonesians were very involved in the training as well. Maintaining the security of this clandestine Jemaah Islamiyah training may well have been a key reason behind Hashim's acceptance of the new cease-fire.

From the Jemaah Islamiyah perspective, the Philippines was part of Mantiqi 3, which included all of Borneo (including the Malaysian provinces of Sabah and Sarawak, as well as independent Brunei) and the eastern Indonesian island of Sulawesi. The mission of Mantiqi 3 was almost purely training, whereas the mission of Mantiqi 1 (peninsular Malaysia, southern Thailand, and Singapore) was primarily to serve as a headquarters, transit point, banking center, and safe haven for planning. In general, military operations in these regions were avoided in order to maintain the security of the primary mission. The primary long-term target of Jemaah Islamiyah operations

---

[572] Cited in Maria A. Ressa, Seeds of Terror: An Eyewitness Account of al-Qaeda's Newest Center of Operations in Southeast Asia (New York: Free Press, 2003), 128.

[573] Further details in Ressa, Seeds of Terror, 128, and Abuza, Militant Islam in Southeast Asia, 45, 136–137.

[574] Ressa, Seeds of Terror, 134. The first trainees that virtually built the new Camp Hudaibayah were MILF recruits who used machetes to clear the jungle for the camp that was said to be up and running by April 1995, the same month the ASG attacked and destroyed the Christian town of Ipil. International Crisis Group, "Southern Philippines Backgrounder," 14.

[575] Ressa, Seeds of Terror, xv.

was clearly Mantiqi 2, the main islands of Indonesia. Although from the beginning *Jemaah Islamiyah* had a pan-Malay perspective and envisioned the eventual unity of all the Malay Muslim areas of Southeast Asia under a single Islamic government, the destabilization and eventual capture of Indonesia was clearly the short-term goal of *Jemaah Islamiyah* operations. The *Jemaah Islamiyah* leadership was Indonesian, as were most of its foot soldiers. The opportunity to launch such operations came only with the fall of the Suharto government in Indonesia in May 1998. In the meantime, its foot soldiers prepared, primarily in the MILF camps.

From the *al'Qa'ida* perspective, support for the *Jemaah Islamiyah* was part of its overall global strategy after the Soviet withdrawal from Afghanistan to support militant Islamist movements throughout the Islamic world that were striving to put an end to the generally authoritarian secular regimes, most often supported by the Western powers, and especially the United States, which had come to dominate most Islamic states during the 20th century. A second aspect of *al-Qa'ida* strategy, at least at the beginning, appears to have been to make use of the linkages that had been created as a means of gaining access to the Philippines as a base from which to conduct global operations, particularly against the United States. The failed Operation Bojinka, directed by Ramzi Yousef and uncovered by Philippine authorities in January 1995, was evidence of this intent, but the failure appears to have ended *al-Qa'ida* efforts to make use of the Philippines for this purpose, at least temporarily.

That *al-Qa'ida* and the MILF did not always share the same objectives was demonstrated on October 14, 1997, when two Arab trainers from Camp Hudaibiyah-Muhammad Gharib Ibrahim Sayid Ahmad and Ragab al-Makki-conducted a suicide attack on a Philippine Army headquarters near Cotabato, killing six. Clearly designed to disrupt the 3-year cease-fire that had been signed between the MILF and the government of the Philippines in July, it failed to achieve its end, as President Ramos and Salamat Hisham both interpreted the action for what it was and agreed to maintain the peace. Although Abuza interpreted this event as an effort to bolster the morale of MILF fighters who had been disillusioned by Hashim's agreement to the cease-fire, a more likely interpretation is that *al-Qa'ida* disapproved of the cease-fire agreement and sought to disrupt it.

Following the bombing of the U.S. embassies in East Africa in August 1998, the *al-Qa'ida* training centers in the Philippines and elsewhere assumed increased importance, as U.S. and Pakistani authorities intensified efforts to make it more difficult for *al-Qa'ida* recruits to use Pakistan as a transit point for individuals to reach the training camps in Afghanistan. Accordingly, Salamat Hashim acceded to requests from the *al-Qa'ida* leadership to open two more camps in the MILF areas that came to be called Camps Vietnam and Palestine, to be used exclusively by Arab and other Middle Eastern personnel.[576]

---

[576] Ressa, *Seeds of Terror*, 7, 133.

How much Philippine authorities knew about the clandestine training occurring in MILF camps in Mindanao at this time is unclear. Most information about it emerged from later interrogations of arrested individuals after the resumption of fighting in 2000. While Ramos remained President, both he and Salamat exerted strong efforts to maintain the cease-fire and to overlook isolated incidents that could have led to a resumption of fighting. Despite the cease-fire with the MILF, the government had no such agreement with the Abu Sayyaf Group, however, and on December 18, 1998, early in the term of Ramos's successor, President Joseph Estrada, Philippine constabulary forces managed to locate and kill ASG founder Abdurazak Janjalani in a shootout in Lamitan on Basilan Island.[577]

Impact of the Death of Janjalani

The death of Janjalani had the impact of splintering the ASG into at least five groups, each claiming to be the real ASG, but in fact operating more or less independently. Of these, two major factions were those commanded by the founder's brother, Khaddafi Janjalani, on Basilan Island and by Galib Andang, alias Commander Robot, operating in the Sulu Archipelago.[578] If the Philippine government believed it had resolved the problem of Abu Sayyaf by eliminating Janjalani, events soon proved it sadly mistaken. At best, Janjalani had played an important role in maintaining the ASG's cohesion, strategy, and tactics. With his death as a martyr to those who had followed him, the successor Abu Sayyaf groups emerged as not only vengeful, but more vicious and terrifying.[579]

A revived ASG, now headed by Khaddafi Janjalani, was heard from again when, on March 20, 2000, his group kidnapped more than 50 people from two elementary schools on Basilan Island, including a number of school children. Calling for release of three al-Qa'ida-linked prisoners held in United States prisons in exchange for the hostages, the incident clearly implied an international dimension that transcended the local Moro struggle in the Philippines. Although most of the school children were soon released in return for food and medicine, the kidnapping crisis went on for 44 days before the last hostages were released. In the meantime, the ASG kidnappers had murdered several of the hostages, including two by beheading, and others were killed by government forces while securing their release by force.[580]

---

[577] Turbiville, "Bearers of the Sword," 6.

[578] Ressa, *Seeds of Terror*, 109.

[579] Eusaquito P. Manalo, "The Philippine Response to Terrorism: The Abu Sayyaf Groups," unpublished master's degree thesis (Monterey, CA: Naval Postgraduate School, December 2004), 35–36.

[580] Ressa, *Seeds of Terror*, 109–110. The three *al-Qa'ida*-linked prisoners in the United States were the Egyptian Shaykh Omar Abd al-Rahman, imprisoned because of his alleged role in the February 1993 World Trade Center bombing, Ramzi Yousef, and Abu Haidal (Mir Aimal Kasi), imprisoned because of his role in killing two and wounding three CIA employees in northern Virginia in January 1993.

Not to be outdone, on April 23, 2000, Commander Robot's group of Abu Sayyaf in the Sulu Archipelago crossed over to Sipidan Island off the coast of Sabah in Malaysia and kidnapped 21 tourists from seven countries whom they brought back to Sulu as hostages. Although the kidnappers lectured the hostages about the ASG's struggle for an independent Islamic state, in the end all that was demanded for their release was $20 million – $1 million for each hostage — which was duly delivered in September by the government of Libya, allegedly under pressure from the affected European governments which were said to have reimbursed Libya for at least part of the ransom.[581]

In the early stages of the crisis, ARMM governor Nur Misuari, who had access to the Abu Sayyaf kidnappers, was tasked by the Estrada government with resolving the crisis. On May 8, however, he was replaced by the former Libyan ambassador to the Philippines, Rajab Azzarouk, who in 1996 had played an important role in facilitating the Jakarta Agreement between the Philippine government and the MNLF. European Union emissary Javier Solana also arrived in the Philippines to play a role.[582] The end result was the $20 million ransom that finally secured the release of the hostages on September 9, 2000.

The $20 million made the ASG incredibly rich. For a time, its contribution to the local economy far exceeded any government program, and recruits flocked to join the Abu Sayyaf Group. CNN journalist Marie Ressa argues that media interest in the kidnapping, which led journalists to pay handsome sums for guides and transportation and the right to interview individual hostages, not to mention the king's ransom at the end, transformed ASG terrorist operations into a virtual money-making industry that had benefits for many throughout the Philippine government, including perhaps even President Estrada himself. Some speculated that as much as half of the $20 million went back to *al-Qa'ida*.[583]

---

[581] Ressa, *Seeds of Terror*, 112–116. The kidnapped hostages were from Finland (2), Germany (3), France (2), South Africa (2), Lebanon (1), Malaysia (7), and the Philippines (2). One of the Filipinos was never released and was believed to have joined the ASG.

[582] AIJAC (The Australia/Israel and Jewish Affairs Council), "Asia Watch," in *The Review*, website of the AIJAC. URL: *http://www.aijac.org.au/review/2000/256/aw256.html*. Accessed September 13, 2005.

[583] Ressa, *Seeds of Terror*, 115.

THE DIFFERENT APPROACH OF JOSEPH ESTRADA

Although these Abu Sayyaf operations took place far from MILF areas of control, and MILF leaders distanced their organization from these terrorist operations, even issuing *fatwas* condemning kidnapping and the beheading of kidnapped hostages, the violence of the ASG provoked communal tensions throughout Mindanao. With the three-year cease-fire between the government and the MILF up for renewal in the summer of 2000, the increased tensions had both the Army and MILF fighters on high alert. A ferry bombing off Ozamis City in northern Mindanao on February 25, 2000, which killed 39 passengers, by terrorists whom the Army claimed had taken refuge in MILF Camp John Mack in Inudaran, Lanao del Norte, led to a military stand-off. Denying the presence of the perpetrators, the MILF camp found itself attacked by Philippine Armed Forces on March 17, just three days before the Abu Sayyaf attack on the two elementary schools on Basilan Island. Camp John Mack commander Abdullah Macaapar (Commander Bravo) responded by sending forces out of the camp to attack and occupy the nearby town of Kanswagan, a move that led to full-scale fighting between the two contending forces.[584]

President Joseph Estrada, elected to replace former President Fidel Ramos in June 1998, scorned his predecessor's policies of "coddling" the Muslims of the southern Philippines,[585] although he took no overt steps to undermine the cease-fire with the MILF until it came up for renewal in 2000. A former popular movie actor-turned-politician who was soon to be constitutionally impeached and driven from office in January 2001 because of alleged massive corruption, Estrada believed the Philippine Army should defeat the MILF rather than coexist with it. Accordingly, on April 27, four days after the ASG Sipidan Island kidnapping, he declared an "all-out war" against the MILF and the ASG.[586]

Estrada Takes the Offensive

Although fighting was general throughout the south over the next several months, with many former MNLF fighters again taking up arms and joining the MILF, and upwards of 900,000 civilian refugees being created by the general violence, a particular strategic target was the 15-km road connecting Camp Abu Bakar with the main Cotabato-Marawi highway that recently had been constructed by the Ramos administration. Heavily fortified and guarded by the MILF, the road ultimately could not be defended, and Philippine Armed Forces succeeded in breaking through to Camp Abu Bakar on July 9, taking control of MILF headquarters.[587] The MILF leadership, including Salamat Hashim, escaped, however, to the more remote *Jemaah Islamiyah*-controlled Camp Hudaibiyah, which continued to hold out against government forces

---

[584] International Crisis Group, "Southern Philippines Backgrounder," 6.

[585] Abuza, *Militant Islam in Southeast Asia*, 46.

[586] International Crisis Group, "Southern Philippines Backgrounder," 27.

[587] International Crisis Group, "Southern Philippines Backgrounder," 6.

until April 2001. Unknown publicly at this time, the Indonesian *Jemaah Islamiyah* cadres training in Camp Hudaibiyah began vacating the camp and returning, mainly to Indonesia, to establish new camps there that within a year were receiving MILF recruits for training.[588]

MILF Reactions

Anticipating the outbreak of hostilities with the Philippine government, the MILF in 1999 had begun establishing a Special Operations Group (SOG) under the leadership of Afghan war veteran Mukhlis Yunos.[589] In doing so, Yunos worked closely with Indonesian *Jemaah Islamiyah* figures, the most notable of which was another Afghan war veteran and explosives expert, Fathur Roman al-Ghozi.[590] In April 2000, Salamat Hashim had responded to President Estrada's declaration of "all-out war" against the MILF (the independent Bangsamoro Islamic state, as Hashim preferred to conceptualize it) by labeling the emerging struggle as a *jihad* against the would-be occupiers of the MILF "liberated zones." Very quickly, on May 3, 2000, Yunos' SOG responded by setting off four bombs in General Santos City that killed three. This attack was followed by another bomb at the SM Megamall in Manila on May 21 that killed one, and six more bombs in General Santos City on June 24 that killed two.[591] These clearly terrorist operations against civilian targets marked a departure for the MILF that heretofore had adhered closely to conventional guerilla tactics of attacking military targets and government facilities within the Muslim-inhabited areas of the Philippines. They did not deter government operations, however, which continued on until the capture of Camp Abu Bakar on June 9.

The fall of Camp Abu Bakar and most other MILF camps produced a lull in the fighting, not because the Philippine Army had achieved victory, but because the MILF needed time to undertake a major reorganization, decentralizing what had become a quite centralized military force[592] and making it more capable of conducting guerrilla operations. That MILF retaliation against Philippine "aggression" would have a different dimension, however, became apparent on August 1, 2000, when a bomb exploded outside the residence of the Philippine ambassador to Indonesia, Leonides Caday, in Jakarta, seriously wounding the ambassador and killing two bystanders. Although not known until after his capture in Manila on January 15, 2002, this operation was carried out by Indonesian *Jemaah Islamiyah* operator Fathur Roman al-Ghozi and others, as a kind of "thank-you note," so some said, to the MILF for the training and assistance provided to the *Jemaah Islamiyah* in recent years.[593]

---

[588] Ressa, *Seeds of Terror*, 139.

[589] Abuza, *Militant Islam in Southeast Asia*, 98.

[590] Ressa, *Seeds of Terror*, 136.

[591] International Crisis Group, "Southern Philippines Backgrounder," 11, 27.

[592] International Crisis Group, "Southern Philippines Backgrounder," 10, provides some detailed information about this reorganization.

[593] Abuza, *Militant Islam in Southeast Asia*, 97–98. For details, see International Crisis Group. "Southern Philippines Backgrounder," 18.

The major act of retaliation for the fall of Camp Abu Bakar was to come in Manila on Rizal Day, December 30, 2000, when the MILF SOG carried out five simultaneous bombings, striking a train, a bus, the airport, a park near the U.S. Embassy, and a gas station, killing 22 people and injuring more than 100. A dramatic event, Philippine authorities at this time had no idea that the bombings had an Indonesian connection.[594] Again, unrealized until after the capture of al-Ghozi and also Mukhlis Yunos on May 25, 2003, the bombings were an MILF SOG operation in which al-Ghozi had been a principal advisor. *Jemaah Islamiyah* leader Hambali had come to Manila a few days earlier to examine the plan and give it his seal of approval, as well as funds ($3,600) to Yunos to pay for his expenses.[595] The confusion over the Rizal Day bombings was only complicated by the occurrence six days earlier, on Christmas Eve, of 30 nearly simultaneous bomb blasts in Christian churches across Indonesia, also orchestrated by Hanbali, which killed 19 and injured about 120 people.[596]

The Impeachment of Joseph Estrada

The year 2000 had not been a good year for the Philippines and, in January 2001, President Joseph Estrada faced impeachment proceedings on grounds of massive corruption while in office, including widely believed allegations that he had derived profit from the $20 million ransom paid in September by the Libyan government to the ASG for release of the Sipidan hostages. Never formerly found guilty by the Philippine Senate, Estrada nevertheless was forced to step down from office only after the Supreme Court had declared the Presidency vacant and swore in his Vice President, Gloria Macapagal-Arroyo, as his constitutional successor on January 20. Claiming that he never had been formally removed from office nor resigned, Estrada and his supporters continued to challenge the legitimacy of the Arroyo government in legal disputes likely to keep Philippine politics in turmoil for the foreseeable future.[597]

ARROYO RESTORES THE RAMOS POLICY

Formerly Vice President in the Estrada administration, Arroyo, the daughter of former Philippine President Diosdado Macapagal (1961-65) and a former professor of economics, was elected in her own right as President in June 2001. Meanwhile, she inherited the problems of the Estrada era, including the challenges of the MILF and the ASG in the south. Closely associated with former President Fidel Ramos, one of her principal supporters and advisors, her policies reflected continuity with his administration rather than the Estrada administration-toward the south as well as the rest of the country.[598]

---

[594] International Crisis Group, "Southern Philippines Backgrounder," 19.

[595] Ressa, *Seeds of Terror*, 136–137.

[596] Symonds, "Political Origins and Outlook of Jemaah Islamiyah," Part 3, 3.

[597] The New Filipino Movement, "President Joseph Ejército Estrada," *Neofinoy.info*. URL: *http://www.neofinoy.info/The%20RP%20Presidents/estrada.htm*. Accessed: September 5, 2005.

[598] The New Filipino Movement, "President Gloria Macapagal-Arroyo," *Neofinoy.info*. URL: *http://www.neofinoy.info/The%20RP%20Presidents/arroyo.htm*. Accessed September 5, 2005.

Briefly stated, her policies were (1) renewal of the peace process with the MILF, (2) a search for new leadership of the MNLF as a prelude to facilitating MILF/MNLF cooperation, and (3) "total war" against the ASG and ending the type of terrorism it represented.[599] Soon after her installation as President she declared a unilateral cease-fire and initiated exploratory talks with the MILF aimed at renewing the former mutual cease-fire agreement originally made by President Ramos in 1997.[600] Such an agreement was reached and signed in Kuala Lumpur, Malaysia, on March 24, 2001.[601] Further talks and agreements on various issues such as security, humanitarian assistance, and economic development continued throughout 2001 and into 2002. An MILF condition for these talks was that they be mediated by the OIC and that they be conducted in an OIC country. The Malaysian government of Mahathir Mohamed took an active role in facilitating this process, as did the Libyan government of Mu`ammar Qadhafi.[602] A final aspect of these talks was an agreement, signed in Kuala Lumpur in August 2001, between the MILF and MNLF stating their intention to reunify after a separation of nearly 20 years.

Another Arroyo initiative was to schedule the long-delayed plebiscite, required by the Philippine Constitution, to formalize the expanded ARMM agreed on in the 1996 Jakarta Agreement. This she put on the calendar for August 2001, three months prior to the scheduled gubernatorial elections for the ARMM in November 2001.[603] One who opposed this process as well as the central role being played by the OIC in the talks between the government and the MILF was MNLF leader and ARMM governor Nur Misuari. Misuari's opposition to the Arroyo peace process provoked a split within the 15-man MNLF Executive Council that Arroyo effectively managed to secure the ouster of Misuari as MNLF chairman in April 2001 and his replacement by Parouk Hussein. Hussein later won election in November as the new governor of the ARMM.[604]

The Demise of Nur Misuari

The eclipse of Misuari was complete. His ultimate success in emerging as the governor of the ARMM in 1996 had been in fact the beginning of his downfall. Although simultaneously serving as Chairman of the SPCPD that gave him oversight of the expenditure of large amounts of development funds for the southern Philippines, there was a widespread perception that many of these funds had been squandered on large "showcase" projects or support of Misuari's own profligate lifestyle, and too little had been spent on health services, literacy, problems of malnutrition and infant mortality,

---

[599] Manalo, "The Philippine Response to Terrorism," 5.

[600] United States Institute of Peace, "The Mindanao Peace Talks: Another Opportunity to Resolve the Moro Conflict in the Philippines," *Special Report 131* (Washington, DC: United States Institute of Peace, January 2005), 6. Also Mel C. Labrador, "The Philippines in 2001: High Drama, a New President, and Setting the Stage for Recovery," *Asian Survey*, XLII, 1 (January/February 2002), 146.

[601] International Crisis Group, "Southern Philippines Backgrounder," 32.

[602] USIP, "The Mindanao Peace Talks," 6.

[603] Manalo, "The Philippine Response to Terrorism," 5.

[604] Abuza, *Militant Islam in Southeast Asia*, 43.

or in employment creation.[605] Salamat Hashim's MILF, moreover, had long opposed Misuari's leadership, and the MILF had only grown stronger since 1996, especially in Mindanao, where the MILF assertion of independence against Misuari's acceptance of autonomy led many to accuse the latter of having sold out to the Philippine regime for his own personal benefit. The rallying of many Misuari followers, including some who had been integrated into the Philippine security services under the terms of the Jakarta Agreement, to the MILF during the 2000 fighting while Misuari remained loyal to the government also had weakened his degree of support. Finally, his failure or inability to deal effectively with the Abu Sayyaf threat, particularly in Sulu, his own territory, where the Sipidan Island hostages had been held, caused Arroyo and perhaps even the Malaysian government, whose seven hostages he had been unable to liberate, to lose confidence in him.

Ousted from the leadership of the MNLF, Misuari soon went into opposition, formally denouncing the Arroyo administration in late October 2001, a month prior to the ARMM elections, and threatening to take up arms again.[606] Coming as it did shortly after the September 11, 2001, al-Qa'ida attack on the World Trade Center and the Pentagon in the United States, and at a time when the Arroyo administration was seeking to cooperate with the United States in its rapidly emerging "global war on terrorism," Misuari's stance could not have been more ill-timed. A bombing in Zamboanga City that killed five on October 28, 2001, attributed to the ASG, just at the moment Misuari was expressing his opposition to the Arroyo government, also seriously undermined his credibility.

Undeterred, Misuari succeeded in raising 400–600 loyalists who on November 19 attacked several military posts in Jolo in an effort to halt the gubernatorial election scheduled for November 26. President Arroyo ordered "full force" to be employed in suppressing the Misuari rebellion, and in a week of fighting nearly 1,300 were estimated to have been killed prior to the election. A court order for his arrest having been issued, Misuari finally fled the country, but was detained by Malaysian authorities as he tried to land in Sabah and later extradited to Manila to stand trial.[607] His long run as the favored leader of the Moro resistance movement by the OIC had come to an end. Despite the violence, elections were held as scheduled on November 26, and new MNLF leader Parouk Hussein, with the full support of the Arroyo administration, was duly chosen as the new governor of the ARMM.

Abu Sayyaf Again

Misuari's cause probably was not helped by yet another major ASG kidnapping and hostage crisis that had emerged earlier in the year. As reported by CNN correspondent Maria Ressa,

---

[605] Abuza, *Militant Islam in Southeast Asia*, 42.

[606] Turbiville, "Bearers of the Sword," 7.

[607] Abuza, *Militant Islam in Southeast Asia*, 43.

On May 27, 2001...Khadaffy Janjalani's group [on Basilan Island] used one of the high-speed boats bought by the Sipidan ransom money to get to the southern Philippine Island of Palawan...In the middle of the night, armed men stormed the rooms by the ocean of the Dos Palmas resort, pulling out twenty people, including three Americans...By June 1, the groups had landed on the island of Basilan and kidnapped still more hostages from the Golden Harvest plantation. Pursued by the Philippine military, the Abu Sayyaf and their hostages fled to a hospital and church compound in the town of Lamitan, where a day-long siege ended in a fiasco that spotlighted either the incompetence of the Philippine military or collusion and corruption on a massive scale.[608]

Totally surrounded by more than 1,000 soldiers, Ressa goes on to say, a back entrance of the church was left unguarded after dusk, enabling the apparently informed kidnappers and their hostages to simply walk out of the compound and disappear into the jungle.

The hostage crisis that ensued ended more than a year later, on June 7, 2002, when a Philippine Army operation, supported by U.S. soldiers who now were providing intelligence and training to the Philippine units, managed to rescue the one remaining living hostage, an American, Gracia Burnham, whose husband, Martin Burnham, along with a Filipina nurse, Edilborah Yap, were killed in the course of the operation.[609] In the meantime, the crisis provoked severe recriminations within the Philippine Army and government as well as among the public, especially when an investigation into the church escape fiasco held no one accountable.[610] Unable to negotiate a ransom agreement with either the Philippine or American government, as their colleagues had done with the Sipidan hostages a year before, the ASG kidnappers embarked on a killing spree, attacking a number of Christian villages on Basilan Island and gradually killing several of their hostages, often by cruel torture, and releasing others until only the three were left that the Philippine Army tried to rescue in June 2002. The Zamboanga City bombing of October 28, 2001, that so compromised Misuari's campaign of opposition against the government was also probably a part of this regime of terror.

The Plebiscite of August 2001

Despite the crisis provoked by the ASG kidnapping, Arroyo proceeded with the August 14, 2001, plebiscite on expansion of the ARMM. In Senate Bill 2129, passed in January, just after her assumption of the Presidency, the government had expanded the potential ARMM to 15 provinces and 14 cities in a gerrymandering effort to increase the

---

[608] Ressa, *Seeds of Terror*, 116–117.

[609] The complete story is told in Ressa, *Seeds of Terror*, 104–123.

[610] Ressa, *Seeds of Terror*, 118.

likelihood that most of the Muslim region would fall under the ARMM-a step deemed necessary to comply most effectively with the spirit of the 1976 Tripoli Agreement and the 1996 Jakarta Agreement. Although Arroyo campaigned in 11 provinces and 14 cities for their inclusion in the ARMM, the results proved disappointing to both the President as well as to Muslim leaders in that only Basilan Island (excluding the municipality of Isabela) and Marawi City voted to be included together with the four provinces previously included in the ARMM in 1989.[611] Christian majorities and/ or Muslims disgruntled with the MNFL or MILF in the remaining ten provinces simply opposed becoming part of an autonomous Moro Muslim state as envisioned by the Tripoli Agreement of 1976, which the government of Gloria Macapagal-Arroyo had now accepted.

9/11

Such was the situation in the Philippine Muslim south when, after the September 11, 2001, *al-Qa'ida* attacks in the United States, President Arroyo was asked for Philippine help in supporting the U.S.-led global war on terrorism. Arroyo was eager to cooperate with the United States, and in fact was the first Asian leader to have called U.S. President Bush in the wake of the attacks, but a return of U.S. forces to the Philippines after their departure from Clark Air Force Base and Subic Bay Naval Station in 1992 was a difficult political issue for the new President. Too, although she was pleased to receive help in combating the ASG organization, she at the same time did not want a renewed relationship with the United States to complicate her concerted effort to negotiate a final settlement of the long-standing Moro problem in the south that she felt was now in sight. For his part, MILF leader Salamat Hashim articulated the right words, when on October 8, 2001, the day after the first U.S. strikes in Afghanistan aimed at dislodging the Taliban government and destroying the *al-Qa'ida* organization, he rejected Usama bin Ladin's call for a general Muslim *jihad* against the United States and its allies and stated that the MILF continued to respect the cease-fire agreement with the government of the Philippines and looked forward to peace talks with the government in Kuala Lumpur scheduled for October 15.[612]

Renewed Relations with the United States

In November 2001, during her first state visit to the United States to commemorate the 50th anniversary of the U.S.-Republic of the Philippines Mutual Defense Treaty, Bush and Arroyo issued a joint statement in which the two leaders "agreed that the September 11 terrorist attacks on the United States and the terrorist activities of the Abu Sayyaf Group or ASG (which now hold both Filipino and American hostages in the southern Philippines) underscore the urgency of ensuring that the two countries

---

[611] Labrador, "The Philippines in 2001," 147.

[612] Abuza, *Militant Islam in Southeast Asia*, 99.

maintain a robust defense partnership into the 21st century."[613] Bush had promised both military and economic assistance and help "in any way she suggests in getting rid of the Abu Sayyaf."[614] Arroyo herself was elated at her reception in the U.S. capital, telling reporters after one of her meetings in Washington that she was "at $4 billion and counting."[615]

The details remained to be worked out but became apparent in December, when Manila began allowing U.S. forces to overfly Philippine airspace and use airfields as transit points in support of Operation ENDURING FREEDOM in Afghanistan. In return, the United States agreed to provide antiterrorism training and advice to Philippine military forces engaged in combat operations against the ASG.[616] The agreement gave rise to a joint exercise called Balikatan (Shoulder-to-Shoulder) 02–01, which brought U.S. troops to Zamboanga and Basilan Island during the period February-July 2002. Initially composed of 660 troops, including 200 members of the U.S. Special Forces, the group later grew to nearly 1,000 soldiers by the end of the exercise. Despite speculation that "shoulder-to-shoulder" meant that U.S. soldiers would accompany Philippine Army units on their patrols in search of ASG fighters, the U.S. role remained confined to training, advising, and intelligence support based on aerial reconnaissance of Basilan Island and surrounding regions. Indeed, the mission of the U.S. forces was very narrowly circumscribed in order not to violate provisions of the Philippine Constitution that prohibited the stationing of foreign forces on Philippine soil.[617] In January 2002, moreover, prior to the deployment of the U.S. forces, the United States, Arroyo's government, and the MILF had signed a trilateral agreement that U.S. forces would not enter MILF-controlled territories on Basilan or elsewhere in the Philippines in pursuit of ASG fighters, much to the chagrin of some in both the U.S. and Philippine armed forces.[618]

Confined to Basilan Island, Operation Balikatan 02–01 had some success in capturing or killing a number of ASG fighters and in bringing an end to the Dos Palmos kidnapping crisis, when on June 7, 2002, the Philippine Army was able to deliver to U.S. forces the one remaining American hostage, Gracia Burnham. Most ASG members, including Khaddafy Janjalani, managed to elude the search and destroy mission organized against them and escape, mainly to Sulu, but also into safe havens in Mindanao, where U.S. forces, by the terms of reference of their presence in

[613] The White House, "U.S.-Philippine Joint Statement on Defense Alliance." November 20, 2001. URL: *http://www.whitehouse.gov/news/releases/2001/11/20011120.html*. Accessed: September 5, 2005.

[614] Sonya Ross, "Bush Promises Help Against Philippine Terrorists," *Honolulu Advertiser*, November 21, 2001.

[615] James Hookway, "Manila Proves Key U.S. Ally in Terrorism War-Bush Responds with Aid, but There are Limits to Philippine Support,." *Wall Street Journal*, November 20, 2001.

[616] Angel Rabasa, "Political Islam in Southeast Asia: Moderates, Radicals and Terrorists," *Adelphi Papers* (London: International Institute for Strategic Studies, July 1, 2003), URL: *http://www3.oup.co.uk/adelph/hdb/volume_358/Issue_011*.

[617] Michael J. Montesano, "The Philippines in 2002: Playing Politics, Facing Deficits, and Embracing Uncle Sam," *Asian Survey*, XLIII, 1 (January/February 2003), 161–162.

[618] Abuza, *Militant Islam in Southeast Asia*, 48.

the Philippines, were unable to go. The ASG retaliation was fierce, however, as strings of urban bombings occurred with regularity throughout the southern Philippines and also in Manila throughout 2002 and into 2003, including one on October 2, 2002, in Zamboanga City, in which a U.S. serviceman was killed. Later evidence collected from captured terrorists determined that various Indonesian members of *Jemaah Islamiyah* had actively collaborated with the ASG in perpetrating these bombings,[619] although the campaign appeared to have been directed by Khaddafy Janjalani.[620] Despite MILF denials of any connection with these terrorist attacks and indeed formal condemnation of them, mounting evidence of established relations between the MILF and various *Jemaah Islamiyah* fighters operating in the Philippines kept the MILF on the defensive.

The overall lack of success of Operation Balikatan 02-01 led the United States and the government of the Philippines to undertake Operation Balikatan 03-01 the following year, this time with the focus on Jolo and the Sulu Archipelago, where about 350 U.S. Special Forces personnel were deployed in February 2003 along with approximately 1,000 U.S. Marines positioned on ships offshore. During this campaign, U.S. forces reportedly had been quietly authorized by the Arroyo government to engage in combat operations against ASG forces, despite the fact that such an authorization would technically be in violation of the Philippine Constitution.[621]

Who Is In Charge?

Growing disarray in the Arroyo administration was evident in early 2003. The last week of 2002 had seen a series of murderous attacks in civilian targets in several provinces of Mindanao that the Army high command blamed on the MILF, despite adamant denials from Salamat Hashim and other MILF leaders. Meanwhile, since mid-October 2002, Arroyo, who on December 31, 2002, formally announced that she would not be a candidate in the next Presidential elections scheduled for May 2004, was engaged in peace talks with the MILF in Malaysia that she deemed to be proceeding well. She also continued successfully to urge the United States not to add

---

[619] The continuing violence in the southern Philippines was overshadowed by the August 12, 2002, bombing of the Sari nightclub in Denpasar, Bali, in neighboring Indonesia that killed 202, including 88 Australian tourists. The Bali bombing was the world's deadliest terrorist incident since the September 11, 2001, attacks on New York and Washington. Largely overlooked at the time were the almost simultaneous bombings that same evening of the U.S. consulate in Bali and the Philippine consulate in Manado, the Indonesian city closest to the Philippines. The Bali bombing was immediately understood to be the work of *Jemaah Islamiyah*, and the simultaneity of the other two bombings suggests they were part of the same operation. Later arrests of nearly 30 individuals believed to be associated with the bombings brought to light the fact that many had trained in MILF camps in Mindanao. Although the MILF may have only "hosted" their training, the only reasonable analytical conclusion was that linkages existed between the MILF and the *Jemaah Islamiyah* that conjoined their respective struggles as parts of a common cause or were simply separate manifestations of the same cause. Montesano, "The Philippines in 2002," 135.

[620] International Crisis Group, "Southern Philippines Backgrounder," 22–24.

[621] Michael J. Montesano, "The Philippines in 2003: Troubles, None of Them New," *Asian Survey*, XLIV, 1 (January/February 2004), 100.

the MILF to the list of Foreign Terrorist Organizations,[622] while in February 2003, concurrent with the redeployment of U.S. forces to Sulu for Operation Balikatan 03-01, she presented the Army command with a three-month deadline to "break the back of the ASG."[623]

Apparently without specific Presidential authorization, but acting on these general orders, on February 11, 2003, the Army launched a multi-battalion assault on the "Buliok Complex," a series of towns in the Liguasan Marsh near Pikit, the hometown of Salamat Hashim, southeast of Cotabato City, where the MILF had reestablished its headquarters after the loss of Camp Abu Bakar in 2002.[624] Hardly had the operation begun, however, when President Arroyo issued orders for the military to halt the attack, because the government had approved the final draft of a comprehensive peace agreement with the MILF. On the following day, the President suddenly reversed her decision and ordered the Army to capture and occupy the Buliok Complex-but only to capture the Pentagon Gang, an independent and particularly brutal ASG-like terrorist group that the Army insisted was being given refuge there.[625]

The Pentagon Gang continued to operate in 2005, meaning that the Army did not succeed in its stated mission, but it did succeed in occupying the Buliok Complex-probably the real intent of the operation-over which the Philippine flag was raised on February 14 after the dispersal of an estimated 1,500 MILF fighters and about 40,000 civilian refugees.[626] Following the fall of the Buliok Complex, Mindanao was struck with a series of violent terrorist attacks, the most notable of which were the bombings of Davao International Airport on March 4, 2003, and the Davao wharf at Sasa on April 2, 2003, in which 38 were killed and over 200 wounded.[627] The Army adamantly argued that the MILF was behind these attacks, whereas the "MILF consistently and vociferously denied complicity" in any of these attacks.[628] The situation was admittedly confused by the reported arrival in Mindanao at this time of ASG leader Khaddafy Janjalani and many of his fighters who were escaping growing pressure on them from Operation Balikatan 03-01 in Sulu.[629]

Clearly frustrated by the contradiction between her policy of trying to negotiate with the MILF and that of the Army to pursue the organization as aggressively as possible,

---

[622] Michael J. Montesano, "The Philippines in 2002," 165–166.

[623] Anthony Davis, "Resiliant Abu Sayyaf Resist Military Pressure," *Jane's Intelligence Review*, 15, 9 (September 2003), 14.

[624] International Crisis Group, "Southern Philippines Backgrounder," 7.

[625] Ressa, *Seeds of Terror*, 141.

[626] Anthony Davis, "Philippine Army Prevents MILF Reorganization," *Jane's Intelligence Review*, 15, 3 (March 2003), 16.

[627] International Crisis Group, "Southern Philippines Backgrounder," 23.

[628] Anthony Davis, "Fragile Ceasefire Holds Out in the Philippines," *Jane's Intelligence Review*, 16, 1 (January 2004), 16.

[629] Anthony Davis. "Philippines Fears New Wave of Attacks by Abu Sayyaf Group" *Jane's Intelligence Review*, 17, 5 (May 2005), 11.

on May 7, 2003, on the eve of her departure for her second state visit to Washington, Arroyo called on the MILF to "renounce all terrorist ties" or risk designation as a Foreign Terrorist Organization by the United States.[630] Salamat and other MILF spokesmen quickly did so, noting that "the MILF, as a liberation organization, has repeatedly renounced terrorism publicly as a means of obtaining political ends." Arroyo's visit to the United States at this time was closely linked to U.S. efforts to gain Philippine support for Bush administration policy in Iraq, which U.S. forces had occupied in March, and she was able to obtain a number of favorable concessions, including keeping the MILF off the Foreign Terrorist Organization list.[631] Soon after her return from Washington, Arroyo again met Malaysian Prime Minister Mahathir Mohamed in Tokyo, and on July 19, 2003, through the good offices of the government of Malaysia, a new Mutual Cessation of Hostilities agreement was signed between the MILF and the government.[632]

At this point, two key developments intervened. A military mutiny in Manila on July 27 called for Arroyo's own resignation as well as that of her Defense Secretary, General Angelo Reyes, and the Armed Forces intelligence director, Victor Corpus. Accusing them of staging bombings in Mindanao for the purpose of securing increased American military and economic assistance and of selling arms to Muslim rebels for personal profit, the rebels asserted that they could no longer serve such a corrupt government at such low pay.[633] Perceiving a plot within the Army to overthrow her, Arroyo moved adroitly to secure the resignations of both Reyes and Corpus in August.[634] Widely perceived as a "hawk" over issues of war and peace in Mindanao, Reyes was replaced by another retired general, Edwardo Ermita, who previously had been serving as Arroyo's point man in the peace process with the MILF and the communist New People's Army (NPA). As chief negotiator with the MILF, Arroyo appointed Silvestre Afable, previously the head of her Presidential management staff, whom she believed the MILF respected and trusted.[635]

---

[630] International Crisis Group, "Southern Philippines Backgrounder," 7.

[631] Montesano, "The Philippines in 2003," 100. Among the concessions received were designation of the Philippines as a "major non-NATO ally" of the US, creation of a new combat engineering unit and other counterterrorism support for the Philippines Armed Forces, twenty refurbished helicopters, development assistance for Mindanao and financial support for the Philippines-MILF peace process, improved processes for overseas workers' remittances, aid for Filipino veterans of the U.S. military, and Generalized System of Preferences benefits for selected Philippine exports to the United States.

[632] International Crisis Group, "Southern Philippines Backgrounder," 7.

[633] The issues raised by the mutineers were clearly related to a new book that had appeared in the summer of 2003 by Gracia Burnham, *In the Presence of My Enemies* (Carol Stream, IL: Tyndale House Publishers, 2003). Ms. Burnham, who had been an Abu Sayyaf kidnapping victim for more than a year prior to her being freed by the Philippine Army on June 7, 2002, had written that certain Philippine Army members had connived with her ASG captors to divide millions of dollars the group had raised through their kidnapping operations. See Leslie Davis, "Philippines on Trial over Hostage Issue," *Asian Times*, August 7, 2004. URL: *http://www.atimes.com/atimes/Southeast_Asia/FH07Ae05.html*. Accessed September 22, 2005.

[634] Montesano, "The Philippines in 2003," 96–97.

[635] Davis, "Fragile Ceasefire Holds Out in the Philippines," 16.

Death of Salamat Hashim

The second development was the death (by heart attack) of MILF Chairman Salamat Hashim on July 13, 2003, nearly a week before the signing of the new Mutual Cessation of Hostilities Agreement. Although announcement of his death was delayed until August 5, when it could be said that Haj Ali Murad had succeeded Hashim as Chairman of the MILF, the choice of Murad was positively received by the Arroyo administration. Long the MILF chief of military operations who had remained most of his life in Mindanao, he lacked the strong international connections possessed by Hashim, and was considered less a religious ideologue than his predecessor had been.[636] Because Murad was considered an easier leader to deal with, despite his formidable talents as a military commander, Arroyo was optimistic, given the new team of Philippine negotiators she was putting in place, that a final settlement of the Moro problem could be readied.

Although the cease-fire with the MILF continued to hold up through 2005, further negotiations aimed at reaching a final settlement failed to occur quickly. First, there was the need for Haj Ali Murad to take charge of the organization he now headed. The refusal of the Army to withdraw from the Buliok Complex it had taken in February, a condition set by the MILF, also delayed the resumption of negotiations. So too did the MILF demand for charges to be dropped against 150 MILF leaders accused of organizing the terrorist attacks that had followed the Army's storming of the Buliok Complex. Yet another issue was an MILF demand that third-party cease-fire monitors from OIC countries, primarily Malaysia, be permitted to enter Mindanao prior to the start of negotiations. Although the Arroyo administration agreed to permit such a team to visit the MILF area on a temporary basis to assess the situation and make recommendations to the government, its position was that a permanent observation team could only be permitted after the conclusion of a final agreement, when its function would be to monitor implementation of the agreement.[637]

Government-MILF Talks Begin

These issues were finally resolved, and the first of six rounds of exploratory talks in Kuala Lumpur during 2004 took place in February 2004. Further rounds of talks continued in February, April, and September 2005. Until this point, the talks remained "exploratory" only, and although both parties expressed the desire to enter formal negotiations to reach a final peace settlement, a variety of issues continued to intervene to retard the process. The question of OIC-sponsored multinational observers was addressed in the first meeting in February 2004, and the first team

---

[636] International Crisis Group, "Southern Philippines Backgrounder," 9.
[637] Davis, "Fragile Ceasefire Holds Out in the Philippines," 16–17.

consisting of Malaysian, Brunei, and Libyan observers/monitors arrived in Mindanao in October.[638]

A complicating issue was a United States initiative to become part of the peace process. During her May 2003 visit to Washington, President Arroyo had asked for and had received from U.S. President George W. Bush a promise of financial support for the Philippines-MILF peace process. Thirty million dollars were made available and provided to the Washington-based United States Institute of Peace (USIP) to help facilitate the peace process. Efforts to enter the peace talks in Kuala Lumpur, however, were rebuffed by the Malaysian government and the OIC. The high-level team put together by the USIP, consisting of former U.S. ambassadors to Manila and others, therefore, had to content itself with bilateral meetings with Philippine government and MILF representatives engaged in the peace talks as well as with individual Filipino scholars and civil society activists engaged in promoting peace.[639] The Institute also sought to promote dialogue through research and the holding of seminars on key issues pertinent to the conflict. A major example was a two-day workshop on the thorny issue of ancestral domain held on May 24-27, 2005, in Davao City and attended by nearly 40 participants, including Philippine government and MILF representatives, Philippine scholars, and civil society activists.[640]

The Issues at Stake

Ancestral domain claims, along with security and the economic redevelopment of the southern Philippines after the conclusion of peace, emerged as the three major issues to be resolved in the exploratory talks in Kuala Lumpur prior to moving into final peace talks.[641] Superficially, security seemed to be the easiest issue to resolve. Early in the talks, the two parties established a series of joint Coordinating Committees on the Cessation of Hostilities (CCCH) to coordinate issues arising from the July 2003 cease-fire agreement and to react jointly to cease-fire violations, when they occurred. 71 cease-fire violations in 2004, as opposed to 559 in 2003, were dealt with in this manner.[642]

---

[638] Temario C. Rivera, "The Philippines in 2004: New Mandate, Daunting Problems," *Asian Survey*, XLV, 1 (January/February 2005), 127.

[639] Eugene Martin, "U.S. Interests in the Philippine Peace Process," *United States Institute of Peace* web page, February 8, 2005. URL: *http://www.usip.org/Philippines/reports/mindanao_martin.html*. Accessed September 22, 2005.

[640] For the proceedings of the conference, see Astrid S. Tuminez, "Ancestral Domain in Comparative Perspective," Special Report 151, *United States Institute of Peace* web site. URL: *http://www.usip.org/pubs/specialreports/sr151.html*. Accessed September 22, 2005.

[641] Rivera, "The Philippines in 2004," 127.

[642] Embassy of the Philippines (Washington), "Status of the GRP-MILF Peace Process," *United States Institute of Peace* web site, February 5, 2005. URL: *http://www.usip.org/philippines/reports/ rosario.pdf*. Accessed September 22, 2005.

Security. Although instances of terrorist violence were significantly reduced during this period, at least three major terrorist attacks, each eventually attributed to the ASG with JI support, marred the security environment. The first, on February 27, 2004, as the first government-MILF talks were getting underway in Kuala Lumpur, was the bombing of a superferry off Corregidor Island as it departed Manila for Davao City in Mindanao, killing over 100.[643] The second, on February 14, 2005, again as talks were resuming in Kuala Lumpur, which an ASG spokesman called a "Valentine's Day gift to Mrs. Arroyo," consisted of virtually simultaneous bombings in the Makati financial district of Manila, General Santos City, and Davao City that claimed 12 killed and at least 140 wounded.[644] The third, on August 28, 2005, was another bomb blast on a ferry, the *Doña Ramoña*, departing Lamitan on Basilan Island for Manila, wounding 30.[645] These and lesser instances of violence continued to provoke Philippine government intervention and claims that the MILF continued to harbor terrorists, despite adamant MILF denials and continued cooperation with the government to uncover wanted individuals.

Increased government success in capturing or killing various ASG and JI fighters during the new cease-fire era was indicative of increased cooperation.[646] Philippine government security operations remained intrusive, however, and MILF spokesmen often accused government forces of being in violation of the Cessation of Hostilities Agreement more often than its own "renegade" commanders. Examples occurred on November 19, 2004, and January 27, 2005, when on both occasions Philippine military helicopter gunships and aircraft on the basis of "solid intelligence" attacked villages in MILF territories in which ASG leaders, including Janjalani, were alleged to be meeting with JI operatives from Indonesia to plan future operations. On both occasions, civilian villagers were killed, but the intended targets were not included

---

[643] Sol Jose Varizi, "Abu Sayyaf: From Kidnap to Genuine Terror," *Philippine Headline News Online*, August 26, 2004. URL: *http://www.newsflash.org/2004/02/22/hl/hl100913.htm*. Accessed September 22, 2005.

[644] Anthony Davis, "Filipinos Fear New Wave," *Jane's Intelligence Review*, 17, 5 (May 2005), 10. Also "New Abu Sayyaf," *The Economist*, February 17, 2005. URL: http://www.economist.com/ Printerfriendly. cfm?Story_ID=3675637. Accessed September 22, 2005. Also AFP, Manila, "Abu Sayyaf, Army Clash on Strife-torn Philippine Island," *Taipei Times*, February 20, 2005. URL: *http://www.taipeitimes.com/News/world/archives/2005/02/20/200223815/print*. Accessed September 3, 2005.

[645] Associated Press, "30 Wounded in Blast on Philippines Ferry," *International Herald Tribune*, Asia-Pacific edition, August 29, 2005. URL: *http://www.iht.com/articles/2005/08/28/news/phils.php*. Accessed September 20, 2005.

[646] Among those captured/killed were: Toufik Rifqi, Indonesian, captured October 2003; Fathur Rohman al-Ghozi, Indonesian, killed October 2003; Galib Andang (Commander Robot), ASG commander on Jolo Island, captured December 2003; Hamsiraji Sali, ASG leader in Basilan, killed with five of his men in April 2004; three Indonesians with ASG Filipino guide, captured December 2004; ASG operatives Gamal Baharan and Abu Khalil Trinidad, captured February 2005; ASG fighter Gappal Banna, arrested in March 2005; Indonesian JI operative Zaki, captured in March 2005; ASG bomber Alex Kahal, captured in August 2005; among others. In April 2005, more than 800 alleged militant Muslims, members of the ASG and others, were reported to be imprisoned in Bicutan military camp near Manila. Maulana Alonto, "Sulu Fighting Exposes Filipino Government Claims to Want Peace in Mindanao," *Al-Jazeersh.info*, April 5, 2005. URL: *http://www.maranao.com/articles/Sulu%20fighting%20exposes%20Filipino%20government%20claims.htm*. Accessed September 26, 2005.

among the casualties.[647] Despite the agreements on security cooperation, the security situation in the south remained tense and the parties distrustful of one another.

Agreement on the OIC-sponsored International Monitoring Teams (IMT) that finally arrived in October 2004 was meant to interpose a third party, trusted by both sides, as a mechanism for ameliorating the distrust between the MILF and the Army. The teams were trusted by the MILF that had demanded their presence as a condition for entering exploratory talks with the government. At the same time, they were trusted by the Arroyo administration on the basis of the President's relations with Malaysian Prime Minister Mahathir Mohamed and, after October 2003, Abdullah Ahmad Badawi. The positive effect of the IMT was not immediately apparent in the months immediately after their deployment, however. Whether a third party could play such a role over the longer term remained to be seen.

One remaining difficulty with the OIC role was that, despite its efforts to facilitate talks between the government and the MILF, it still recognized the MNLF (if not Nur Misuari) as the official voice of the Bangsamoro people.[648] Still technically the elected leadership of the ARMM, now under Parouk Hussein, Philippine government, OIC, and MNLF leadership policy was for the MILF ultimately to rejoin and become part of an enlarged MNLF. Meanwhile, the MNLF leadership was being challenged by a breakaway group (MNLF-BG), still loyal to Nur Misuari (who remained under house arrest in Santa Rosa) but headed by religious leader Habier Malik. This group engaged the Philippine Army in pitched battles on Jolo Island in February 2005.[649] Despite the MILF-government agreement on security cooperation, security in the south remained tenuous in ways over which the MILF had no control.

Economic Redevelopment. On the second issue of economic redevelopment of the southern Philippines, the MILF and the government reached ready agreement in principle, although concerted efforts to spur reconstruction in the south necessarily awaited a final peace settlement. Early in the negotiations, agreement was struck on

---

[647] Anthony Vargas, "AFP Checking Report Janjalani Killed in Air Raid," *The Manila Times*, December 21, 2004. URL: *http://www.manilatimes.net/national/2004/dec/21/yehey/top_stories/ 20041221tops.html*. Accessed September 20, 2005. Also Roel Pareña, "AFP Launches Airstrikes on Janjalani Meeting," *Star* (Manila), January 28, 2005. URL: *http://www.newsflash.org/2005/02/hl/ hl101697.htm*. Accessed September 20, 2005. Also USIP, "The Mindanao Peace Talks," 11.

[648] USIP, "The Mindanao Peace Talks," 10.

[649] Davis, "Filipinos Fear New Wave," 10. AFP Manila, "Abu Sayyaf, Army Clash on Strife-torn Philippine Island," *Taipei Times*, February 20, 2005. URL: *http://www.taipeitimes.com/News/world/ archives/2005/02/20/2003223815/print*. Accessed September 3, 2005.

the creation of a Mindanao Trust Fund (MTF).[650] Under the terms of this agreement, a Joint Needs Assessment was conducted by the World Bank during August and September 2004 in which needs were assessed in four areas: human development, rural development, finance and private sector, and governance and institutions.[651] Also created was a Bangsamoro Development Agency (BDA), originally consisting of 135 personnel identified by the MILF to take the lead in managing development projects in the Bangsamoro area. A Malaysian Technical Cooperation Program (MTCP) was also established that provided training for the BDA personnel in 2005.[652]

Easy enough to agree on, perhaps harder to implement, the MTF concept was fraught with problems, even before the conclusion of the hypothetical peace settlement. Most funds provided by the donor countries were matching funds, meaning that they would be made available only to match appropriations by the Philippine government. The government, meanwhile, faced a looming fiscal crisis in 2005, brought on by a massive budget deficit and a ballooning public debt, all aggravated by widespread corruption throughout the government and society, plus the seemingly unending security problem associated with the Moro problem in the south as well as the continuing problem with the NPA in the north. The question of authority over the allocation and spending of available redevelopment funds, most of which were attached to specific projects identified by the World Bank, also loomed as a divisive issue. How authority between the World Bank, Philippine government ministries, and the newly established local BDA in Mindanao-created to provide a stronger sense of Moro self-determination and control of their own destiny-would be divided remained unresolved.

Ancestral Domain. The final issue, ancestral domain, on the table for the Kuala Lumpur meetings during 2005, promised to be an even thornier problem. Gradually driven from their ancestral lands by a hundred years of "colonization" by northern Christian Filipinos, and by more than 30 years of war since its outbreak in 1972, the "ancestral domains" of the Moros had all but been lost. Yet, through the MILF, the struggle for self-determination and independence continued, not strong enough to claim independence by force from the Philippine government, yet strong enough to make it impossible for the Philippine government to impose its will on the Moros of Mindanao. The MILF no longer claimed the whole of Mindanao, but negotiated in terms of the 1976 Tripoli Agreement that allocated 13 provinces as the designated homeland of the

---

[650] Originally called the Multi-Donor Trust Fund, it was put together by the World Bank in cooperation with the government of the Philippines during the summer of 2003 for the purpose of consolidating donor funds from a variety of countries for the redevelopment of the southern Philippines after a final peace settlement had been reached. The Islamic Development Bank, the Organization of Petroleum Exporting Countries (OPEC), Bahrain, the United Arab Emirates, Kuwait, and Saudi Arabia were early contributors to the fund. Clearly aimed at wooing the MILF into peace talks with the Philippine government, President Arroyo advertised it as a "peace dividend" for Mindanao as soon as a peace agreement had been finalized. Rexcel Sorza, "Life in Mindanao Better Once Peace Talks Start: Manila," *IslamOnline.net*, September 26, 2003. URL: *http://islamonline.net/English/ News/2003-09/26/article07.shtml*. Accessed September 26, 2005.

[651] USIP, "The Mindanao Peace Talks," 11.

[652] Embassy of the Philippines (Washington), "Status of the GRP-MILF Peace Process," 3.

Moro people. Yet the Philippine constitutional requirement that such an entity could be created only by a popular plebiscite in each of the provinces so affected had thus far kept this provision of the Tripoli Agreement from being implemented in full. How this dilemma would be resolved remained unclear, although talks in September 2005, in which the adoption of a federal system for the Philippines was seriously addressed, gave hope to delegates from both sides that a final settlement between the government and the MILF might be in the offing.[653]

OUTLOOK

Still, the MILF had not abandoned its historic view that independence for the Bangsamoro Muslim people was its ultimate objective. Nor had the Philippine government backed away from its historic perspective that the south was an integral part of the Philippine state and that the rights of the Moro people had to be accommodated within the context of the right of all other minorities and indigenous peoples of the country. What appears to have become clear, at least to President Arroyo and the MILF leadership, was that after more than 30 years of war final victory for either side was not possible, and close observers of key actors on both sides affirmed that the desire for peace was authentic.[654] Indeed, the desire for peace may be even stronger among the Muslim supporters of the MILF, whose cities and rural countryside have been ravaged by 30 years of war, with their inhabitants severely displaced, than for the government itself. For the government, however, the crisis in the south has involved a long and expensive military campaign that has not been effective and that it no longer can afford. Both sides appear sincere in their desire for a more or less permanent settlement, but on what terms?

The MILF may be content to live indefinitely with the current cease-fire, established in July 2003, that helps to keep the Philippine Armed Forces at arm's length. If so, then it may avoid reaching a final settlement that likely would define the Muslim south as something less than the independent Muslim state for which it has been fighting for many years. Meanwhile, it will continue to operate its shadow government in the south that will be more effective in commanding the allegiance of the Muslims of the south than the authorities representing the central government in Manila. Time, for the MILF, remains on its side as long as it is not confronted by serious violence. If the central government in Manila really wants a less problematic south, it must eventually understand that peace will come as a result of permitting a maximum degree of self-determination for the Bangsamoro people of the south.

---

[653] Agence France-Presse, "RP-MILF Peace Talks in Malaysia Make Major Breakthrough," *inq7.net*, September 17, 2005. URL: *https://news.inq7.net/breaking/index.php?index=1&story_id250494*. Accessed September 22, 2005.

[654] Zachary Abuza, "Crunchtime for the Mindanao Peace Process," *United States Institute of Peace* web site, February 8, 2005. URL: *http://www.usip.org/philippines/reports/mindanao_abuza.html*. Accessed September 5, 2005.

From the point of view of the government in Manila, however, especially under Arroyo, a final settlement that retains the south as a part of the Philippines is vital. Despite her astute management of the peace process up to this point, the problems faced by her administration are manifold and massive, and her hold on political power is precarious. Like her mentor, former President Fidel Ramos, she is accused by some, particularly in sectors of the military, of "coddling" the Muslims unnecessarily. There are "spoilers" on all sides—the ASG, elements of the MILF disgruntled with Murad's leadership, military factions disgruntled with Arroyo's leadership, and others—that could take some action designed to scuttle the current, very fragile peace process. Even if successful, a peace process that did not result in a high degree of perceived self-determination on the part of the Moro population will likely leave a restive Muslim population under Philippine government rule.

Map of Southeast Asia today. Source: CIA.

CHAPTER 7

ISLAM AND POLITICS IN SOUTHEAST ASIA

In the West, the domain of religion, represented by the church, and the domain of politics, represented by the state, are separate and coexist with their own distinct laws and claims of authority...In Islam, however, religion and politics are inseparable.

—Mir Zahir Husain, 1995

THE FIRST ISLAMIC STATE

The joining of religion and politics has been a feature of Islamic doctrine since the establishment of the faith by its Prophet Muhammad beginning in 620 C.E. In large measure, this doctrine became implanted because of the example of the Prophet himself who, during his lifetime, joined both religious and political authority in his own person. As noted by W. Montgomery Watt, Muhammad was both "Prophet and Statesman."[655] The importance of the Prophet's example (*hadith/sunna*), moreover, in the later elaboration of Islamic law (*shari`a*) and doctrine virtually guaranteed that Muslim scholars would have little choice but to uphold this unity of purpose.

Throughout most of Islamic history, however, this doctrine of the inseparability of religious and political authority has been more theoretical than real. Aside from the Shi`a faction who hold that the Prophet did indeed designate `Ali bin Abu Talib, his cousin and son-in-law, and the latter's descendants as his heirs in both spiritual and temporal authority, most Muslims-the prevailing Sunni majority—have held that the Prophet left no clear instructions about how his community should be governed following his death, only that it should be guided by the divine revelation that he had received on behalf of all mankind. Following a *hadith* of the Prophet—"My community cannot agree on an error."—the close companions of the Prophet after his death chose one of their own—"the best among us"—as his successor (*khalifa*/caliph). Although the successor Caliph held clear temporal authority, his claim to religious authority became increasingly problematic, particularly after the passing of years and the transformation of the Caliphate into a dynastic institution in which periodically individuals of an impious character held the office.

The Sunni solution was to gradually devolve religious authority on the `*ulama*, the body of professional Islamic scholars who collectively worked to formulate Islamic law and doctrine, to propagate it to successor generations, and to implement it throughout Islamic society by serving the Caliphs as *qadis* (judges) in Islamic courts, *muftis* (givers of legal opinions) in the Caliph's courts, and as teachers in *madrasas* (Islamic

---

[655] W. Montgomery Watt, *Muhammad: Prophet and Statesman* (London: Oxford University Press, 1961).

schools). Although religious authority theoretically remained vested in the figure of the Caliph, in fact it flowed from the collective consensus (*ijma'*) of the scholarly profession who came to form the lawyer, teacher, and pastoral class in Islamic society that was patronized by the Caliphs in return for legitimizing their rule as the "Shadow of God on Earth" and technically as successor to the inseparable religious and political authority of the Prophet Muhammad.

Evolution of the Original Model

The theoretical linkage between religious and political authority became even further compromised with the gradual decline of the political authority of the Caliphate beginning as early as the second century of the Islamic era, when various governors in peripheral parts of the Islamic empire began to succeed in establishing dynastic claims of their own. Such dynasties as the Rustamids (777–909), Idrisids (78–926), and the Aghlabids (800–909) in North Africa; the Samanids (819–1006) and Saffarids (867–913) in Central Asia and Iran; and the Tulunids (868–905) in Egypt all continued to recognize the overall religious authority of the Abbasid Caliph in Baghdad. In return, the Caliph recognized their local political authority as *sultans* (power holders) as long as they ruled in accordance with Islamic law.

The process of political dissolution of the Caliphate culminated with the establishment of the Turkish Seljuk sultanate in Baghdad in 1056. After this time, the former Abbasid Empire was in fact a collection of more or less independent sultanates that were only theoretically united under the overall authority of the Abbasid Caliph. The ultimate demise of the Abbasid Caliphate in 1258 as a result of the sack of Baghdad by the Mongol chieftain, Hulagu, grandson of the famous Chengis Khan, was in a sense anti-climactic. The office of Caliphate no longer wielded power or even influence. Islamic (religious) authority was in the hands of the network of `ulama that existed in every Islamic sultanate, whereas political and military authority was in the hands of a number of dynastic sultanates. The Caliphate was in fact no longer necessary, and no serious effort to revive it occurred until the last decades of the 19th century.

Reaction to the End of the Caliphate

It is perhaps the nature of dynastic authority that caused the `ulama, dependent as they were on the patronage of the ruler for positions of leadership and authority he was able to bestow upon them, to adjust themselves to the changing realities of powerholding in the Islamic world. At the same time, so entrenched had the `ulama become throughout the world that had become Islamic that new *sultans* coming to power generally perceived it in their interest to seek the blessing of the `ulama as a basis of their legitimacy as a ruler once the Caliph was not longer present to provide it. Such a relationship between the *sultan* and the `ulama was solemnized by the ceremony of *bai`a* (pledge of alliegance)[656] that typically inaugurated a new *sultan's* rule. In this coronation ceremony, as it were, the `*ulama* formally acknowledged the legitimacy of the new *sultan*, and he in turn committed himself to govern in accordance with Islamic law-that is, to rely on the `*ulama* as the principal administrators of justice, education, and religious affairs over which he held legitimate authority accorded him by the `*ulama*.

This revised formula for Islamic governance that had evolved over several centuries provided a basis for a renewed expansion of Islam during the 12th-15th centuries C.E. In some cases, such as with the Ottoman *sultans* of Anatonia, the Ghaznavid *sultans* of Afghanistan, and the Almoravid and Almohad *sultans* of Morocco, this expansion occurred as a result of renewed military conquest. In many other instances, however, as in southeast Asia and Sub-Saharan Africa, it was the result of missionary work by traders and traveling `*ulama* who, as representatives of a dominant, successful, and prosperous civilization, succeeded in drawing converts to Islam. The new formula whereby an indigenous local ruler could through conversion transform his realm into a sultanate, thereby associating himself and his people with the extensive Islamic civilization, was a particularly powerful means by which Islam continued to spread during the post-Caliphal era.

The Role of Sufism

Closely associated with this second expansionist period of Islamic history was the flourishing of *Sufi* (mystical) orders associated with Islam during this same era. Although the origins of Sufism predate this era, most of the great *sufi* teachers and founders of orders—such as al-Ghazali (d. 1111), al-Jilani (d. 1166), al-Rifa'i (d. 1182), Chisti (d. 1233), al-Suhrawardi (d. 1234), Ibn al-`Arabi (d. 1240), al-Shadhili (d. 1258), Rumi (d. 1273), Hajji Bektash (d. 1337), and Naqshbandi (d. 1389)—date from the early part of this period.

The growth and widespread acceptance of esoteric Sufi concepts and practices added a new dimension to Islam. The diverse approaches represented by the various Sufi orders (chanting, singing, dancing, whirling, and silent meditation) to realizing direct consciousness of God (*Allah*), albeit within the confines of Islamic doctrine and law, added a liberal dimension to the faith that not only respected diversity, but honored it. Sufi teaching made it possible to bridge the gap between Islam and other religious traditions, facilitating conversion without the necessity of totally abandoning pre-Islamic religious practices.

---

[656] The Arabic term *bai`a* carries the meaning of contract, deal, transaction, or sale, as well as homage or pledge of allegiance. In the traditional Islamic states, it represented the "social contract" between the ruler and the ruled, as represented by their `*ulama*.

Although later Wahhabi, Salafi, and other religious purists in the 19th and 20th centuries would criticize and condemn Sufism for enabling non-Islamic concepts and traditions to be introduced into Islam, during the post-Caliphal era and prior to the age of European colonialism and imperial outreach, the Sufi orders were a source of great strength and appeal for Islam, facilitating its spread and widespread acceptance in territories far beyond what Marshall Hodgson has called the Islamic *Oikoumeni*—the lands between the Nile and the Oxus.[657] The attraction of Sufistic Islam was not just confined to the expanding border regions of the Islamic world, however, but became a powerful current in the central, historic Islamic lands as well, especially under Ottoman rule, until the collapse of the Ottoman empire in the aftermath of World War I (1914–1918). In many respects, Sufistic Islam represented the true face of Islam, particularly at the popular level, if not at the governmental level, during the post-Caliphal era until very recent times.

SPREAD OF ISLAM TO SOUTHEAST ASIA

As Islam spread in the post-Caliphal era, it nevertheless did so in a fairly common political pattern—through the establishment of sultanates, centers of Islamic governance by rulers that relied on the `ulama of their realms to uphold their legitimacy and in turn empowered the `ulama to administer their realms in accordance with Islamic law (*shari`a*) and custom. This was precisely the pattern that marked the spread of Islam in Southeast Asia.

The gradual spread of a network of relatively small, coastal Muslim trading states throughout Southeast Asia occurred at the expense of the former Java-based Hindu Majapahit kingdom that had dominated most of the southeast Asian archipelago and Malay peninsula since the mid-14th century. Majapahit had in turn replaced the even stronger and longer-lived Sumatra-based Malay Hindu kingdom of Srivijaya that had dominated most of the region since at least the 6th century. Whether one of the new Muslim states—perhaps Malacca—would eventually have emerged as a strong new state dominating most of the region, displacing Majapahit, cannot be known.

The process of Islamization in Southeast Asia was at this time impacted by the arrival of European naval armadas and trading missions. As was noted in the first chapter of this study, aside from the Portuguese conquest and capture of Malacca in 1511, which had the impact of disrupting the unity of the Muslim-dominated trading states that had been centered on this strategic port, the European impact in the region was not at first great. The Dutch in particular, who eventually came to dominate the largest portion of the archipelago, were for more than a century little more than just another trading state in the region, albeit a Christian one, headquartered at the Company's fort in Batavia.

---

[657] Marshall G. S. Hodgson, *The Venture of Islam: Conscience and History in a World Civilization, Vol 1, The Classical Age of Islam* (Chigago, IL: University of Chicago Press, 1974), 120–124.

The End of Islamic Rule in Southeast Asia

It was only in the late 18th and 19th centuries that Britain in Malaya, Thailand in the north, and the Dutch and the Spaniards in the archipelago began to embark on those competing and centralizing policies that led to the formation of the large political entities that today we call Malaysia, Thailand, Indonesia, and the Philippines. Prior to this time, the Islamic states in the region continued to survive, expand in number, engage in trade, and participate in shifting alliances that included relationships with the European companies designed to augment the regional strength of each. In the end, however, it was the English, Thais, Dutch, and Spaniards that prevailed, and as they did so Islam as a political force in the region was gradually disenfranchised. Although the pattern of imperial rule over the increasingly Muslim archipelago differed in each case, Islamic political authority was gradually ended. At the beginning of the 20th century, only the sultans in the southern Philippines still claimed any degree of independent political authority, and their status was soon ended by American colonial policy in the Philippines.

As elsewhere in the Islamic world during this era, the collapse or co-opting of Islamic political authority by the prevailing imperial power left religious leadership in the hands of the `ulama, who no longer had the benefit of a protecting political leadership. As Robert Hefner has noted in his brilliant study on Islam in Indonesia:

> Foreign control of the state led Muslim leaders to develop a cautious and critical attitude toward government, and forced them to rely on their own resources to develop their institutions... The tendency was for Muslim institutions to distance themselves from the state by locating themselves deep in native society. In Java and other areas of the archipelago, for example, the eighteenth and nineteenth centuries saw the spread of a vigorous little institution known as the *pesantren*, a Javanese variant of the...Qur'anic school...their educational function was made all the more important by state hostility toward Islam. [The] *pesantren* were also important because they provided a translocal network for native authority apart from the state.[658]

What was true in Indonesia was at least partially true in the rest of the Muslim archipelago. Lacking judicial institutions in which to apply Islamic law as *qadis* or a seat at the Sultan's court as *muftis* to advise the ruler on aspects of Islamic law, the `ulama focused on the one role that remained available to them, their traditional educational role of imparting Islam and its requirements to the young generation of Muslims and advising the local community as required. The message they tended to impart, however, was that true political authority lay not with the colonial masters, but with God Himself whose will could be known in the absence of true political authority

---

[658] Robert W. Hefner, *Civil Islam: Muslims and Democratization in Indonesia* (Princeton, NJ: Princeton University Press, 2000), 33–34.

only by consultation with themselves. Under their tutelage, Islam increasingly became an authority structure outside of and apart from the state that tended to manifest itself as sullen, and unwilling, acquiescence to foreign ruling authorities, be it the Thai, British, Dutch, American, or Philippine ruling establishments.

Origins of the New Ruling Class

At the same time, however, the ruling colonial authorities embarked on educational programs of their own, designed to prepare a class of civil servants capable of assisting them in providing effective administration to the states they ruled. These programs, which often involved schooling in the home country or capital, tended to co-opt mainly the traditional ruling class associated with the historic ruling families (*sultans/rajas*) of the archipelago. As Indonesia and Malaysia began to move toward independence during and after World War II, it was individuals of this class who were best positioned to lead the movement toward independence, to bargain with the imperial authorities, and to lead their new countries in the modern international environment. Such leaders as the Cambridge-trained Tunku Abdul Rahman of Malaysia or the Dutch-educated Ahmad Sukarno of Indonesia, as well as their key associates, had a far different vision for the states they inherited than the far larger number of *pondok*- and *pesantren*-educated individuals who also had to be included in the new democratic institutions adopted by the newly independent states. Conflict between these two competing visions of what independence from foreign rule should mean was inevitable and has been characteristic of the politics of both Malaysia and Indonesia since independence.

Malaysia

In Malaysia, the conflict between the more modern, secular, and cosmopolitan leadership and those who envisioned a return of a more traditional Islamic political order has been muted by the perceived need to maintain Malay-Muslim unity in the face of the large non-Malay Chinese and Indian population that also inhabits the country. UMNO and the *Barisan Nasional* (National Front) that has dominated Malaysian politics from the beginning has been the primary vehicle for maintaining this unity. PAS, the party representing the more traditional vision within the Malay community, makes a strong showing in the northern and eastern, more nearly all-Malay states, but has failed to have strong appeal at the federal level and especially among the non-Malay communities. The aggressive and on the whole successful economic policies of the UMNO leadership over the years has also tended to co-opt the Islamist opposition, as has the adoption of a number of administrative procedures designed to make Malaysia appear more Islamic in character. The success of the UMNO in dominating Malaysian politics since independence in 1957, however, has also given Malaysia the appearance of being a one-party state that governs in a too authoritarian manner. Closely linked with the traditional ruling families that have governed the Malay peninsula for centuries, UMNO represents continuity with the past as well as change in response to the demands of modernity. Yet beneath the surface lies a level of dissent with the rather high-handed methods of the ruling party. Such dissent, of which the Islamic opposition is a part, tends to keep Malaysian politics in turmoil and keeps alive the prospect that political change of a quite radical nature is not unthinkable at some point in the country's future.

Indonesia

In Indonesia, the conflict between the two competing visions-the secular nationalist vs. the Islamic-has been present from the beginning. The *Darul Islam* movement that envisioned independent Indonesia as an Islamic state and competed with nationalist leader, Ahmad Sukarno, for leadership in the country's war for independence (1945-1950) was only the military vanguard of a much larger Islamic movement embodied in the *Masjumi* party. This party, which grouped together Indonesia's two largest Islamic mass organizations—the modernist Muhammadiyah movement and the traditionalist *Nahdlatul Ulama*—competed for ascendancy in the newly independent country's democratic institutions. Fully expecting to win Indonesia's first parliamentary elections in 1955, the party hoped to use electoral victory to achieve what military action had not.[659] That they did not enabled Sukarno, leader of the Nationalist Party (PNI), in alliance with other secular parties, but particularly the Communist Party (PKI), to consolidate his nationalist agenda for the country. Sukarno's growing reliance on the Communist party tended only to empower this group that also had rapidly growing support in Indonesia. With Sukarno's support, the communists behaved ever more aggressively, polarizing Indonesian politics even further.

The denouement came in 1965, when an army *coup* d'état led by General Ahmad Suharto put an end to the Sukarno regime and the communist movement in Indonesia. Suharto's action was not carried out on behalf of the Islamist factions of Indonesian politics, however, although he at first had their active support. Rather, Suharto, using the army as his political base, sought to put an end to the anarchy he believed had characterized Indonesian democratic politics during the Sukarno era by constructing a strong, authoritarian state dominated by his own personal rule. As Benedict Anderson put it, Suharto's policy was to make the state triumph over "society and nation."[660] Suharto succeeded by suppressing both the Islamic and secular-nationalist wings of Indonesian politics, forcing them to merge into two competing political parties, the Islamic PPP and the secular-nationalist PDI, which he successfully sought to dominate through the construction of his own political party, Golkar, of which all government employees — military and civilian — had to be members. Meanwhile, paying lip service

---

[659] The *Nahdlatul Ulama* had withdrawn from the *Masjumi* in 1952 and therefore ran as a separate party in the 1955 elections, gaining 18.4 percent of the parliamentary vote as opposed to 20.9 percent for *Masjumi*. Together, the two were still considered the Islamic party in Indonesian politics at the time, but their combined vote of 39.3 percent was insufficient to give them control of the parliament. M.C. Rieklefs, *A History of Modern Indonesia Since c 1200* (Stanford, CA: Stanford University Press, 2001), 298, 304.

[660] Benedict R. O'G. Anderson, "Old State, New Society: Indonesia's New Order in Comparative Historical Perspective," in Benedict R. O'C. Anderson, ed., *Language and Power: Exploring Political Cultures in Indonesia* (Ithaca, NY: Cornell University Press, 1972), 109.

to capitalism as the basis of the country's economy, Suharto also placed emphasis on state-owned corporations as the primary means to facilitate Indonesia's economic development, thus transforming the employees of most of the country's engines of economic growth into civil servants who also had to be members of Golkar.

For more than three decades, Suharto's *étatist* policies worked, gradually transforming Indonesia into a dynamic economic powerhouse in Southeast Asia. With this transformation, however, came other changes, most notably the growth of an increasingly large, better-educated middle class that was increasingly less enchanted with the corrupt and authoritarian nature of the Indonesian state. Closely associated with this change was the nearly simultaneous emergence of what Robert Hefner has called "civil Islam." Articulated by a body of new intellectuals, the most notable of which was Nucholish Madjid, this school of thought argued that Muslims were wrong to work for the establishment of an Islamic state and in fact diminished the "high values" of Islam when they did so. Rather, Muslims should work to ensure that the high values of Islam were reflected in the state as well as the society, and such values did not support the corruption, cronyism, brutality, and authoritarianism of the current state.[661] Such an argument that accepted the political disenfranchisement of Islam was in fact encouraged by the Suharto government and found resonance in the newly emerging middle class, which underwent a general process of "santrification" (becoming more conscious of Islamic observance) during this same era.

So powerful did the movement become that, by the 1990s, Suharto decided to bestow his favor on it by authorizing the establishment of the Association of Indonesian Muslim Intellectuals (ICMI). His official support of this Islamic movement was not intended to empower it, however, as much as to control it and ensure that it did not join forces with other groups in Indonesian society seeking to end his system of authoritarian rule.[662] He might have succeeded in this ploy had it not been for the Asian financial crisis of 1997, which seriously undermined his control of Indonesian politics and led to his resignation in May 1998 in the face of a united opposition that joined the proponents of civil Islam and the secular nationalists in a popular movement to restore true democratic rule in Indonesia.

With the election of Islamic reformist leader Abdurrahman Wahid, a proponent of civil Islam, as President of Indonesia in October 1999, it appeared that the authoritarian New Order regime of Ahmad Suharto was finally over, and forces favoring change solely on a democratic basis had achieved ascendancy. As Robert Hefner has noted, "the proponents of civil Islam" were "a key part of this renaissance," and proponents of "statist Islam" had become a minority.[663] For the moment, at least, those elements favoring radical political change, be it from the left or from the Islamic right, have been marginalized, despite efforts of the militant Islamist group, *Jemaah Islamiyah*,

---

[661] Hefner, *Civil Islam*, 116–119.

[662] Hefner, *Civil Islam*, 129.

[663] Hefner, *Civil Islam*, 218.

to make its presence felt and to influence public opinion by continued periodic terrorist operations.

Thailand and the Southern Philippines

The situation of the Malay Muslim populations of southern Thailand and the southern Philippines was far more bleak. Unlike the inhabitants of Malaysia and Indonesia, those "colonial powers" which had come to dominate them politically were not distant European powers for whom colonialism was no longer fashionable nor profitable. Their "occupiers" were nearby regimes who considered the territories they inhabited integral parts of the nation state of which they were a part. Despite being the inheritors of proud local histories, they had become "indigenous minorities" of rapidly modernizing states of which most did not wish to remain a part. A result of this cultural alienation has been, since the 1960s in the case of southern Thailand and the 1970s in the case of the southern Philippines, long-term insurgencies aimed at demonstrating to the ruling governments the difficulty of ruling a restive population that rejects the authority of "foreign" rule.

During the earlier phase of these insurgencies, the "national" character of the insurgent movement—Malay in southern Thailand and Moro in the southern Philippines—was stressed. Since the late 1980s and 1990s, however, the "nationalist" appeal has given way to a more Islamist appeal in both cases. In the southern Philippines, the MILF has become the principal source of resistance to the central government rather than the MNLF, and in southern Thailand the secretive GMIP appears to have replaced PULO as the most active agent of the continuing insurgency. The change certainly reflects the general Islamic resurgence that has been apparent throughout the Islamic world since the 1970s, but more specifically it reflects the inspiration of the successful *jihad* conducted by the Afghan resistance against the Soviet occupation of that country in the 1980s.

Western and other international supports of the Afghan resistance to the Soviet occupation of Afghanistan may or may not have perceived that their support was empowering a *jihad* movement. To those who were actually engaged in the combat, however, but especially the foreign fighters who came to lend their support, it was indeed a *jihad*, a sanctified and holy resistance movement against an infidel whose power seemed irresistible.[664] The success of the Afghan *jihad* in leading one of the two major global superpowers of the day to reverse its course and withdraw from Afghanistan raised hopes among Muslim minorities throughout the world, including those in southern Thailand and the southern Philippines. If one of the major superpowers

---

[664] In fact, for the Afghans themselves, it is uncertain that many perceived their resistance as a holy war for Islam. Many simply saw the conflict as a national resistance movement against a foreign occupier. The foreign fighters involved, to include the Pakistani government of Zia al-Haq, as well as some of the more radical Afghan groups, justified their involvement on a religious basis, that is, they were engaged in a *jihad* that was larger than the Afghan conflict and would not necessarily end after the Soviet withdrawal.

could be forced to lift its occupation, then perhaps it was possible for the governments of Thailand and the Philippines to reach a similar conclusion.

Statist Islam vs. Civil Islam

Unlike Indonesia and to some degree Malaysia as well, where "statist Islam," to use Robert Hefner's terminology, has been and continues to be effectively marginalized politically, in southern Thailand and the southern Philippines, it appears to be ascendant. As far as we know, the goal of both the GMIP and the MILF is to achieve the independence of the Muslim peoples, whom they claim to represent, by the establishment of an "Islamic state." In support of this objective, they have had at least a degree of support from two other clandestine organizations-the globally-oriented *al-Qa'ida* movement, established by Usama bin Ladin in Afghanistan in 1988, and the regionally-oriented *Jemaah Islamiyah* movement founded by the Indonesians Abdullah Sungkar and Abu Bakar Ba'asyir in Malaysia in 1993. Although the leadership of *Jemaah Islamiyah* from the beginning had a fundamentally Indonesian orientation, which became readily apparent after the fall of Suharto in 1998, it began as an organization having a regional objective of facilitating the transformation of the whole Muslim archipelago that has been the focus of this study into an Islamic state. The formation of *Jemaah Islamiyah* appears to have been a result of meetings between bin Ladin and the two Indonesian clerics in Pakistan in 1991. The organization had difficulty maintaining focus on the larger regional perspective after the fall of Suharto, however. It nevertheless continued to pose a terrorist threat in Indonesia until at least 2005. The Abu Sayyaf Group (ASG) in the southern Philippines appears to have originated as a unique group having ties primarily to *al-Qa'ida*. No evidence has been uncovered during this research of linkages between the ASG and *Jemaah Islamiyah*.

Islam, whether in its more modern civil variety or the more traditional statist version, has played and will continue to play a significant role in the politics of Southeast Asia. The traditional view that religion and politics are inseparable in Islam, repeatedly articulated over the centuries by traditional Islamic scholars from Ibn Taymiyya to Sa`id Qutb still holds sway over the minds of many Muslims around the world. In this view, there can be no security for Islam or the Muslim peoples without the protection of an Islamic state, one in which Islamic law (*shari`a*) is the law of the land and is effectively administered by competent authorities. Unfortunately, the former western colonial powers as well as the current Thai and Philippine governments have done little to disabuse the Muslims of Southeast Asia of this view.

As Robert Hefner has noted, however, we all — Muslims included — live in a complex, modern world that is characterized by "migration, urbanizations, and communications that render borders permeable to transcultural flows." In such a world, "the markets, media and migrations...make any enduring institutionalization of...statist Islam difficult...The arrangement fails because it is so out of step with the pluralism and movement of our age.[665] In today's globalized marketplace of ideas, opinions and sources of information come from many sources. Every idea is challenged, and ultimate truth is elusive. In the end, Muslims may find, as they apparently are finding in Indonesia, that the high values of Islam are more effectively maintained in an environment in which freedom of religion is guaranteed rather than one in which religion is coerced.

---

[665] Hefner, *Civil Islam*, 219–220.

BIBLIOGRAPHY

Islam and Politics

Abu Sulayman, Abdul Hamid A. *The Islamic Theory of International Relations: New Directions for Islamic Methodology and Thought.* Herndon, VA: International Institute of Islamic Thought, 1987.

El-Affendi, Abdelwahab. *Who Needs an Islamic State?* London: Grey Seal, 1991.

Al-Ahsan, `Abdullah. *The Organization of the Islamic Conference: An Introduction to an Islamic Political Institution.* Herndon, VA: International Institute of Islamic Thought, 1988).

Asad, Muhammad. *The Principles of State and Government in Islam.* Gibraltar: Dar al-Andalus, [1961] 1980.

Ayoob, Mohammad, ed. *The Politics of Islamic Reassertion.* London: Croom Helm, 1981.

Ayubi, Nazih N. *Political Islam: Religion and Politics in the Arab World.* London: Routledge, 1991.

Bannerman, Patrick. *Islam in Perspective: A Guide to Islamic Society, Politics, and Law.* London: Routledge for the Royal Institute of International Affairs, 1988.

Brown, L. Carl. *Religion and State: The Muslim Approach to Politics.* New York, NY: Columbia University Press, 2000.

Carré, Olivier. *Islam and the State in the World Today.* New Delhi: Manohar Publishers, 1987.

Dawisha, Adeed. *Islam and Foreign Policy.* Cambridge: Cambridge University Press, 1983.

Eickelman, Dale F., and James Piscatori. *Muslim Politics.* Princeton, NJ: Princeton University Press, 1996.

Enayat, Hamid. *Modern Islamic Political Thought.* Austin, TX: University of Texas Press, 1982.

Esposito, John L., ed. *Islam and Development: Religion and Socio-Political Change.* Syracuse, NY: Syracuse University Press, 1980.

Esposito, John L. *Islam and Politics.* 2nd ed. New York: Syracuse University Press, 1987.

Esposito, John L., ed. *Voices of Resurgent Islam.* New York: Oxford University Press, 1987.

Farah, Caesar E. *Islam: Beliefs and Observances.* 6th ed. Hauppauge, NY: Barron's Educational Series, 2000.

Fuller, Graham E., and Ian O. Lesser. *A Sense of Siege: The Geopolitics of Islam and the West.* Boulder, CO: Westview Press, 1995.

Gaiduk, Ilya V. *The Great Confrontation: Europe and Islam through the Centuries.* Chicago, IL: Ivan R. Dee, 2003.

Gilsenan, Michael. *Recognizing Islam: Religion and Society in the Modern Middle East.* New York: I.B. Tauris, 2000.

Hamidullah, Muhammad. *The Muslim Conduct of State.* 7th revised and enlarged edition. Lahore, Pakistan: Kashmiri Bazar, 1977.

Hodgson, Marshall G.S. *The Venture of Islam: Conscience and History in a World Civilization.* 3 volumes. Chicago: University of Chicago Press, 1974.

Hunter, Shireen T., ed. *The Politics of Islamic Revivalism: Diversity and Unity.* Bloomington, IN: Indiana University Press, 1988.

Hussain, Asaf. *Political Perspectives on the Muslim World.* New York: St. Martin's Press, 1984.

Ibn Khaldun (d. 1409). *The Muqaddimah: An Introduction to History.* 2nd ed. Trans. by Franz Rosenthal. Princeton, NJ: Princeton University Press, 1967.

Ismael, Tareq Y., and Jacqueline S. Ismael. *Government and Politics in Islam.* New York: St. Martin's Press, 1985.

Khadduri, Majid. *War and Peace in the Law of Islam.* Baltimore, MD: Johns Hopkins Press, 1955.

Khan, Qamaruddin. *Political Concepts in the Quran.* Lahore: Islamic Book Foundation, 1982.

Kramer, Martin. *Political Islam.* Beverly Hills, CA: Sage Publications, 1980.

Kramer, Martin. *Islam Assembled: The Advent of the Muslim Congresses.* New York: Columbia University Press, 1986.

Kurzman, Charles, ed. *Liberal Islam: A Sourcebook.* New York: Oxford University Press, 1988.

Lambton, Ann K.S. *State and Government in Medieval Islam: An Introduction to the Study of Islamic Political Theory.* Oxford: Oxford University Press, 1981.

Landau, Jacob M. *The Politics of Pan-Islam: Ideology and Organization.* Oxford: Clarendon Press, 1990.

Lewis, Bernard. *The Political Language of Islam. Chicago,* IL: University of Chicago Press, 1988.

Al-Mawardi, Abu-l-Hasan. *Kitab al-ahkam al-sultaniyya* [Book of the Principles of Governance]. Cairo: n.p., 1960.

Al-Maududi, Abu-l A`la. *Political Theory of Islam.* Lahore: Islamic Publications, 1976.

Al-Maududi, Abu-l A`la. First Principles of the Islamic State. 6th ed. rev. Trans. and edited by Khurshid Ahmad. Lahore: Islamic Publications, 1983.

Migdal, Joel S. *Strong Societies and Weak States: State-Society Relations and State Capabilities in the Third World.* Princeton, NJ: Princeton University Press, 1988.

Moinuddin, Hasan. *The Charter of the Islamic Conference: The Legal and Economic Framework.* Oxford: Clarendon Press, 1987.

Mortimer, Edward. *Faith and Power: The Politics of Islam.* London: Faber and Faber, 1982.

Mutalib, Hussin, and Taj ul-Islam Hashmi, eds. Islam, *Muslims and the Modern State: Case Studies of Muslims in Thirteen Countries.* Hampshire: The Macmillan Press, 1996.

Piscatori, James P., ed. *Islam in the Political Process.* Cambridge: Cambridge University Press, 1983.

Piscatori, James P. *Islam in a World of Nation-States.* Cambridge: Cambridge University Press, 1986.

Rosenthal, Erwin I.J. *Islam in the Modern National State.* Cambridge: Cambridge University Press, 1965.

Roy, Olivier. *The Failure of Political Islam.* Trans. from the French by Carol Volk. New York: Cambridge University Press, 1994.

Seiple, Robert A., and Dennis R. Hoover, ed. *Religion and Security: The New Nexus in International Relations.* Lanham, MD: Rowman and Littlefield Publishers, Inc., 2004.

Sivan, Emmanuel. *Radical Islam: Medieval Theology and Modern Politics.* New Haven and London: Yale University Press, 1985.

Sivan, Emmanuel, and Menachem Friedman. eds. *Religious Radicalism and Politics in the Middle East.* Albany: State University of New York Press, 1990.

Smith, Donald E., ed. *Religion and Political Development.* New Haven, CT: Yale University Press, 1974.

Watt, W. Montgomery. *Islamic Political Thought: The Basic Concepts.* Islamic Surveys, No. 6 Edinburgh: Edinburgh University Press, 1968.

Watt, W. Montgomery. *Muhammad: Prophet and Statesman.* London: Oxford University Press, 1961.

Contemporary Islamic Trends

Adams, Charles C. *Islam and Modernism in Egypt: A Study of the Modern Reform Movement Inaugurated by Muhammad `Abduh.* New York: Russel & Russel, 1968.

Ahmed, Akbar S., and Donnan Hastings. *Islam, Globalization and Postmodernity.* London: Routledge, 1994.

Anderson, J.N.D. *Law Reform in the Muslim World.* London: Athlone Press, 1976.

Arkoun, Mohammed. *Rethinking Islam: Common Questions, Uncommon Answers.* Trans. and ed. by Robert D. Lee. Boulder, CO: Westview Press, 1994.

Ayoob, Mohammed, ed. *The Politics of Islamic Reassertion.* London: Croom Helm, 1981.

Bennabi, Malek. *Les grandes thèmes de la civilisation, de la culture, de l'idéologie, de la démocratie en islam, de l'orientalisme.* Préface et annotations par Nour-Eddine Boukrouh. Algiers: O. Benaissa, c1976.

Burke, Jason. *Al-Qaeda: Casting a Shadow of Terror.* London: I.B. Taurus, 2003.

Cesari, Jocelyne. *Faut-il avoir peur de l'Islam?* Paris: Presses de Sciences Po, 1997.

Clifford, James, and George E. Marcus. *Writing Culture: The Poetics and Politics of Ethnography.* Berkeley and Los Angeles: University of California Press, 1986.

Crane, Robert Dickson. *Shaping the future: Challenge and response.* Acton, MA: Tapestry Press, 1997.

Esposito, John L, ed. *Islam and Development: Religion and Sociopolitical Change.* Syracuse, NY: Syracuse University Press, 1980.

Esposito, John L. *The Oxford Encyclopedia of the Modern Islamic World.* 4 volumes. New York: Oxford University Press, 1995.

Fluehr-Lobban, Carolyn. *Islamic Societies in Practice.* 2d ed. Gainesville, FL: University Press of Florida, 2004.

Geertz, Clifford., ed. *The Interpretation of Cultures.* New York: Basic Books, 1973.

Gibb, H.A.R. *Modern Trends in Islam.* Chicago: University of Chicago Press, 1947.

Gilsenan, Michael. *Recognizing Islam: An Anthropolotist's Introduction.* London: Croon-Helm, n.d.

Gunaratna, Rohan. *Inside Al Qaeda: Global Network of Terror.* New York: Columbia University Press, 2002.

Haddad, Yvonne, John Obert Voll, and John L. Esposito. *The Contemporary Islamic Revival: A Critical Survey and Bibliography.* New York and Westport, CT: Greenwood Press, 1991.

Hourani, Albert. *Arabic Thought in the Liberal Age*. London: Oxford University Press, 1970.

Hunter, Shireen. *The future of Islam and the West: Clash of civilizations or peaceful coexistence?* Westport, CT: Praeger, 1998.

Huntington, Samuel P. *Political Order in Changing Societies*. New Haven, CT: Yale University Press, 1968.

Huntington, Samuel P. *The Clash of Civilizations and the Remaking of the World Order.* New York: Simon and Schuster, 1996.

Islam outside the Arab world. Eds. David Westerlund and Ingvar Svanberg. Richmond, Surrey: Curzon, 1999.

Jansen, Geoffrey H. *Militant Islam.* New York: Harper and Row Publishers, 1979.

Kepel, Gilles. *Intellectuels et militants de l'Islam contemporaine.* Paris: Editions du Seuil, 1990.

Kepel, Gilles. *Jihad: The Trail of Political Islam.* Trans. by Anthony F. Roberts. Cambridge, MA: The Belknap Press of Harvard University Press, 2002.

Kepel, Gilles. *The Revenge of God: The Resurgence of Islam, Christianity, and Judaism in the Modern World.* Trans. by Alan Braley. University Park, PA: Pennsylvania State University Press, 1994.

Kerr, Malcolm H. *Islamic Reform: The Political and Legal Theories of Muhammad `Abduh and Rashid Rida.* Berkeley, CA: University of California Press, 1966.

Kettani. M. Ali. *Muslim Minorities in the World Today.* New York: Mansell Publishing Ltd., 1986.

Khadduri, Majid. *War and Peace in the Law of Islam.* Baltimore, MD: The Johns Hopkins Press, 1955.

Khadduri, Majid. *The Islamic Conception of Justice.* Baltimore, MD: The Johns Hopkins Press, 1984.

Lapidus, Ira M. *A History of Islamic Societies.* Cambridge: Cambridge University Press, 1988.

Lawrence, Bruce. *Defenders of God: The Fundamentalist Revolt against the Modern Age.* New York: Harper and Row, 1989.

Lewis, Bernard. *What Went Wrong? Western Impact and Middle Eastern Response.* London: Phoenix, 2002.

Marty, Martin E., and R. Scott Appleby, eds. *Fundamentalisms Observed.* Chicago, IL: University of Chicago Press, 1991.

Mehmet, Ozay. *Islamic identity and development: studies of the Islamic periphery.* London and New York: Routledge, 1990.

Al-Nayhum, Sadiq. *Al-Islam didd al-Islam [Islam against Islam].* London and Beirut: Riyad El-Rayyes Books, 1994.

Pʻanjikize, Tʻeimuraz. Muhamedi, Islami, *Vahabizmi, da Sakʻartʻvelos problemebi.* Tʻbilisi: Tʻbilisis universitetis gamomcʻemloba, 1999.

Rahman, Fazlur. *Islam and Modernity: Transformation of an Intellectual Tradition.* Chicago, IL: University of Chicago Press, 1982.

Roy, Olivier. *Globalized Islam: The Search for a New Ummah.* New York: Columbia University Press, 2004.

Roy, Olivier. *Généalogie de l'islamisme.* Paris: Hachette, 1995.

Schacht, Joseph, with C.E. Bosworth, eds. *The Legacy of Islam.* 2nd ed. Oxford: Clarendon Press, 1974.

Shaikh, Farzana, ed. *Islam and Islamic Groups.* Essex, UK: Longman Group UK Ltd., 1992.

Siegel, James T. *The rope of God.* Ann Arbor: University of Michigan Press, 2000.

Sifaoui, Mohamed. *Inside Al Qaeda: how I infiltrated the world's deadliest terrorist organization.* Trans. by George Miller. New York: Thunder's Mouth Press, 2004.

Sivan, Emmanuel. *Radical Islam: Medieval Theology and Modern Politics.* Enlarged edition. New Haven, CT: Yale University Press, 1990.

Smith, Wilfred Cantwell. *The Meaning and End of Religion: A New Approach to the Religious Traditions of Mankind.* New York: Macmillan, 1963.

Voll, John. *Islam: Continuity and Change in the Modern World.* Boulder, CO: Westview Press, 1982.

Weekes, Richard V., ed. *Muslim Peoples: A World Ethnographic Survey.* 2d ed. Westport, CT: Greenwood Press, 1984.

Youssef, Michael. *Revolt against modernity: Muslim zealots and the west.* Leiden: E.J. Brill, 1985.

Yurdatapan, Sanar. *Opposites: Side by side.* Foreword by Aron Aji. Afterword by Jonathan Sugden. Trans. by Isfendiyar Eralp. New York: George Braziller, 2003.

Southeast Asia

Abdullah, Taufiq, and Sharon Siddique, eds. *Islam and Society in Southeast Asia.* Brookfield, VT: Gower, 1986.

Abuza, Zachary. *Militant Islam in Southeast Asia: Crucible of Terror.* Boulder, CO: Lynn Reinner Publishers, 2003.

Alagappa, Muthiah. *Political Legitimacy in Southeast Asia: The Quest for Moral Authority.* Stanford, CA: Stanford University Press, 1995.

Brown, David. *The State and Ethnic Politics in Southeast Asia.* New York: Routledge, 1994.

Christie, Clive J. *A Modern History of Southeast Asia: Decolonizaton, Nationalism and Separatism.* London: Tauris Academic Studies, 1996.

Christie, Clive J. *Southeast Asia in the Twentieth Century: A Reader.* London and New York: I.B. Tauris, 1998.

De Jonge, Huub, and Noco Kaptein, eds. *Transcending Borders: Arabs, Politics, Trade and Islam in Southeast Asia.* Leiden: KITLV Press, 2002.

Diamond, Larry, Juan J. Linz, and Seymour Martin Lipset, eds. *Democracy in Developing Countries, Volume Three: Asia.* Boulder, CO: Lynne Rienner Publishers, 1989.

Embree, Ainslie T. *Encyclopedia of Asian History.* Volume 3. New York: Charles Scribner's Sons, 1988.

Esposito, John L., ed. *Islam in Asia: Religion, Politics, and Society.* New York: Oxford University Press, 1987.

Federspiel, Howard M. "Islam and Development in the Nations of ASEAN," *Asian Survey* 25, no. 8 (August 1985), 805-821.

Friend, Theodore. *The Blue Eyed Enemy: Japan Against the West in Java and Luzon.* Princeton, NJ: Princeton University Press, 1988.

Gordon, Alijah, ed. *The Propagation of Islam in the Indonesian-Malay Archipelago.* Kuala Lumpur: Malaysian Sociological Research Institute, 2001.

Government of Singapore. *White Paper: The Jemaah Islamiyah Arrests and the Threat of Terrorism.* Singapore: Ministry of Home Affairs, 2003.

Hefner, Robert W., ed. *Democratic Civility: The History and Cross-cultural Possibilities of a Modern Political Ideal.* New Brunswick, NJ: Transaction Publishers, 1998.

Hefner, Robert W., and Patricia Horvatich, eds. *Islam in an Era of Nation States: Politics and Religious Renewal in Muslim Southeast Asia.* Honolulu: University of Hawaii Press, 1997.

Hooker, M. B., ed. *Islam in South-East Asia.* Leiden: E.J. Brill, 1988.

Hunt, Robert A. *Islam in Southeast Asia: A Study for Christians.* New York: GBGM Books, 1997.

Ibrahim, Ahmad, Sharon Siddique, and Yasmin Hussain, eds. *Readings on Islam in Southeast Asia.* Singapore: Institute of Southeast Asian Studies, 1985.

Isaacson, Jason F., and Colin Rubinstein, eds. *Islam in Asia: Changing Political Realities.* New Brunswick, NJ: Transaction Books, 2002.

Keyes, Charles F., Laurel Kendall, and Helen Hardacre, eds. *Asian Visions of Authority: Religion and the Modern States of East and Southeast Asia*. Honolulu: University of Hawaii Press, 1994.

Leifer, Michael. *Dictionary of the Modern Politics of Southeast Asia*. London: Routledge, 1996.

McAmis, Robert Day. *Malay Muslims: The History and Challenge of Resurgent Islam in Southeast Asia*. Grand Rapids, MI: William B. Eerdmans Publishing Company, 2002.

McCloud, Donald G. *Southeast Asia: Tradition and Modernity in the Contemporary World*. Boulder, CO: Westview Press, 1995.

Mutalib, Hussain. "Islamic Revivalism in ASEAN States: Political Implications." *Asian Survey* 30, no. 9 (September 1990), 877-891.

Nakamura, Mitsuo, Sharon Siddique, and Omar Farouk Bajunid, eds. *Islam and Civil Society in Southeast Asia*. Singapore: Institute of Southeast Asian Studies, 2001.

Neher, Clark D. *Democracy and Development in Southeast Asia: The Winds of Change*. Boulder, CO: Westview Press, 1995.

Neher, Clark D. *Southeast Asia in the New International Era*. Boulder, CO: Westview Press, 1998.

Osborne, Milton E. *Southeast Asia: An Introductory History*. St. Leonard's, New South Wales, Australia: Allen & Unwin, 1997.

Osman, Mohmmad Taib, ed. *Islamic Civilization in the Malay World*. Kuala Lumpur, Malaysia: Dewan Bahasa dan Pustaka and the Research Centre for Islamic History, Art and Culture, Istanbul, Turkey, 1997.

Peacock, James L. *Muslim puritans: Reformist psychology in Southeast Asian Islam*. Berkeley: University of California Press, 1978.

Pearn, P.R. *An Introduction to the History of South-East Asia*. Kuala Lumpur, Malaysia: Longman Malaysia SDN, 1970.

Rabasa, Angel M. *Political Islam in Southeast Asia: Moderates, Radicals and Terrorists*. Adelphi Paper 358, International Institute of Strategic Studies (IISS). London and New York: Oxford University Press, 2003.

Ramakrishna, Kumar, and See Seng Tan. *After Bali: The Threat of Terrorism in Southeast Asia*. Singapore: World Scientific Publishing and the Institute of Defence and Strategic Studies, 2003.

Readings on Islam in Southeast Asia. Eds. Ahmad Ibrahim, et al. Singapore: Institute of Southeast Asian Studies, 1985.

Reid, Anthony, ed. *The Making of an Islamic Political Discourse in Southeast Asia*. Monash Papers on Southeast Asia, No. 27. Clayton: Monash University, 1993.

Reid, Anthony, ed. *Southeast Asia in the Early Modern Era*. Ithaca, NY: Cornell University Press, 1993.

Ressa, Maria A. *Seeds of Terror: An Eyewitness Account of Al-Qaeda's Newest Center of Operations in Southeast Asia*. New York: Free Press, 2003.

SarDesai, D.R. *Southeast Asia:* Past and Present. Boulder, CO: Westview Press, 1994.

Smith, Paul J., ed. *Terrorism and Violence in Southeast Asia: Transnational Challenges to States and Regional Stability*. Armonk, NY, and London: M.E. Sharpe, 2005.

Tan, Andrew, and Kumar Ramakrishna, eds. *The New Terrorism: Anatomy, Trends, and Counter-Strategies*. Singapore: Eastern Universities Press, 2002.

Tarling, Nicholas. *Nations and States in Southeast Asia*. Cambridge and New York: Cambridge University Press, 1998.

Tarling, Nicholas, ed. *The Cambridge History of Southeast Asia*. 2 volumes. Cambridge: Cambridge University Press, 1992, 1999.

Taylor, John G., and Andrew Turton, eds. *Southeast Asia*. New York: Monthly Review Press, 1988.

Trocki, Carl A., ed. *Gangsters, Democracy and the State in Southeast Asia*. Ithaca, NY: Cornell University Press, 1998.

Van Esterik, Penny, ed. *Women of Southeast Asia*. DeKalb, IL: Northern Illinois University, Center for Southeast Asian Studies, 1996.

Von der Mehden, Fred R. *Religion and Modernization in Southeast Asia*. Syracuse, NY: Syracuse University Press, 1986.

Von der Mehden, Fred R. *Two Worlds of Islam: Interaction between Southeast Asia and the Middle East*. Gainesville: University Press of Florida, 1993.

Wurfel, David, and Bruce Burton, eds. *The Political Economy of Foreign Policy in Southeast Asia*. New York: St. Martin's Press, 1990.

Wurfel, David, and Bruce Burton, eds. *Southeast Asia in the New World Order: The Political Economy of a Dynamic Region*. New York: St. Martin's Press, 1996.

Malaysia

Ackerman, Susan, and Raymond Lee. *Heaven in Transition: Non-Muslim Religious Innovation and Ethnic Identity in Malaysia*. Honolulu: University of Hawaii Press, 1988.

Andaya, Barbara Watson, and Leonard Y. Andaya. *A History of Malaysia*. 2d ed. Honolulu: University of Hawaii Press, 2001.

Barlow, Colin, ed. *Modern Malaysia in the Global Economy: Political and Social Change into the 21st Century*. Northampton, MA: Edward Elgar, 2001.

Brown, C. C. *Sejarah Melayu*, or *Malay Annals*. Kuala Lumpur: Oxford University Press, 1970.

Bunge, Frederica M., ed. *Malaysia: A Country Study*. 4th ed. HQ, Department of the Army, DA PAM 550-45. Washington, DC: U.S. Government Printing Office, 1985.

Crouch, Harold A. *Government and Society in Malaysia*. Ithaca, NY: Cornell University Press, 1996.

Enloe, C.H. *Multi-Ethnic Politics: The Case of Malaysia*. Berkeley: Center for South and Southeast Asian Studies, University of California, 1970.

Funston, John. *Malay Politics in Malaysia: A Study of UMNO and PAS*. Kuala Lumpur: Heinemann, 1980.

Gladney, Dru C., ed. *Making Majorities: Constituting the Nation in Japan, Korea, China, Malaysia, Fiji, Turkey, and the United States*. Stanford, CA: Stanford University Press, 1998.

Hooker, Virginia Matheson. *A Short History of Malaysia: Linking East and West*. Crows Nest, Australia: Allen and Union, 2002.

Ibrahim, Anwar. *The Asian Renaissance*. Singapore: Time Books, 1996.

Jumper, Roy Davis Linville. *Power and politics: the story of Malaysia's Orang Asli*. Lanham, MD: University Press of America, 1997.

Kahn, Joel S., and Francis Loh Kok Wah, eds. *Fragmented Vision: Culture and Politics in Contemporary Malaysia*. London: Allen & Unwin, 1992.

Kaur, Amarjit, and Ian Metcalfe. *The Shaping of Malaysia*. London: Macmillan Press, 1999.

Kessler, Clive S. *Islam and Politics in a Malay State: Kelantan, 1838-1960*. Ithaca, NY: Cornell University Press, 1978.

Khoo Boo Teik. *Paradoxes of Mahathirism: An Intellectual Biography of Mahathir Mohamad*. London: Oxford University Press, 1995.

Kratoska, Paul H. *The Japanese Occupation of Malaya: A Social and Economic History*. London: Hurst and Co., 1998.

Leake, David, Jr. Brunei: *The Modern Southeast-Asian Islamic Sultanate*. Jefferson, NC: McFarland, 1989.

Lee, H.P. *Constitutional Conflicts in Contemporary Malaysia*. New York: Oxford University Press, 1995.

Lee, Raymond, ed. *Ethnicity and Ethnic Relations in Malaysia*. DeKalb, IL: Center for Southeast Asian Studies, Northern Illinois University, 1986.

Mackie, J.A.C. *Konfrontasi: The Indonesia Malaysia Dispute, 1963-1966.* For the Australian Institute of International Affairs. London and Kuala Lumpur: Oxford University Press, 1974.

Means, Gordon P. *Malaysian Politics: The Second Generation.* Singapore: Oxford University Press, 1991.

Metzger, Laurent. *La minorité musulmane de Singapour.* Paris, France: L'Harmattan, 2003.

Metzger, Laurent. *Stratégie islamique en Malaisie: 1975-1995.* Paris: L'Harmattan, 1996.

Milne, R.S., and Diane K. Mauzy. *Malaysia: Tradition, Modernity, and Islam.* Boulder, CO: Westview Press, 1986.

Milne, R.S., and Diane K. Mauzy. *Singapore: The Legacy of Lee Kuan Yew.* Boulder, CO: Westview Press, 1990.

Milne, R.S., and Diane K. Mauzy. *Malaysian Politics under Mahathir.* London and New York: Routledge, 1999.

Mohamad, Mahathir. *The Malay Dilemma.* Singapore: Donald Moore, 1970.

Mohamad, Mahathir. *The Challenge.* Petaling Jaya, Selangor: Pelanduk Publications, 1986.

Mohamad, Mahathir. *The Way Forward.* London: Weidenfeld and Nicolson, 1998.

Mohammad Kamal Hassan. *Towards actualizing Islamic ethical and educational principles in Malaysian society: some critical observations.* Petaling Jaya, Selangor: Muslim Youth Movement of Malaysia, 1996.

Mutalib, Hussain. *Islam and Ethnicity in Malay Politics.* Singapore and New York: Oxford University Press, 1990.

Mutalib, Hussain. *Islam in Malaysia: From Revivalism to Islamic State?* Singapore: Singapore University Press, 1993.

Muzaffar, Chandra. *Islamic Resurgence in Malaysia,* 2d ed. Selangor: Penerbit Fajar Bakti, 1987.

Nagata, Judith A. *The Reflowering of Malaysian Islam: Modern religious radicals and their roots.* Vancouver: University of British Columbia Press, 1984.

Nair, Shanti. *Islam in Malaysian Foreign Policy.* New York: Routledge, 1997.

Ongkili, James. *Nation-Building in Malaysia, 1946–1974.* Singapore: Oxford University Press, 1985.

Roff, William R. *The Origins of Malay Nationalism.* New Haven, CT: Yale University Press, 1967.

Ryan, N.J. *A History of Malaysia and Singapore*. London: Oxford University Press, 1976.

Short, Anthony. *The Communist Insurrection in Malaya, 1948–1960*. London: Frederick Muller, Ltd., 1975.

Sloane, Patricia. *Islam, Modernity and Entrepreneurship Among the Malays*. London: Macmillan Press, Ltd., 1999.

Turnbul, C.M. *A History of Malaysia, Singapore and Brunei*. Rev. ed. London: Allen and Unwin, 1989.

Verma, Vidhu. *Malaysia, State and Civil Society in Transition*. Boulder, CO: Lynne Rienner, 2002.

Zainah, Anwar. *Dakwah Among the Students: Islamic Revivalism in Malaysia*. Kuala Lumpur: Pelanduk Publications, 1987.

Thailand

Baker, Chris, and Pasuk Phongpaichit. *A History of Thailand*. Cambridge: Cambridge University Press, 2005.

Bunnay, Tej. *The Provincial Administration of Siam, 1982–1915*. Kuala Lumpur: Oxford University Press, 1978.

Carment, David. "Managing Interstate Ethnic Tensions: The Thailand-Malaysia Experience," *Nationalism and Ethnic Politics 1*, no. 4 (Winter 1995), 1–22.

Che Man, Wan. K. *Muslim Separatism: The Moros of Southern Philippines and the Malays of Southern Thailand*. Quezon City: Ateneo de Manila University Press, 1990.

Department of the Army. *Ethnographic Study Series: Minority Groups in Thailand*. DA Pamphlet No. 550-107. Washington, DC: Department of the Army, February 1970.

Farouk, Omar. "Malaysia's Islamic Awakening: Impact on Singapore and Thai Muslims," *Conflict 8*, no. 2/3 (1988), 157–168.

Forbes, Andrew, ed. *The Muslims of Thailand: Volume II: Politics of the Malay-Speaking South*. Bihar: Centre for Southeast Asian Studies, 1989.

Gilquin, Michel. *The Muslims of Thailand*. Trans. by Michael Smithies. Cheng Mai, Thailand: Silkworm Books, 2002.

Jock, Lim Joo, and S. Vani, eds. *Armed Separatism in Southern Thailand*. Singapore: ISEAS, 1984.

Pitsuwan, Surin. *Islam and Malay Nationalism: A Case Study of Malay-Muslims of Southern Thailand*. Bangkok: Thai Khadi Research Institute, Thammasat University, 1985.

Pojar, Daniel J., Jr. "Lessons Not Learned: The Rekindling of Thailand's Pattani Problem." Unpublished M.A. thesis. Monterrey, CA: Naval Postgraduate School, March 2005.

Sugunnasil, Wattana, ed. *Dynamic Diversity in Southern Thailand.* Cheng Mai, Thailand: Silkworm Books, 2005.

Syukri, Ibrahim. *History of the Malay Kingdom of Patani.* Trans. by Conner Bailey and John N. Miksic. Athens: Ohio University Press, 1985.

Indonesia

Alatas, Syed Farid. *Democracy and Authoritarianism in Indonesia and Malaysia: The Rise of the Post-Colonial State.* New York: St. Martin's Press, 1997.

Algadri, Hamid. *Dutch policy against Islam and Indonesians of Arab Descent in Indonesia.* Jakarta: LP3ES, 1994.

Anderson, Benedict R.O.G., ed. *Language and Power: Exploring Political Cultures in Indonesia.* Ithaca, NY: Cornell University Press, 1972.

Aveling, Harry, ed. *The Development of Indonesian Society: From the Coming of Islam to the Present Day.* New York: St. Martin's Press, 1980.

Azra, Azyumardi. "The Transmission of Islamic Reformism to Indonesia: Networks of Middle Eastern and Malay-Indonesian `Ulama' in the Seventeenth and Eighteenth Centuries." Unpublished Ph.D. Dissertation, Columbia University, 1992.

Baker, Richard W., M. Hadi Soesastro, et. al. *Indonesia: The Challenge of Change.* Singapore: Institute of Southeast Asian Studies, 1999.

Barton, Greg. *Indonesia's Struggle: Jemaah Islamiyah and the Soul of Islam.* Sydney: University of New South Wales Press, 2004.

Barton, Greg, and Greag Fealy, eds. *Nahdlatul Ulama: Traditional Islam and Modernity in Indonesia.* Clayton, Victoria: Monash Asia Institute, Monash University, 1996.

Bayly, Susan. *Saints, Goddesses, and Kings: Muslims and Christians in Southeast Asian Society, 1700–1900.* New York: Cambridge University Press, 1990.

Bell, Coral, ed. *Politics, Diplomacy and Islam: Four Case Studies.* Canberra: Department of International Relations, The Australian National University, 1986.

Bhattacharjee, G.P. *Southeast Asian Politics: Malaysia/Indonesia.* Calcutta: Minerva Associates, 1976.

Boland, B. J. *The Struggle of Islam in Modern Indonesia.* The Hague: Martinus Nijhoff, 1982.

Bowen, John. *Muslims through Discourse: Religion and Ritual in Gayo Society.* Princeton, NJ: Princeton University Press, 1993.

Brown, Colin. *A Short History of Indonesia.* Crows Nest, Australia: Allen & Unwin, 2003.

Budiman, Arief, ed. *State and Civil Society in Indonesia.* Clayton, Victoria: Monash University, 1990.

Budiman, Arief, Barbara Hatley and Damien Kingsbury, eds. *Reformasi: Crisis and Change in Indonesia.* Clayton, Victoria: Monash Asia Institute, 1999.

Crouch, Harold A. *The Army and Politics in Indonesia.* Ithaca, NY: Cornell University Press, 1988.

Effendy, Bahtiar. *Islam and the State in Indonesia.* Singapore: Institute of Southeast Asian Studies, 2003. Copublished: Athens: Ohio University Press, 2003.

Eliraz, Giora. *Islam in Indonesia: Modernism, Radicalism, and the Middle East Dimension.* Portland, OR: Sussex Academic Press, 2004.

Emmerson, Donald K., ed. *Indonesia Beyond Suharto.* Armonk, NY: M.E. Sharpe, 1999.

Federspiel, Howard M. *Islam and Ideology in the Emerging Indonesian State: The Persatuan Islam (PERSIS), 1923 to 1957.* Leiden: Brill, 2001.

Federspiel, Howard M. *Muslim Intellectuals and National Development in Indonesia.* New York: Nova Science Publishers, Inc., 1992.

Federspiel, Howard M. *Popular Indonesian literature of the Qur'an.* Ithaca, New York: Cornell Modern Indonesia Project, Southeast Asia Program, Cornell University, 1994.

Feener, R. Michael. "Developments of Muslim Jurisprudence in Twentieth Century Indonesia." Unpublished Ph.D. Dissertation, Boston University, 1999.

Forrester, Geoff, ed. *Post-Soeharto Indonesia: Renewal or Chaos?* Singapore: Institute of Southeast Asian Studies, 1999.

Frederick, William H., and Robert L. Worden, eds. *Indonesia: A Country Study.* HQ, Department of the Army, DA PAM 550-39. Washington, DC: U.S. Government Printing Office, 1993.

Freitag, Ulrike, and William G. Clarence-Smith, eds. *Hadhrami Traders, Scholars and Statesmen in the Indian Ocean, 1750s–1960s.* Leiden: Brill, 1997.

Geertz, Clifford. *Islam Observed: Religious Development in Morocco and Indonesia.* Chicago: University of Chicago Press, 1968.

Geertz, Clifford. *The Religion of Java.* Chicago: University of Chicago Press, 1960.

Hefner, Robert W. *Civil Islam: Muslims and Democratization in Indonesia.* Princeton, NJ: Princeton University Press, 2000.

Hill, Hal. *Indonesia's New Order.* Honolulu: University of Hawaii Press, 1994.

Holt, Claire, ed. *Culture and Politics in Indonesia.* Ithaca, NY: Cornell University Press, 1972.

Hooker, M. B. *Indonesian Islam: Social Change Through Contemporary Fatawa.* Honolulu: University of Hawaii Press, 2003.

Hurgronje, C. Snouck. *Mekka in the Latter Part of the 19th Century: Daily Life, Customs and Learning of the Moslims of the East-Indian-Archipelago.* Trans. by J.H. Monahan. Leiden: Brill, 1970.

International Crisis Group (ICG). *Aceh: A Slim Chance for Peace.* ICG Indonesia Briefing. Jakarta/Brussels: ICG, March 27, 2002.

International Crisis Group (ICG). *Al-Qaeda in Southeast Asia: The Case of the "Ngruki Network" in Indonesia.* ICG Indonesia Briefing. Jakarta/Brussels: ICG, August 8, 2002.

International Crisis Group (ICG). *Indonesia: Overcoming Murder and Chaos in Maluku.* ICG Asia Report No. 10. Jakarta/Brussels: ICG, December 19, 2000.

International Crisis Group (ICG). *Indonesia: The Search for Peace in Maluku.* ICG Asia Report No. 31. Jakarta/Brussels: ICG, February 8, 2002.

International Crisis Group (ICG). *Indonesia: Violence and Radical Muslims.* IGC Indonesia Briefing. Jakarta/Brussels: ICG, October 10, 2001.

International Crisis Group (ICG). *Indonesia Backgrounder: How the Jemaah Islamiyah Operates.* ICG Asia Report No. 43. Jakarta/Brussels: ICG, December 11, 2002.

International Crisis Group (ICG). *Jemaah Islamiya in South East Asia: Damaged But Still Dangerous.* ICG Asia Report No. 63. Jakarta/Brussels: ICG, August 26, 2003.

International Crisis Group (ICG). *Recycling Militants in Indonesia: DarulIslam and the Australian Bombing.* IGC Asia Report, No. 92. Jakarta/Brussels: IGC, February 22, 2005.

Kingsbury, Damien, and Arief Budiman, eds. *Indonesia: The Uncertain Transition.* Adelaide: Crawford House Publishing, 2001.

Kipp, Rita Smith, and Susan Rodgers. *Indonesia Religions in Transition.* Tucson: The University of Arizona Press, 1987.

Laffan, M.F. *Islamic Nationhood and Colonial Indonesia: The Umma Below the Winds.* London and New York: Routledge Curzon, 2003.

Lee Khoon Choy. *A Fragile Nation: The Indonesian Crisis.* Singapore: World Scientific Publishing Company, 1999.

Lev, Daniel S., and Ruth Thomas McVey, eds. *Making Indonesia: Essays on Modern Indonesia in Honor of George McT. Kahin.* Ithaca, NY: Cornell University Press, 1996.

Lloyd, Grayson, and Shannon Smith. *Indonesia Today: Challenges of History.* Singapore: Institute of Southeast Asian Studies, 2001.

Manning, Chris, and Peter van Diermen, eds. *Indonesia in Transition: Social Aspects of Reformasi and Crisis.* Singapore: Institute of Southeast Asian Studies, 2000.

McCreedy, Amy, ed. *Piety and Pragmatism: Trends in Indonesian Islamic Politics.* Asia Program Special Report. Washington, DC: Woodrow Wilson Center, April 2003.

McDonald, Hamish. *Suharto's Indonesia.* Honolulu: University of Hawaii Press, 1981.

Mobini-Kesheh, Natalie. *The Hadrami Awakening: Community and Identity in the Netherlands East Indies, 1900–1942.* Ithaca: Cornell University Press, 1999.

Noer, Deliar. *The Modernist Muslim Movement in Indonesia 1900–1942.* Singapore: Oxford University Press, 1978.

Peacock, James L. *Muslim Puritans: Reformist Psychology in Southeast Asian Islam.* Berkeley: University of California Press, 1978.

Peacock, James L. *Purifying the Faith: the Muhammadijah Movement in Indonesian Islam.* Menlo Park, CA: The Benjamin/Cummings Publishing Co., 1978.

Perwiranegara, Alamsyah Ratu. *Development of the Indonesian Moslems.* Jakarta: [s.n.], 1979.

Porter, Donald J. *Managing Politics and Islam in Indonesia.* London and New York: Routledge-Curzon, 2002.

Ramage, Douglas. *Politics in Indonesia: Democracy, Islam and the Ideology of Tolerance.* London: Routledge, 1995.

Ricklefs, M. C. *A History of Modern Indonesia: Since c. 1200.* 3rd ed. Stanford, CA: Stanford University Press, 2001.

Ricklefs, M. C., ed. *Islam in the Indonesian social context.* Clayton, Victoria: Centre of Southeast Asian Studies, Monash University, 1991.

Riddell, Peter G. *Islam and the Malay-Indonesian World: Transmission and Responses.* Honolulu: University of Hawaii Press, 2001.

Studies on Indonesian Islam. Ed. B.B. Hering. Townsville, Qld., Australia: Centre for Southeast Asian Studies, James Cook University of North Queensland, 1986.

Schwarz, Adam. *A Nation in Waiting: Indonesia in the 1990s.* Boulder, CO: Westview Press, 1994.

Schwarz, Adam, and Johnathan Paris, eds. *The Politics of Post-Suharto Indonesia.* New York: Council on Foreign Relations Press, 1999.

Stauth, Georg. *Politics and Cultures of Islamization in Southeast Asia: Indonesia and Malaysia in the Nineteen-Nineties.* New Brunswick, NJ: Transaction Publishers, 2002.

Steenbrink, Karel. *Dutch Colonialism and Indonesian Islam: Contacts and Conflicts, 1596–1945.* Vol. 7 of Currents of Encounter. Atlanta, GA: Rodolpi, 1993.

Suryadinata, Leo. *Military Ascendancy and Political Culture: A Study of Indonesia's Golkar.* Athens: Ohio University, Center for International Studies, 1989.

Syamsuddin, M. Din. "Religion and Politics in Islam: The Case of Muhammadiyah in Indonesia's New Order." Unpublished Ph.D. Dissertation, University of California at Los Angeles, 1991.

Taylor, John G. *Indonesia: People and History.* New Haven, CT: Yale University Press, 2003.

Weinstein, Franklin B. *Indonesian Foreign Policy and the Dilemma of Dependence.* Ithaca, NY: Cornell University Press, 1976.

Woodward, Mark R., ed. *Toward a New Paradigm: Recent Developments in Indonesian Islamic Thought.* Tempe: Arizona State University, Program for Southeast Asian Studies, 1996.

Woodward, Mark R. *Islam in Java: Normative Piety and Mysticism in the Sultanate of Yogyakarta.* Tucson: University of Arizona Press, 1989.

Philippines

Agoncillo, Teodoro A. *History of the Filipino People.* 8th ed. Quezon City, RP: Garcia Publishing Co., 1990.

Barreveld, Dirk J. *Terrorism in the Philippines: The Bloody Trail of Abu Sayyaf, Bin Ladin's East Asian Connection.* San Jose, CA: Writers Club Press, 2001.

Bauzon, Kenneth España. *Liberalism and the Quest for Islamic Identity in the Philippines.* Durham, NC: Acorn Press, 1991.

Bonner, Raymond. *Waltzing with a Dictator: The Marcoses and the Making of American Policy.* New York: Times Books, 1987.

Brennan, John. *Crisis in the Philippines: The Marcos Era and Beyond.* Princeton, NJ: Princeton University Press, 1986.

Burnham, Gracia. *In the Presence of My Enemies.* Wheaton, IL: Tyndale House, 2003.

Che Man, Wan. K. *Muslim Separatism: The Moros of Southern Philippines and the Malays of Southern Thailand.* Quezon City: Ateneo de Manila University Press, 1990.

Coate, Austin. *Rizal: Philippine Nationalist and Martyr.* Hong Kong: Oxford University Press, 1968.

Curaming, Lilian M., and Leonardo N. Mercado. *100 years of Filipino Muslim-Christian Relations.* Zamboanga City, Philippines: Silsilah Publications, 1999.

Davis, Leonard. *Revolutionary Struggle in the Philippines.* New York: St. Martin's Press, 1989.

Day, Beth. *The Philippines: Shattered Showcase of Democracy in Asia.* New York: M. Evans and Company, Inc., 1974.

Doland, Ronald E., ed. *Philippines: A Country Study.* 4th ed. Federal Research Division, Library of Congress. Washington, DC: U.S. Government Printing Office, 1993.

Filipinas Foundation, Inc. *An Anatomy of Philippine Muslim Affairs: A Study in Depth on Muslim Affairs in the Philippines.* Manila: Filipinas Foundation Inc., February 1971.

Fowler, Dennis Bryce. "The Moro Problem: An Historical Perspective." Unpublished M.S. Thesis. Monterey, CA: Naval Postgraduate School, June 1985.

Friend, Theodore. *Between Two Empires: The Ordeal of the Philippines.* New Haven, CT: Yale University Press, 1965.

Gaerlan, Kristina, and Mara Stankovitch, eds. *Rebels, Warlords, and Ulama: A Reader on Muslim Separatism and the War in Southern Philippines.* Quezon City: Institute for Popular Democacy, 2000.

Goodno, James B. *The Philippines: Land of Broken Promises.* London, Zed Books, Ltd., 1991.

Gowing, Peter Gordon. *Mosque and Moro; a study of Muslims in the Philippines.* Manila: Philippine Federation of Christian Churches, 1964.

Gowing, Peter Gordon. *Muslim Filipinos—Heritage and Horizon.* Quezon City: New Day Publishers, 1979.

Gowing, Peter Gordon. *Understanding Islam and Muslims in the Philippines.* Quezon City: New Day Publishers, 1988.

Jones, Gregg. *Red Revolution: Inside the Philippine Guerrilla Movement.* Boulder, CO: Westview Press, 1989.

Jubair, Salah. *Bangsamoro: A Nation Under Endless Tyranny.* 3rd ed. Kuala Lumpur: IQ Marin SDN BHD, 1999.

Kamilan, Jamail A. *Bangsamoro Society and Culture: A Book of Readings on Peace and Development in Southern Philippines.* Iligan: Iligan Center for Peace Education and Research, 1999.

Karnow, Stanley. *In Our Image: America's Empire in the Philippines.* New York: Random House Press, 1989.

Kerkvliet, Benedict J. *The Huk Rebellion: A Study of Peasant Revolt in the Philippines.* Berkeley: University of California Press, 1977.

Kiefer, Thomas M. "Tausig Armed Conflict: The Social Organization of Military Activity in a Philippine Moslem Society." Unpublished Ph.D. Dissertation. Bloomington: University of Indiana, 1969.

Kiefer, Thomas M. *The Tausig: Violence and Law in a Philippine Moslem Society.* New York: Holt, Rinehart and Winston, Inc., 1978.

Laarhoven, Ruurdje. *Triumph of Moro Diplomacy: The Maguindanao Sultanate in the 17th Century.* Quezon City, RP: New Day Publishers, 1989.

Larousse, William. *A Local Church Living for Dialogue: Muslim-Christian Relations in Mindanao-Sulu, Philippines: 1965–2000.* Rome: Pontificia Università Gregoriana, 2001.

Lucman, Norodin Alonto. *Moro Archives: A History of Armed Conflicts in Mindanao and East Asia.* Quezon City: FLC Press, 2000.

Majul, Cesar Adib. *The Contemporary Muslim Movement in the Philippines.* Berkeley, CA: Mizan Press, 1985.

Majul, Cesar Adib. *Muslims in the Philippines.* Quezon City: University of the Philippines Press, 1973. Reprint: Berkeley, CA: Mizan Press, 1985.

McKenna, Thomas M. *Muslim Rulers and Rebels: Everyday Politics and Armed Separatism in the Southern Philippines.* Berkeley: University of California Press, 1998.

Mercado, Eliseo R. *Mission and Dialogue: Challenges for Muslims and Christians in the Philippines.* Cotabato City, Philippines: Center for Policy Advocacy and Strategic Studies, Notre Dame University, 1999.

Mercado, Monina Allarey. *People Power: An Eyewitness History of the Philippine Revolution of 1986.* New York: Tenth Avenue Editions, 1986.

Miller, Stuart Creighton. *Benevolent Assimilation: The American Conquest of the Philippines, 1899–1903.* New Haven, CT: Yale University Press, 1982.

Muslim, Macapado Abaton. *The Moro Armed Struggle in the Philippines: The Nonviolent Autonomy Alternative.* Marawi City: Mindanao State University, 1994.

Nimmo, H. Arlo. *The Sea People of Sulu.* San Francisco, CA: Chandler Publishing Co., 1972.

Orosa, Sixto Y. *The Sulu Archipelago and its People.* Yonkers-on-Hudson, NY: World Book Co., 1923. Updated, enlarged, and republished by the author in the Philippines in 1970.

Phelan, John L. *The Hispanicization of the Philippines: Spanish Aims and Filipino Responses, 1565–1700.* Madison: University of Wisconsin Press, 1967.

Ramos, Fidel V. *Break Not the Peace: The Story of the GRP-MNLF Peace Negotiations, 1992–1996.* Quezon City: Friends of Steady Eddie, 1996.

Rasul, Jainal D. *Muslim-Christian land: Ours to share.* Quezon City: Alemar-Phoenix Pub. House; Manila: Sole distributor, Alemar's, 1979.

Reed, Robert R. Colonial *Manila: The Context of Hispanic Urbanism and Process of Morphogenesis.* Berkeley: University of California Press, 1978.

Reeve, Simon. *The New Jackals: Ramzi Yousef, Osama bin Ladin, and the Future of Terrorism.* Boston, MA: Northeastern University Press, 1999.

Richardson, Jim. *The Philippines.* Denver, CO: Clio Press, 1989.

Stanley, Peter W. *Reappraising an Empire: New Perspectives on Philippine-American History.* Harvard Studies in American-East Asia Relations, No. 10. Cambridge, MA: Harvard University Press, 1984.

Steinberg, David J. *The Philippines: A Singular and A Plural Place.* Boulder, CO: Westview Press, 1982. 2nd ed., 1990.

Torres, Jose Jr. *Into the Mountain: Hostaged by the Abu Sayyaf.* Quezon City: Claretian Publications, 2001.

Vitug, Marites D., and Glenda M. Gloria. *Under the Crescent Moon: Rebellion in Mindanao.* Quezon City: Ateneo Center for Social Policy and Public Affairs and the Institute for Popular Democracy, 2000.

JOURNALS

Annual Review of the Social Sciences of Religion
Asian and African Studies (Israel)
Asian Studies Review
Asian Survey
Asian Thought and Society
Asia-Pacific Review
Australian Journal of International Affairs
Conflict
Contemporary Southeast Asia
Far Eastern Economic Review
Indonesia
Inside Indonesia
Jane's Intelligence Review
Journal of Asian and African Studies
Journal of Asian Studies
Journal [of the] Institute of Muslim Minority Affairs
Journal of Southeast Asian Studies
Muslim World
Nationalism and Ethnic Politics
Sojourn
Studia Islamika
Survival
Terrorism and Political Violence
Third World Quarterly

INDEX

A

Abduh, Muhammad 16, 49, 99
Abdul Kadir, Tengku 64
Abdul Rahman, Kabir 69
Abdul Rahman, Tunku 16, 32, 238
Abhangen 24, 25, 26, 85, 86, 99, 113
ABIM (*Angkatan Belia Islam Malaysia*—Malaysian Islamic Youth Movement)
    v, 38, 39, 40, 41, 43, 71, 91
Abu Jibril (Muhammad Iqbal Rahman) 47
Abu Zubayda 105, 131, 209
Aceh vii, 166, 167, 168, 190, 259, 267, 268, 270
Act of Free Choice 141
Afable, Silvestre 223
Ahtisaari, Martii 166
Al-Azhar University (Cairo) 182, 187, 195
Al-Ma'unah 53
al-Mukmin 48, 49
Alonto, Datu Abulkhayr 188, 226, 263
Al-Qa'ida v, ix, 3, 46, 47, 48, 50, 51, 52, 54, 74, 76, 82, 103, 104, 105, 106,
    107, 108, 114, 129, 131, 133, 136, 137, 160, 162, 197, 201, 203, 204,
    205, 208, 209, 210, 211, 212, 219, 242
Ambon 117, 123, 124, 125, 126, 127, 129, 138
AMCJA (All-Malayan Council of Joint Action) 15
AMM (Aceh Monitoring Mission) 166, 167
Ancestral Domain 225, 228
Anglo-Siamese Treaty of 1909 62
Aquino, Agapito 200
Aquino, Benigno 186, 199
Aquino, Corazon (President of the Philippines, 1986-1992) 193, 199, 202,
    203, 204, 205, 207
Arismanandar 132
ARMM (Autonomous Region of Muslim Mindanao) 207, 208, 209, 212, 216,
    217, 218, 219, 227
Arroyo, Gloria Macapagal (President of the Philippines, 2001-   ) 215, 216,
    217, 218, 219, 220, 221, 222, 223, 224, 225, 226, 227, 228, 229, 230
ASG (Abu Sayyaf Group) 103, 108, 203, 204, 205, 206, 207, 208, 209, 211,
    212, 213, 215, 216, 217, 218, 219, 220, 222, 223, 226, 242
Asian Financial Crisis 42
Atef, Muhammad 50, 103, 160, 205
Autonomous Region 192, 193, 194, 195, 198, 200, 202, 206, 207

Dwikarna, Agus 136, 160

E

East India Company 10, 11, 13, 19, 60
EDCOR (Economic Development Corps) 180
Eluay, Theys Hiyo 144, 146
England/Great Britain 9, 10, 11, 62, 175
Ermita, Edwardo 223
Estrada, Joseph (President of the Philippines, 1998-2001) 211, 212, 213, 215
Ethical Policy 22, 23

F

Fadillah, Haris (aka Abu Dzar) 131, 132
Farouk, Omar al- 105, 131, 136, 160, 209
Federation of Malay States (Malay Federation) 12, 13, 14, 64, 65
Federation of Malaysia 15
Foreri (Forum for the Reconciliation of Irian Jaya Society) 144, 147
FPI (*Front Pembala Islam*—Islamic Defenders Front) 167
Freeport-McMcRan Copper and Gold, Inc. 142, 143, 148
Fretilin 118, 119, 120, 142

G

GAM (*Gerakan Aceh Merdaka*—Free Aceh Movement) 151, 155, 156, 157,
        158, 159, 160, 161, 162, 163, 164, 165, 166, 167, 168
General Santos City 214, 226
Gestapu coup 89, 95, 154
Ghamdi, Hemaid H. 51
Ghozi, Fathur Rahman al- 96, 108, 135, 214, 215, 226
GMIP (*Gerakan Mujahideen Islam Pattani*—Pattani Islamic Mujahideen
Movement) 73, 74, 77, 82, 241, 242
Golkar (*Golangan Karya*) 81, 90, 92, 109, 110, 112, 115, 154, 165, 239, 240
Gusmao, Jose Alexeandre (aka "Xanana") 120

H

Habibie, B.J. 93, 110, 111, 112, 144, 150, 157, 158, 159
Hambali (Riduan Isamuddin) 47, 48, 50, 51, 52, 76, 78, 107, 134, 135, 140,
        203, 215
Hamza, Tenku Razaleigh 41, 42, 113, 114
Hashim, Salamat 173, 185, 188, 192, 194, 196, 197, 198, 199, 200, 203, 208,
        210, 213, 214, 219, 221, 222, 224
Hatta, Muhammad 3, 23, 25, 26, 28, 153

Haz, Hamza 113, 114, 128
HDC (Henri Dunant Center for Humanitarian Dialogue) 162
Hekmatyar, Gulbuddin 195
HMI (*Himpunan Mahasiswa Islam*—Islam University Student Movement)
    90, 91
Horta, Jose Ramos 120
Huk (Hukbalahap) rebellion 179, 180, 186
Hussein, Parouk 216, 217, 227

I

Ibrahim, Anwar v, vi, 36, 38, 39, 40, 43, 44, 45, 54, 55, 56, 91, 205
Ibrahim, Ustaz 45
ICFM (Islamic Conference of Foreign Ministers) 187, 189
ICMI (Association of Muslim Intellectuals) 93, 111, 113, 240
IIRO (International Islamic Relief Organization) 201, 203
IMF (International Monetary Fund) 108, 109
IMT (International Monitoring Team) 227
Indies Party 23
INTERFET (U.N. International Force in East Timor) 121
Internal Security Act 41, 53
Ipil 204, 209
Irian Jaya (West New Guinea or Papua) 50, 88, 107, 117, 129, 141, 142, 145,
    146, 147, 150, 151, 153, 156, 160, 168
Isamuddin, Riduan, see Hambali
ISI/ISID (Inter-Services Intelligence Directorate, Pakistan) 196
Iskandar Muda 155
Islam Hadhari (Civilized Islam) 56
Ismail, Zainon 52, 53
Ittihad-i Islami 196

J

Jabida "massacre" 183
Jakarta 96, 98, 101, 108, 110, 113, 116, 123, 125, 126, 128, 129, 131, 139,
    140, 141, 143, 145, 151, 154, 156, 159, 162, 164, 168, 206, 207, 208,
    212, 214, 216, 217, 219
Jakarta Agreement 206, 207, 208, 212, 216, 217, 219
Jamaat Tabligh 34, 35, 36, 37, 38
Jamiyat-i Islami (Pakistan) 36, 39, 196
Janjalani, Abdurajak 48, 196, 197, 200, 203, 204, 205, 211
Janjalani, Khaddafy 211, 220, 221, 222, 226, 227
Japan (World War II) 3, 64, 65, 87, 175

Java 4, 5, 7, 8, 10, 19, 20, 21, 22, 23, 24, 26, 27, 28, 48, 61, 85, 87, 88, 94, 95, 97, 107, 123, 126, 133, 140, 152, 153, 154, 155, 156, 236
Java War (1825-1830) 19, 20
Jogjakarta (see Yogjakarta)
Johore 5, 10, 11, 14, 17
Jolo 171, 188, 189, 191, 217, 221, 226, 227

K

Kalimantan 4, 50, 107, 108, 117, 124, 133
Kalla, Yusef 138, 164, 165, 167
Kartosuwiryo, Soekarmadji 87
Kebatinan 85
Kedah 10, 11, 14, 16, 17, 37, 44, 45, 59, 60, 62, 65, 67
Khalifa, Muhammad Jamal 48, 201, 203
Khomeini, Ruhollah 100, 104
Kiram II, Jamal al-, Sultan of Sulu 172, 191
Kiram, Datu Mahakutta, Sultan of Sulu 191
KISDI (Committee for Islamic Global Solidarity) 128
Kittikachorn, Thanom 71
KMM (*Kampalan Mujahidin Malaysia*) 52, 53, 54, 56, 57, 58
Komando Jihad 96, 97, 155
Konsojaya Trading Company 51
Kopassus 147, 148, 149
Kota Baru 40, 51, 52
Krue Se mosque 79
Kuala Lumpur 6, 12, 15, 18, 32, 35, 36, 37, 45, 52, 53, 54, 107, 216, 219, 224, 225, 226, 228

L

Laskar Jihad 123, 125, 126, 127, 128, 129, 131, 132, 133, 137, 138, 140, 145, 149, 150, 167
Laskar Jundallah 136, 138, 160
Laskar Mujahidin 125, 129, 131, 132, 134, 167
Lhokseume 158, 160, 161
Liberal Policy 21, 22
Libya 70, 182, 187, 188, 190, 195, 205, 212
Loncar, Badimir 162
Lucman, Datu Rashid 185, 192

M

Macapagal, Diosdado (President of the Philippines, 1961-1965) 18, 215
Madjid, Nurcholish v, 91, 113, 240

S

Sabah 8, 13, 18, 19, 41, 50, 107, 139, 171, 183, 185, 187, 189, 190, 197, 209, 212, 217

Sabil-illah 71

Saesaeng, Nasori ("Sori"—alias for Wae Ka Raeh) 73

Samudra, Imam (alias for Abdul Aziz) 194, 134, 140

Sandakan 139

Santa Cruz "massacre" 120

Santri 24, 25, 26, 85, 86, 89, 99

Sarawak 8, 13, 18, 19, 50, 107, 209

Sarekat Islam 23

Sayyaf, Abd al-Rasul 102, 196

SBPAC (Southern Border Provinces Administration Center) 71, 75

SBPPBC (Southern Border Provinces Peace Building Command) 78

Sedition Act of 1948 32

Selangor 11, 17, 35, 107

Shah, Wali Khan Amin 51, 203

Shari`a 90, 99, 100, 112, 114, 153, 167, 168, 169, 173, 176, 181, 209, 233, 236, 242

Shinawatra, Thaksin 75, 80

Singapore 1, 10, 11, 15, 17, 18, 19, 38, 46, 50, 66, 69, 76, 85, 90, 102, 103, 104, 106, 107, 108, 114, 131, 135, 185, 209

Sipidan Island 212, 213, 215, 217, 218

SIRA (*Sentral Informasi Referendum Aceh*—Information Center for a Referendum on Aceh) 159

Solana, Javier 212

Solo (Surakarta) 48, 97, 101, 108, 132, 134

Solossa, Jacobus ("Japp") 148

Spain 8, 9, 13, 171, 172, 175

SPCPD (Southern Philippines Council for Peace and Development) 206, 207, 216

Strait of Malacca 10, 48, 56

Sufism 7, 235, 236

Suharto, Ahmad 19, 43, 46, 47, 49, 50, 89, 90-124, 131-135, 141-144, 151, 154-158, 165-168, 210, 239-242

Sukarno, Ahmed vii, 3, 18, 19, 23-28, 37, 48, 86-90, 93, 110, 112, 141, 152-154, 162, 238, 239

Sukarnoputri, Megawati 112, 113, 128, 146, 150, 161, 164

Sulu 6, 9, 10, 13, 18, 108, 171-175, 180-185, 188-193, 199, 202-204, 211, 212, 22-222, 226